LIBRARY LIT. 13-
The Best of 1982

edited by

BILL KATZ

The Scarecrow Press, Inc.
Metuchen, N.J., & London
1983

ISBN 0-8108-1624-5
Library of Congress Catalog Card No. 78-154842

Copyright © 1983 by The Scarecrow Press, Inc.
Manufactured in the United States of America

CONTENTS

Introduction   v

PART I: LIBRARIES AND LIBRARIANS

Ortega Revisited (Lester Asheim)   3
Where Does It Hurt? Identifying the Real Concerns in
    the Ethics of Reference Service (Samuel Rothstein)   14
Ignoring the User: How, When and Why (Maurice B. Line)   26
Something There Is That Doesn't Love a Professor: "The
    Mismanagement of College Libraries" Revisited (Daniel
    Gore)   37
Libraries, Technology, and the Information Marketplace
    (Richard De Gennaro)   48
Jewish Libraries in the Polish Ghettos During the Nazi
    Era (David Shavit)   70
Views of a Luddite (Paul A. Lacey)   90
The Terminal and the Terminus: The Prospect of Free
    Online Bibliographic Searching (John Budd)   104
Is There a Catalog in Your Future? Access to Information
    in the Year 2006 (Nancy J. Williamson)   113
Questions Sheehy Can't Answer: Reflections on Becoming
    Head of Reference (Mary W. George)   129

PART II: COMMUNICATION AND EDUCATION

Who Can Own What America Knows? (Anita R. Schiller
    and Herbert I. Schiller)   138
The Long Road From Byblos (Wallace Stegner)   143
On Biography (Stanley Olson)   155
The Case for Quality Book Selection (Murray L. Bob)   161
The Public Library and the Alternative Press (Celia
    Minoughan)   169
Photography as Historical Evidence and Art: Steps in
    Collection Building (Juan R. Freudenthal and
    Josette A. Lyders)   195
Sweet Dreams for Teen Queens (Margo Jefferson)   209
Lies, Damned Lies, and Crime Statistics: The FBI Story
    (Joe Morehead)   216

Girls' and Boys' Reading Interests: Keeping the
  Options Open (Elizabeth Segel) 226
Research on Library Services for Children and Young
  Adults: Implications for Practice (Shirley Fitzgibbons) 232
Automation in School Library Media Centers (Russell &
  Mary Anne Driver) 258
Static in the Educational Intercom: Conflict and the School
  Librarian (Alixe Hambleton) 269

PART III: THE SOCIAL PREROGATIVE

From Adam Smith to Ronald Reagan: Public Libraries as
  a Public Good (Miriam Braverman) 277
Book Banning in America (Colin Campbell) 287
The Only Gentleman (Russell Baker) 296
Information Justice (Patricia Glass Schuman) 299
Anti-Intellectualism in American Libraries (David Isaacson) 314
'These Are Little Battles Fought in Remote Places' (Nat
  Hentoff) 326
Are School Censorship Cases Really Increasing? (Kenneth I.
  Taylor) 331
Home Information Systems: The Privacy Debate (Alan F.
  Westin) 343

Notes on Contributors 359

INTRODUCTION

After thirteen years of compiling these collections I say with confidence that library literature is better than ever. The writing, both in terms of content and style, improves each year. There is more thought, more challenge, more research, more careful consideration of pressing problems than when the series began in 1970.

This volume, and the twelve others which precede it, is witness enough that library literature is as good, often considerably more refined, than the literature of any profession. If you think this exaggerated, just check out a current issue of almost any trade or professional journal from PMLA to the Annals of the American Academy of Political and Social Science. While comparison is often unfair, even odious, the fact of the matter is that librarians tend to underestimate their own skills when handling language and ideas.

The present collection indicates that there are numerous places where one may publish. Somehow the notion that quality must be equated with only well-known, large circulation journals dominates the thinking not only of librarians, but laypersons. This simply is not true. Regional and local and more specialized journals--both here and abroad--are represented. In fact, many quite superior articles appear in other than the expected places. Here, then, is a corrective to the notion that immediate recognition of a journal title is a major aspect of importance of published material.

Over the years librarians have been kind to this effort. They have appreciated the desire of the compiler and the jury to honor what is considered the best of the year's thousands of articles. Few agree entirely with the 30 selected. Immediately after each volume is published I normally receive letters asking why "x" piece was included, and how in the name of common sense was "y" excluded. Granted, even the best-meaning and qualified jury make mistakes from time to time, yet on balance it seems to me (admittedly a trifle biased) that the selection pretty well holds up, does, in fact represent the year's best.

Candidates are selected in one of two ways. First, the editor looks at material in the 200 library literature periodicals available in the School of Library and Information Science Library at the State University of New York at Albany. (Fortunately, finding the magazines is not as difficult as writing out the title of the school.)

In addition, anything from The Village Voice to Nation is a possible point of entry for an article concerned with libraries and librarians. Second, readers and jury members throughout the year make many valuable suggestions. From all of this a group of articles is chosen, and from the chosen the jury then narrows it down to the winners-- the magic 30.

The jury and the editor determine what is best by intuition, experience, and luck. It is a situation familiar to the librarian who must select materials. Objectively, one must and does consider the style of writing, the originality of ideas, the excitement of the argument, the thoroughness of the research, and other aspects on the yardstick of quality. Balance, too, is important. We try to have various aspects of the profession--from cataloging and reference services to user studies and censorship--represented in each volume.

The time frame is from 1 November 1981 to 1 November 1982, although because of some vagaries of publishing and the activities of the post office, we may include material missed in the previous volume which was published, say, in September or October of 1981, but did not arrive at our library until November or December of 1981.

And with that, the usual annual request: if you come across a piece you think should be in the 1983 volume, please send it to me. It requires no more than a citation on the back of a postcard. I promise to reply and you can be sure your candidate will be dutifully considered. There is, by the way, nothing wrong in suggesting your own article.

The 1982 Jury

The jurors were: Ms. Bertha M. Cheatham, Associate Editor, School Library Journal; Ms. Pat Schuman, President, Neal-Schuman Publishers; John Berry, Editor of the Library Journal; William Eshelman, President, Scarecrow Press; Arthur Curley, Deputy Director of the New York Public Library; and the undersigned.

--Bill Katz

Part I

LIBRARIES AND LIBRARIANS

ORTEGA REVISITED*

Lester Asheim

It was in 1934 that José Ortega y Gasset defined the future role of the librarian as that of "a filter interposed between man and the torrent of books."[1] Long before Ortega, of course, there were library leaders who also had attempted to articulate the mission of the librarian, but few had his ability to state it in terms that capture the imagination, serve as a slogan, and at the same time cut through to a universal truth underlying both daily practice and its philosophical underpinnings. What is fascinating today about Ortega's figure of the filter is that the image takes on new and even more challenging implications in the light of current developments in library practices and new challenges to the library's social role.

During the dissident period of the 1960s and until very recently, the librarian's function as a selector took on a certain negative image, as an arrogation of control over content inconsistent with the move toward an absolutist view of free access to ideas. The filter function was taken to be a negative mechanism for governance, an instrument of the Establishment; and the assumption was implicit that the Establishment must always be on the other side from the "people."

The perception that the filter role implied the imposition of standards was not an altogether incorrect interpretation of Ortega's intent, of course. His concern about the "torrent of books" was indeed a reaction against the number of "useless" and "stupid" ones whose "existence and ... conservation is a dead weight upon humanity which is already bent low under other loads." But he was equally disturbed by the absence of needed materials, and he looked to a utopia in which there would be a "regulation of the production of books, [not only] ... to avoid the publication of superfluous ones [but to] ... guard against the lack of those demanded by the complex of vital problems in every age." This "collective organization of book production" he saw as the responsibility of librarians in the future [1, p. 21].

---
*Reprinted by permission of the author and publisher from The Library Quarterly, 52:3 (July 1982) 215-226. Copyright © 1982 by The University of Chicago.

What sent me back to Ortega and his filter metaphor was my recent reading of a book by Orrin Klapp called Opening and Closing [2], in which once again we find a concern, even more urgent than in the mid-thirties, over the proliferation of communications which, instead of filling our need for more and more information, has proved instead to have complicated communication even further because of the problem of "overload." In quite another context, and from quite another point of view, Klapp seems to be pointing once again to the need for a filter which will screen out the redundant, the banal, and the irrelevant, or at least facilitate their control. The purpose is still to make it possible for each seeker of information to obtain that part of the total store which is pertinent to his or her need and interest, but the angle of vision is sufficiently different to justify an exploration of the contemporary relevance of Ortega's half-century-old insight.

Klapp challenges a long-standing liberal view that an open mind is always better than a closed one. My first reaction was to bridle at such a proposition; surely it is better to be open to all information at all times, is it not, instead of closing off a chance to be exposed to new ideas and new challenges? Well, says Klapp in effect, yes and no. Any living system (whether a person or a society) has to maintain a balance between intake and outgo if it is to continue to operate. There can be "bad opening" as well as "good opening," "good closing" as well as bad.

> The sea anemone in a tide pool outstretches and retracts its green tentacles. The turtle and snail withdraw into shells when openness gets to be too much ... the pupil dilates when light is dim and contracts when it is bright ... what we call aliveness--resilience, adaptability--is not continual intake, nor any constant policy, but sensitive alternation of openness and closure. The mind listens alertly, then turns off to signals. The natural pattern is alternation, and the more alive a system is, the more alertly it opens and closes.... A perpetually open society would suffer the fate of a perpetually open clam. [2, pp. 14-15]

An even more apposite comparison is with a ventilating system; if it "failed either to keep out fresh air or let in fresh air at the appropriate times, it could not maintain the needed balance" [2, p. 156]. Perhaps the human mind bears the same relation to fresh ideas as a ventilating system to fresh air; there are appropriate times for keeping them out as well as for letting them in, if the needed balance is to be maintained.

In communication theory the need for closure is recognized in the concept of noise. Noise is anything that interferes with the clear reception of the message. It is not a matter of decibels, but of "unwanted" content. To the dedicated concert-goer, a whisperer in the seat behind is more noise than the blast of the trumpet section. The intrinsic value of the content as such is not at issue (the whisper may have contained important information for its intended receiver). What matters is the subjective reaction of the individual receiver to the particular message at the moment. The music lover resents the whisper that interferes with the clear reception of the symphony; the loving couple in the next row takes exception to the symponic noise that drowns out the whispered sentiment. "So we may think of opening and closing as part of a shifting strategy to get the most of the best information and the least of the worst noise.... When the environment becomes adverse, from noise or information overload, more closing is needed" [2, p. 20].

This is, then, an individual matter, not an absolute measure. "Useless" and "stupid" are not so easily identified and dismissed as Ortega would have it. One person's useless may be another person's essential. For the mediator in communication exchange, which is what the librarian is, the task is to gauge the point of diminishing return in each communication transaction and then alter the flow in order to reduce that which functions as noise and foster that which promotes clarification or supplies reinforcement. Among the factors to which the mediator must be sensitive is the fact that the receiver must be allowed time to reflect and to think as well as simply to receive; an unexamined openness to everything flowing in becomes at some point--which varies for each individual--a channel for "unwanted" messages.

This view of the filter--operating as in a ventilating system-- is not opposed to openness; it is simply sensitive to the overload or the irrelevance of the inflow. And this, of course, was what many of us meant by selection, even in a more traditional context. The librarian's selection of materials was based upon the greatest openness that is consistent with effective assimilation of the information. It was not meant, for example, to let in only those points of view with which he or she agreed, but rather to make sure that all aspects of a topic were accessible so that the library patron could choose that which best met the need of the time. Where selection (i.e., rejection as well as acceptance) was forced upon us by limited funds, limited space, and the particular needs of a given community, the selection was designed to bring in, as Klapp phrased it, the "best information and the least of the worst noise" as determined by the nature of the particular audience served by each library. The criteria for determining "best" and "worst" were not the selectors' personal preferences, but the purposes of the individual users.

It is with these several elements in mind that I find another look at Ortega instructive. The "torrential abundance" of print that horrified him is, if anything, more a problem than ever before. The need for information is probably greater--or at least the awareness of the need is keener--than it was fifty years ago. The capability of gathering, storing, and retrieving more of the record is constantly increasing. But the capacity of the human receiver is essentially as limited as ever, which means that the probability of overload is even greater than before. One of the benefits of our society--the tremendous access we have to information--is one of its detriments as well. The overload, the burden of noise, can have many undesirable psychological results, not the least of which (in our context of the need for information) is simply the rejection of messages, even when they could be messages that meet the potential user's need. Too much, even of a good thing, can become a bad thing, and the remedy for "too much" is closure.

An easy first reaction to the problem of overload is--of course--to reduce the amount of input. But that is only apparently easy. As has been pointed out, the criterion for the librarian should in each case be the need of the particular user, and the dilemma is that no two persons will consistently agree on what constitutes noise or at what point the amount of content begins to become a source of noise. Klapp reminds us of the familiar paradox of "museum fatigue," where the inability to take in one more picture or one more piece of sculpture has nothing to do with the quality and value of the works of art themselves. The answer to museum fatigue is not to do away with half of the museum's collection. What is needed-- between the visitor to the museum and all of that beautiful and valuable communication--is an individual filter.

This suggests, then, that the librarian has more than one selector role to play: one, as the builder of the store of information; the other, as the intermediary between that store and the user's present need. As collection builder, the librarian's openness is a virtue. Precisely because one person's banality is another person's revelation, it becomes necessary to have as wide a variety of information sources as possible, and with today's move toward systems, resource sharing, and other varieties of access far beyond any one institution's storage capacity, the complete record is almost a possible goal. The major problem therefore is no longer that there is not enough information but that there is too much for any one receiver. Even so--and this is part of the collection-building dilemma-- the overload of information on some topics does not guarantee that needed information in other areas exists in any retrievable form or, even if it does, that our collection has it.

The problem continues to be the one Ortega defined: both too much information and not enough. And so the second selector role comes into play, and it requires a much more sensitive ability to recognize when to close and when to keep open. The balance between the user's need and the material pertinent to it, even within a carefully defined and limited field, requires a more refined mechanism than our library procedures have yet designed.

The need, and recognition of it, are not new. Without overtly using the communication jargon, librarians have long recognized their need to assist the user to screen out noise and zero in on the wanted information. Classification schemes and cataloging processes are an early form of just such measures. Reference and readers' advisory services attempted to carry them further. Departmentation and information services pinpointed specific information needs and separated them from the welter of other information that the total collection encompassed. The multiplication of approaches to information which the computer makes possible, and the refinement of descriptors to narrow the range of the user's attention, are additional steps in this direction. But with the growth of information and access, each of these steps must eventually and inevitably prove to be inadequate.

Librarians are now able to multiply avenues to information, types of content, and varieties of formats; to set no limit to the size of accessible collections, because we now have ready access to collections other than our own. But this has provided more information than a patron can use even on a topic in which he or she has an interest; great amounts of information encoded in ways that convey meaning only to a limited few; and great amounts which might well be useful at some other time, but not now. This mass of information, "irrelevant, redundant, or in sheer overload," explains why, although it has so much more information than ever before, our society seems even less able to cope with its problems [2, p.4].

The task for the librarian then would seem to be to work on the problem of the transaction between the source (which needs to be as wide-ranging as possible) and user (who is always going to be limited, in interest and in capacity). The mechanical devices we now have for making our resources greater and more complex push us toward entropy unless we can devise some means for trimming the transaction itself down to human scale.

The librarian has two different ways of making this important contribution. One is through direct intervention, refining and extending the interpersonal exchange by which the user's need can, by fine tuning on the part of the knowledgeable librarian, be focused on the usable part of the total information available. The need is to reduce noise to a minimum and, through a delicately balanced alternation of opening and closing, constantly to readjust to take advantage of both strategies.

The other responsibility of the librarian is to redesign library processes and procedures so that the users themselves can more easily accomplish the desirable opening and closing that will facilitate their passage through the maze of too much and too little. The library's organization is an important part of the system. Its purpose is to provide for clear access to the needed information, but it can itself introduce noise if it does not permit users to adjust the flow and select what will serve them best. Librarians, if they are sensitive to the user's needs as well as to the organization's complexity, could devise better ways to control the information flow so that the desirable balance is achievable.

In other words, there are two kinds of filter function performed by the librarian, but both of them serve to bring to the user a manageable store of information from which to select. Original selection by the librarian in the building of the collection attempts to provide the largest possible store, so that all needed items are available for a potential user. This selection process usually precedes the entrance of the user on the scene. But once a library patron comes with a request for information of whatever kind, a new filter function faces the librarian: the manipulation of the flow of information from the total store to focus on that part of it that meets the user's need insofar as the librarian understands the expression of that need. As the negotiation proceeds, new questions may be raised, additional information may be sought, the focus may be shifted, and a reformulation of the need may even be required. The constantly adjusting filter of the librarian responds to the constantly adjusting filter of the user; they work side by side until the user says, "This is what I want."

  The function of the librarian, then, is not only to act as a filter but also to make it possible for the users to act as their own filters. Control of the flow is adjusted, through a variety of techniques and devices, to provide the pertinent information in the appropriate amount to be useful in the patron's evaluation, assimilation, and utilization of the information. The point is to avoid the inundation of the users with so much information, however relevant, that they reject it all and impose closure before their need is satisfied, but at the same time to provide users with enough information for them to be able to identify what more they may want. Given the different search styles and techniques that different patrons bring to their problems; given the different thresholds that individuals perceive as representing too little or too much, the librarian's task demands great sensitivity and flexibility. One approach, one method, one set of markers along a predetermined path is not the answer. The prerecorded message is an example of the problem with an imposed filtering of information which assumes that all or most information searches are essentially the same. A theater, for example, prerecords the show times because that is the most frequent question posed by people who phone in. It is therefore the answer for a large majority of questioners, and a tremendous saver of time and money for the theater. But the questioner who wants something other than that gets noise, not useful information. The problem of dealing with the unusual as well as the typical requires personal interchange and flexibility that permits the adjustment to the individual request. The librarians' goal should be to use our special knowledge of sources, content, retrieval techniques, and bibliographic control inventively and imaginatively in each case to help the individual find his or her way--not ours--through the complex and many-faceted store of information.

  This is the librarian's ideal gatekeeper role, and of all the many gatekeepers in the communication complex, the librarian may be the one best prepared to define that function in such a way as to reconcile the conflict between as complete a store as possible, and the problem of individual overload. More than any other gatekeeper in the field of formal communication, the librarian is devoted to the tradition of individual service and individual response. The lecturer and the teacher aim at an audience; the mass media seek an even larger target group. The librarian operates at both the group and the individual levels, but the individual exchange remains the keystone of the library's service. When we conduct community surveys and other techniques for identifying the major components of our "audience," we are utilizing a group approach, but always within that strategy there is the recognition that the audience is made up of individuals and that there may be a few people, or even one person, whose different drummer should also be represented in our store of information and ideas. In the mass media, a program may be cancelled if only several hundred thousand people are watching or listening; in the library, one person's interest can justify the acquisition of material he or she wants. Above all, in the library there is on hand the living human being--a librarian--who speaks directly to another human being--the patron--when the patron wishes that kind of face-to-face assistance.

But the library's ability to respond to the need of the individual is not confined to the face-to-face contact, although this is a feature of library service that is well worth preserving in an increasingly impersonal society dominated by machines. Equally central to the concept of individual service is the fact that in the search for information through the library, it is the user who initiates the transaction, and it is the user's interest, not the librarian's, that shapes the nature of the service rendered. This has been identified as a weakness by some students of the professions [3, pp. 17-18], but it is one of librarianship's greatest assets, if the concern is with reducing to human scale the tremendous overload of information in today's society.

Any librarian who turns to subject experts for assistance in selecting materials in a special field discovers how much narrower a limit the experts apply to their definition of what would be useful in the library. Their view is frequently colored by their personal prejudices, by their adherence to a particular "school of thought" in their field, by the personal animosity they feel for the writer or the approach, by the arrogant assumption--shared by Ortega--that they can define and eliminate, for everyone else, the "useless" and the "stupid." Librarians, almost alone among professionals, do not, in that sense, "prescribe." Their aim is to find for the user what the user is seeking, and where that search is at all complex, overload can inhibit the user's willingness or ability to carry on the pursuit. The librarians' expertise lies, not in their superior knowledge of every subject area as such, but rather in their knowledge of sources and search strategies and in their willingness to put themselves in the user's place. Since overload can be an inhibiting factor in the search for information, control of the flow, not just of the nature of the content, is the librarian's responsibility. Traffic control in the information search does not seek to inhibit the expression of ideas, but rather to facilitate their assimilable movement and display.

A frequent criticism of the mass media as a stimulus to individual thought is that they introduce a mechanism between the sender of the message and the designated receiver--the TV set, the film projector, the broadcasting system. The mechanism in itself, however, need not be the inhibiting factor. It is salutary to remember that the book too is, in effect, an intervening device, yet it has long been recognized as eminently responsive to individual needs. Today new developments in communication technology are beginning to add to the mechanical devices, a number of the kinds of individual adaptation that once were possible only with the book, or the intervention of a helping hand. Random access, replay, slowdown and speedup, portability, query and response, feedback and readjustment, reproduction in a format that permits temporary storage for comparison or deferred attention--all are now possible through technological improvements in communications. The library should not turn its back on these aids to the librarian's function, but rather use them in support of its aim: response to user-initiated transactions--at the users' time, speed, and level of interest and capacity. There is nothing wrong in itself with a recorded message (a book is a recorded message); what is wrong--and what introduces noise on the channel--is a nonresponsive message; a message prerecorded to fit the purposes of the sender rather than that of the user. The librarian--as filter--monitors the traffic, not as an authoritarian controller, but to foster the smooth flow, and to assist each traveler to find the avenue that leads to his or her chosen destination.

In the librarians' self-image, this is what we have been doing all along. We have been dedicated to serving the user; we have fought long and hard for users' right to freedom of access to ideas; we have conscientiously attempted to keep our own preferences from taking over in the selection process; we have attempted to facilitate the individual's own search rather than to construct a mystique around our procedures that would require their dependence upon our intervention. To dramatize the extremes, contrast the kind of choices a library user has with the kind of choices a television viewer has, when specific information is sought. Television may well, in the course of a year, cover a great many subjects in which users are interested, but the timing, the depth, the duration, and the focus are all dictated by TV's programming schedule, not the user's moment of interest. The comparison points up something more than just the freedom of choice; it underlines also the importance of storage and preservation of the record, and the machinery for access to that record which is sufficiently discriminating to get to the particular piece or pieces of information that will match the user's special requirements. Both timing and content are important if it is the receiver rather than the sender who is to be accommodated.

Libraries and Librarians   11

    The librarian, among all the communicators, has a head start at playing the new filter role effectively. In defining the strategies for coping with the problem of overload, Klapp prescribes "a response involving: 1) scanning to see what is at hand; 2) awareness of gain or loss (interest awakened, gratification, bafflement, boredom, and so on) perhaps by comparison with a standard such as noise/signal ratio; 3) decision (closure) to some pattern as a goal; 4) opening and closing to get more of that goal and to avoid the rest.... Coping requires continual maneuvering, depending on feedback" [2, p. 159].

    This is indeed a description of the ideal that librarians hold of the way they carry out their information, reference, and advisory functions. It suggests that the preparation of filter/librarians will build upon the traditional principles of library service rather than force a departure from them. What will be required is more attention than has been typical in the past to the user/librarian relationship, the interpersonal exchange, and the sensitivity to human feedback during the transaction. It suggests a greater emphasis on the social and psychological aspects of the librarians' relation with their clients, not at the expense of efficient operations but certainly in addition to them, and with far greater application of user satisfaction as an appropriate measure of effectiveness. It certainly suggests that librarians must develop a greater awareness of their operation as a communication activity, and of communication problems as well as financial and organizational problems, as possible barriers to the successful achievement of the service objectives.

    Librarians have learned a lot about management, organization, processes, and procedures as these affect library operations from the administrators' and practitioners' points of view. What is needed now is an evaluation of these elements in terms of the end result as seen by the patron. Basic to this evaluation is the paradox of information overload: increasing the amount of information or speeding up the communication process does not necessarily improve the ability of the receiver to get the benefit of the information delivered. Indeed, the reverse may be true: the faster the messages pour in, the more there are of them, the more confused and resistant one's responses become [2, p. 70]. The danger of overload is not only that people are receiving a lot of messages that are of no value to them; it is also that the individual may, in frustration with too much information--even intrinsically useful and valuable information--resort to rejection of the messages, perceiving them as noise. Someone must scan, process, and select from the great domain of total information the needed information to suit the individual seeker--and I suggest that the librarian should be that monitor.

    Commercial communication agencies are well aware of the problem of information glut and have already begun to apply the new technology to capitalize on it.[4] The direction they take, typically, is to pinpoint specific audiences and design "customized information

services" for them. But while the subject matter can be narrowed
down to quite specialized areas--"metals news for a scrap-metal
company, grain news in a grain elevator"--these services are still
prepackaged and prerecorded. They respond to a generalized rather
than a specific, immediate need of a single person. They are highly sophisticated updates of the special library/special collection/"Current Contents" approach which narrows the field, but they are not
the reference interview that separates A's interest in metals on Tuesday from B's interest in metals on Wednesday, nor A's newly discovered interest during the course of the transaction. One can, with
these new data services, dip into the flow of information as it goes
by, but it is still a flow of considerable proportions and responds to
the interest of a paying audience large enough to justify the expense
of the automated system that supplies it. It is an <u>audience,</u> if not
a major mass audience, that is served. The idiosyncratic need of
the individual can still be overwhelmed by even this smaller extract
from the total data bank.

So none of these does quite the job that the library is expected to do: store information on virtually every subject field until it is wanted and respond from that general store to a specific,
immediate request, however atypical or singular it may be. The
library still represents the best example of combining both the broad
store and the special response, with equal access to both the permanent bank of information and the ephemeral and highly individual
part of it that fits no standard category of preestablished demand.

In the end, after all, it is not just information as such that
the library user is seeking, but the meaning of the information in a
specific context. To attain to an understanding of the meaning requires, as Klapp points out, "a complex process of interactive support that always takes longer and that cannot keep up with the information flood" [2, p. 72]. The sensitive, directed filter can help
to provide the necessary room to move around in which makes possible the derivation of meaning from what might otherwise be only
noise. If librarians will bear this simple fact in mind, and are
willing to subject their operations and their long-established habits
of retrieval and interpretation to evaluation by this standard, they
could achieve the role that Ortega y Gasset proposed for them:
not just "the simple administration of the things called books, but
the adjustment, the setting to rights, of that vital <u>function</u> which is
the book" [1, p. 22, italics added]. For "book," <u>read</u>, not a material object, but Ortega's concept of a "living function"--a stimulus
to thinking, assimilating, making the content truly the user's own.

Conclusion

The rich store of information to which librarians can now provide
access has a tremendous potential for good--to the individual and
to the society. It was our awareness of this that led most of us
to choose librarianship as a career, and to acquire and organize
these riches for public use. It now appears that, as collectors,

librarians have contributed to the information overload which inhibits rather than promotes achievement of the goal we had in view. Do we not have an obligation now to provide a solution to the problem we have helped to create?

That solution--as Ortega foresaw and as recent communication study has verified--may require access to some kind of filter process, which can be interposed, when needed, between potential users and the overwhelming store of information we have accumulated and continue to augment. For librarians to see the constructive values of the filter role may take some rethinking, but less for librarians than for many of the other gatekeepers in the communication community. For us it represents, not a repudiation of our traditional role, but a logical extension and enhancement of it through which the library may, at long last, be able convincingly to demonstrate the indispensable function it can serve in the developing communication society.

References

1. In an address to the International Congress of Bibliographers and Librarians in Paris. All quotations from Ortega y Gasset in this paper are from: Ortega y Gasset, José. The Mission of the Librarian. Translated by James Lewis and Ray Carpenter. Boston: G.K. Hall & Co., 1961. (Reprinted from Antioch Review 21, no. 2 [Summer 1961]: 133-54.)

2. Klapp, Orrin E. Opening and Closing: Strategies of Information Adaptation in Society. Cambridge: Cambridge University Press, 1978.

3. Goode, William J. "The Librarian: From Occupation to Profession?" In Seven Questions about the Profession of Librarianship: The Twenty-sixth Annual Conference of the Graduate Library School, June 21-23, 1961, edited by Philip H. Ennis and Howard W. Winger. Chicago: University of Chicago Press, 1962.

4. Bulkeley, William M. "Electronic Gear Aims to Help Folks Cope with Data Deluge." Wall Street Journal (August 14, 1981).

WHERE DOES IT HURT? IDENTIFYING
THE REAL CONCERNS IN THE ETHICS
OF REFERENCE SERVICE*

Samuel Rothstein

What is the right thing to do--for our clients, for our employers, for our government and society, for our colleagues and ourselves? In theory no subject would seem to be of more importance to reference librarians than the ethical considerations that underlie their activities. In fact the topic gets little attention.[1]

Bernard Vavrek, who is himself one of the few people to make a serious study of ethical issues, has deplored reference librarians' lack of interest in this subject.[2] His concern is commendable but the sad reality is that, considering the way in which the subject has usually been treated and presented, the apathy with which it has been received is understandable and perhaps even warranted.

The most common type of presentation has taken the form of a library association promulgating an official "code" or formal statement which presumes to set forth the principles and precepts by which the librarian is to be guided into righteous behavior. Some examples of such codes or statements are those issued by the American Library Association (1938 and 1975),[3] the Institute of Professional Librarians of Ontario (1975),[4] the Ohio Library Association (1976),[5] the California Library Association (1976),[6] the American Library Association (the 1979 revision of the 1975 version),[7] and the Library Association (1980).[8]

The failings of these documents are not difficult to detect. In a number of instances, notably that of the ALA Code of Ethics of 1938, the writing itself is so bad as to have prompted severe criticism. The "vague idealism,"[9] "fatuous adjurations"[10] and pompous platitudes[11] of such a statement are reason enough for ignoring it. Another problem is that the documents often mix up major points of principle with minor matters of etiquette.[12] Still another

---
*Reprinted by permission of the author and publisher from The Reference Librarian, (1982) 1-12. Copyright © 1982 by The Haworth Press, Inc. All rights reserved.

Libraries and Librarians 15

drawback, in this case more the fault of the library profession itself than of its codes of ethics, is that the codes are "toothless."[13] Librarians, in North America at least, are not yet so organized as to provide for investigation and punishment of malfeasance. Accordingly the precepts enunciated in the codes are regarded as pieties rather than rules of conduct.[14] Lastly, it should be noted that the codes tend to take a more unitary view of library practice than is actually the case. This is to say that the codes address themselves to librarians in general rather than specifically to public librarians, cataloguers, etc. In a profession as notoriously heterogeneous as librarianship, it thus becomes all too easy for librarians of a particular kind to dismiss the codes as having little direct relevance to their own situation.

As it happens, at least as of 1979, most of the above criticisms do not apply to reference librarianship. The revised version of "A Commitment to Information Services: Developmental Guidelines," which was originally issued by the Reference and Adult Services Division of the ALA in 1976[15] as simply its set of standards for information services, has added a section on "Ethics of Service."[16] This means that reference librarians have in effect a code of ethics of their very own.

The statement on "Ethics of Service" has much in its favor. The writing is refreshingly direct and succinct and for the most part its meaning is unequivocal. For example, reference librarians are enjoined to treat their "information contacts with users ... with complete confidentiality" and are obligated to codify their rules and practices so that a "reference policy statement is to be made available to the user in written form."[17] It is to be noted that both of these "commandments," highly debatable though they are, are presented without qualification of any kind. The RASD statement on "Ethics of Service" is not afraid to speak its mind.

With so much to commend it, then, one would think that the RASD statement would have elicited considerable attention from reference librarians and perhaps even their applause. If this has in fact happened, I am wholly unaware of it. My own guess is that the statement has met with much the same sullen silence accorded to all its predecessor codes.

Assuming the accuracy of the above analysis, it seems to me that there can be only two tenable conclusions deriving from it: either reference librarians simply do not care about ethical issues or the whole matter has thus far not been presented to them in a way in which they would recognize the subject as being significant to them.

There being no hard facts to support either conclusion, I naturally prefer to take the most favorable view of myself and my fellow reference librarians. I assume therefore that reference workers will be ready to tackle their problems in ethics--i.e., in "doing things right"--if these problems can be accurately identified and properly analyzed.

Now, by far the best way of making such identification and analysis of ethical problems is simply to ask the reference librarians themselves--what conflicts, what difficulties, what tensions in their work lead them to question or to worry about whether they are doing the "right thing?" Unfortunately, we have had no such survey undertaken among reference librarians, but we can gain some idea of what such an investigation might yield by examining examples from allied fields. A very good case in point is the recent article by Eleanor Blum (herself a librarian) and Clifford Christians of "Ethical Problems in Book Publishing."[18] Blum and Christians adopted what they called "an inductive approach for [the] inquiry".[19] That is, instead of attempting to even define ethics, let alone enunciate precepts, they allowed "practitioners ... to describe their own perceptions"[20] of the problems that had actually perturbed them. In almost all cases, they found out, the ethical problems of publishers center on conflict of legitimate interests. For example, concern about maintaining quality runs up against the need to show a profit; one's loyalty to the firm conflicts with one's obligation to the author, and so on. It should be added that the length, candor and emotional nature of the replies indicated clearly that the respondents did feel keenly about ethical issues if they were allowed the opportunity to say "where it really hurt."

It seems to me that the approach taken by Blum and Christians--to discuss the ethical problems of a group by focussing on the perplexities and anxieties actually felt by the practitioners--is also amenable and useful to a study on the ethical problems of reference librarianship. I propose, then, to do just that. Of course, not having seen or made a survey of reference practitioners' experience and options, I do not have any solid data at my disposal. No matter; I will make do as best I can without facts and, drawing simply on my own knowledge and imagination, attempt to describe what I think to be the actual situation. Acting then as both questioner and universal respondent, I now present my survey of the "real" ethical problems of reference librarians.

The most frequent and probably also the most important problems derive from the relationship between the reference librarian and the client. Because there is seldom any monetary advantage to be gained by the librarian whether his or her service be good or bad, the very considerable ethical conflicts and tensions implicit in the librarian-client "encounter" can easily be overlooked or misunderstood. Such problems, moreover, can be greatly compounded by virtue of the fact that the client seldom has the capacity or opportunity to judge the librarian's performance.

A good part of the difficulty in the librarians' dealings with inquirers arises, it seems to me, from the fact that the expectations placed upon the librarians seem so straightforward and simple-- deceptively straightforward and simple. As a professional and therefore someone obligated to render service of an appropriate standard, the reference librarian must be, it is generally agreed, competent, assiduous, courteous and nondiscriminatory. Such agreement, I suggest, is mostly the product of a rather superficial advocacy of what may look like the obvious "motherhood virtues." Examined more closely, each of the above desiderata may involve a sharp conflict between the librarian's self-interest and the interest of the client. Moreover, it is a conflict which the librarian may not necessarily or even usually be willing to resolve in favor of the client. Take, to begin with, the librarian's obligation for competence in the performance of his or her duties. This obligation implies not only the possession of the requisite initial qualifications (e.g., an M.L.S. with appropriate training in reference work) but also the requirement for keeping these qualifications up-to-date and up-to-scratch by a lifetime program of continuing education. This requirement for maintaining one's competence is, of course, no more than that which is demanded of professionals in almost every field. However--and here lies the ethical dilemma--unlike most other professionals, librarians are unlikely to receive much financial assistance or direct rewards for their efforts in continuing education, or, for that matter, to be subject to any penalty for failing to do so. Given also the fact that reference librarians are generally underpaid as it is and that their clients seldom recognize or complain of incompetence, should reference librarians realistically be expected to assume the burden of continuing education? The ethical problem here is substantial. It is also widely evaded, probably because, if seriously examined, it would really "hurt."

A comparable set of considerations apply to the other desiderata in the reference librarian-client relationship. It has been pointed out that reference librarians are frequently less than assiduous in the information service they render,[21] notably in respect of the degree of effort taken in the interview to find out exactly what the inquirer needs. Similarly, there is evidence to indicate that reference workers often discriminate among clients in the amount of service rendered. For example, questions from students and "contest" participants are likely to be treated quite differently than would the same questions asked by governmental officials or faculty members. Lastly, as librarians themselves have attested, courtesy and thoughtfulness are by no means the constant attributes of the reference worker. Crawford cites as particularly reprehensible the "casual disregard of confidentiality" in many reference departments and the "many put-downs" ranging from the "superior half-smile" to the "cold glare of indifference" by which librarians are apt to establish their superiority to their clients.[22]

The incidence of such failings among reference librarians in general is not known and is probably not even determinable with any statistical accuracy. Nor is it likely that individual librarians' performance in these respects is known either to themselves or to their supervisors. And yet knowledge is crucial in deciding whether an ethical problem is at issue here. Given the fallibility of mankind, some deficiencies in courtesy, effort or impartiality are inevitable in each of us. On the other hand, consistent failings in these respects would represent a kind of arrant insensitivity to the client's welfare that is tantamount to a dereliction in professional duty. And unfortunately the only way in which to answer that question of "guilt or innocence" is to have the individual librarians look within themselves and render conscientious and accurate judgment.

Clearly a substantial conflict of interest is implicit in such self-assessment. Quite apart from the normal human tendency to rationalize away one's failings and to take the most favorable view of oneself, reference librarians have some very good reasons to excuse or mitigate their blameworthiness. Others seldom appreciate in what extraordinarily difficult circumstances the librarian must operate within the "reference encounter." The reference librarians must serve anonymous clients whose needs and capabilities they cannot really know; they must be prepared to give instant answers to questions covering almost every conceivable subject; they must operate in full public view and under harassing requirements for speed. In most reference departments five minutes is considered a long time to allocate to one customer! Add in the facts that many of the questions asked may be repetitive to the point of numbing boredom and that the questioners themselves may be ignorant or rude, and is it any wonder that reference librarians may be tempted to take a self-exculpatory view of the imperfections in their relationships with clients? Here once again, then, the reference librarian's ethical problem will be "real" and substantial--and the dilemma will not be easily resolved.

Thus far in my analysis, I have dealt with the ethical problems of the librarian-client relationship solely in terms of the responsibilities devolving on the individual reference librarian. There is, however, another and very troublesome set of ethical problems in reference service which derive essentially from the policies set by the employing library rather than from the performance of the librarians themselves.

Perhaps the most publicized question of this sort relates to the quality of the information services rendered. The "unobtrusive testing" done by Childers and others has drawn attention to the fact that reference questions are often answered badly.[23] Allan Angoff has even suggested, albeit mostly facetiously, that libraries may be subject to malpractice suits if the erroneous or incomplete information which they supply leads to damaging consequences for the users thereof.[24] There seems to be no immediate likelihood of such suits but the mere possibility is enough to raise the significant issue of to what extent the library can and should "stand behind its wares."

And even if the library feels it can offer no guarantees, should it at least assume a commitment to quality in service? The Reference and Adult Services Division of the American Library Association evidently thinks the library should do something very like that. In the RASD's "A Commitment to Information Services: Developments Guidelines," it is specified that "a professional librarian/information specialist should be available to users during all hours the library is open."[25]

If the library is able but unwilling to meet that standard of quality, is it reprehensible? If it is unable, whether usually or in a given instance, to have a professional librarian on reference duty, is it morally bound to notify the public of that fact? If the library refuses to remedy or even give fair warning of its shortcomings in reference service, are its professional staff members and their library associations duty bound to take action against it? It will be readily seen that a whole hornets' nest of ethical problems opens up once one seriously examines the issue of quality control.

An even more explosive (pun intended, please note) issue in institutional responsibility was recently raised by Robert Hauptman's intriguing experimental study of libraries' attitude to the presumed uses of the information service they offered. Hauptman asked thirteen libraries for information on how to blow up a house; not one refused, on ethical grounds, to supply the information even though they were given reason to believe that the inquirer had a criminal purpose in mind.[26] D.J. Foskett once stated, in a memorable phrase, that the creed of a librarian vis-à-vis a client should be "no politics, no religion, no morals."[27] Apparently the libraries examined by Hauptman acted on those "hands-off" precepts to the point of being willing to aid and abet, so to speak, in the commission of a crime.*

Interestingly enough, the unanimity of viewpoint reported by Hauptman seems not to be unusual. In a rather similar vein, the library's obligation to respect the confidentiality of information about and for the client is one of the very few points to find a place in all the more recent codes of ethics. Such views probably derive from the present-day insistence on the paramount importance of freedom of information. However, as Hauptman points out,[28] in their anxiety to avoid imputations of censorship, discrimination and bias, libraries may well be abjuring other responsibilities to society. There is a real conflict of values here, no less strong for being generally unrecognized.

The issues of neutrality and privacy are also interesting in that they are examples of what may be said to be "gray areas" in reference ethics.

Doubt breeds dispute, and in such gray areas there are likely to be many instances of where conflicts of principle and interest arise as between the librarian and the library. An example may illustrate the point. How much reference service is the client entitled to? The conscientious librarian may well feel that anything less than an effort at full satisfaction is "short-changing" the client. Such a view may run counter to a library's policy of limiting service in the interest of economy.

---

*Robert Pierson has called attention to the fact that reference librarians quite frequently "aid and abet" in the commision of academic "crimes" such as plagiarism and cribbing. Cf. his "Is Moby Dick the Whale or the Captain?" RQ 7:21-24 (Fall, 1967).

It is probably a safe generalization to say that within the last decade, public libraries have been willing to go much further in the provision of legal reference service than ever before. There is no evidence to suggest that similar courage or initiative has been applied to other categories of "sticky questions." The traditional reluctance of libraries (as distinguished from their staff) to deal with matters of controversy is still evident in the way in which they tend to treat inquiries regarding the merits of specific encyclopedias, dictionaries and other reference books. Here on their very own ground of expertise, so to speak, reference librarians are usually not permitted to offer their personal knowledge or opinions and can only direct inquirers to such information as may be available from published sources, such as reviews. The libraries' caution is presumably occasioned by fear of prompting criticism or legal action by publishers. But such pragmatic considerations can run counter to the conscience of reference librarians themselves, who may see themselves as ready and able to do a far better job of information service than the needless timidity of their employing institutions allows them to offer.

Some of these conflicts between reference librarian and library might be obviated or alleviated if the libraries were required, as the RASD "Developmental Guidelines" demand,[29] to prepare and make public a written statement of reference service policy. The conscientious reference worker, who finds a given program of reference service to be substandard, would then presumably know that fact in advance and not go to work for such an employer. One may even visualize library associations protesting against and imposing sanctions upon such an offending library, much as the Library Association (of the U.K.) urges its members to blacklist libraries held to be in violation of standards of proper practice. Moreover, the poor old clients, now almost always completely ignorant of their rights with respect to reference service, would then at least know what they are entitled to expect, and might even press for a higher standard of service.

It is worth noting, however, that the result of requiring libraries to make a public statement on their reference policy might well yield the opposite outcome to that visualized above. My own guess is that such publication would prompt many libraries to play it even safer than they do now. They would simply employ opaque or evasive language to cover themselves against troublesome demands or criticisms. In a sense their commitment to a really good reference service might be weakened rather than strengthened.

Some Personal Conclusions

The fact is that there is probably no way in which the conflicts of interest or priorities as between librarian and library can be wholly reconciled. The same is probably true for all the examples of conflict which I have given in this paper. Moreover, I am convinced that it is a very good thing that the problems described here are not all that easily to be remedied.

Libraries and Librarians   21

I may well be deluding myself into taking an unreasonably optimistic view of an intractable situation, but it seems to me that it is the very existence of numerous and substantial ethical problems that attests to librarians' claim to professionalism. It is just because we recognize ourselves as having obligations and duties that may well outweigh our self-interest; it is because we espouse principles and standards that may well bring us into conflict with our employing institutions and even governments (as in the matter of confidentiality cases); it is because we may place duties upon ourselves (e.g., for continuing education) which our employers do not even see as necessary--it is largely because of issues such as these that we may distinguish our responsibilities as professionals from those of law-abiding persons of any calling.

I note with relish, moreover, that reference librarianship provides more and keener instances of such ethical concern than do most other types of library work. Reference work provides the practitioner with a clearly visible (if usually anonymous) client and a readily available and reasonably accurate judgment of success or failure in one's efforts on behalf of that client. By contrast, the technical services librarians cannot usually obtain nearly so immediate or sharp a sense of the consequences of their actions on the people they serve.

Accepting, then, that reference librarians not only _do_ but _should_ have ethical problems, how do I suggest that they _deal with them?_ My recipe consists of three steps. The first is to dispense with attempts at preparing or following codes of ethics. The consistent lack of attention given to such codes, not only in librarianship but in other fields,[30] indicates that they are of little use.* Almost inevitably they are apt to be pompous and orotund in wording and vague in meaning. More important, they are likely to be pointless and boring. People at any time do not wish to be harangued by precepts (I seem to recall that even the Ten Commandments did not go down very well with its intended audience)--all the more so if those precepts are unenforceable and, because of their generality, of doubtful relevance to any one group.

Nevertheless--point two--ethical issues _can_ be confronted. Indeed they must be if we reference librarians _are_ to regard ourselves as anything more than technicians. The first requirement in such confrontation is to identify the issues that really matter. I have suggested that the way to do so is look within ourselves and

---

*For a contrary conclusion regarding a field closely related to librarianship (information science), see the recent and interesting article by B.J. Kostrewski and Charles Oppenheim, "Ethics in Information Science," Journal of Information Science, 1:282-283, (January, 1980). A code of ethics, say Kostrewski and Oppenheim, would be useful in committing the professional association "to a certain stance in the case of a dispute between an information scientist and his employer." (p. 283)

see what troubles us--where it hurts. Many such troubles--our
anxieties about the right thing to do, our conflicts of interest--will
be easily apparent from such self-analysis. (Whether to charge fees
for reference service is a pertinent and at present frequent case in
point.) Other problems we, like all other humans, may well have
tried to repress or ignore. (The ethical obligation to maintain our
professional proficiency is an example of such generally unacknowledged problems.)

My last point is that, having (perhaps at some pain) identified
our ethical problems, we must reconcile ourselves to not solving
them. As distinguished from minor questions of deportment, which
are amenable to prescription in "codes of practice,"[31] major questions of principle, priority and conscience can only be discussed and
debated, not decided. But such "inconclusive" debate and discussion
are still well worth undertaking. At worst, it will indicate to ourselves and to the general public that librarianship is not the bland,
colorless, routinized activity that it is too often reputed to be.* At
best, we reference librarians will individually receive useful guidance
on the very biggest and most significant of the problems that beset
us.

And it all begins by finding out "where it hurts."

References

1. Robert Hauptman notes that Daniel Gothie's extensive Selected
   Bibliography of Applied Ethics in the Professions 1950-1970
   does not include a single citation in the field of library science. Cf. Robert Hauptman, "Ethical Commitment and the
   Professions," Catholic Library World 51:197 (December,
   1979).

2. Bernard Vavrek, "Ethics for Reference Librarians," RQ 12:56
   (Fall, 1972). Much the same complaint is made by Shirley
   Fitzgibbons, "Ethics," ALA Yearbook 1977. (Chicago: American Library Association, 1977), p. 116.

3. American Library Association. Code of Ethics Committee,
   "Code of Ethics for Librarians ... Adopted ... December,
   1938," A.L.A. Bulletin 33:128-30 (February, 1939); American Library Association. Special Committee on Code of
   Ethics," Statement on Professional Ethics ... 1975," reprinted in ALA Yearbook 1976 (Chicago: American Library
   Association, 1976), p. 155.

---

*Cf. John Sharp's biting criticism of librarianship in this regard. He
avers (mistakenly, in my opinion) that "the professional ethic is relevant only to situations in which there is potential for good or evil. Librarianship is sterile in that respect." ("For Good or Evil, Librarianship is Sterile," Library Association Record, 83:192. April, 1981.)

4. Institute of Professional Librarians of Ontario, "I.P.L.O. Code of Ethics," I.P.L.O. Quarterly 17:88-91 (July-October, 1975).

5. Ohio Library Association, "Library Code of Ethics, of the Ohio Library Association," Ohio Library Association Bulletin 46:7-9 (January, 1976).

6. California Library Association, "Draft Statement of Professional Responsibility for Librarians," reprinted in Recurring Library Issues: A Reader, ed. by Caroline M. Coughlin (Metuchen, N.J.: Scarecrow Press, 1979), p. 413-419.

7. American Library Association. Professional Ethics Committee, "Draft: Statement on Professional Ethics, [1979]," American Libraries 10:666 (December, 1979).

8. Library Association, "Draft Code of Professional Ethics: a Discussion Document October, 1980," Library Association Record 82 (October, 1980). Unpaged insert.

9. Martha Boaz, "Code of Ethics, Professional," in Encyclopedia of Library and Information Science (New York: Marcel Dekker, 1971), v. 5, p. 246.

10. Samuel Rothstein, "In Search of Ourselves," Library Journal 93:156 (January 15, 1968).

11. John G. Fetros, "The Search for a Code of Ethics," American Libraries 2:744 (July 1971). Cf. also Eric Moon, "Ethical Bones," Library Journal 93:131 (January 15, 1968) and Helen Crawford, "In Search of an Ethic of Medical Librarianship," Bulletin of the Medical Library Association 66:331 (July, 1978).

12. E.g. the A.L.A. Code (1938), point I.8; the Ohio Library Association code, points V.2, 3, 4; the I.P.L.O. Code point 7.

13. Crawford, "In Search of an Ethic of Medical Librarianship," p. 331.

14. The Library Association and the California Library Association codes are interesting exceptions to this statement in that they do make provision (not yet implemented, I believe) for the associations to review complaints of misconduct against members and to impose sanctions if need be.

15. American Library Association. Reference and Adult Services Division. Standards Committee. "A Commitment to Information Services," Library Journal 101:973-74 (April 15, 1976).

16. RQ 18:275-78 (Spring, 1979).

17. Ibid., p. 277.

18. Eleanor Blum and Clifford Christians, "Ethical Problems in Book Publishing," Library Quarterly, 51:155-69 (April, 1981).

19. Ibid., p. 156.

20. Ibid.

21. Donald Davinson, Reference Service (London: Clive Bingley, 1980), p. 93-96. Davinson bases his conclusions largely on the research by G. Carlson, Search Strategy by Reference Librarians: Final Report on the Organization of Large Files, Part 3 (Sherman Oaks, Calif.: Advanced Systems Division Hughes Dynamics Inc., 1964) [NSF Contract C 280].
    Cf. also Thomas Childers, "The Test of Reference," Library Journal 105:926 (April 15, 1980); David E. House, "Reference Efficiency or Reference Deficiency," Library Association Record 76:222-23 (November, 1974); William A. Donovan, "The Reference Librarian and the Whole Truth," RQ 8:196-99 (Spring, 1969).

22. Crawford, "In Search of an Ethic of Medical Librarianship," p. 334-35.

23. Thomas Childers, "Managing the Quality of Reference/Information Service," Library Quarterly 42:215 (April, 1972).

24. Allan Angoff, "Library Malpractice Suit: Could It Happen to You?," American Libraries 7:489 (September, 1976).

25. "A Commitment to Information Services: Developmental Guidelines," p. 277.

26. Robert Hauptman, "Professionalism or Culpability? An Experiment in Ethics," Wilson Library Bulletin 50:626-27 (April, 1976).

27. D.J. Foskett, The Creed of a Librarian--No Politics, No Religion, No Morals (Library Association. Reference, Special and Information Section. North Western Group. Occasional Papers No. 3 [London: Library Association, 1962]).

28. Hauptman, "Professionalism or Culpability ...," p. 627.

29. "A Commitment to Information Services: Developmental Guidelines," p. 277.

30. Boaz, "Code of Ethics, Professional," p. 246.

31. Cf. Institute of Professional Librarians of Ontario 'Recommendations re Professional Conduct: Some Do's and Don'ts for I.P.L. Members" [I.P.L.O.] Information Bulletin No. 4 (March, 1962).

Additional References

Anderson, John F., "Ethics: the Creaking Code," Library Journal 91:5333-35 (November 1, 1966).

Dalton, Jack, "Ethics" in ALA Yearbook 1976 (Chicago: American Library Association, 1976), p. 155-56.

Donovan, William, "Seemingly Unjustified Complaints Repay a Second Look," RQ 8:265-67 (Summer, 1969).

Gibson, Barbara, "Professional Ethics for Librarians," British Columbia Library Quarterly 27:10-13 (April 1964).

Grogan, Denis, Practical Reference Work. London: Clive Bingley, 1979, p. 16-17, 110-112.

Katz, William A., Introduction to Reference Work: Volume II, Reference Services and Reference Processes. 3d ed. New York: McGraw-Hill, 1978.

Roberts, Anne, "Prescriptive, Descriptive or Proscriptive? Implications of the Developmental Guidelines, A Commitment to Information Services," RQ 17:223-25 (Spring, 1978).

Vavrek, Bernard, "Implications of the New Information Service Guidelines," American Libraries 6:295-96 (May, 1975).

IGNORING THE USER: HOW, WHEN AND WHY*

Maurice B. Line

I do not propose to go into the history of ignoring users, since there is not time to give an account of librarianship from its beginnings, even in summary. Rather, I wish to say what I mean by users and their needs; to give some examples of how information providers (including libraries, but including also information systems and channels of other kinds) have ignored, and still ignore, users; to explain that to give users what they want it is sometimes necessary to ignore what they say; and to suggest ways in which users can be served in spite of themselves.

It is useful first to distinguish between needs, wants, demands and uses. At this point I am reminded of the story that appeared in American Libraries some months ago, of a middle-aged lady who came into a public library and asked the young man who served her if he was aware of an opinion poll that had shown that American women were a lot more interested in sex than in reading. He replied, "No, ma'am, but I do know that a lot more women come in here asking for books than for sex." Who is to say what the lady's needs, wants, demands or even uses were? Did the information she gave the young man satisfy any of his needs, or was it perhaps added to his store of knowledge for future use? Was he right in assuming most women came to the library for information, and how narrowly should the library define its role of serving information needs? How many people come to libraries for company, conversation, or even warmth, and is it utterly wrong to dissociate these needs and uses from information needs and uses?

In my definition, an information need is a basic requirement for information that is of value--for one's job, one's hobby, one's recreation or even one's life, private or social. A person may not--and this is a crucial point--always be aware of his needs. A want is a felt need; a demand is an expressed want; and a use is what it says it is. Use can occur without a demand being expressed or even without a want being felt--few felt the need to use pocket calculators until they became common, but now so many use them

---
*Reprinted by permission of the author and publisher from The Nationwide Provision [Aslib/IIS/LA Joint Conference] London: The Library Association, 1981.

that use can be said to have created a need, which would now have to be satisfied in other ways if calculators ceased to be produced. More commonly, information use--such as random browsing in a library--can help people to perceive needs as wants and articulate wants as demands.

"Users," by the way, are not some kind of special animal. They are not mice to be kept out or exterminated by all possible means, nor pandas that will eat only highly specific foods, nor buffaloes that will turn a place into a shambles if left untended. They are ordinary human beings like ourselves; and we could do worse than observe ourselves in a strange library, especially one in a foreign country, or using a new information system of whatever kind.

As ordinary human beings, users will take the shortest road that they know of, use the least effort possible, resent it if they think their time is being wasted, be unprepared to learn difficult or complex or inconvenient systems, and use systems only if they are rewarded for doing so or penalized for not doing so. Indeed, if libraries can convince their users that they are reducing the time and effort required to use them they are well on their way to winning the battle.

At this point it should also be noted that most information services are "free" to most users most of the time--that is, they do not pay money for using them. There are, it is true, costs of time and effort that are incurred, and, as just noted, users try to minimize these as best they can. This feature of information services--that they are mostly not paid for in money by their consumers--has both good and bad features. It means that there is no market evaluation (bad). It also means that the poorer do not get worse service because they are poor (good), though they may if they are also less informed about the system; and that long-term benefits can take precedence over short-term ones (mainly good but can be bad).

The simplest and most obvious element of library and information service is the library's collection. Librarians have built, and continue to build, their collections in various ways. The main ways are direct suggestion by users (very important in academic and special libraries); selection by library staff in anticipation of likely (mainly short-term) demand--this occurs particularly in public libraries; and aiming towards a "balanced" stock, with "fair" representation of different subjects and perhaps languages (this aim is commonest in national libraries and public reference libraries). Direct suggestions by users may be subject to vetting by library staff on grounds of desirability or money available--it may be preferred to buy material of wider interest than to a specific individual; in either case one of the other two principles of collection building may be underlying. The "balanced stock" concept is least user-orientated, regarding the library stock as almost a thing in itself-- although it might be argued that a balanced stock offers the best statistical probability of meeting future demand over the long term.

The middle option--meeting known and anticipated needs--seems the best in most circumstances but requires knowledge of or empathy with users; if it is badly done it is worse than the other options. A library designed solely to serve actual needs would receive fewer uses than one that anticipated demands and needs well (by stimulating use according to interest), while a library planned as a balanced collection may both fail to serve many short-term needs and become too out of date to serve many long-term needs as well.

To serve whom, though? All potential users (Mills and Boon readers included), or only some users? And if only some, which? In industrial libraries, and to a lesser extent in academic libraries, the clientele is already defined for the librarian, but this is not so in public libraries, for whom most non-users are potential users: should they serve the using "middle class" or the non-using "working class," and which interests and appetites should they serve? Is pandering to lonely old ladies by supplying them with romances any worse than pandering to a technological society by providing technological information to industry? There is not so much a danger as an inevitability of moral and cultural judgement in defining users, either implicitly or explicitly. Even when it is known or decided who a library's users are, it cannot serve them all of the time: a library that tries to respond to every individual demand or provide for every individual need is liable to end up by serving no one properly.

The above brief and crude analysis of one aspect of library service illustrates several things. It illustrates the weakness both of following users' demands slavishly and of ignoring present demands completely: "ignoring" can be either not bothering to find out or not listening when told--or both. It illustrates also the problems of anticipating their needs and demands.

Stock selection is perhaps the simplest example, but an emphasis on stock is itself something that may not be best for the user. The concept of a library as a collection of books available for use arises naturally enough from the monastic library and the private library: the idea of an information service to either monks or individual gentlemen is rather ludicrous, particularly in cases where books were collected as possessions rather than as stores of knowledge. The treasury/repository concept is still very much alive in some academic and a few public libraries--and rightly so for a proportion of their stock. At the other extreme are industrial libraries that are essentially information services and contain books only because books contain in a convenient form much information that is needed. This concept has influenced academic libraries, many of which perform both functions, but with significant differences in the balance between them.

In determining the balance, the librarian, in particular the academic librarian, has, in theory at least, the choice not only of selecting stock according to different models, as suggested above, but of deciding between stock and service--or, perhaps more neutrally, between passive service (well selected stock) and active service. His concept of the library will be crucial in deciding the balance--in essence, the question is whether he is library-orientated (building a "good" stock) or user-orientated. He may believe that a good stock is the best way of serving users, and he may even be right; he may also be wrong, and if so he is ignoring his users' needs (but not necessarily their words). The question has never been properly tested, and surely it is a matter of great importance to find the answer to it. If, however, he does not believe that a good stock is the best way of serving users, he will have to resist some suggestions for books that his users say they would like to have but do not want to buy for themselves; he may have to persuade his customers that an information service would serve them better. This is difficult to do in the abstract, and he may therefore have to take a risk by giving them the service first and seeking approval afterwards.

All this is rather theoretical. In practice the librarian may be so ruled by his committee or by other influences that may be brought to bear on him that he cannot do what he thinks he should do. His committee may consist largely of "politicians" (local or institutional) who have stopped using the library long ago. Nevertheless, they speak--again in theory--on behalf of users, and to ignore them is far from easy; in fact, ignoring the words of committees is a lot more difficult than ignoring the needs of users.

There is of course a higher level at which resources are allocated. In a university, the balance between scientific equipment and library expenditure has to be decided (often by default), and similar "decisions," deliberate or not, have to be made in other academic institutions, local authorities, industries and elsewhere. An <u>organization</u> may be neglecting its clientele or members by neglecting its library and information services. Librarians have to educate their authorities, through committees and in other ways. (Of committees, more later.)

On the micro-level also, librarians have ignored users in both senses--ignored what they said in order to give them what they wanted, and ignored, or not bothered to find out, what they needed. Wilful ignorance of established fact is rare mainly because there are so few established facts about users' needs, and what facts there are are open to different interpretations, or may be truly valid only for a particular place and time. However, even when several surveys, carried out at different places and times, point clearly in the same direction, librarians appear to be either unaware of the findings or reluctant to believe them or unwilling to act upon them.

Several studies have shown, for example, that simple catalogue entries serve most users better most of the time than complex entries, that classification schemes are not understood, and that classified catalogues are almost totally unused. Yes, a librarian may say, but although <u>users</u> may not use these tools, surely they can be invaluable in aiding library staff to serve users? To this I would reply that libraries with the most conventional catalogues and classification systems tend to be the last to devote much of their resources to information services.

These issues become more important as automation is being used more and more for the production of catalogues. As with the invention of printing the first typefaces copied manuscript letters, and as with the coming of railways coaches like those drawn by horses were put on rails and pulled by engines instead, so the cataloguing and classification styles designed for catalogue cards were initially transferred to the new medium; few people seemed to consider how the new medium could be used to serve users' needs most effectively, although the medium itself, with its flexibility of access and output, invited experimentation.

One of the problems of meeting users' needs is that it is difficult to ask them what they want, because they do not know what the ranges of possibility are, and even if told what is possible cannot imagine what it is like to use it. In any case, they may all give different answers, and even when they do not their individual desires cannot all be met. For example, every user would like the books he uses--"his books"--to be conveniently shelved altogether in one place--and preferably never moved thereafter. It is possible to find out how people use existing services and what they like and dislike about them, and this information can be interesting and useful, but it is of limited prescriptive value. In such circumstances it is hardly surprising if librarians stick to what they know and do, on the "father knows best" principle ("eat up your porridge, it is good for you").

One function, incidentally, that surveys can perform, apart from yielding useful information (if they are well designed, executed, analysed and interpreted--that rules out not a few), is that of showing concern for users, getting them to think a little about the service and to see that the library cares. A good survey is quite a potent instrument of propaganda (and a bad one can do much damage).

What users say they need of a service will depend very much on how they perceive the service. Their perception is rarely what we would like it to be, and it certainly differs from our perception of our own service, but we must admit that it is often uncomfortably close to reality. People ask more, and ask different things in a different way, of a good service. The best, if not the only way round the problem of how to serve users who cannot say what services would help them, is to develop new services and evaluate their use, in as real circumstances as possible. One recent example of this is the series of Bath University catalogue experiments, which, unusually for any research project, led to actual significant changes in practice. One reason why there have been so few experiments is that many librarians have shown little imagination, but another is that experiments can be costly. However, there are such great differences between libraries serving very similar clienteles that

Libraries and Librarians   31

we have in effect an actual situation that is quite close to an experimental one. Carefully designed studies of users in this natural experimental situation could provide some very useful comparisons. For example, provision of stock and services for medieval history in two libraries in universities with similar departments of medieval history may be very different in quantity and nature. It should not be difficult to find out which suits and serves the historians better. In such ways as these the time and cost of experimentation and evaluation can be greatly reduced: we need a Co-operative Library Experiment and Evaluation Programme (CLEEP).

To experiment it is necessary to hypothesize. Guesswork can be reduced by studies of the present system, especially comparative studies of different systems, but any major change requires a leap of the imagination. The librarian therefore needs to have not only a systematic design approach, but imagination and empathy. In any case, not all changes can be monitored without great effort and cost, and some can be implemented fairly safely without evaluation.

Some quite simple guidelines can be laid down for designing library and information systems. The first is that simplest is usually best: complexity increases costs disproportionately to any benefits to users, and may actually give an inferior performance. Secondly, when there is a choice of existing systems, the commonest one should normally be chosen, because there is a much higher chance that the user will be familiar with it. Why should the user have to learn a new classification scheme every time he uses a new library? This principle would in my view rule out Bliss and Colon entirely, whatever their theoretical virtues. The third principle is that, for rather similar reasons, refinements are to be avoided: at least a user going into a library that uses Bliss realises that it is not Dewey, but one going into a library that uses Dewey in an idiosyncratic way may be much more seriously misled. As Ranganathan said, "Save the time of the user" (a precept, incidentally, that I wish he had followed when writing his books). Systems should <u>not</u> be designed by bringing together committees of librarians, however experienced the librarians are and however many meetings they have: it is hard to think of a case where this procedure has resulted in any movement for anyone. The fundamental law underlying all guidelines for designing systems is that they should be <u>designed round users</u>--a point to which I shall return later.

Users do not by any means always react to changes, however well designed for them, with enthusiasm; they may prefer the bad old system. Some libraries have had this experience with computerized issue systems, especially when they are not working. People have to be persuaded and convinced, especially when they have been ignored in the past.

To act on behalf of users as <u>we</u> perceive their real needs can appear authoritarian. After all, some appalling things have been done by people who think they know what is best for others, and today we do not have to look far to find examples of people who

want to change a society that does not want to be changed, or at
least not in that way. "You'll feel better when you have fully recovered from the operation" is not a very comforting saying if it
is followed by "but it may take many years," or worse, by "... and
once you've adjusted to living with your handicaps." The solution
lies, as suggested, in building evaluation into change or new development--and also in not introducing too many changes at once. There
is another check to authoritarian change in libraries and information
services--users can get their own back by becoming non-users, unlike citizens who cannot opt out of an authoritarian society of which
they are inevitably members. If we do not make our systems usable
we do not deserve to have users.

If the advice of users is often not only useless but against
their own interests, should it be sought at all? To seek opinion and
then to ignore it is not calculated to please users, even if it serves
them. On the other hand, not to consult at all may be worse, and
it may be worse still to have some consultative machinery and use
it only for trivial and non-controversial issues. The question of
how much to tell committees, when and in what way, is a difficult
and important one, to which each librarian will have his own answer;
there is not time to go into the politics of librarianship here. The
more information that is given, the more awkward questions can be
raised, but a committee that suspects that information is being hidden from it is not likely to be very supportive. The best solution
in theory is a full statement of the problem and the factors that
lead the librarian to present a particular case, but this approach
has the difficulty that the committee may not be aware there is a
problem at all. Ultimately, much will depend upon how much trust
the committee places in its librarian; even the most unperceptive
committee will usually work out sooner or later (sooner rather than
later in most cases) whether a librarian is concerned primarily with
status--the library's or his own--or with the interests of his users.

At this point it may be remarked that, whatever the virtues
of committees, innovation is not one of them. Any bright idea,
especially one involving expenditure, has a very good chance of
being talked out or watered down. This is particularly so when
existing interests appear to be threatened or longstanding orthodoxy
is challenged. The creation of the National Lending Library for
Science and Technology is an especially interesting case. It was
approved by a committee of ultimate users--that is scientists--who
clearly did not see how it could do anything but lead to a greatly
improved service to them; but it is as good as certain that a committee of intermediate users--librarians--would never have approved
it. When the concept was first publicly discussed, the reactions of
many if not most librarians were very hostile, and it is greatly to
their credit that after two or three years nearly all of them not only
used it but began to admire its progenitor, in due course honouring
him with the Presidency of the Library Association. Dr. Urquhart
clearly perceived the needs of libraries better than their librarians
did. If ever there is a case of serving users in spite of themselves
this is it. It has been fascinating to watch from across the Atlantic

the same debate going on over the last few years in the USA. The concept of a National Periodicals Center took a long time to gain a fair measure of support, has still not been accepted by all librarians, and may now never be translated into reality. If such a centre had been established, say, ten years ago, or if the Center for Research Libraries in Chicago had been able to move more quickly in the direction of a comprehensive national service, it is safe to say that it would now be receiving such massive use that the whole debate would have seemed unreal.

Up to now no direct mention has been made of the possibility of ignoring users <u>completely</u> to the extent of gradually reducing their number with the <u>long-term</u> prospect of their total elimination. We all know how to do this, because libraries we have entered or inherited at some time have done a very good job along these lines, and because some of us have been guilty of practising the black art ourselves. We all know forbidding buildings, unhelpful staff, unguided shelves, unusable catalogues and out-of-date and badly chosen stock. Some exceptional libraries manage to combine all these features, and there may well be a good case for preserving one such library, so that it is not necessary to waste time going round several to find out how to ignore users in different ways.

More common than totally ignoring the user is despising him, because he is too stupid to use our system, organized as it is in accordance with all the best library manuals. Some libraries add insult to injury by first of all despising the user because he cannot use their libraries, and then "educating" him to bring him up to their elevated standards. To make myself clear, I must distinguish between guidance such as almost any system needs, and courses of training. Even courses of training may be necessary to enable customers to use bibliographic tools that are thrust upon libraries and users by producers and publishers, but "education" in basic use of an ordinary library is always patronizing and should never be necessary. That many people are stupid is a fact of life: if God had intended us all to be high fliers, he would not have invented the ground.

I have hitherto used libraries as an example, but everything said so far applies equally, <u>mutatis mutandis,</u> to information services such as indexing and abstracting services and even to forms of publication such as microforms. Microforms are an excellent way of storing the barely readable in the form of the barely legible, though I question whether some microform producers should go so far as to ensure that it is quite impossible to produce legible hard copies from their films. Microforms have been the "system of the future" for about 50 years, and I hope that this future never comes. While librarians may have to tolerate microforms, they should not-- and most of them do not--advocate their extension.

Librarians also have to accept the published indexing and abstracting tools that are published, but it is distressing that they seem unwilling or powerless to exert some influence over them. Last year saw the completion of a long-term research programme

into information problems and systems in the social sciences. The
research team found a great proliferation of indexing and abstracting
services in the social sciences; they were growing very much faster
than primary journals. Overlap between them was massive, but no
worker in a particular field of the social sciences could expect to
obtain even 70-80 per cent of relevant references unless he used
four or five different services. Not only was their coverage of
journals poor, but their coverage of non-journal literature, which
accounts for about half of the literature and half of the usage in the
social sciences, was barely covered at all. Secondary services also
varied greatly in their arrangement, frequency, currency and style
of entry. How such a system can conceivably serve users at all
well is hard to imagine. Few individual secondary services seem to
be really well designed, and secondary services as a total system
are virtually unusable. It is hardly surprising that they are grossly
under-used. Even if their libraries could afford to buy them all,
users would be totally confused and ill-served. Since no library can
afford more than a fraction of them, the situation is even worse.

There is more than one lesson to be learned here. The first
is that most producers can hardly have bothered to study their potential users before designing the service, or to evaluate the service when it was produced. In many cases it is hard to guess the
audience at whom the service is aimed. Problems of this kind are
normally sorted out by market evaluation, but this has not occurred
with secondary services because the purchasers (libraries) are not
the users. The second lesson is that librarians, as the purchasers,
have made little if any effort to find out which secondary services
serve their users best. To do so is not easy, whether "objective"
criteria such as coverage and overlap are used or "subjective" criteria such as acceptability and ease of use, but since library budgets
are everywhere very tight and cancellations are having to be made,
it is surely most important that librarians find out what to cancel.
If some of the unnecessary secondary services were eliminated because librarians ceased to buy them, there might be more chance
of the remaining ones improving. As it is, almost any secondary
service will find buyers, even if it finds no users in the libraries
that buy it.

There have been signs that similar neglect of users was oc-
curing in the online information services, but there is a major difference in that the use of these can be directly monitored, so that
evaluation is relatively easy. This does not of course mean that
they cannot be improved, but there is a strong element of competition that does not exist for published secondary services. It has
been amusing and interesting to hear more and more about "user-
friendly" systems and even terminals, indicating that this is an area
where the user can and does have a say and influence. But if we
talk about user-friendly online systems, we should also think about,
and should long ago have thought about, user-friendly published secondary services and user-friendly libraries. Indeed, if some libraries and their staffs do not become rather more user-friendly,
the friends they have may desert them for computer terminals,

which may have their limitations but may also have fewer user-hostile elements.

In parenthesis, the possible disbenefits of a good library and information service should not be forgotten. Not only may one good library spoil users and make them unable to use or tolerate other, more typical, libraries, but a good library system may do as much harm as a succession of excellent but excessive meals, inducing users to put on mental fat to an extent where they become incapable of clear or creative thought. Information overload is a serious problem. It is all very well to say that users can ration themselves--this is rather like putting boxes of chocolates in front of children and telling them to control their eating habits. A good service is one that drip-feeds rather than swamp-feeds its users. It would, however, be going a little far to cultivate deprivation deliberately because Bunyan wrote Pilgrim's Progress in prison.

Earlier I mentioned as the most fundamental principle of all information systems design the need to build the system round the user. One reason why I object so much to a good deal of user education is that it attempts to mould the user to fit the system, and quite apart from any considerations of humanity, I believe it is a good deal easier to modify systems than to modify human nature. If we are to serve users we must know our users--and this is not very different from saying that we must understand human beings better. We can observe them, we can survey them--as unobtrusively as possible; we can study the effect of any changes in our systems upon them, but above all we have to get to know them personally. In some environments, for example, industry, this is much easier than in others such as a public library, but in all cases it is vital. I suggested earlier that we might do worse than observe ourselves when using unfamiliar libraries and information systems. If we are totally unrepresentative of ordinary mankind, this exercise will not be very useful, but I would suggest that such a degree of abnormality would not equip us very well for our job in the first place.

Getting to know people better is not in itself enough. We have to gain their confidence, convincing them that we are on their side, and that our only concern is to give them the best service we can within the resources we have. I suspect that if you ask many people whether their librarian is giving them a good service, they would reply along the lines of "Don't shoot the librarian, he is doing his best"--to which a reasonable reaction would be that if what he has done in many places is the best that a librarian can do, he probably ought to be shot.

People in the information world seem to have more conferences than any other profession--something that has always been rather a mystery to me, because there must be other professions in which it is possible to learn from those who are better and to gain comfort from the observation of those who are worse. With all these discussions we keep having with one another, could we not do more to pool our experience of users? Of all the surveys of library and information use that have been carried out, how many are comparable or replicable? And apart from systematic studies of users, surely it would be useful to pool reactions to our services and to changes in them, however impressionistic these are? Can we have fewer papers on "How I run my library good" and more on "What my users feel about my service"?

Having sensitive antennae is of no use unless the sensations are put to some practical purpose. Being in tune with one's users should not put one in the position of a passive receiver. Understanding one's users should lead to a continuous exploration of ways in which the service can be improved. To improve services requires an extensive knowledge of the techniques for doing so, and it requires also imagination, commonsense and courage. This all sounds very idealistic, too far away from the brass tacks of librarianship; but a librarianship that consisted entirely of brass tacks would be neither aesthetically pleasing nor physiologically comfortable, and to put together a bulky structure with brass tacks is no better than putting it together with tin tacks. Librarianship and information science should have its philosophy as well as its technology.

SOMETHING THERE IS THAT DOESN'T LOVE A PROFESSOR:

"THE MISMANAGEMENT OF COLLEGE LIBRARIES" REVISITED*

Daniel Gore

Sixteen long years have now passed, and still a pungent air of cooling brimstone hovers about the thick file of letters I received from wrathy colleagues who read my paper, "The Mismanagement of College Libraries," when it came out in the March 1966 issue of the AAUP Bulletin (p. 46-51). One naturally expects to provoke a certain measure of hostile response on any occasion of speaking plainly about the shortcomings of one's profession. But neither I nor the editor of the Bulletin really anticipated the firestorm of outrage, scathing denunciation, and violent language that quickly began to roar my way, and his. Journal editors hear a lot of harsh comment from readers and learn to relish it: somebody out there is actually reading their publication! But this editor was not enjoying what he was hearing then from librarians around the nation. He rang me from Washington to ask, anxiously, "Why am I getting mail like this? I've never seen anything like it, and most of it is just too violent to publish."

    Well, I told him I was getting some pretty warm correspondence myself, a lot of it also unpublishable, and I was a little puzzled too about the unprecedented hysteria in many of the letters--some of which were sent unsigned, while others bore the signatures of a number of persons, suggesting a posse of vigilantes in hot pursuit of a candidate for hanging. I tried to calm that editor down by offering him a fresh new paper entitled "A Modest Proposal for Improving the Management of College Libraries," but that was not his idea of comfortable words. So instead I comforted him with the news that I had also received letters from a number of librarians saying they had found the paper to be an honest, accurate, and welcome depiction of the unpleasant reality of academic libraries as they had known them too. The editor could at least stop worrying whether my unflattering view of academic libraries was a nightmare vision unique to myself--and to his wife, who had worked in academic libraries and had encouraged him to publish the piece in the first place.

---

*Reprinted by permission of the author and publisher from Library Journal, 107:7 (April 1, 1982) 686-691. Published by R.R. Bowker Co. (a Xerox company). Copyright © 1982 by Daniel Gore.

As a matter of fact, that Bulletin essay was only a rewrite of a paper I had published the year before in the journal of a regional library association. The readers of that journal let it sail by them on a sea of almost unbroken calm. Yet when essentially the same paper appeared in the AAUP Bulletin, the president of the same regional association publicly censured me for publishing an "unscientific paper." He seemed not to realize that his own journal had published virtually the same paper a year before, thus making us equal partners in the sin against science. My motive for placing the revised essay in the Bulletin was to obtain a wider audience of both librarians and professors on an issue that I assumed concerned both groups equally. Since the earlier published version of the paper provoked so little reaction from librarians, I had some difficulty comprehending why the revised version in the Bulletin was now arousing so many cries of outrage and alarm.

Some correspondents plainly told me I had no business publishing unflattering words about librarians in their enemy's own journal: they felt betrayed. In those days I could not see how the faculty could be the enemy. Like many other librarians, I held a faculty appointment myself and was also a member of the AAUP. So the Bulletin seemed to me, logically, simply to be our journal, and certainly not the organ of some hostile, opposition group. Moreover, in those days most of my friends were young, easygoing, good-natured faculty members, still untenured but confident that some day they would be, and I spent a lot of time drinking beer and playing tennis with them. Certainly such amiable folk could never be foes of librarians--their allies in scholarship--and publishing in their journal, which I understood to be our journal too, could hardly be called treason.

My faith in the modesty, good sense, and natural good-heartedness of professors even soared to the extreme height of my believing they could actually help solve management problems in their own libraries, if only they would put their minds to it--as I naïvely called upon them to do in that Bulletin paper. Clearly I had drunk too much beer, and played too much tennis with professors, to have a proper understanding of their ludicrous incapacity for solving any problem having to do with libraries.

"But now the fancy passes by, and nothing will remain," as the poet says, and years of dealing with the vagaries and perversity of sometimes mischievous professors have taught me to feel genuine sympathy for the writers of those sulfurous letters in my files. They knew perfectly well who the enemy was, but like other afflicted minority groups they hadn't been risking public announcements. Rarely in our vast professional literature will you find any hint of the strong resentment librarians feel towards faculty as a class. The curses we send their way are like those Macbeth feared: not loud, but deep. The general desire among academic librarians to hold faculty rank must be at least partly attributable to the Freudian theory of the desire for identification with the enemy. Since he is overwhelmingly powerful, our best hope is to become indistinguishable

Libraries and Librarians   39

from him. We have gone far in that direction, but still the old tensions remain.

Howling frustrations

It is easy for me now to guess how this tradition of bad feelings between librarians and professors arose. In recent years, as we began to regard libraries as inventories for answering present demands, rather than treasuries for future generations to plunder, we've learned that people coming to an academic library in quest of a book or whatnot have probably suffered less than a 50 percent chance of finding it there. Libraries have brought scholars not just rich satisfactions, but immense, howling frustrations too. If you were looking for frustration--and even if you weren't--you'd find plenty of it in the library. And when you felt you must finally ventilate it, what better target than a librarian to aim your fury at? After all, the librarians caused your misery--and, better yet, the librarian is powerless to retaliate. Your cause is just and your tormentor weak: the perfect combination for initiating hostilities any time you feel like it. Faculty often feel like it--or so they say themselves. Consider one professor's baleful views of his colleagues that surfaced in the New York Times Op-Ed page on December 12, 1977. The writer is Charles Steinberg, professor of communications at Hunter College since 1972. For 16 years prior to that, he was vice-president of CBS-TV; not the sort of person to frivolously condemn his own associates in a place so public as the editorial pages of the Times. Here is what Professor Steinberg has to say about professors:

> Having spent five years in the lofty academic post of full professor at a prestigious university, I can't puzzle out why my former colleagues in industry look with envy on my new affiliation. Most of them applaud my "courage" in walking away from a lucrative executive position. And wish that they had the guts to abandon the rat race for the tranquil groves of academe. I assure them that their idea of a university bears little resemblance to reality, and that their notion that they will find tranquility in academe is a gross canard. Pay no heed to those stories of backbiting on Madison Avenue. They are a mild broth compared to the witches' brew that professors are capable of stirring up in the deceptively mild environment of the campus.
> Academe, in short, can be a jungle--more terrifying than the real jungle, where predators kill out of a natural need for food. But academic people on the make have an instinct for the jugular that is driven by a deadly combination of ruthless ambition and sheer, malevolent, sadistic pleasure.

Here I will suspend the professor's diatribe in order to give you the first of three examples from my own experience of what Professor Steinberg is talking about.

At one of my many stops along the academic trail, a professor decided to offer an undergraduate course in the American novel, loftier than others in that it would focus exclusively on the works of unknown 19th Century women authors. Of course, the library owned none of these rarities. The professor's idea was to acquire them all on interloan, and naturally he told us nothing of his intentions, and placed no requests until the day the course began. As it turned out, only the Library of Congress and the Boston Athenaeum owned these elusive titles, and they weren't about to lend them to us or anyone else. Upon learning of the embarrassing dead end his course was speeding towards, the professor did not think to look upon himself and curse his fate, or his own lack of foresight. Instead he launched a bitter attack upon our hapless interloan librarian. Repeatedly I tried to halt the attack by pointing out to this choleric professor that the interloan person could not be fairly blamed for failing to deliver what other libraries would not provide. But the attacks continued, and culminated with the professor's writing a letter denouncing the incompetency of the interloan librarian and proposing his early dismissal.

At that point, I told the professor flatly that his charge of incompetency was unfounded and indefensible--and that a letter of retraction would now be welcomed from him, since he had elevated the issue to the epistolary mode. This professor was not used to having his assaults upon a mere staff person blunted, let alone turned back upon himself, and he declined to retract his harsh and unjust words. Whereupon I told him I would then be obliged to pass his malignant letter along to the person he had so freely condemned, and let the victim decide for himself whether the slander he had suffered was worth discussing with a lawyer. The professor suddenly realized he was on strange new ground, where even tenure afforded no protection. He shot out of my office like Zacchini, the human cannonball, and in a few days I was hearing around campus that I had threatened to sue the professor myself and that other faculty should take warning and mind their manners around library staff lest I sue them too. At the end of this dark comedy, the professor did retract his malicious words, and thanks to his false or confused reporting of my litigious disposition, the library staff suffered very little thereafter from the faculty's "malevolent, sadistic pleasures," whereof Professor Steinberg was speaking in the <u>Times</u> piece. Now a few more excerpts from Steinberg's phillippic:

> Strangely enough, for five years I have heard little talk of students' needs. Teaching and learning are rarely mentioned. Instead the burning issue usually involves political action against the misfeasance--real or imagined--of the administration. [And often of the library too.] The administration is the enemy and the particular target of professors who operate behind the sanctuary of permanent tenure; the administration is autocratic and evil when it confronts an issue, and pusillanimous when it does not. [And so, I have learned, is the library.]
>
> As a full, tenured professor, I am considered fortunate

> in being immune to these pressures. Indeed, no business corporation can boast of executive authority remotely comparable to the arrogance of power emitted by the tenured professor. As a result, many of my sacrosanct colleagues are utterly contemptuous of their peers, autocratic with their students....

Putting my own words in the professor's mouth, some of them are demanding and insolent with librarians, haughtily indifferent to the limitations that reality imposes on every kind of library service, and paragons of ingratitude when it comes to making any acknowledgment of the valuable things we regularly do on their behalf ... But I let myself get swept away by the strong undertow of the professor's rhetoric. Back to the professor, and the peroration of his diatribe:

> C.P. Snow once called the academic world a community of "strangers and brothers." That is actually a better description of the corporate executive hierarchy. Despite the jockeying for position, despite the uncanny ability of some to succeed without really trying, the corporate organization men have a sense of loyalty and obligation that reveals an instinct for morality. It is a profound shock to discover that in the academy ethics and obligations are just that--academic.
>
> In the desperate need to publish or perish, in the savage struggle for tenure, there is a lethal combination of ambition and malevolence that shortchanges the students and demeans the idea of what a university should represent. That's why I urge my former colleagues to stay put in their precarious executive suites. The grass is not greener in academia, and the ivy can be very poisonous.

Steinberg's bleak view of the faculty matches that of Wilhelm von Humboldt, founder of the University of Berlin. "It was in no small measure the arrogance and vanity of the professors that drove him to distraction," Prof. Ziolkowski of Princeton states in the <u>Chronicle of Higher Education</u> (April 24, 1978, p. 44).

> The true father of the university, who had been commissioned by the Prussian government to bring about its establishment, Humboldt resigned his position only a few weeks after the first lectures began in 1810. "To direct scholars," he confided to his wife, "is not much better than being in charge of a troupe of comedians." Scholars, he complained, constitute "the most unruly and least easily satisfied class of human beings, with their jealousy, their envy, their lust for power, their one-sided views, in which each one believes his discipline alone deserves support and advancement."

Both Steinberg and Humboldt have probably overstated their case against the captains of erudition. At any rate, one of Steinberg's departmental colleagues at Hunter College soon gave him the retort direct in a letter to the Times, arguing that only a few "misfits" in the otherwise wholesome academy justly deserved Steinberg's harsh words. For charity's sake, and honesty's too, in my own experience, let us accept this temperate view, and agree that it is these misfits who make such great mischief for academic librarians. Though they may be few in number, they are powerful in effect, both on our work, and on our nerves. All of us could provide dramatic examples from our own experience. To exemplify further Steinberg's generalities and also to reassure you that you are listening to a respectably scarred veteran, not a smoothskinned theorist, I offer the following two examples from my experience.

Classify for vanity

A professor of literature comes to me with the demand that our many volumes of The Huntington Library Quarterly be reclassed from Z, where the Library of Congress places them, to PR. The professor's argument is that the Quarterly frequently publishes literary studies and should, therefore, be classed with literature, rather than with the publications of libraries. I tell him his argument is entirely reasonable, and the only problem with it is that for nearly every publication in the library a good case could also be made for putting it in some class other than the one LC chose. And if ever we started responding favorably to such arguments, the library would begin to whirl in a vortex of perpetual reclassification. The professor is unsatisfied with this answer, and peppers me with a shower of specious reasons why our entire run of HLQ must immediately be reclassed. Finally I say to him, "Your insistence upon having this journal reclassed surpasses anything I've ever seen. Something very personal seems to be at stake for you here, and I wonder if you would mind telling me what it is?"

Astonishingly, he tells me. The Quarterly had recently accepted a paper of his for publication, and his colleagues might eventually stumble upon it through browsing, if only I would remove the journal from class Z, where they never browse, and put it in PR, where they sometimes do. Then they might discover that this distinguished journal had published his paper! "Why don't you just send them a reprint?," I innocently ask. "That way they're sure to know about your paper." The professor explodes at what I thought was a pretty useful piece of advice.

"Don't you know my colleagues will accuse me of vanity if I do that? The journal must be shelved where they'll come upon my paper by chance!"

Outside the academy, a story of such bizarre egotism could neither be understood nor believed. I tell it as a light prelude to something graver. My final narrative has to do with the profaning of holy things, with the ethical emptiness that Professor Steinberg was shocked to discover in the academy.

Several years after I submitted my mismanagement piece to the wrong journal, I found myself caught in the middle of what must surely be the worst situation a librarian can get into professionally: a censorship issue. I wasn't actually in the middle of the issue: I was on one side of it, the side that holds that principles of academic and intellectual freedom require us to guard libraries against censorship. Some indignant parent wanted <u>The Evergreen Review</u> thrown out of the college library I directed, and I wasn't about to comply. I put the matter before the faculty library committee, whose chairman, by chance, was also the local chapter president of the AAUP. The issue was discussed amiably and sporadically for several months, and then a member of fundamentalist persuasion moved to expel <u>The Evergreen Review</u> forthwith from the library. The committee chairman was much dismayed when the vote came to a tie--leaving him, our AAUP chapter president and local champion of academic freedom, to break the tie. Stunned by his bad luck, he meditated in silence for at least ten minutes, with his forehead cradled in his fingers and the committee nervously trying to avoid taking open notice of his silent anguish. Finally he raised his head and broke his long silence to deliver as fine a brief discourse as you will ever want to hear in defense of academic freedom. And then he voted to throw out <u>The Evergreen Review</u>. Had he voted the other way, as the central ethic of the academy plainly required him to do, then his own livelihood would have been in jeopardy.

The unpleasant secret

Experiences such as these prove nothing at all, but they do help me to understand what it is that drives Professor Steinberg to make such a damaging public assessment of his fellow teachers--and what it was that so angered my library colleagues when I wrote of their managerial shortcomings in the leading journal of their natural enemy. Steinberg can rail securely against the professors, with the shield of tenure before him. Most of us cannot. For even if we possess the shield, we are still caught in a service relationship to the faculty, as Steinberg is not. Somehow we must get along with them, misfits and all, and by various stratagems we manage pretty well, keeping the unpleasant secret of our longstanding tensions hidden from public view.

Although we cannot afford to speak openly about the strained relationship between professors and librarians, I see things happening in librarianship that will, on the one hand, release the tension, and on the other increase it to the point of open rupture. The strain will be eased by our dramatically growing capacity to deliver to scholars a very high percentage of the publications they wish to see. The rapid spread of highly efficient interloan networks, the development of computerized bibliographic services, and the better management of local collections through automated inventory control, all point to a time in the rather near future when faculty will have to abandon their immemorial complaint that we give them too little, and too late. The grief instead will be that we routinely give them more than they can possibly use. They may eventually come to regard us with the sort of awe one feels for a broken dam or an active volcano.

Ten years ago few of us took seriously the optimistic forecast that the computer would bring revolutionary change to libraries. We enjoyed hearing of the comic disasters that befell pioneering efforts to make computers work in libraries. Failure after failure confirmed our fixed belief that no mere computer could cope with the vastness and intricacy of our collections, nor with the variety, complexity, and unpredictability of library transactions. Hopes were blighted, careers damaged, and sometimes an entire library administration would collapse when an expensive automated system turned out to have not bugs but dragons in it. But out of that rich compost of seeming failures, success is suddenly flowering up, and everywhere we look we are beginning to see automated circulation, cataloging, and retrieval systems functioning efficiently and reliably--and truly revolutionizing the capacity of libraries to provide real service. The long age of frustration and disappointment in using libraries draws rapidly to a close.

We have mainly ourselves to thank for that approaching end to our professional frustrations. Within the academy, no group has rivaled librarians in their willingness, and in their capacity, to bring about beneficial changes. For all their heady talk about innovations in teaching, faculty still appear to go about their work much as they did in the middle sixties, or the Middle Ages. Not that that is necessarily a bad thing. The point is that while professors love to urge radical change upon everybody else, they are notoriously hostile to the introduction of any change that touches their professional life. Indeed I have learned over the years that the principal obstacle to change in academic libraries is not the librarians, as I once thought, but the professors. They clamor for better library service, but bristle at the idea of changing any library practice to obtain it.

In my own work I have sometimes introduced innovations that brought about unmistakable improvements in service--and often discovered that one or more professors would be inconsolably distressed when they learned about it. Showing them the plain before-and-after facts of the matter would do nothing to abate their anger. A change had been imposed upon them, and they were bound to hate it regardless of its favorable consequences, simply because it was a change.

Diffuse dictatorship

Adverse faculty reaction to library change is such a common and predictable phenomenon, I marvel when any change at all takes place in an academic library. If one seeks to introduce change in the sole manner endorsed by the academy--that is to say, by gaining the approval and support of every faculty member on campus--

then no change will ever take place, because the only change that
ever receives unanimous faculty approval is a raise in their salaries.
This requirement for unanimity is called academic democracy, but
it seems more a diffuse sort of dictatorship, where everyone believes he or she is by right entitled to block any action initiated by
other persons. In the Old South, we call that principle Nullification.

None of this is news to any library director, but it may be
to other staff. When a director sets a library on a course of
change, even with the enthusiastic support of library staff and maybe even a majority of the faculty, he can be quite certain that some
professors will denounce him as autocratic and impulsive for not
consulting them ahead of time in order to obtain their predictable
veto. Making changes in an academic library involves not only
risks--things sometimes do not work out as hoped, and occasionally
they crash in flaming disaster--but even the successful changes involve the certainty that some part of your faculty clientele will never
forgive you for having brought off a beneficial change.

An academic library director eventually grasps that either
there will be no change, nothing but stagnation and sullen discontent
until the revolving years whirl him into the Elysium of retirement--
or there will be change, and along with it, a growing coterie of disaffected faculty to bring a very special misery into the director's
life. The courage of those directors, and their staffs, who have
suffered over the years to make computers work in libraries, is
something I admire mightily. I can unabashedly praise their daring,
and their successes, and their failures too--without which there
never could have been any successes--I can praise all those things
unhampered by personal modesty, because they are things I've had
nothing directly to do with myself. I have only watched, and waited,
and wondered how the computer might eventually transform libraries,
once we had tamed it and taught it to do properly most of the routine tasks that human hands and heads have done in the past.

Curbing scholarly excess

The brightest mission I see ahead for the computerized library is
the exposure, and possibly the curbing of the great scholarly excesses of the 20th Century. The faculty do not even suspect it yet,
but we librarians are pretty well poised to show that a scandalously
large proportion of their published work is rarely used by anyone.
You have seen the facts trickling in over the last few years; but the
rapid spread of automated circulation systems will soon turn that
trickle into a stream, and thence into a mighty river to wash away
the persistent illusion that the enormous outpourings of scholarship
are actually useful to mankind. For the most part it appears they
are not useful, in the sense that they do not get used. But scholarly
tradition has disposed us to believe otherwise, and ensures their endless multiplication through the requirement that professors emit such
things at decent intervals as a primary condition of promotion. Our
libraries are storehouses not only for the advancement of learning,
but of careers as well.

Those libraries are fast running out of space. Where are you going to shelve all the scholarly contributions that are coming your way over the next decade? The present outlook is that you will not be able to shelve them much longer in ever larger numbers on your own campus. You will instead be entering into a variety of off-campus storage arrangements for economically housing the vast quantities of dead and dying material that presently burdens your shelves.

When large numbers of academic libraries begin to do that openly--some have done it furtively for years--then we may have to endure a professorial resentment on the epic scale, as when the blinded Cyclops learned that Odysseus had absconded with his sheep. For nothing offends a professor as the deliberate ejection of a book from the library by librarians, even on a clear showing that the book never gets used. It is easy to understand why they take offense, when you consider that most of the little or never-read books were written by the professors themselves. Our shelves aren't jammed with Shakespeare's plays--there are only 37 of them--but by the hundreds of books about them, mostly the work of scholars, many of them unreadable and unread. "There is more ado to interpret interpretations than to interpret things," says Montaigne, "and more books upon books than upon all other subjects; we do nothing but comment upon one another."

How will we develop the nerve to announce to the faculty what we are learning about the usefulness and durability of their publications? Partly, I think, from losing that old sense of impotency that came from knowing that much too often we simply could not produce the book or article that the professor wanted. Multiply such failures to deliver by millions of times, and spread the sense of failure among thousands of librarians over the span of decades, and what you get is a nervous profession easily intimidated by the faculty, and envious and resentful of them, too. That sense of impotency will vanish as we and the faculty come to see that we can deliver virtually everything that is wanted, and a good deal more than can actually be used.

We will be even more strengthened by discovering, through the use of computers, exactly what is going on in our vast library collections. When the first shock of discovery wears off and faculty come to understand the exceedingly low utility of so many of their publications, they may be grateful to us for revealing the absurd consequences of the old publish-or-perish mandate. Most professors I have known regard publishing as only a slightly more attractive option than perishing, and would cheerfully cease to publish if administrators would remove the pressure. Perhaps administrators will, when they see the end results of that pressure: namely the enormous capital and operating costs of housing an expanding heap of unread books that got written only because administrators thought publishing was the only sure-fire test of professorial competency. Looking at those piles of unread books, and contemplating the pressures that brought them into being, administrators may ask themselves whether all this forcing-house scholarship was really worth it, and whether some better and cheaper way of assessing teacher competency cannot be found. If the pressures to publish were removed, academic life might become at least as pleasant as the life of corporate executives, which Professor Steinberg unhappily forsook for the halls of poison ivy. Certainly our life as librarians would be made more agreeable by slowing the torrent of tepid scholarly work that keeps flowing into our already flooded stack areas.

"Ye shall know the truth, and the truth will make you free." That great New Testament prophecy has a special relevance to our situation as librarians. We have never really known the truth about libraries. The facts were just too numerous to assess, or even obtain, and most of our decisions about library management have perforce been made in near-total ignorance of the facts. The state of our knowledge may be likened to that of biologists prior to the invention of the microscope: we have grossly misconstrued the fundamental nature of the organism under study simply because we were unable to see what was going on. Like microscopes, computers will enable us to see a whole universe of activity hitherto seen by no one. The computer is on the way to revolutionizing librarianship as the microscope did biology two centuries ago. We can make it show us the truth about libraries, and the truth will set us free from many things that plague and perplex us--including our uncomfortable relationships with professors. When we can all finally see and know what is going on in libraries, then we should be able to get on amicably together in the common enterprise of helping young people discover the durable ideas, and value the unfading beauties of feeling and imagination that also repose on library shelves, and make libraries the noblest, and most humane, of all institutions.

LIBRARIES, TECHNOLOGY, AND THE
INFORMATION MARKETPLACE*

Richard De Gennaro

"Reports of my death are greatly exaggerated." With that brief rejoinder Mark Twain squelched the stories of his death that appeared in the New York papers when he was living in London in 1897. Unfortunately, it is not so easy to squelch the equally false reports of the death of libraries that have been appearing in the press since the 1960's. The truth is that libraries are alive and well and adapting to a changing world. They continue to serve millions of grateful users in both old ways and new, despite the ravages of inflation and budget cuts. It is true that a variety of new and expensive commercial information services are mushrooming to serve the special needs of business and industry, but for most of us, libraries are, and will be for years to come, the only affordable information game in town or on campus.

Beware of predictions

There is a growing consensus among a new wave of technologists and futurists that books and other forms of print on paper are on their way out, along with the libraries and librarians whose stock in trade they are. They are telling us that books and libraries are being made obsolete or irrelevant by new electronic technologies in the hands of an aggressive new breed of information entrepreneurs. If this sounds familiar, it is because similar predictions were being made during the early 1960's in the first flush of enthusiasm that greeted computers and electronic media.

The current wave of predictions that electronic technology will soon replace books and libraries is inspired by a rapidly accelerating series of developments in that technology which multiplies its power while drastically reducing its costs. Among these developments are communications satellites, cable TV, inexpensive

---

*Reprinted by permission of the author and publisher from Library Journal, 107:11 (June 1, 1982) 1045-1054. Published by R.R. Bowker Co. (a Xerox company). Copyright © 1982 by Xerox Corporation.

Libraries and Librarians   49

mass-storage in the form of optical and digital videodisks, and powerful microcomputers on chips. With them we are acquiring a level of technology which fires the imagination and gives credence to even the most fanciful forecasts. In this heady environment, there is a danger that those responsible for the financial support of libraries will neglect or prematurely abandon traditional libraries in favor of more glamorous alternatives in promising, but as yet untested or even nonexistent, technologies.

We have seen many advances in information technology and we will see many more, but our experience in the last 20 years should teach us that they frequently take longer, cost more, or come in ways that we do not expect and cannot foresee. Meanwhile, we need to continue to develop and support libraries because they work, and because they contain the knowledge resources upon which our information society is based.

The experts who are predicting the early demise of books and libraries have impressive credentials. They include management consultants, information entrepreneurs, government officials, university professors, and popular futurists. Their forecasts of things to come are based on insights that come from solid knowledge and years of experience. They can neither be ignored nor accepted uncritically. There were two recent essays that put forecasting into perspective: "Why Forecasters Flubbed the 70's" (Time, January 21, 1980, p. 91-92) and "For the 1980's Beware All Expert Predictions" (Science, January 18, 1980, p. 287-88). They remind us that no one, no matter how impressive his or her credentials, can predict the future with any degree of accuracy--and those who try are more frequently wrong than right. Life is full of surprises, and as a Chinese philosopher said: "Prediction very difficult, particularly of future."

These are the same kinds of experts who, in the 1960's, were predicting the end of books and libraries along with a revolution in education based on teaching machines and new media. Important advances were made, but the extravagant forecasts failed to materialize. The publishing industry in the U.S. is thriving (it published about 15,000 titles in 1960 and 45,000 last year) and libraries have grown proportionately. The use of media in education is still a promise unfulfilled. And no one predicted the hand-held calculator or the energy crisis. Librarians will remember the bad timing of the predictions made by Florida Atlantic University, MIT's Project INTREX, the King Report on Technology in the Library of Congress, and countless others. We can all recall the predictions that were made about picture phones and flying family cars. Nothing dates faster than our fantasies about the future. It is also worth noting that during the 1960's, there was another, equally impressive and much larger body of experts, who thought that electronic and print media would coexist and complement each other, that books would survive, and that technology would reinforce and revitalize libraries. Those more conservative experts were closer to the mark, but moderate forecasts are never as newsworthy as the dramatic ones. There is a similar silent majority of experts at work today.

The most dramatic predictions about the future of books, libraries, and information technology tend to be made by men of thought rather than men of action--by writers, professors, and committees that do not have to implement their ideas in the marketplace and take personal responsibility for the results. Nothing is impossible to the man who does not have to do it. The practitioners who are charged with managing libraries and information businesses tend to be more realistic and focused in their views. Theoreticians who are not responsible and accountable for implementing change can afford to be a few years or even decades off in their predictions of the replacement of one technology, product, or service by another. They get credit for hitting close to the mark and even for trying. However, those in operating positions must have the right timing as well as the right idea and approach. The right idea at the wrong time spells failure; they get no credit for near misses and no A's for effort. Entrepreneurs and managers have a limited number of options and opportunities. Resources committed to a course of action today are no longer available for tomorrow's more promising course. The stakes are higher; they bet their money, jobs, and sometimes even the future of their organizations on their decisions. And timing is everything. Here are some examples:

- One major science library building was planned and built in the late 1960's on the assumption that books and journals would soon be replaced by microforms and electronic media. No provision was made for normal growth of the collections beyond five years. The planners were wrong in their assumption and the building was inadequate.
- Another library was planned at that time with similar assumptions. A large computer room was provided in the basement in lieu of stacks. The room never housed a computer, but no real harm was done because it was converted to much-needed stack space a few years after the building was opened.
- In several instances, colleges and universities delayed or decided against building new library space in the 1960's on the assumption that books and libraries would be replaced by electronic media.
- Numerous business ventures in the information field have failed because they were based on faulty assumptions about technologies and markets. Two well-known examples are the ill-fated attempts by National Cash Register and the Encyclopaedia Britannica, Inc. to market ultrafiche libraries in the early 1970's.

Anyone can enjoy the intellectual sport of speculating about the wonders of information technology in the year 2000 and beyond, but some of us--managers, trustees, entrepreneurs--must try to see and assess the near-term future of that technology and make plans to use it appropriately. I define near-term future as five to ten years ahead; trying to see and plan beyond that is largely guesswork.

The insights and perspectives of theoreticians and futurists are useful; they help us to see and understand the complex social, economic, and technological forces that are at work in our larger environment, but only those with authority and responsibility can decide how and when those forces might affect any particular enterprise. Futurists can tell us what the future may be like, but they cannot tell us how to get there or when to make our moves. The really important long-term decisions about any organization or institution must in the end be made by those responsible for it, based on their best judgment and as much practical wisdom as they can muster.

Books already have many strong and articulate defenders and need no help from me. I will merely cite two recent defenses of the book and move on to discuss the future of libraries in our emerging information society. They are Herbert S. Bailey's Bowker Lecture, "The Traditional Book in the Electronic Age"[1] and John P. Dessauer's "Why Books Won't Die."[2]

The "Paperless Society"

Prominent among and representative of those who are predicting an early end to books and libraries are Dr. F. Wilfrid Lancaster, Professor of Library Science at the University of Illinois, and Dr. Vincent E. Giuliano, Senior Consultant with Arthur D. Little, Inc. in Cambridge, Massachusetts. Lancaster sums up his views as follows:

> We are moving rather rapidly and quite inevitably toward a paperless society. Advances in computer science and in communications technology allow us to conceive of a global system in which reports of research and development activities are composed, published, disseminated, and used in a completely electronic mode. Paper need never exist in this communication environment. We are now in an interim stage in the natural evolution from print on paper to electronics.[3]

Lancaster is one of the most thoughtful and articulate spokesmen for this point of view.[4] To the extent that he is concerned with electronic systems in support of research and communication in science and technology and other scholarly areas in the 20-year time frame, his views have considerable validity as a conceptual framework. However, when he predicts the coming of a paperless society by the year 2000 and the passing of books, journals, and libraries in that time-frame, his writings must be treated as mere speculation or a kind of science fiction.

In any event, if the paperless society comes on Lancaster's schedule, it will be but a small part of a massive transformation of our society and our way of life. In that society not only libraries, but the institutions and scholars they serve, may also become obsolete. We cannot do much now to prepare for that kind of massive change. The best we can do, and this is difficult enough, is to try to cope with the changes that are coming now and in the next few years, and to try to plan for those that are coming in the next five, ten, or even 15 years when books and paper will surely coexist with electronic media.

Giuliano's Manifesto

Giuliano is a spokesman of a different kind. A mathematician and former dean of a library school, he has been a consultant for Arthur D. Little, Inc. (ADL) on information technology and organizations for many years. In his position, he advises government, business, and professional societies and associations. He is well-known and respected as a friendly and articulate critic of libraries. When Giuliano concludes, as he did as the senior author of a recent ADL report entitled Into the Information Age, A Perspective for Federal Action on Information[5] that libraries are becoming irrelevant and are not information age institutions, his views carry considerable authority and demand a response. The gist of Appendix A of the ADL report, which dealt with the future of libraries, was summarized in a popular and provocative LJ article by Giuliano entitled: "Manifesto for Librarians."[6]

Ironically, the ADL Report itself is a good example of the hazards of scenario writing and forecasting. The report was sponsored by the National Science Foundation in 1978 when the economy was booming and the federal government seemed poised to take decisive action in the information arena. Three years and one presidential election later the report was made obsolete by a massive shift in government spending policy.

Giuliano begins his Manifesto by calling attention to the paradox that libraries everywhere are in decline while our economy is booming and our society is rushing into the Information Age. Library budgets are being cut, use is down, staff are being laid off, hours are being reduced, branches are being closed, and book and journal purchases are being severely curtailed. Libraries, he says, are in year five (i.e. 1979) of a retrenchment and the situation is desperate and hopeless.

To Giuliano we are seeing the beginning of the end of libraries and librarians as we know them. He says we cannot save traditional libraries, which have outlived their usefulness anyway, but it is not too late for librarians to save themselves. They can do it either by transforming their libraries into centers for contemporary information which serve their constituents by any and all appropriate means and media, or by abandoning libraries completely and setting themselves up as independent information professionals or moving into other Information Age jobs.

Yes, libraries have been retrenching for the last several years; their situation is grim now and will get worse in the years ahead, but it is by no means desperate or hopeless. The reason for the decline of library budgets in the last five years is not that society has in some mysterious way concluded that libraries are not Information Age institutions and is, therefore, withdrawing support, as Giuliano and others suggest. Libraries are not being singled out for extinction; they are just being squeezed like other educational, cultural, and civic institutions on campuses and in towns and cities all across America.

There is no evidence of a nationwide decline in the use of libraries. If the use of libraries is down in some cities and regions, it is not because people no longer need or want them. Where use is down, it is largely due to changing demographic trends and shifting populations in the cities. There is a well-documented migration from the old cities of the Northeast and Mid-West to the Sun Belt states. The postwar babies have grown up. Just as many schools are closing for a lack of children to fill the classes, so library use is declining in many places for the same reason. Young people and students are among the heaviest library users, and as their numbers diminish library use falls.

Giuliano seems to include all libraries and not just public libraries in his doomsday scenario. It is an oversimplification to talk about libraries as though they were all alike and share a uniform fate. It may seem obvious, but it should be said that public, academic, and special libraries serve different purposes and user groups and are funded from a wide variety of sources. Some libraries or types of libraries may be more vulnerable than others to the effects of recession and new technology. Naturally, if one starts with the premise, as Lancaster and Giuliano do, that print on paper is passing, then libraries, to the extent that they deal with this medium, are threatened. But no convincing case for the end of print on paper has been made. In any event, libraries--and especially research libraries of record--are still the only practical means of access to the records of human achievement and therefore merit society's continued support until other means are developed. The fact that library support is faltering is not necessarily proof that society's need and appreciation for libraries is declining. On the contrary, the need for libraries has never been greater and it is our duty to make the case for libraries and to make them worthy of continued support.

Information professionals

Libraries and librarians do have a future, but not as the overarching information agencies and managers of our society. Let's face it, they never have been that. Some librarians and other information professionals are in danger of being carried away by the current rhetoric about the postindustrial or information society. There seems to be a widely held view that the library profession has an opportunity to become the principal manager of information in the information society, and that if it fails to seize that opportunity, it will richly deserve the early demise that is in store for it. I don't believe this. I believe that librarians are going to survive and continue to play the same essential but limited role in the future that they have in the past, but there simply is no chance that they will become the principal handlers of information as it is defined in the context of the information society.

The information society was defined into existence in the 1960's and 1970's by a number of prominent sociologists, futurists, economists, and Department of Commerce statisticians. They took an array of economic activities which used to be classed in various categories and grouped them together into a single category called the Information Sector of our economy. Thus, what used to be called commerce, communications, postal services, banking, publishing, education, libraries, and practically all other activities based on information transfer are now defined as the information sector of our economy. By that definition, information work employs half the labor force and accounts for half the GNP.

This may be a valid way of viewing our economy in the 1980's. The problem is that librarians and other information handlers started calling themselves "information professionals" and "information scientists" in the 1960's before the information society was born. With the coming of the information society, many of these information professionals have come to believe that they somehow have a right or a responsibility to go forth and become the principal managers of information in this newly defined sense. It will not happen that way. A banker is still a banker, a publisher is still a publisher, and a librarian is still a librarian, even though they are now all classed together as "information workers" in the information society.

Abandon libraries?

According to Giuliano, "Establishing libraries and the library profession as central in our current information-oriented society does not take a big change; it requires only a shift in perspective, a change in view." He continues: "My main message is that it is time now for librarians to shift context--to start looking at the situation from the other end of the telescope. The shift has to be away from libraries and their institutional structures as the main focal point, towards providing contemporary and needed information services to their constituents, using whatever means, media, or structures that are appropriate. For some, the shift in perspective may mean working outside a library; for many, it may mean transforming a library institution."[7]

Giuliano is saying, in other words, that librarians should stop being librarians and become something else. That is becoming the conventional view among a growing number of librarians and particularly library school deans who are deemphasizing or even dropping the word library from the names of their schools.[8] They believe that a growing number of interesting and well-paying jobs will be outside the library institution in the future and that many librarians would do well to go after them. They may be right about the jobs, and librarians and prospective librarians cannot be blamed if they take that advice because librarianship is a poorly paid, low status, and somewhat overcrowded field now.

Those who remain committed to libraries will continue to define librarians as persons who are responsible for libraries and to define libraries as institutions which, in the aggregate, contain and provide access to man's recorded knowledge. At the present time, this recorded knowledge is largely in the form of print on paper, film, and in electronic forms. As technology advances, new forms will appear and the proportion of books to film, tapes, disks, and other media will change but the function of the library will continue. Libraries cannot exist without librarians and librarians cannot exist without libraries. The names may change in the future, but their functions will continue as long as there are users who need to gain access to the record in whatever form it takes and wherever it is located.

The continuing role and importance of libraries as the repositories of society's records in various forms was reconfirmed in a dramatic way in 1980 by a gift to the University of South Carolina Library of 60 million feet of film from the old 20th Century Fox Movietone News. Along with the film are 1.87 million index cards used by Movietone News librarians and the logs of the shooting turned in by the cameramen. The process of cataloging the film on the computer for use by scholars and the public is in progress.

Other examples of libraries taking responsibility for preserving the history and creations of new media and technology are the Library of Congress's unique collection of early Hollywood films, Vanderbilt University's growing archives of CBS television news broadcasts, and the University of Pennsylvania's recent acquisition of papers and records of John W. Mauchley, the co-inventor of the first stored-program computer.

Giuliano says that "reading is not now, and never was, the way most people get the information that counts to them." He may be right, but the information that counts always comes to them in one way or other from people who do read and have information. The ultimate source of most of that information is in printed form in libraries. He says that "for those who do read, the library is of less and less importance as a place to get reading" and cites the proliferation of mass-market paperbacks, book clubs, and specialized magazines. This may be true, but the authors of these books and magazine articles are among the heaviest library users--the Barbara Tuchmans and the Arthur Haleys could not write their books without libraries. The library has always been the court of last resort, the place where serious researchers go to find collections of materials that are not available elsewhere or that they cannot afford to buy.

Are libraries obsolete?

Of all the statements that Giuliano makes about the declining role of libraries in our society the one that is potentially the most important, and therefore the most demanding of a careful response, is this one: "As far as information institutions in our society go, libraries are of minor importance. Technology has already evolved to a point where access to most of the world's literature can be obtained within a couple of days through a combination of the online bibliographic searching utilities and vendor-supplied, computerized order fulfillment systems for books, documents, and periodical articles."[9]

If Giuliano is right on that point then libraries have indeed served their purpose and can quietly fade away. But I believe his assertion is totally unfounded. It is one of those "big lies" that should be refuted before it gains wide acceptance through repetition. The truth is that most of the new technology-based information businesses are still largely dependent on the library market for survival and the new information brokers ultimately rely on libraries as the source for most of the documents they supply to their clients. Just as Willie Sutton robbed banks because that is where they kept the money, so information brokers use libraries because that's where we keep the information--in the form of print on paper.

It is still true that libraries--public, academic, governmental, and special--provide the only means of access in our society to any book, journal, or document that is out of print or more than a few years old. Bookstores, even in major cities, carry only a small selection of current English language in-print books; the rest have to be ordered from publishers or jobbers. Most books and journals go out of print within a few years or even months of their publication and are no longer available except in libraries. The time that books are in print is decreasing rapidly as the cost of warehousing books increases. The recent Thor Power Tool Decision will make that time even shorter.

Most foreign books and journals and most specialized documents are not obtainable at all through regular book-trade channels. Only a few score major research libraries in North America and Europe manage to acquire and preserve any more than a small fraction of the universe of materials that are currently published. The rest of the recent materials, when they are available at all, are dispersed among thousands of smaller and more specialized libraries in every country of the world. Older publications, from recent out-of-print titles all the way back to Gutenberg, can be obtained from libraries or not at all.

Document delivery

Several major nonlibrary information vendors have recently gone into the document supply business for selected research materials. One of the most frequently cited as the forerunner of things to come is ISI (Institute for Scientific Information) in Philadelphia. ISI is a very successful computer-based information company which indexes a selection of some 6500 of the world's principal and most-cited research journals. It publishes the results in a variety of printed services which are sold to individual subscribers and libraries. As a by-product of that process, and as an additional service to subscribers, it undertakes to supply them on request with copies of articles from most of the journals it indexes.

ISI's OATS Service (Original Article Tearsheets), as it is called, is used by researchers in business, industry, and government as a convenient means of obtaining papers which are cited in ISI's current awareness services. Libraries also use OATS as a convenient source for articles in journals they do not receive. ISI's prices and delivery times are reasonable. The problem is that ISI only retains these journal files for the latest four years and 6500 titles are but a small fraction of a larger universe of useful journal titles which is estimated at upward of 50-75,000 titles. No books or parts of books are included in the service. OATS is a specialized service which serves only a small fraction of the total need and demand for journal articles and poses no threat to libraries. In 1980, it filled 156,000 requests.

Chemical Abstracts Service has begun offering its subscribers an attractive Document Delivery Service covering the 12,500 periodicals and other documents it abstracts. The cost for a photocopy or document loan is $10-20 including copyright fees. Orders can be placed via the online search services, OCLC, or by Telex/TWX. The service is good and payment is convenient. Like OATS, libraries will use CAS service to purchase articles on demand from journals to which they do not subscribe.

The BLLD (British Library Lending Division) offers a similar service from some 50,000 journal titles and a lending service from its growing collection of approximately one million books. Since it is a library of record, it attempts to maintain complete historic files of its journals. The BLLD charges fees for this service, but it is a subsidized library as are most libraries. In 1980, BLLD's journal service filled over a million orders of which one third came from outside the United Kingdom.

The Center for Research Libraries (CRL) in Chicago provides its members with a Journal Access Service which is backed-up by the BLLD via an online computer ordering system. Libraries are the principal users of both the CRL and BLLD services. CRL and BLLD are examples of a new kind of libraries' library which complement and expand the collections and services of other libraries and enable them to better serve their users.

Another type of major commercial work that is frequently cited as offering the kind of information age document delivery service which will make libraries obsolete is University Microfilms, Inc. (UMI), a Xerox company in Ann Arbor, Michigan. UMI started by microfilming and selling copies of dissertations along with Dissertation Abstracts. It later expanded its scope and added a service to film and supply back runs of journals and out-of-print books on demand. It creates its master negative file by filming books and journals, some of which it borrows from libraries. UMI does most of its business selling copies to libraries. UMI, Bell & Howell, and other similar firms could not exist without their library suppliers and customers, and the libraries would be poorer without their vast collections and useful services.

Some may see these growing document delivery services as a serious threat to the continued existence and development of libraries. I believe, on the contrary, that these new services are essential to the continued well-being of libraries. They enable libraries to gain easy access to a range of resources which would be out of reach otherwise.

Despite the commendable efforts of ISI, CAS, UMI, and some others, there is simply no way "to gain access to most of the world's literature within a couple of days" or even a couple of months unless one turns to conventional libraries--public, academic, special, or government--all of them subsidized one way or another and none of them profitable or even self-supporting. Libraries have a near-monopoly on one of the most important but unprofitable pieces of the information business--that of selecting, acquiring, preserving, organizing, and providing free access to the retrospective records of our civilization. That is both their strength and weakness. For-profit information companies will be offering an increasing number and range of information services, but it is unlikely that any of them will ever find it profitable to acquire and maintain comprehensive retrospective collections. UMI, Bell & Howell, and similar suppliers of research materials in microform seem to be exceptions, but their business is to supply libraries. If they develop truly effective electronic storage, retrieval, and delivery systems to replace their cumbersome film files, they could become the forerunners of commercial libraries of record. The viability of commercial libraries is a technical and economic issue, but their desirability in our society is a serious political issue which will be hotly debated.

Online services

What about the online bibliographic searching utilities with their computerized ordering systems? Are these helping to put libraries out of business as Giuliano and others suggest? Let's look at the evidence.

In the 1960's and 1970's, most of the major indexing and abstracting services such as Index Medicus, Chemical Abstracts, Physics Abstracts, BIOSIS, etc., computerized their data handling and publishing operations and created machine readable data tapes as a by-product. NLM provides its own online MEDLARS service, but most of the other A&I services sell or lease these tapes to commercial

Libraries and Librarians   59

online bibliographic utilities such as Lockheed's DIALOG, SDC's ORBIT, and BRS. These firms are sometimes referred to as data base spinners because they maintain searchable online files containing hundreds of bibliographic records. Searching these online data bases from computer terminals in libraries, offices, and laboratories in technologically advanced countries began in the 1970's and is becoming an accepted way of doing literature searches in all subjects, including the humanities. The vast majority of searches, however, continue to be done from the printed indexes in libraries. The product of these computer searches is a printout of a bibliography (sometimes with abstracts) of retrieved records numbering from a few to hundreds of items. It is important to note that a search retrieves only the bibliographic descriptions of documents and not the full text. Carrying the full text of documents online is still too expensive for all but a few specialized systems covering law and current news.

When searchers have their computer-produced bibliographies in hand, they must then turn to the library or send someone else to the library to retrieve the documents. They must turn to the library because that is still the only place where most of the documents can be found. Recently the three principal online search services began to offer online document ordering services whereby searchers can order copies of many of the documents listed in the bibliographies they retrieve. The database spinners do not supply the documents because they do not have them in their computer files. They are middlemen. They forward the orders to other vendors, sometimes the publisher, but usually to information brokers who, in turn, use conventional libraries as the source for filling most of them.

The bibliographic search function is being successfully computerized, but the document delivery function is not. It is still largely dependent on libraries, copying machines, postal services, interlibrary loan, and other nonelectronic methods. The promise of computerized bibliographic searching (and library networking) cannot be fully realized until the full text of documents is accessible in electronic form, either directly online or in secondary storage, and text access is brought into line with bibliographic access. Affordable telefacsimile or videodisc systems for storing, transmitting, and receiving copies of existing documents would be a significant interim advance, but several years may pass before they are widely available and used.

Six of the largest commercial journal publishers recently launched the ADONIS project, an exploratory effort to make the contents of their journals available on videodisc. However, no significant results can be expected for three to five years in my opinion.

There are at least two important full-text online systems already commercially available--LEXIS and NEXIS, services by Mead Data Central. They may be forerunners of things to come.[10] LEXIS is putting a growing corpus of legal materials, including compilations of statutes and decisions, online in full text. Searching and retrieval of these specialized, high-use materials is very effective and very expensive. NEXIS has the New York Times, the Washington Post, and a selection of other important current news and business publications searchable and retrievable online in full text.

As the cost of full text services come down, they will become increasingly important for specialized fields and uses. The commercial providers of such services may well skim off certain parts of the library business. However, they will also create and satisfy a whole new market for those services, and libraries will be a part of that market. Their gain need not be the library's loss.

The main business of Abstracting and Indexing (A&I) services is to abstract or index the literature of a subject field or discipline and to publish printed volumes which are then sold almost entirely to libraries. Sale or lease of the data base for online searching provides them a secondary source of income, but the cost of creating and maintaining the data bases are still covered largely by the sale of printed volumes. A BIOSIS official said in 1979, "if the full cost of producing the data base were to be recovered from online use, we would have to charge about $700 a connect hour."[11]

Clearly, the financial viability of both the A&I and the online search services rests firmly, now and for some years to come, on the sale of printed volumes to libraries. Eventually, the printed volumes may be superseded by electronic forms, but the library market will continue to be a major support for these services. Why? Because libraries are and will continue to be the principal point of interface between researchers and the collections being indexed and abstracted.

The bulk of online searches are done in libraries, by librarians, for library users. Online searching is enhanced reference service using new tools. Just as few users had the necessary skills or the desire to do their own searching in printed indices, so few users have the skills or the desire to do their own computer searches. Those library users are the same scholars and researchers who do the research and write the books and papers that are being abstracted and indexed by the A&I services. They work in universities, in commercial firms, in industrial laboratories, and government agencies--the same institutions that create and maintain research libraries. It is unlikely that the principal market for A&I services (whether in printed or online form), and for scholarly and scientific information will move somewhere far from libraries and those who own and use them.

Online searching is not putting libraries out of business; libraries have helped put online searching into business and constitute its principal market. The online services will, in turn, generate new business for themselves and for libraries.

Libraries and Librarians

Information brokers

Another interesting development of the information society is the appearance on the scene of a growing number of small, for-profit information firms which provide a wide variety of specialized information services to commercial and industrial customers.[12] Staffed largely by people with library backgrounds, they do online literature searches, retrieve and supply documents, compile bibliographies, prepare research reports, and serve as consultants on a variety of information problems. The firms range in size from a freelance librarian working at home, to well-established firms like FIND/SVP, Inc., Warner-Eddison, Inc., and Information-on-Demand, Inc. They came into existence during the last 10-15 years when both the need and the means for fulfilling the need for special information services to special clients developed.

Some people see these aggressive new firms as a threat to libraries and possibly as the beginning of either a deplorable or a desirable trend toward the displacement of free libraries by for-profit vendors or "information supermarkets." These first, in my view, pose no threat to libraries. Like online services, they supplement them by filling needs and demands that publicly supported libraries cannot and should not try to meet--providing special and expensive services to business, professional, and other users who can afford them.

Some libraries already sell special services to corporate users. A few others have spun off for-profit service units physically and administratively separate from their regular free public service departments. As times get harder, more libraries will try to find acceptable ways of earning money by selling services. The danger, of course, is that they could jeopardize or alienate their main support base while trying to earn this extra income.

Most librarians, however, will continue to find it offensive in principle and difficult in practice to offer a range of services to users, some of which are free and some of which carry high charges. Inevitably, those who can afford to pay will get preference and those who cannot will feel discriminated against and object. With some few exceptions, libraries are not and cannot be staffed sufficiently to offer, at no charge, the kinds of services provided by the new information brokers. If they did offer these special services, demand for them would quickly soar to a level where the staff would be overwhelmed and costs would exceed the budget. In these times of retrenchment, it is naïve to think that additional staff will be added to meet the added demands. Libraries cannot cope with too much success in their labor-intensive free reference services, but they can absorb considerable increases in the self-service use of their collections and facilities without incurring significant additional costs.

Information brokers rely heavily on library collections as their ultimate source for documents and information. It is no

accident that FIND/SVP, one of the leaders in the field, is located
across the street from the central research collections of New York
Public Library. A number of others are located near and make extensive use of large research libraries such as the University of
California at Berkeley and Los Angeles. The brokers are a new
kind of library user. Libraries support the brokers and make it
possible for them to skim off a profitable piece of the library and
information business.

The existence of these new commercial information services
and consultants could, however, make it attractive for many corporations which now maintain their own special libraries to reduce or
eliminate them in favor of purchasing services as needed--to rent a
librarian instead of buying one.

Business vs. free libraries

Back in 1974, when the Information Industry Association (IIA) was
young and brash, a spokesman testified at a hearing of the National
Commission on Library and Information Science that pay libraries
were inevitable and would be forced on the nation by the information
explosion and technological advances.[13] The IIA was registering
its disapproval of libraries giving scientific and technical information free to the public in competition with some of its members.
More mature now, the IIA appears to have softened its position on
this issue or at least lowered its voice. In any case, there is little
evidence of pay libraries displacing free libraries or of free libraries
inhibiting the development of for-profit information services.

If we have an information or knowledge society today, it is
because we have had for the last century a strong tradition and an
effective system of free public education with free libraries as an
integral component. Giuliano and other prophets of the information
society are now telling us that free libraries are a creation of the
passing industrial society and are no longer viable institutions in
our postindustrial information age. They are urging librarians to
abandon the "free" library ethic and either go into the information
business themselves or transform their libraries into self-supporting
information businesses by charging fees for services. This is bad
advice. The "free" library ethic is what makes libraries worthy of
society's support. It would be a blunder and a tragedy for librarians to turn their backs on free libraries and try to make them self-
supporting by charging fees. Subscription libraries have never flourished. Libraries are subsidized because a basic premise of American society has been that an informed citizenry is essential to a
free society.

I do not agree with those libraries who insist as a matter of
principle that libraries should never charge fees. Many libraries
do charge fees for a variety of special services including photocopies,
online computer searches, certain interlibrary loan requests, and
the fines for overdue books. Some libraries also impose special

Libraries and Librarians   63

card fees for those who come from outside the jurisdiction or constituency that the library is mandated to serve. In nearly all cases, those fees are primarily administrative devices and serve to ration or regulate the use of a special service that is partially subsidized, particularly expensive, or of limited availability. I know of no libraries that charge fees with the intention of becoming fully or even substantially self-supporting. It is hard to see how a library could earn enough money through fees to support its operations and building, and to accumulate the capital needed to replace physical plant and purchase new technology.

Librarians should not try to transform their libraries into businesses, and businessmen should not try to get into the library business. Libraries are by their very nature unprofitable. The use of new technology will not change the basic functions of libraries: to acquire, preserve, organize, and make available the records of human achievement. They also serve as powerful and visible symbols of our culture--a function that is frequently overlooked or undervalued.

This is not to say that businessmen cannot or should not make profits assisting librarians to do their job better by creating and selling them useful products and services. Nor is it to say that it is improper for businessmen to make profits by identifying and meeting special information needs and demands that libraries cannot adequately satisfy for lack of resources. Librarians and businessmen both have essential roles to play in the information society as they did in the industrial society, and those roles are complementary and mutually supportive. Librarians, publishers, and the new information entrepreneurs are not adversaries, or even competitors; they are natural allies who need each other's services and products in order to prosper.

The information business is not a static, zero sum game where one player's gain is necessarily another player's loss. It is a rapidly expanding business where all the players can win if they recognize and accept that each one has a unique and important contribution to make. We need to lay to rest the simplistic idea that electronic technology in the hands of information entrepreneurs is going to put an end to libraries. Libraries are here to stay, but by no means are they going to stay the same. Their basic functions will remain, but the ways and means they use to perform those functions will change in varying degrees and at varying speeds for different kinds of libraries in different countries.

Every library has specific functions to perform for a particular institution or constituency. Academic libraries, for example, exist to serve the educational and research activities of their parent institutions. Whether they survive or not depends less on what their librarians do or do not do about new technology than on the fate of the institutions that support them. If academic libraries become obsolete in the information society, it will be because the institutions they serve have also become obsolete or have no further use

for them. Libraries cannot exist apart from the needs and wants
of their constituents and they should cease to exist when they are
no longer needed or used.

Changing libraries

The stereotype of libraries as static, unchanging institutions is no
longer valid if it ever was. Libraries, and especially large libraries of record, are necessarily and by nature conservative institutions. However, in the last hundred years they have demonstrated
a remarkable ability to grow, to adapt to changing conditions, to
meet new demands, and to implement new technologies. American
research libraries used to double in size every 16 years on the
average during the last century. Growth at that rate means constant
change. Most of this country's library physical plant was replaced
or built during the last 30 years and the large bulk of library collections have been accumulated during that same period. It is this
explosive rate of growth and change that keeps our libraries in what
may seem like a state of chronic fiscal and managerial crisis.

In 1950, there were fewer than 20 research libraries in the
U.S. and Canada with more than one million volumes. In 1980,
there were nearly 100. Derek Price concluded, in his much cited
Little Science, Big Science, that most of the scientists who ever
lived are alive and working.[14] The same can be said of librarians.
And it may well be that most of the libraries in existence today were
established or revitalized in the last 30 years and most of the books
and journals in those libraries were published or acquired in the
same period. Libraries and librarians as we know them are relatively new phenomena.

Far from being conservative, librarians are eager, sometimes too eager, to change and to embrace new technology. They
are frequently dangerously ahead of their governing boards and users
in that regard. If libraries were inflexible and slow to change, they
would have been overwhelmed by the enormous increases in the number and variety of new publications and in the demands made on
them for new and expanded services in the last 30 years. If libraries have been able to cope with this flood of publications and demands, which were largely created by new technology and a growing and more affluent population, it is because they have begun to
make effective use of that same technology.

Partners for progress

The relationship between librarians and the vendors who serve them
has been badly strained in recent years. Two divisive issues were
the "fair use" copying provisions of the Copyright Act of 1978 and
the proposal by librarians for a federally-sponsored National Periodicals Center. These conflicts, now fortunately subsiding, have
made it difficult for both camps to see how mutually dependent they

are, and how effective their collaboration has been in the past and could be in the future. A brief look at some notable examples of past collaborations will help make this point.

In the 1950's, American research libraries were being overwhelmed by a flood of doctoral dissertations and the problems involved with acquiring and cataloging them. They helped and encouraged a small commercial firm, University Microfilms, Inc. to design and implement a systematic program to regain control of this valuable but difficult form of research material. UMI now systematically collects and microfilms the dissertations and provides full bibliographic control over them in its published and computerized version of Dissertation Abstracts. It also supplies films or paper copies on demand and this makes it unnecessary for individual libraries to acquire, organize, and preserve these numerous and elusive materials. Libraries save money while access to dissertations is now greatly facilitated.

Librarians pioneered the use of microfilm for document reproduction, preservation, and storage, and created a market for library materials in that form. Newspapers were a troublesome problem for libraries--expensive to acquire and service, space-consuming, and impermanent. They were a prime candidate for the new medium of microfilm. Libraries collaborated with other libraries and then with commercial vendors to film and make available copies of back files of thousands of newspaper titles which would otherwise have been lost. Current files of major newspapers, foreign and domestic, are now available through commercial vendors and the newspaper problem has been brought under control.

To provide the retrospective materials needed to strengthen the collections of existing libraries and to stock the thousands of new libraries that have come into existence in the last 30 years, a number of commercial vendors went into the business of reprinting and republishing out-of-print books and journals on a massive scale. Several of them made significant contributions to research by assembling, organizing, and publishing comprehensive collection[s] of research materials that were heretofore practically inaccessible to scholars. The Kress-Goldsmith Collection of Economic History, The Court of Arches Archives, the collections contained in the Short Title Catalogue of Books Published in English to 1600, the American Periodical Series, and the Landmarks of Science are but a few examples of the genre.

Other companies have greatly expanded the resources available to scholars through libraries by assembling and publishing in book form a whole array of library catalogs. The many catalogs of firms such as G.K. Hall, Edwards Brothers, Mansell, Kraus-Thompson, and others come to mind.

The commercial publishers of abstracting and indexing services make an incalculable contribution to the use of library collections by providing efficient access to materials that would be inaccessible without the existence of these services.

The rapidly growing mass of local, state, federal, and foreign government publications, which were threatening to inundate libraries, are being brought under control and made accessible to users through libraries by a number of imaginative commercial entrepreneurs who organize, index, and publish collections of them and guides in various paper, micro, electronic, and other formats.

There are other firms that expand the resources and service capabilities of libraries by providing and marketing a variety of specialized catalogs and collections of materials for specialized groups of users. These include art exhibition catalogs, photograph collections, annual reports of companies, college and university catalogs, and countless others.

Still other firms design and provide libraries with a variety of computer-based systems and services to perform a number of functions ranging from circulation control to searching online bibliographic data bases.

These are examples of the kind of collaboration that take place between libraries and vendors and the kinds of products and services that some of the new information industry firms are bringing to libraries and those who use them. Not to be overlooked, of course, are the thousands of traditional publishers of books and journals and the hundreds of library suppliers that have been serving libraries for decades.

In sum, commercial firms invest millions of dollars every year in developing and supplying new products and services to libraries and library users. Without that capital investment, and that investment of entrepreneurial know-how, libraries would, in fact, be the static and unchanging institutions that the conventional wisdom believes them to be.

With Andrew Carnegie as the all-time champion, American business and the philanthropic foundations it spawns and nurtures have been among the most generous and faithful supporters of libraries. Librarians could do more to recognize these friends and strengthen the special relationship that exists between libraries and business--a relationship that is unique to this country.

I have stressed the importance of the contributions that business makes in keeping libraries dynamic and responsive by expanding and improving library resources and services, but the flow of benefits is not one way. In 1980, 104,000 libraries spent $5.6 billion on staff, materials, and services.[15] The library market may not be large by some measures, but it is critically important for many of the businesses that serve it, and virtually the sole support of many others.

Libraries provide many of the new ideas and resources that make this business contribution possible. For example, librarians first started indexing and abstracting journal literature and parts of books (making "analytics" for card catalogs) on a cooperative basis in the 19th century. This approach proved to be impractical and the function was taken over and perfected by commercial firms and professional societies. A number of firms that provide computerized bibliographic services to libraries are dependent for their machine readable data on the Library of Congress's MARC tapes. Nearly all the applications of computer technology to library operations such as circulation, serials control, acquisitions, online cataloging, etc., have been (and continue to be) developed by libraries and library networks. When the systems prove their potential and create a market, commercial vendors develop and offer their own improved systems and services based on the best available designs and experience. Specialized reference services, book-form catalogs, and many forms of library equipment are among the other products and services that were pioneered by librarians and picked up by vendors.

In general, whenever a sufficient market is created to make a particular library service profitable, it will be skimmed off and provided by commercial vendors--usually, but not always, to the ultimate benefit of all concerned. Libraries can develop prototype products and services for local use, but they usually lack the capital, the organizational capability, and the legal mandate to complete the development and market them successfully.

The emergence in the last decade of not-for-profit library corporations in the form of consortia and networks such as OCLC, Inc., the Research Libraries Group (RLG), and the Washington Library Network (WLN) has opened new possibilities for libraries to create and satisfy their own market for certain services without the intervention of commercial vendors. It is becoming increasingly clear, however, that in order to succeed, these library networks or utilities, will have to adopt the same sound business practices and marketing skills that characterize successful vendors.[16]

The library future

Is information technology in the hands of commercial vendors making libraries obsolete? I conclude that libraries are and will continue to be a critical link in the chain that produces, preserves, and disseminates the knowledge that has created and sustains our information society. The information industry is not making libraries obsolete. Rather, it is revitalizing them with new technology and services. Libraries, in turn, nourish that industry with the knowledge resources it needs while providing a vital and ready initial market and distribution system for its new services and products. Libraries are becoming more, not less, important in our information society even though their relative share of the total information market is declining.

Technology in the hands of businessmen and librarians has been responsible for the enormous growth and expansion of libraries that has occurred since Gutenberg invented movable type and started mass-producing printed books in 1452. The coming of computer and related electronic technologies in the last two decades represents a development of similar magnitude and significance. The difference is that the development and effects of printing technology took centuries to unfold while the development and effects of electronic technology are compressed into decades and are transforming our entire technological society.

Gutenberg's invention made libraries as we know them necessary and possible. It is already a fact that our electronic computer technology is making new kinds of electronic "libraries" or data banks necessary and possible, but whether or when it will make Gutenberg-type libraries obsolete, nobody really knows. In the meantime, those charged with the stewardship of libraries should be assured that librarians and businessmen are using electronic technology to give libraries the enhanced capabilities they need to continue to function effectively in the present mode and to make the transition to new and as yet unknown future modes.

References

1. Bailey, Herbert S. "The Traditional Book in the Electronic Age," Publishers Weekly, December 5, 1977, p. 24-29.

2. Dessauer, John P. "Why Books Won't Die," Publishers Weekly, November 26, 1979, p. 23-25.

3. Lancaster, F.W. "Whither Libraries? or, Wither Libraries," College and Research Libraries, September 1978, p. 356.

4. See especially: Lancaster, F.W., Toward Paperless Information Systems, Academic Pr., 1978.

5. Into the Information Age, A Perspective for Federal Action on Information. Vincent Giuliano and others. Arthur D. Little, Inc. American Library Assn., 1978. (A Report prepared by Arthur D. Little, Inc. for the National Science Foundation.)

6. Giuliano, Vincent E. "A Manifesto for Librarians," LJ, September 15, 1979, p. 1837-42.

7. Giuliano, "Manifesto," p. 1838.

8. See, for example, Pauline Wilson, "Taking the Library out of Library Education," American Libraries, June 1981, p. 321-25.

9. Giuliano, "Manifesto," p. 1840.

10. For a more conservative view see: Richard Kollin and Brett Butler, "Beyond full text: Indexing and Abstracting in Legal

and other information services," a presentation at the 89th Cranfield Conference on Mechanized Information Transfer, 21-24 July 1981. Cranfield Institute of Technology, Cranfield, Bedford, UK.

11. Elias, A.W. "The Economics of Online Data Base Creation," Text of a presentation at the ASIS Annual Meeting in Minneapolis, Michigan, October 16, 1979.

12. See Lorig Marangian and Richard W. Boss. Fee-Based Information Services, Bowker, 1980.

13. For a more complete discussion of this subject see: R. De Gennaro, "Pay Libraries and User Charges," LJ, February 15, 1975, p. 263-67.

14. Derek De Sola Price. Little Science, Big Science. Columbia Univ. Pr., 1963, p. 14.

15. Quirk, Dantia and Patricia Whitestone. The Shrinking Library Dollar. Knowledge Industry Pub., 1982. (Source: KIP Estimates based on data from US National Center for Education Statistics, Bureau of the Census, Department of Labor, and Association of Research Libraries.)

16. See R. De Gennaro, "Libraries and Networks in Transition," LJ, May 15, 1981, p. 1045-49.

JEWISH LIBRARIES IN THE POLISH GHETTOS DURING THE NAZI ERA*

David Shavit

Jewish Libraries in Poland before World War II

On January 1, 1930, the Polish Ministry of Religious Creeds and Public Education made a survey of all public libraries in Poland. The survey recorded 748 Jewish libraries (that is, libraries in which the majority of books were in Yiddish and Hebrew) with combined collections of 860,806 books[1].

This is evidence that the Jews of Poland maintained a vital community and cultural life even when living in adversity. Before the outbreak of World War II there were 3,300,000 Jews in Poland, of whom 350,000 lived in Warsaw, 200,000 in Lodz, and 55,000 in Vilna. The great majority were lower-middle-class workers, small businessmen, and a proletariat, employed or unemployed. They lived in a hostile atmosphere, under an oppressive governmental economic policy, in a country with rampant anti-Semitism and pogroms. Nevertheless, however low their economic level, the Jews in Poland had networks of religious, educational, social, and cultural institutions.

Jewish secular libraries began to appear in the Jewish pale (the western part of the Russian Empire) during the last quarter of the nineteenth century. Many were destroyed during World War I, but they were rebuilt after the war in Independent Poland and Lithuania and played an important role in the secular cultural life of the Jews in Poland during the 1920s[2-3].

During the early 1930s, two other surveys of Jewish libraries were conducted in Poland. One was made by "Tarbut," the educational and cultural network of the General Zionist Organization. One of the two largest secular school systems, Tarbut was Zionist-oriented, with Hebrew as the language of instruction and an emphasis on Hebrew culture. The other survey was made by the

---

*Reprinted by permission of the author and publisher from The Library Quarterly, 52:2 (April 1982) 103-121. Copyright © 1982 by The University of Chicago.

Kultur-Lige, the cultural adjunct of the General Jewish Labor Bund (commonly referred to as the "Bund"). This was a Jewish Socialist party that opposed Zionism and stood for international socialism, the preservation of Jewish identity, and the advocacy of cultural and religious autonomy. It favored the Yiddish language.

One hundred twenty-four libraries had responded to the Tarbut questionnaire (although many answers were fragmentary and incomplete). These libraries contained 166,522 books (an average of 1,370 books per library). However, sixty-nine libraries had less than 1,000 books and only six had more than 5,000 books. The libraries had 13,382 readers (an average of 109 readers per library).

The Kultur-Lige survey reported 133 libraries (these figures were also fragmentary and incomplete) having 166,213 books (an average of 1,250 per library) and 15,271 readers (an average of 115 readers per library). It is interesting to compare the composition of the readers in both the Hebrew and Yiddish libraries (table 1)[4-5].

TABLE 1

COMPOSITION OF READERS IN JEWISH LIBRARIES IN POLAND IN THE EARLY 1930s

	Hebrew Libraries (%)	Yiddish Libraries (%)
Workers (including unemployed)	10.6	60.9
Merchants and tradesmen	9.9	12.0
Pupils	54.8	14.7
Professionals	6.2	3.2
Youth	18.5	7.6
Not specified	....	1.6
Total	100.0	100.0

Source--[4, pp. 219-24].

Jewish book collections existing before World War II in the countries occupied by the Nazis were surveyed at the end of the war. The survey, which included only libraries containing a minimum of 1,000 volumes, listed 251 libraries in Poland with 1,650,000 volumes[6-7].

There were, of course, hundreds of additional libraries which had less than 1,000 volumes. They existed in almost every city and town. They were provided by political and social organizations, such as political parties, professional societies, sport associations, clubs,

and particularly youth organizations. Indeed, the library was the
most important secular institution in town. It was the center of
Jewish youth life, no less than the synagogue was the center of the
religious life. Writing about life in the Lithuanian town, a later
commentator remembered: "In the area of secular culture, the local
library--whether the Hebrew one of Zeiri Zion or the Yiddish one of
the Yiddishists or Kultur-Lige--had been the meeting place of the
Lithuanian Jewish youth.... This youth has already swallowed most
of the library's books, torn and shabby from much use, and came to
the librarian to look for something new and stimulating among the
newly arrived books. During the visit to the library, the youth exchanged words with friends and discussed the politics of the Lithuanian parliament, the question of the Yiddish and Hebrew languages,
the long-ranging debate between the Zionist and the Yiddish-Folkist
newspapers, and the latest show of the traveling Jewish theater
troupe"[8, p. 255]. (All translations are the author's.)

Each political party and youth organization tried to establish
a library in the town. It was important to have one's own library,
not only for reasons of prestige, but also because it attracted un-
affiliated youth who were looking for material to read. Indeed, many
writers on Jewish life in Poland between the world wars comment on
the importance of reading among the Jewish youth. Moshe Kligsberg,
who used a collection of autobiographies of young Jews which had
been collected in Poland during the 1930s, wrote: "Reading, and
much reading, played a very important role in the life of the Jewish
youth. Mostly poor, they could not buy books, and this was one of
the reasons why social libraries were established in every town and
city" [9, p. 161]. Kligsberg assumes that two-thirds of the some
450,000 Polish Jewish youth between the ages of fourteen and twenty
read books systematically, that is, on an average of 1 book a week.
The most frequent types of books read were: (1) fiction; (2) party
and ideological publications, including magazines and pamphlets;
(3) history and social sciences; (4) poetry and philosophy; and
(5) natural science [9, p. 167].

In a survey of the Jewish libraries in the city of Warsaw,
conducted in 1934 by a Jewish librarian, over fifty Jewish libraries
(owned by Jewish individuals or organizations) whose readers were
Jewish and which included a separate section of books in Hebrew or
Yiddish, were recorded (tables 2 and 3)[10]. The most important
public libraries in Warsaw included the Grosser Library of the
Kultur-Lige, established through the amalgamation of eight smaller
libraries, belonging mostly to various labor unions, and of a children's library. By 1936 it had some 30,000 volumes and 4,580
readers. Located in the center of Jewish Warsaw, the Grosser Library was active seven days a week, twelve hours a day without
interruption. It employed twenty-two workers, eleven salaried and
eleven students and volunteers. It included a reading room, with
newspapers and magazines, and even a study room. Like all other
Jewish libraries, its income was derived from users' fees[11, pp.
571-73].

TABLE 2

BOOK COLLECTIONS OF JEWISH LIBRARIES IN WARSAW, 1934

Number and Type of Libraries	Number of Books				
	Total	Yiddish	Hebrew	Polish	Other
10 private lending libraries	152,500	22,500	3,350	103,950	22,650
2 Judaica libraries	34,700	6,000	18,460	500	9,740
13 labor libraries	48,500	29,100	....	15,900	3,500
6 libraries of professional societies	18,436	5,697	82	10,576	2,133
11 Zionist libraries	6,325	2,010	1,348	....	....
3 "Hamizrachi" libraries	1,115	535	405	140	35
3 "Agudah" libraries	1,560	950	260	350	....
2 other	2,200	650	....	1,500	50

Source--[10].

The library of the Life Society, belonging to the Communist-oriented Textile Workers Union, had 12,000 volumes. Two smaller labor libraries were the Hazomir library, belonging to Poalei Zion Right and having 5,000 volumes, and the Borochow library, belonging to Poalei Zion Left and having 4,000 volumes. The largest Zionist library was Merkaz (Center) with 3,000 volumes. Among the libraries belonging to various professional associations were the library of the Jewish Traveling Salesmen (6,500 volumes), the Society of Commercial Employees of the Jewish Faith (about 8,000 volumes), and the library of the Jewish Printers Union (4,000 volumes).

There were several large private lending libraries. Humanita with 60,000 volumes, Pantheon with 20,000 volumes, and Lektura with 12,000 volumes were the largest.

Among the significant libraries of Lodz were the library of the B'nai B'rith Lodge, the Ivriah library, belonging to the Tarbut organization, and the A.D. Gordon library, each of which had several thousand volumes. The Borochow library had more than 11,000 volumes and more than 1,500 readers and included a childrens' library, and the Grosser Library which also contained some 11,000 volumes and more than 1,200[12; 13].

TABLE 3

READERS IN JEWISH LIBRARIES IN WARSAW, 1934

Number and Type of Libraries	Number of Readers			
	Total	Yiddish	Hebrew	Polish
10 private lending libraries	12,150	1,410	85	10,655
2 Judaica libraries	...	...	...	...
13 labor libraries	3,080	...	...	1,923
6 libraries of professional societies	1,144	345	3	796
11 Zionist libraries	693	323	164	206
3 "Hamizrachi" libraries	179	61	93	25
2 "Agudah" libraries	180	90	10	80
2 other	...	...	...	...

Source--[10].

Vilna had two major libraries. Mefitse Haskalah, the library of the Association to Spread Enlightenment, which belonged to the Jewish community, was a large popular library. In the beginning of World War II there were 45,000 volumes in this library, including 10,000 books in Yiddish, 5,500 in Hebrew, 10,000 in Polish, 18,000 in Russian, 500 in Lithuanian, 500 in English, and 500 in French. It had some 2,000 readers[14]. The children's library, belonging to the Central Committee for Education, a Jewish school system, contained in 1939 over 20,000 volumes (of which 9,500 were in Yiddish, 4,900 in Polish, 1,300 in Hebrew, and 4,500 in Russian). It had 1,479 readers, children and youth up to the age of twenty. In 1937 it had circulated 58,286 volumes. Adjacent to the circulating library there was a reading room which was used in 1937 by 11,000 children who had access to a collection of 13,000 books. The reading room was used mostly by children from poor families who could not afford to pay the monthly subscription fee [15, pp. 213-14]. There were several other small libraries and reading rooms in Vilna--in clubs and sport associations and also the library of the Cultural Committee of the Jewish Construction Workers Union which had, by 1939, some 1,900 books in Yiddish.

In 1939 Vilna came under Soviet occupation. The Soviet

authorities purged from the Jewish libraries books which were considered "reactionary," undesirable, or contrary to Soviet ideology or opposing the Soviet regime and its policies. This included all books in the Hebrew language. The Soviet authorities tried also to standardize and centralize all libraries. Both trends caused great difficulties for the Jewish libraries. All libraries were nationalized. The Mefitse Haskalah library was nationalized in November 1940, became the property of the municipal cultural department, and was renamed Public Library No. 5. The children's library was also nationalized and became the State Children's Library. As the monthly fee and deposit were canceled, 800 new readers were added in the first month after the Soviet occupation. The number of Yiddish readers increased by more than ten times, probably because poorer readers could now use the library. The monthly circulation reached 16,000. The Jewish newspaper Der Emes (The Truth) was much interested in the problem of libraries and service to Jewish readers and published several supplements dealing with this subject, the last one on May 28, 1941, a few days before the German invasion of the Soviet Union and the occupation of Vilna [16, pp. 119-24].

It should be noted that many of the small libraries in Poland between the world wars, both Hebrew and Yiddish, were in poor condition. Most were run by amateurs, and only a few had their own facilities. Cataloging and other technical matters were primitive. A reviewer of Jewish cultural life in Poland in the middle 1930s complained that "to our sorrow the question of the library and librarianship has been completely neglected in our cultural life. In the Hebrew publications there is almost no mention of it" [4, p. 219]. The situation in the Yiddish libraries was somewhat better, and there were efforts to correct the problems, particularly by the Kultur-Lige. It had organized a library center, based on the Grosser Library in Warsaw, using modern library techniques. Headed by Herman Kruk, it helped the small local Jewish libraries. The library center organized a commission of librarians which reworked the catalog, adopted the decimal classification system, prepared many informative and bibliographical publications for readers, established an office of readers' adviser, and spread knowledge about modern library practice. It published a monthly bulletin, prepared several pamphlets about modern library administration, helped establish internal library work, and compiled lists of recommended books on current affairs and other subjects. Das Yidishe Buch (The Jewish Book) was a selected catalog for public libraries and a guide for librarians and readers. Four hundred libraries in various cities and towns all over Poland were connected to the library center. Through the library center libraries could obtain various aids and printed materials for library work, such as catalog cards, readers' cards, etc. The library center helped to open new libraries, gave legal advice, and even intervened when Jewish libraries were persecuted by the Polish authorities [17, pp. 351-53].

One must mention the three major Jewish reference libraries in Poland. These were the Library for Jewish Studies of the Great Synagogue on Tlomackie Street in Warsaw, and the Straszun Library and the library of the YIVO Institute of Jewish Research in Vilna [18-20].

Nazi Destruction of Libraries

Destruction of Jewish and other "undesirable" books was part of Nazi policy from its beginning. After the invasion of Poland in 1939 the German conquerors embarked there, too, upon a policy of book destruction and looting. The libraries in occupied Poland were hard hit. It has been estimated that approximately 70 percent of the libraries in Poland, both Jewish and non-Jewish, were looted and destroyed by the Nazis [6, p. 11]. Chaim A. Kaplan, a Warsaw schoolteacher, wrote in his diary on October 25, 1939: "The day before yesterday, like true Vandals, the conquerors entered the Tlomackie Library, where spiritual treasures were stored. They removed all the valuable books and took them to some unknown place. This is burning of the soul of Polish Jewry, for this library was our spiritual sanctuary where we found respite when troubles came to us. Now the fountain which slaked our thirst for Torah and knowledge is dried up." And a few weeks later he wrote again: "In general the conqueror displays a weakness for libraries which other hands have accumulated and preserved" [21, pp. 57, 89].

The destruction of the famous library of the Lublin Yeshiva was reported gleefully in the German press: "For us it was a matter of special pride to destroy the Talmudic Academy which was known as the greatest in Poland.... We threw the huge Talmudic library out of the building and carried the books to the marketplace, where we set fire to them. The fire lasted twenty hours. The Lublin Jews assembled around and wept bitterly, almost silencing us with their cries. We summoned the military band, and with joyful shouts the soldiers drowned out the sounds of the Jewish cries" (Frankfurter Zeitung, March 28, 1941) [6, pp. 5-6].

After the German occupation of Poland, the Jews were concentrated in the larger cities. Eventually they were forced into ghettos. The first major ghetto was established in Lodz, in May 1940; the Warsaw ghetto was established six months later, in November 1940, and the Vilna ghetto was established in September 1941, following the German conquest of the western part of the Soviet Union [22, pp. 396-97; 23; 24, pp. 33-39].

The Lodz Ghetto Libraries

All Jewish libraries in Lodz were liquidated by order of the Propagandaamt during the first winter of the war (1939/1940). Only one circulating library, owned by U.W. Zonenberg, which has been active since 1931, continued to operate. In the beginning, Zonenberg had some 1,900 books in Polish and his readers were mostly from among the middle class. Beginning with April 1940 he was buying books in various languages, including even German and English, from Jews who were deported to Lodz. In addition to fiction, Zonenberg bought textbooks, encyclopedias, nonfiction books, and textbooks for studying foreign languages. Beginning with May 1942 each German-reading Jew who wanted to register in the library had to provide a German book as a registration fee and the German section of the library reached some 800 books. By the beginning of 1944 there were some 7,500 volumes in the library; by the spring of 1944 Zonenberg's library had 4,000 readers.

The borrowing fee was 1 mark in the beginning, rising later to 2 marks per month. In addition, 5 marks were required as deposit payment. On June 9, 1942, the Lodz ghetto bulletin recorded that long lines were stretching outside Zonenberg's circulating library and that readers were ready to pay the high monthly fee and the deposit.

A second circulating library was opened somewhat later by the private bookseller S. Atlasberg. It had 2,000 volumes and some 2,000 readers. In this way, all the books were always in circulation. There were a few other small circulating libraries in private apartments, containing Yiddish books. Libraries were publicized by signs on the front doors of the buildings: "Attention! I lend Yiddish books for reading." When people were deported from the ghetto, their books remained. Some were collected, and out of this collection several small rotating libraries were established in institutions for children and youth.

The authorities allowed the libraries to exist, although they were all forbidden to keep German war books and books which were forbidden in the Reich.

The small libraries were liquidated in time. Zonenberg's library existed until the final liquidation of the Lodz ghetto in August-September 1944 [25, p. 35; 26, pp. 115-39; 27, pp. 400-401; 28, p. 51].

Warsaw Ghetto Libraries

The Germans closed all Jewish libraries and bookstores in Warsaw. After a few months a number of libraries were permitted to function, but when the Jews were forced into the ghetto, all libraries were ordered closed again. In consequence a large number of small underground libraries came into being, each containing a few hundred volumes. They were circulating libraries, most of which were "mobile." Their owners went from one reader's home to another, each carrying a briefcase and giving each reader a book in exchange for the one returned. One of the courier librarians recalled: "In the mornings, until 1 p.m., I am the 'lady from the library,' since people come to see me; between 1 p.m. and 9 p.m., I am the 'girl from the library,' since I run around town." Running around town meant going "to different apartments, up and down many flights of stairs, with a heavy briefcase." There were also a few private lending libraries in private apartments [22, p. 258].

Of the two public libraries existing in the Warsaw ghetto, one was organized and operated by Leyb Schor, who was a publisher of

Hebrew books in Vilna before the war. In his home in the ghetto he accumulated some 10,000-12,000 books. Some of them he acquired illegally, with funds received from the Jewish Self Help Assistance. Other books he acquired from the collection of "The Life" library which remained closed within the ghetto walls. He also bought several book collections from private persons, using his own funds. Schor and his assistant organized the library and prepared a catalog. The library collection forced Schor and his family to sleep in the kitchen and cold corridor of his apartment, keeping the books in the living room. In the beginning he also circulated his books, going with a briefcase full of books to the readers, but by the spring of 1941 he received a license and the readers began to come to the library.

The other library in the Warsaw ghetto was the children's library operated by CENTOS, the National Society for the Care of Orphans. It was established in November 1940 and was directed by Batia Temkin-Berman. The directors of CENTOS saw the library as serving two important roles: a circulating library lending books to individual readers for a small fee, and, what was even more important, a supplier of books to the score of children's institutions. The CENTOS library was located in a facility previously occupied by a branch of the municipal library. It received books from various sources, including children and other private persons. Schor gave it many of the children's books from his collection. In the end it contained some 5,000 books. Since it was an illegal library, it was called the "Committee for Children's Toys" of CENTOS. The apartment was decorated accordingly with dolls and other toys. Originally, for security reasons, the children's library served only CENTOS institutions: orphanages, kitchens, dormitories for child beggars, the children's hospital, and quarantines (for which a special book collection was used, because of the danger of contagion). Some fifty children's institutions received book collections of 10-20 books each.

In the spring of 1941 libraries were again permitted to function in the ghetto. The children's library received a license and began to lend books to individuals. In a short time it had some 700 subscribers and could not serve any more children, since each child could borrow 2 books, one in Yiddish and one in Polish. The fee was small, and many children did not have to pay anything. The library served mostly the poorer children; the well-to-do were sent to a private children's circulating library. Many children worked as volunteers in the library, repairing books, preparing the catalog, going to readers' homes and demanding overdue books, and helping the librarian. The library also conducted literary programs for children.

By July 1942 there were no more children in the Warsaw ghetto and the library stopped functioning. Some time later the books burned when the ghetto went up in flames. In August 1942 the street on which Schor's library was located was placed outside the ghetto's boundaries. On the night before his books were thrown into the street to be destroyed, Schor hanged himself among the bookshelves. In mid-May 1943 the Warsaw ghetto was liquidated following a futile and heroic uprising [29, pp. 521-24; 30, pp. 40-44; 31, pp. 167-71].

Vilna Ghetto Libraries

Luckily, Mefitse Haskalah library was situated within the boundaries of the Vilna ghetto. The first cultural institution to be opened there, it was operated by the Cultural Department of the Jewish Council [32; 33; 34, pp. 241-42; 35, pp. 104-5].

"The appearance of the library was a pleasant surprise," wrote one visitor, who later became a librarian in that library. "Unchanged from the old days, the floor was washed clean--impressive lines of shelved books, a quietness, an intellectual passion, a modern corner in the ghetto" [36, p. 1672].

In September 1942 the Vilna library had 39,000 volumes (10,000 in Yiddish, 5,000 in Hebrew, 7,000 in Polish, 16,000 in Russian, and 1,000 in other languages) [32, table 1]. It was used extensively (tables 4-5). During the period December 1-20, 1942 (the library was closed the rest of the month of December 1942), an average of 425 books were loaned per day, 8,507 in all [32, table 14]. In the first two years the library had 6,800 readers. In May 1943, 14,400 books were borrowed--a record number considering the fact that there were less than 20,000 residents in the ghetto. On September 1, 1943, out of the remaining 10,000-12,000 residents in the smaller ghetto, there were 2,500 active readers [37, p. 333]. Some idea about the number of books circulated by the ghetto on several dates can be obtained from table 6.

TABLE 4

NUMBER OF REGISTERED READERS IN VILNA LIBRARY,
SEPTEMBER-DECEMBER 1941

Month	Number of Registered Readers
September 1941	1,485
October 1941	1,739
November 1941	2,260
December 1941	2,560

Source--[40, p. 131].

TABLE 5

NUMBER OF BOOKS READ IN THE VILNA GHETTO LIBRARY, OCTOBER-DECEMBER 1941

Language	October 1941	Percent	November 1941	Percent	December 1941	Percent
Polish	6,277	80.41	7,156	77.62	6,338	74.5
Yiddish	1,306	16.72	1,743	18.88	1,884	22.2
Hebrew	61	.78	45	.5	38	.4
Lithuanian	67	.86	138	1.5	125	1.4
Russian	87	1.12	92	.8	50	.6
French	5	.05	14	.15	18	.2
English	3	.04	14	.15	36	.4
Other	...	...	32	.4	23	.3
Total	7,806	100.00	9,234	100.00	8,512	100.00

Source--[40, p. 131].

The reading room had originally a separate book collection of 2,895 volumes, but later the whole library collection was placed at the disposal of the reading room users. There were on the average 200 visitors per day. The reading room was opened eleven hours a day, seven days a week. During the first year, 40,762 people used the reading room. They were composed of 21,896 men, 4,440 women, and 14,426 children.

On October 1, 1941, there were ten workers employed in the ghetto library and four in the reading room. To raise the professional qualifications of his staff, special courses were organized in which Kruk read a series of lectures on library techniques, and other scholars presented lectures on the pedagogic approach to the reader and on Yiddish literature and children's literature. The library was originally open seven hours a day, six days a week, and after August 1, 1942, it was open every day of the week. However, the lines in the library were huge, and it was necessary to divide the library into two sections--one for adults and one for children. The librarians complained that they were overworked and falling off their feet because of too much work. "One would have thought [seeing the long queues] that sugar was being distributed rather than books being lent" [37, p. 337]. Readers who did not return the books they borrowed on their due date received an "invitation" from the ghetto police, where they faced a fine.

On December 13, 1942, the residents of the ghetto celebrated

TABLE 6

STATISTICS OF NUMBER OF BOOKS CIRCULATED IN
VILNA GHETTO LIBRARY ON SELECTED DATES

Language and Type of Books	November 22, 1942	December 1, 1942	January 3, 1943	June 20, 1943
Polish fiction	298	203	266	353
Polish children	35	36	...	...
Polish nonfiction	17	8	19	20
Yiddish fiction	94	75	69	118
Yiddish children	47	45	...	...
Yiddish nonfiction	8	15	2	8
Hebrew fiction	10	2	1	5
Hebrew nonfiction	...	...	...	2
Russian	55	38	69	100
Other	10	5	12	13
Total	574	426	438	592

Source--[14, p. 441].

the lending of 100,000 books from the ghetto library. The celebration is mentioned by many who participated. One boy wrote in his diary:

> Today the ghetto celebrated the circulation of the 100,000th book in the ghetto library. The festival was held in the auditorium of the theater. We came from our lessons. Various speeches were made and there was also an artistic program. The speaker analyzed the ghetto reader. Hundreds of people read in the ghetto. The reading of books in the ghetto is the greatest pleasure for me. The books unite us with the future. The books unite us with the world. The circulation of the hundred thousandth book is a great achievement for the ghetto and the ghetto has the right to be proud of it. [38, p. 106].

Zalman Kalmanovich, a scholar of Yiddish literature, recorded that "the lectures are good. The speeches, not worth mentioning" [39, p. 94]. Kruk recorded that in addition to the assembly, a demonstration newsstand was established in which were exhibited the books one could obtain in the ghetto. "It has shown that regardless of our suffering and anguish and regardless of the hard and bitter situation of the Vilna ghetto, a cultural life throbbed in the ghetto. The stage of the assembly was adorned with pretty diagrams of readers and reading in the ghetto" [32; 40, pp. 418-19].

On March 9, 1942, a decree by the Vilna ghetto chief ordered that all books held by the ghetto residents be turned over to the library. Only a few copies of textbooks and prayer books could be kept in private apartments. The final date for the delivery of books to the library was March 12, 1943, after which date there would be an inspection in all the houses. A few days later there was another official announcement which explained the decree:

> The situation of the ghetto library becomes more difficult from day to day. New books cannot be acquired and the old books are wearing out; pages are lost; they get torn and some get lost. Our library is already facing difficulties when it tries to serve its reading public. On the other hand, there are many books in private hands that are seldom or never read by their owners. It will be better, therefore, if these books are transferred to the possession of the ghetto library. In this way, wider circles of the ghetto population will be able to benefit from them, including their previous owners. This is a wiser and a more practical situation than the current one, when many books lie in attics and narrow rooms--where they will only accumulate more dust or cause misunderstanding during an inspection. [41, p. 330]

Due to financial difficulties, on April 30, 1942, the Jewish Council gave the library permission to charge a fee for using the reading room. The fee was 0.03 mark for one time and 0.2 mark for a ten-day use.

At the same time the library called upon the ghetto residents with slogans such as:

> Your only comfort in the ghetto is the book.
> The book makes you forget the sorrowful realities.
> Books carry you to worlds far from the ghetto.
> The book can be a medium to satiate you in time of hunger.
> The book has kept faith with us, let us keep faith with the book. [14, p. 440]

The intensity of reading was less than before the war, but considering the conditions of life in the ghetto, it was high indeed. In 1937 each subscriber to Mefitse Haskalah library borrowed on the average 67 books a year, in 1939 the average rose to 74 books a year, and in 1942 the figure was 40. Polish remained the major language read. The coefficient of adult book use (that is, the ratio of the number of books borrowed to the number of books in the library) was: Polish 8.19, French 2.4, Yiddish 1.54, English 1.3, Lithuanian 0.92, German 0.82, Russian 0.38, and Hebrew 0.2. The coefficient children's book use was: Yiddish 9.4, Polish 9.0, and Hebrew 2.0.

Of 88,697 books loaned between September 1941 and September 1942, 78.3 percent were adult fiction, 17.7 percent were

children's books, and only 4.0 percent were nonfiction. In respect
to language, 70.4 percent were in Polish, 19.4 percent in Yiddish,
7.5 percent in Russian, 1.3 percent in Hebrew, and 1.5 percent in
other languages [32, tables 4-5]. It seems that there were several
reasons for the success of Polish books in the Vilna ghetto:

1. There was a significant number of refugees from Warsaw,
many of whom were members of the assimilated intelligentsia, who
used mostly the Polish language.

2. The books in the Polish language were concerned mostly with
the outside world. Many of the Yiddish books dealt with Jewish
troubles, which paled in comparison with the present situation, at
the time when readers wanted to escape from the present in which
they were living.

3. There were many fewer "literary trash" books and detective
stories in Yiddish, and this was the kind of literature most read in
the ghetto.

In April 1943 several smaller branches of the Vilna ghetto
library were established and placed in two butter factories. There
were also movable libraries in several other working places, in the
ghetto jail and the theater, in the children's home, in the youth and
children's club, and in the technical school [33].

By September 1943 the Vilna ghetto was liquidated and with
it its libraries, its books, and all its readers.

The Librarians

Among the Jewish librarians working in the various libraries in the
ghettos, two were particularly influential: Batia Temkin-Berman in
Warsaw and Herman Kruk in Vilna. Batia Temkin was born in Warsaw in 1907 to a poor family. Despite the difficult material conditions at home, she graduated from the Free Polish University, studied social science, and completed her studies in librarianship. She
was the director of a department in the Polish public library system
of Warsaw. She worked also in the Department of Judaica of the
Polish National Library. In 1934 she published the important survey
of the Jewish libraries in Warsaw mentioned above. She acquired
many friends, particularly among the Polish librarians, who helped
her during the war years in her underground activities. After September 1942 she acted as an "aryan" in the Jewish and Polish underground outside the ghetto. She looked after scores of help and rescue cells for Jews, as part of the secret National Jewish Council.
She survived the war and later became a school librarian in Israel [42].

Herman Kruk was born in 1897 in the city of Plotsk. In 1920
he was conscripted into the Polish army and at about the same time
he joined the Bund. He was involved in party work for the rest of
his life. He eventually became involved with cultural work, providing

workers with theater, concerts, lectures, etc. In 1925 he was appointed secretary of the cultural section of Zukunft, the Bund youth organization. He organized traveling libraries, which traveled from organization to organization, staying in each place several weeks to several months, and then moving on. In 1930 Kruk became the director of the Grosser Library in Warsaw. He also managed the library center of the Kultur-Lige, edited its monthly bulletin, and wrote several articles and pamphlets in Yiddish and Polish on library work and other subjects. After the German occupation of Poland, Kruk left Warsaw and escaped to Vilna. After the liquidation of the Vilna ghetto, Kruk was deported to the Klooga camp in Estonia, where he became one of the 6 million Jews murdered by the Nazis [40, pp. xi-xlv].

Readers and Reading

In a report dated September 1942, on the first anniversary of the opening of the Vilna ghetto library, Herman Kruk wrote: "How thirsty were the new ghetto residents for the book. The terrible happenings ... not only could not stop the children but even a large number of the adult reading element. In the book they have searched for a narcotic, a medium for becoming drunk, in order to forget [32]. A well-to-do woman, a refugee from Warsaw, wrote in her diary: "Now when even a cigarette is difficult to obtain, books are a narcotic for me. After reading three detective stories my head is clogged up so that I forget about the world around me, and that is my good fortune" [43, p. 73].

Among the documents found in the remains of the Vilna ghetto was a small piece of paper written with pencil by an unnamed librarian: "Sometimes it seems to the ghetto librarian that he is a provider of narcotics; it is so clear that the time is not for reading, but for getting drunk. There are people here who do not take up any other book but detective stories, often of the worst kind" [37, p. 330]. These quotes provide an answer to the question, Why did the ghetto residents read?

No less interesting is the question, What did they read? As stated, the readers, especially the women, immersed themselves in light reading. In addition to detective and adventure stories, there was in the Lodz ghetto a great demand for classical authors in the Polish language, such as Stefan Zeromski, Andrzej Strug, Eliza Orzeszkowa, Henry Sienkiewicz, and Boleslas Prus. Among the Soviet authors the more popular were Boris Pilniyak, Ilya Ehrenburg, Maxim Gorky, and Mark Aldanov. Those who read German had a special inclination for books on history and philosophy and classics of German literature. Heinrich Heine, Lion Feuchtwanger, and Emil Ludwig were the most liked. Among the Yiddish authors, the most in demand were Y.L. Peretz and Sholem Asch [25, p. 35].

One of the librarians of the Vilna ghetto library recalled that there were several categories of readers. In the morning came the

well-to-do women, whose husbands worked in the city. They read
Russian sentimental novels of the type that were popular between
the world wars, and mystery stories. The "better" readers read
books by Margaret Mitchell, Ethel M. Dell, and Vicki Baum. In
the early afternoon came the children, directly from school. They
were looking for adventure stories, such as The Children of Captain
Grant, Around the World in Eighty Days, and The Prince and the
Pauper. Young adults were interested in Soviet fiction, such as
How the Steel Was Tempered by Nikolay Ostrovsky. Adult men
came in the later afternoon and particularly on Sundays, when men
who worked outside the ghetto came to the library. The most active
readers were young men and women, members of Zionist youth organizations and often refugees from Warsaw. They read mostly
world literature in Polish translation and books on political and social subjects. The intelligentsia read books by Roger Martin du
Gard, Jakob Wassermann, and Aldanov.

There was little demand for such authors as Flaubert or
Gorky, and even less demand for Dostoevski and Romain Rolland.
Among the more popular authors were A.J. Cronin, who wrote
about miners' life in England; Galsworthy; Ignazio Silone, author of
Bread and Wine; and Upton Sinclair and Theodore Dreiser. Among
books by Jewish authors who wrote in German, The Jewish Wars
by Lion Feuchtwanger and Franz Werfel's The Forty Days of Musa
Dagh, the story of the annihilation of the Armenian minority by the
Turks during World War I, were favored. One reader explained,
"The heart stood still reading such an amazing analogy to our own
situation, that we have read the book with a shiver--as a prophetic
vision of what our fate unfolds before us" [32;36, p. 1672].

The serious Jewish reader, noted Ringelblum on June 25,
1942, was fascinated by war writings: "People particularly enjoy
descriptions of the year 1918 and the downfall of the Germans."
The ghetto Jews read about Napoleon, delighting in accounts of the
march on Moscow. For the same reason, Ringelblum remarked,
Tolstoy's War and Peace was enormously popular in the ghetto.
"In a word, being unable to take revenge on the enemy in reality,
we are seeking it in fantasy, in literature" [22, p. 259]. Other
war novels--such as Erich Maria Remarque's All Quiet on the
Western Front, Jroslav Hasek's The Good Soldier Schweik, and
Emile Zola's La Débâcle--were also popular, as were World War I
memoirs by, among others, the White Russian generals Denikin and
Wrangel.

Some of the intelligentsia began to be interested in Jewish
history, particularly medieval history, and especially the history of
the Crusades and the Inquisition. Historical fiction also had a
large following. Books such as The Witch of Castile and Kiddush
Hashem by Sholem Asch and The Dreamers of the Ghetto by Israel
Zangwill were in great demand. "Reading was not only narcotic
and escape, but also a discipline of the mind, an attempt to retain
the habits of a civilized existence. Reading about past wars and
catastrophes involving other peoples and nations universalized the

Jewish experience and transcended the misery within the ghetto walls" [22, p. 259]. A fourteen-year-old Jewish boy living in the Vilna ghetto wrote in his diary:

> 24 September 1942. I have not been feeling well for several days. Occasionally I have fever. I have a very bad taste in my mouth. I cannot eat. I feel cold. There is no limit to my ennui and boredom. A good part of the day I spend lying down. It will probably pass. Fortunately I have an extraordinary book, Kellermann's The Ninth of November. The book made a strong impression upon me. The book is a picture of the former World War. We see the whole horror of war which puts such a dark stamp on the human life....
> 11 October 1942. Today I feel much better. I read Gorki's Three.... The book made a strong impression on me.
> 15 October 1942. Today I went to school. It was rainy and bleak outdoors. It is cold.... I am reading Bergelson's Penek.
> 17 October 1942. A boring day. My mood is just like the weather outside. I think to myself what would be the case if we did not go to school, to the club, did not read books. We would die of dejection inside the ghetto walls.
> 27 October 1942. I am now reading in Polish The Yellow Cross by Andrzej Strug. A good book, a picture of the first World War. There is much that is comparable to our war, the same blood bath, the same tragedy. [38, pp. 58, 66, 67, 75].

As we know, in less than a year from this entry, the libraries, books, and readers of Vilna ghetto were violently destroyed.

References

1. Poland. Ministerstwo Wyznan Religijnych i Oswiecenia Publicznego. Biblijoteki Oswiatowe spis na dzien 1 Stycznia 1930 Roku Oraz Tablice Statystyczne. Warsaw, 1932.

2. Weisberg, Moshe. "Unzere Biblioteken un die Statistik fun die Leyner." Literarishe Bleter, no. 117 (July 30, 1926), pp. 503-5; no. 123 (September 10, 1926), pp. 603-5.

3. Meyer, D. "Bibliotek-vesen." Bicher-velt; Kritish-bibliografisher Zhurnal 1 (May-June 1922): 215-18, 331-36; 1 (July-October 1922); 467-76.

4. Levinson, Avraham. Ha-Tnuah Ha-Ivrit Ba-Golah. Warsaw: Executive of the World Hebrew Union, 1935.

5. Schweizer, Shlomo. 'Dos Yidishe Kultur-leben in Poylen Tzvishen Beyde Velt Milkhomot." Sefer Ha-Shanah shel Ha-Federatzya shel Yehudey Polin 2 (1958): 112-209.

6. Friedman, Philip. "The Fate of the Jewish Book during the Nazi Era." Jewish Book Annual 15 (1957-58): 3-13.

7. Shatzki, Yaacov. "Yidishe Biblioteken." Poylisher Yid 5 (April 1945): 11-13.

8. Khasman, Rephael. "Ha-Mechora Sheeyna Od." In Yaadut Lita. Tel Aviv: Ha-Agudah Le-Ezra Hadadit Le-Yoyzey Lita Be-Israel, 1967.

9. Kligsberg, Moshe. "Die Yidishe Yugent-bewegung in Poylen Tzwishen Bayde Velt-Milchomot (a Sotziologishe Studie)." In Studies in Polish Jewry 1919-1939, edited by Joshua A. Fishman. New York: YIVO Institute for Jewish Research, 1974.

10. Temkin, Batia. "Die Yidishe Biblioteken in Varsha in Licht fun Tzifern." Das Virtshaftliche Leben, Zeitschrift far Ekonomish-Statistishe Fragen fun Yidishen Leben in Poylen 1 (September-October 1934): 20-27.

11. Kruk, H. "Grosser Bibliotek." In Yidisher Gezelschaftlicher Leksikon, edited by R. Feldshuh. Vol. 1. Warsaw: Yidisher Leksikografisher Farlag, 1939.

12. Commission on European Jewish Cultural Reconstruction. Tentative List of Jewish Cultural Treasures in Axis-occupied Countries. Supplement to Jewish Social Studies, vol. 8, no. 1 (1946).

13. Lodzer Gezelshaftlechkayt Almanach, edited by M. Frankental. Vol. 1. Lodz: Aygener Farlag, 1938.

14. Balberyszki, Mendel. Shtarker fun Eisen. Tel Aviv: Hamenorah, 1967.

15. Kilkes, Sheyna. "Die Kinder-Bibliotek baym Tzentralem Bildungs-Komitet." In Vilner Almanach, edited by A.I. Gradzanski. Vilna: Farlag Avant-Kurier, 1939.

16. Levim, Dov. "Sefarim Mita'am, Sifrey Limud Ve-Kriah Be-Yidish Be-Lita Ha-Sovyetit (1940-1941)." Yad La-Kore 16 (April 1977): 111-24.

17. Kazdan, Kh. S. "Di Shul un Kultur-tetikayt." In Die Geshichte fun Bund, edited by S. Dubnov-Erlich and others. Vol. 4. New York: Farlag Unser Tzayt, 1972.

18. Gazvet, A. "Die Yidishe Hoypt-bibliotek in Varsha." In Haynt Yovel Buch 1908-1938. Warsaw, 1938.

19. Klausner, Israel. "Batey Aked Sefarim Be-Yerushalayim De-Lita." In Sefer Raphael Mahler, edited by Shmuel Yevin. Merhavia: Sifriyat Poalim, 1975.

20. Berger, Mira. "Sifriait Straszun Be-Vilna." In Ha-Hinuch Veha-Tarbut Ha-Ivrit Be-Eyropa beyn Shtey Milchamot Ha-Olam. New York: Ogen, 1967.

21. Kaplan, Chaim A. The Warsaw Diary of Chaim A. Kaplan. Revised ed. New York: Collier Books, 1973.

22. Dawidowicz, Lucy S. The War against the Jews 1933-1945. New York: Holt, Rinehart & Winston, 1975.

23. Trunk, Isaiah. Judenrat: The Jewish Council in Eastern Europe under Nazi Occupation. New York: Macmillan Co., 1972.

24. Katz, Alfred. Poland's Ghettos at War. New York: Twayne Publications, 1970.

25. "Antziklopedia shel Geto Lodz." Yediot Beyt Lohamey Ha-Getatot, nos. 9-10 (1952).

26. "Min Ha-Metzr." Deapim Le-Haker Ha-Shooh Veha-Mered. Pt. 1. Tel Aviv: Hakibutz Hameuchad, 1951.

27. Trunk, Isaiah. Lodzer Geto; a Historishe un Sotziologishe Shtudie. New York: YIVO Institute for Jewish Research, 1962.

28. Spizman, Leib, comp. Khalutzim Ba-Makhteret Uba-Krav. Jerusalem: Kiryat Sefer, 1964.

29. Temkin, Batia. "Sifriyot Yehudiyot." In Antziklopedia shel Galuyot. Vol. 1. Jerusalem: Hevrat Antziklopedia shel Galuyot, 1953.

30. Berman, Adolph Avraham. Asher Ya'ad Li Ha-Goral: im Yehudey Varsha 1939-1942. Tel Aviv: Beyt Lohamey Hagetaot, 1978.

31. Auerbach, Rachel. Be-Khutzot Varsha. Tel Aviv: Am Oved, 1950.

32. Kruk, Herman. "Geto Bibliotek un Geto-Leyner." Sutzkever-Katcherginsky Collection of Materials from the Vilna Ghetto. New York: YIVO Library. Document 369-70.

33. Ran, Leyzer, comp. Yerushalayim De-Lita Illustrirt un Dokumentirt. Vol. 2. New York: Vilner Farlag, 1974.

34. Dworzecki, Marc. Yerushalaym DeLita in Kampf un Umkum. Paris, 1948.

35. Sutzkever, Avraham. Vilner Geto 1941-1944. Paris: Farband fur die Vilner in Frankreich, 1946.

36. Abramovich, Dina. "Vilner Geto-Bibliotek." In Lite, edited by Mendel Sudarsky and others. New York, 1951.

37. Belis, Shalomo. "Farvus und Vos Hot Man Geleynt." In Fartraten un Problemen. Warsaw: Yidish-Buch, 1964.

38. Rudashevski, Yitskhok. The Diary of the Vilna Ghetto June 1941-April 1943. Tel Aviv: Beyt Lokhamey Hagetaot, 1973.

39. Kalmanovich, Zalman. "A Diary of the Vilna Ghetto." YIVO Annual of Jewish Social Science 8 (1953): 9-81.

40. Kruk, Herman. Togbuch fun Vilner Geto. New York: YIVO Institute for Jewish Research, 1961.

41. Korchak, Reizel. Lehavot Ba-Efer. 3d ed. Merhavia: Moreshet-Sifriat Poalim, 1965.

42. Le-Zichra shel Lokhemet: al Batia Temkin Berman Le-Yom Ha-Shanah Ha-Asiri Le-Mota. Tel Aviv, 1963.

43. Solowejczyk, Aleksandra. "Dray Fertel Yar Unter die Daytshen in Vilna." YIVO Bleter 30 (Fall 1946): 59-93.

VIEWS OF A LUDDITE*

Paul A. Lacey

I am pleased to be invited to speak about what the next decade might mean to my work as a teacher and researcher because so much of my work and my enjoyment depends on libraries and librarians. What happens to librarians will also happen to me. In fact, my temperament and training are such that, where others would turn to a crystal ball, a computer projection, or their own imaginations to approach today's theme, I went to the library. Or, more technically, I began a documents search for materials on what libraries might be like ten years from now. I clipped articles from Change and the Chronicle of Higher Education (my own copies!), I turned to my reference librarian--my friend and colleague Evan Farber--and I read all the material he put in my hands. I also tried to experience what the future will be like by pursuing three computer searches of databases--one in modern poetry, one in the history of British dissenting academies, and one in a new therapy in psychology.

As you know from your own work, the predictions about these next ten years contain good news and bad news. The bad news is that no library will be adequate, in itself, to meet all the demands that will be placed on it; and that the cost of acquiring new materials--which will continue to pour forth in geometrically increasing quantities--will continue to rise so steeply that every academic and university library will have to become more selective in its own holdings. Some colleges are planning to stabilize their collections at some specific number of volumes (rather than increasing holdings indefinitely), then maintain that number by careful culling, on the one hand, and vigorous use of cooperative and network arrangements, on the other, to supply what students and faculty need. The good news, of course, is that such cooperative arrangements, networks, and computer-accessible databases are already largely in place and at present make far more material available to the researcher than ever before. Moreover, it is good news that computer indexing of databases will be followed rapidly by immediate computerized access to the documents themselves. A recent New York Times article on

---
*Reprinted by permission of the author and publisher from College & Research Libraries, 43:2 (March 1982) 110-118. Copyright © 1982 by the American Library Association.

the computerization of the library of Congress catalog notes that the electronic catalog now has 81 million entries, with room for scores of millions more, and that in the future electronic processes will allow the retrieval of actual book contents on the cathode screen. In the future, we also know, it will become ever more common that such retrieval of materials will allow for hard-copy reproduction as well.

We are in the middle of a sweeping revolution in the ways we generate, collect, store, retrieve, and use the products of the human mind--the products we rather casually call information or data. Work that would previously have taken years of drudgery to accomplish will be done in a fraction of the time and of the drudgery. Questions that would not have occurred to us to ask, because their answers would have required methods of comparison and analysis too complex to keep straight in our minds, might soon be commonplace to ask and answer. The very forms in which we index and catalog materials will permit multiple studies in word frequency, stylistic profiles, concordances, and the like--to speak of only one kind of literary study. Problems involving many variables can be studied in ways too complicated to have been attempted in the past. The very ways we collect and store information will produce more information; we will be able to wring out the last drop of significance from every piece of data--which is the scholar's dream.

As this brief survey of what is already happening reminds us, the ways we use libraries in the future are likely to be vastly different from what they have been in the past. Some of the predictions I have read speak exultantly of the end of libraries as we have known them, the end of dependence on print, and the end of the book. In place of the vast building with its many holdings and many services, the most radical predictions envisage the "disembodiment of the library," and in its place a system of information retrieval operated by a keyboard at the scholar's desk. They see the scholar alone in his or her office, typing out instructions that will call up, in moments, virtually anything that has ever been committed to print or entered into a memory bank. According to this vision, publishing will also change radically; articles and books will be entered directly into a memory bank or database, to be called up if and as anyone is interested. Books will virtually disappear--not only as physical objects, print on paper, but as extended argument or discussion. "Instead, bibliographic technicians will have already broken down the book into fragments suitable for storage in giant computers and for transmission through a variety of audio-visual systems" [1]. No one will want to labor to make a book a coherent whole if everything of that sort is destined to be dismantled into fragments suitable for storage and retrieval.

Perhaps you've noticed that I stopped talking about good news and bad news. That is because I am no longer sure whether what I am describing is one or the other. I see the marvelous possibilities in having so much material so readily available, but I also recognize that the technological developments that are confidently

predicted to lead to the end of print, the end of the book, and the
end of the library, strike me with horror. I cannot imagine doing
my work as a teacher and a researcher with pleasure in such a
world.

By training and interest I am a teacher and student in the
humanities. I spend my professional time, and much of my recreational time, reading literature and making connections between literary works and between literature and other disciplines--especially
psychology, philosophy, theology, and history. Like the majority
of college and university teachers in America, I see myself primarily as a teacher. I write and publish modest amounts, and I keep
a number of research projects working all the time, but virtually
all of my writing and research relates directly to my teaching,
which in turn grows largely out of my intellectual interests. I am
drawn not only to aesthetic questions, but to social, political, and
philosophical ones, and these help shape what I teach and how I do
research to prepare for my teaching.

My job, then, is to read literature carefully, to understand
what writers have written and the contexts out of which their writings have come. I do this job for my own satisfaction--for the
pleasure I receive from the beauty of literature, from the wisdom
and the insight into human motives and actions it offers, and from
the truth it contains. I also do this job because it brings me into
meaningful relations with other people--my undergraduate students
and my teaching colleagues--with whom I share the pleasure, beauty,
wisdom, insight, and truth of literature.

As a teacher and a student of literature, my methods are
analytical, but I am ultimately concerned with wholes rather than
with parts. My effectiveness must be judged according to how well
I bring the whole text, the complete work, before my students, and
how well I demonstrate my respect for the whole text in my attention
to the smallest detail. I must, in turn, assess the value of a library or an information-retrieval system by how well they help me
come to a close, informed examination of a whole text.

As a teacher and a student of the humanities, I must come
clean on something else about myself that profoundly influences how
I look at what will be happening to libraries in the next ten years.
I am a Luddite. The first Luddites--named for an English factory
worker who was said to be mentally retarded--broke machinery that
was threatening to put them out of work. To say I am a Luddite
is to say I approach technological developments, which others call
progress, with fear and hostility, and my stock reaction to the introduction of a new piece of machinery into my life is to hope it
will break down ignominiously. I love to see machines fail, and I
believe they reciprocate the feeling. My experiences with computerized technology have frequently been catastrophic. The only time
I ever tried to withdraw money from a bank machine was on a Saturday afternoon, just before I was to leave on a business trip. The
machine housed a persona named something like Auntie Em--warm,

chatty, eager to help. In the middle of our transaction, Auntie Em
ate my card and then pretended never to have heard of me. When
in desperation I left to make a futile effort to phone someone from
the bank, the public telephone swallowed my only dime. Like most
Luddites, I am selective as well as ambivalent about the technology
I wish to eliminate. I drive a car, fly in airplanes, use the telephone, radio, and television, but deep down in my heart I have only
accepted the radio fully. I prefer to write with a fountain pen--not
even a cartridge pen but a real fountain pen. Do not expect me to
greet the future with unalloyed pleasure.

Undoubtedly my feelings are made up of a lot of sentimentality
and wrongheadedness, but let me indulge them for a few minutes because there are a great many people like me--perhaps especially
among people in the humanities--and what we can forsee as the shape
of our work in the future rests only in part on what technology can
offer us. The larger part rests on how we feel about what technology can do for us. The first Luddites were weak, fighting a desperate losing battle; those I am talking about are strong and influential; they can make systems fail simply because they will not
cooperate. So, for a few minutes, I will indulge myself.

I have strong emotions about libraries. The feel and look
of books matter to me. I love the touch and smell of a clean new
book and an old leather-bound secondhand one. Every library I
have ever worked in evokes memories of the first one I used, a
branch public library in a bankrupt grocery store on a side street
in Philadelphia. When I was a child, I not only played cowboys and
war and school; I also played library. I put cards in my books,
and I used to like to hold my pencil between my first and second
fingers, the way librarians did when they wrote in one's card number and then reversed the pencil to stamp in the date. The library
not only had the books one wanted, it was a place to be on rainy
Saturdays. It had heavy oak tables to sit at and read; it was intimate and personal and run like a cottage industry. It was a mom
and pop library. In the years since then I have learned to use bigger and better libraries--Widener, Houghton, the New York Public,
the British Museum, and many others--but they have all felt familiar
to me because they were still essentially cottage industries.

But of course libraries have also changed enormously since
the days when the librarian wrote your card number on the book
card and then stamped the date. I recall when I first became aware
of the rapidity of the changes. I was finishing college at the University of Pennsylvania in 1957, and the university was just beginning to use a computer for course registration. (I recall with pleasure that the first experiment was disastrous.) Several of us found
ourselves speculating about how this new thing could be used in libraries. We spent a hilarious couple of hours capping each other's
wildest fantasies about what might be possible with the new technology. I recognize now that every outrageous science fiction invention we imagined has since been surpassed by what happens every
day now with computer searches, telephone transmission of printed

data, and new forms of bibliographies, concordances, and indexes. I mention this not only to put you on your guard about me as a forecaster but also to put in stark relief the differences between the library of my memories and the library I seem to be destined to work in in the future.

If I were a Luddite only out of nostalgia and mechanical incompetence, I would not be worth listening to; but even when we have been wrongheaded, we Luddites have raised important value questions. The first Luddites had three anxieties that you and I, and our colleagues, must also face now and in the decade ahead. They can be put in the form of three questions:

1. Will the new technology put us out of meaningful and valuable jobs?
2. Will the fine old crafts we practice be cheapened or lost as a result of the new technology?
3. Will the new machinery alienate us from our work and from our fellow workers?

These, I suggest, are crucial questions for us to ask as we speculate on what will happen in the study of the humanities in the next ten years, and I will try to reflect on each in some detail.

Will the new technology put us out of meaningful and valuable jobs?

I have already indicated that I am a teacher first of all, and a researcher in large part as a result of my teaching. My work, then, brings me into close and rich association with people who study as well as produce literary works. Dame Helen Gardner describes the study of literature this way:

> In no other subject is the pupil brought more immediately and continuously into contact with original sources, the actual material of his study. In no other subject is he so able and so bound to make his own selection of the material he wishes to discuss, or able so confidently to check the statements of authorities against the documents on which they are based. No other study involves him so necessarily in ancillary disciplines. Most important of all, no other study touches his own life at so many points and more illuminates the world of his own daily experience [2].

Both studying and teaching literature are, preeminently, library work. To teach a student how to study literature is to introduce him or her to systematic library research methods--going to original sources, selecting judiciously, checking authorities against the documents, reaching out into other fields of study to get more light on the meaning of our documents. Such study is an end in itself and the means to other ends. It teaches us how to read accurately, and in the process it lets us share the pleasure, beauty, insight, and wisdom that literature offers to those who approach

it with openness and respect. Will technology put me out of that
job, or are there ways it can enhance and extend the effectiveness
of that work--whether or not I am the one who does it?

My ultimate end may be to find truth and beauty in literature,
but my means require making discriminations, studying fine details.
Analysis must precede synthesis. In these kinds of tasks, which
Professor Donald Bond has called "scholarship preparatory to scholarship," new technology is invaluable. Discovering and classifying
documents, making descriptive bibliographies, editing texts, establishing sources and analogues are essential but painfully time-consuming tasks. Now indexes and bibliographies can be searched
in instants instead of weeks. Collating editions, textual studies,
concordances, word-frequency counts and stylistic profiles, formerly among the slowest, most tedious of work, can now be done with
the assistance of the computer in a fraction of the former time and
quite possibly with more fertile results, since the computer-generated
tracings and cross-references can help us see far more elaborate or
deeply embedded literary patterns than we have seen before. To
cite a single example, the Chronicle of Higher Education (March 16,
1981, p. 19) reports that Professor Colin Martindale of the University of Maine at Orono used a computer to trace trends in language
usage among English poets over a five-hundred-year period. Choosing the work of five leading poets in twenty-year time periods, Professor Martindale fed fifty-eight line samples of each poet's work--
taken at random--into the computer. The resulting computer analyses showed a trend in each period toward "incongruous or unpredictable imagery as the younger poets within the tradition succeeded."
And as one tradition gave way to another, the new poets wrote once
more "in more familiar images." According to Professor Martindale, this study would have been difficult if not impossible without
the computer.

Historical and critical approaches, literary biography, social
history, intellectual history, and a variety of cross-disciplinary approaches to literary works may in time all be made less exhausting
as more and more relevant material gets entered into memory banks.
Surveys of lists, book-sale records, names on registers, wills and
legal documents are some of the raw material of such studies.
Meyer Abrams has described indifference to boredom as "the sine
qua non of scholarship," but it is possible that in the future we will
be able to get more useful conclusions out of our surveys of such
material at the cost of less weariness of flesh and spirit.

The kinds of scholarly tasks I have been describing, though
they are highly valuable, are only a small part of what students of
the humanities find useful to do. Moreover, not everything we
might want to examine minutely will be fed into a computer in time
for us to avoid the tedium of a hand search; indeed, most of such
tedious material will get into a computer only after someone has
gone through it minutely to program it. And despite all the promise
of easy access, there will have to be selections of what is going to

be made retrievable in the great databases. Even if microforms and computer memory are easy to store, the expense of collecting material will continue to increase, as will the cost of retrieving it. The librarian who helped me with my computer searches discouraged one line of approach by saying gently that computer time was pretty expensive for playing around. He is right, of course, but we must remember that <u>playing around</u>, hunting and poking around in unexpected places, imagining unorthodox ways to get at information, are the very heart of research. <u>Playing around</u> is cheap when only the scholar's time is being considered, since in fact we never put an hourly cost to that, but when we have to pay for machine time instead of human time, we may find that some things we would like to do simply are not affordable.

Information is not merely exploding, it is undergoing fission. Even the great storage capacity we have will not allow us to keep up with the rapidly moving present while simultaneously reaching ever more deeply into the distant past. For economic reasons, if no other, we may be unable to do both. Some of the more radical projections of changes in research methods acknowledge, perhaps a bit condescendingly, that people who deal in earlier ages will still have to look at books, original documents, and other antique data sources. I hope they will not waste too much pity on us, for that is our greatest strength. As C. P. Snow pointed out, whereas something like 90 percent of the natural scientists who have ever lived are alive now, about 90 percent of the writers who have ever lived are dead. Snow thought that the latter fact was regrettable, but I consider it a great benefit. The humanist does not live only in the immediate present or in anticipation of a swiftly arriving future; he or she lives in distant times or several ages. The humanist is a time traveler into the past, studying and honoring and seeking to understand writers whose canon is forever closed, writers who, in representing their own time, offer something for ours.

What I say about literary study also applies to much philosophical, theological, and historical work. Plato and Thucydides, Isaiah, Socrates, and Jesus are not our contemporaries, but they speak to us precisely because they are so deeply rooted in the existential problems of their times and places. Will the new technology put us out of meaningful and valuable jobs? No. The new technologies have enormous promise for us, but not everything we consider worth doing will benefit from the laborsaving new machines. Some things will never get into the memory banks or will be too expensive to call up in meaningful form. This cautionary point leads directly into the Luddite's second question.

<u>Will the fine old crafts we practice be cheapened or lost as a result of the new technology?</u>

This is not a trivial question. We know already how easy it is to let machines dictate what we will do. Natural scientists find themselves deciding to study one topic rather than another because they have the necessary equipment to study the first topic.

The equipment may not only determine what we will study, it will significantly determine what will be accepted as meaningful data. A number of scientists and philosophers have warned against the growing tendency to let what we study, how we study it, and what will be taken as acceptable conclusions to our study be determined by the equipment we have available. We know how hard it is to go outside the limits of the field, however they are established, yet just that breaking the limits of the field, conceiving of new ways to approach a topic, is what vitalizes research. It is not merely fear of the future, or sentimental longing for the past, that leads the humanist teacher and researcher--like our counterparts in the natural and social sciences--to worry about the craft of research, the skill of mind and hand and eye that turns up the fruitful lead, or the telling bit of information. That craft can be lost if we do only what the machinery knows how to do rather than what we believe is worth doing.

What is the craft of research? For me it is being able to frame a significant question. This is the same craft which is at the heart of teaching. To frame a question means making a judgment about what is worth asking on a subject, what will produce the most important connections between ideas and bits of information, and what can lead us into more sophisticated or far-reaching questions. In speaking of framing rather than asking questions, I am trying to get at the process by which one examines a body of material, an event or a phenomenon at the same time as one examines the tools or the means by which a further examination of the subject can be best made. Framing the question is not simply requesting information; it is more like framing up a building, that preliminary roughing out of the space one is going to occupy, putting in the supports that allow one to do the substantial building in a more orderly fashion. I have to consider the materials I have to work with, the terrain I am working in, the tools I have at my disposal. If I am framing a question, I have to ask what I want to know and how I am likely to find out what I want to know in the most dependable fashion.

As a teacher I ask myself what I want my students to be able to do after they have reviewed research, what I want to come out of their writing of papers, what form I want those papers to take--and all of that leads me to thinking how my assignment should be constructed. When I am most fully engaged in reflecting on these questions, I am framing the questions that will organize a course within the content to be examined and what my students will be able to do with it.

For those of us in the humanities and social sciences certainly, and for natural scientists pretty substantially, the library is the most important and largest toolbox we have for framing our questions. Yet most of us who are teachers and researchers are poorly instructed in how to use the tools a library provides. We have been accustomed to having the hardest courses we took and the hardest we teach introduce the longest list of books on reserve.

Our professors gave us fine bibliographies that directed our reading, and we may do the same for our students. Often it has been our experience that the most challenging graduate seminars we took specified both the paper topics and the works we were to consult. Our best graduate and undergraduate courses gave exclusive attention to mastering the content of major works in our field. We would go to a reference librarian as a last resort, and rarely if ever imagine that we could learn a generalizable method of research that might give us more interesting questions to pursue.

Several consequences flow from that kind of experience. We are only experienced in a very small part of the research tools a library offers. We only know a small part of the library's holdings--the eighteenth century or the American colonial period. Because of our limited, though deep, experience with a specialized set of holdings and the specialized tools for studying them, we may automatically turn away from stimulating new questions to work in the same and familiar. We become passive in the presence of a new problem. We decide it is uninteresting or impossible to pursue.
I consider myself quite at home in a library, but I occasionally catch myself evading a topic when a preliminary survey shows that it will not yield to my standard methods. Confessing ignorance is good for us, we know, but most of us will pass up the opportunity to admit our ignorance, when we can. In this connection it is worth noting that approaching a database through programs that are not, in the jargon, "user friendly," is far more daunting than asking a librarian for help in a strange new area.

We also like to postpone wrestling with the hard work of a study, making the material make sense, constructing the questions that will probe the data. Dreary though note taking is, it is not the hard work of thought--which is what we tend to avoid when the problem we are studying is resistant. Have you noticed how often people stand feeding coins into the Xerox machine, copying pages, instead of reading the pages to decide which are really worth having? Searching for more material is a familiar way for avoiding coming to grips with what one already has. Research technologies that show us how to amass great quantities of bibliographies, indexes, lists, bits of books, may--unless we do something about learning a more subtle craft--cause our ability to frame questions to deteriorate even further.

So behind the question of whether the new technology will ruin our craft lie two concerns. First, there is already a danger that researchers ask only the questions they are certain they have the means of answering. We and our students can become passive and ask only what our machines can answer, rather than venturing beyond those limits. Second, for people who are already overspecialized and too narrow in their acquaintance with a library, the kinds of new technologies we have may help confirm the overspecialization, both because they let us mine familiar territory more extensively and because they are daunting when we enter new territories. One of my computer searches came to a temporary standstill as the printout repeated "invalid command" time after time, while my helper, trained to negotiate such obstacles, tried unsuccessfully for about ten exchanges to puzzle out what would satisfy this mechanical servant which had just become so finicky. Need I say that, had I been on my own, I would have typed something like "Forget the whole mess, let me out of here"? Of course, the machine would have replied "invalid command," and my private nightmare would have continued.

To put the matter as I have is to remind us of the maxim that it is a poor craftsman who blames his tools when something goes wrong. The enormous possibilities of new technology show us that many of us, both as teachers and researchers, have asked the same kind of question again and again about familiar material and have done the same research project on several different texts. We have had little experience in framing new questions, new approaches. It is universally agreed that there is a great deal of garbage being published in all fields, but how do we deal with that fact when we ask for a research paper from students? Typically, such papers are required to begin with a thorough review of the literature, and the student is rewarded for going through the literature with the thoroughness and indiscriminacy of a powerful vacuum cleaner. Apparently we see no way of dealing with the garbage except to wade through all of it. The computer will not solve that problem for us. Technologies that produce longer lists of titles, more piles of data, and which break books down into fragments for suitable storage cannot, in themselves, give us better research.

In speaking of the value of social science indexing for perceiving complex social systems, Kenneth Boulding has said, "It is fundamental to all knowledge that we gain knowledge by the orderly loss of information." Most of us, at the start of our careers as teachers and researchers, assumed that one never dared to lose any information. It was always to be piled on more and more; knowledge was the sum total of one's information. That is a false model of learning, but some of the most exultant celebrations of the libraries of the future speak of research and learning only under that model. Will the new technology make us lose or cheapen our crafts as researchers? It will not, in itself, either cheapen or improve our craft. That depends on us. Computer databases will be selective and discriminating only if we tell them to be so. They make a craft possible, but they are not a craft in themselves. This brings me to my third Luddite question.

<u>Will the new technology alienate us from our work and from our fellow workers?</u>

That question has to be considered on at least two levels. I have already begun to address one level in discussing the problems by considering study and research as first and foremost the amassing of data. To work in the humanities means to treat the text, the original source, with the utmost respect. Every piece of research we do ought to have as a major goal bringing us closer to the text, to the composer of the text, and to the society that created it. Our study ought always to be a celebration of human hopes and accomplishments. Counting word frequencies or beating out a poem's meter on the desk top may be very far away from these noble goals, but they must somehow participate in these goals or they mean nothing. As teachers and researchers in the humanities, some of our most significant work involves not great quantities of material but a small body of material studied deeply. As I have suggested, that is both a strength and a problem.

On the second level we must consider research as a social activity, something that we do with other people. The stereotype of the scholar in the humanities places him or her in a lonely study, occasionally sending a little signal to the outside world in the form of an article, learned note, or query. Scholarship is something we do alone, but we also pursue it in company. Not only do we want to be in touch with those who are working on similar issues, we want friends and colleagues around--working on very different things-- who can share with us the delight in a new insight, a fruitful line of inquiry.

When I first started teaching at Earlham, there was only one coffee urn in our building. If one went for coffee, it was with the expectation of spending half an hour or longer. One was away from the desk and the telephone, and more important, one was with colleagues from the whole faculty. A lot of very good conversations generated a lot of good ideas while we were drinking coffee. As time went on, people started thinking it would be cheaper and more efficient if departments bought their own coffeepots, so we would not have to walk three flights to get coffee or expect to spend half an hour over it. And now, to be sure, every department has its coffeepot, and most of us walk across the hall, fill our cups, return to our offices, and keep on working. There are no half-hour breaks; I at least drink coffee all day long now, instead of three or four cups; and I see less of my immediate colleagues and virtually nothing of people in other departments unless I seek them out. The gathering place disappeared when we found a little bit of a timesaver to ease our work. The work, perhaps, is also less satisfying, because it is not shared with others.

If advances in information retrieval technology really lead to every scholar sitting at a console, calling up data and books and articles in splendid isolation, I believe we will be the worse for it, just as we will be worse off if "publishing" comes to mean dropping one's little pebble of information into the deep well of a database with no hope of hearing the faintest splash. The projections that foresee the disappearance of libraries, and librarians working themselves out of a job, fill me with despair, unless I conclude that what those writers mean by a library is very different from what I mean.

Let me acknowledge once again that books have great aesthetic appeal to me, and I love to browse through stacks of them. But I do not think of a library as simply a giant warehouse for books. If the library of the future becomes a storehouse of computer memories and microforms, rather than of books, my aesthetic enjoyment will be reduced; but that is really a minor consideration. For a library is far more than a storage or retrieval center. At its best, a library is a model for the teaching-learning process. I am going to describe that model, using the Lilly Library at Earlham College, which I know best, but intending to make the model widely generalizable.

First of all, the building is designed for a multiplicity of uses, all of which are essentially voluntary. Materials for both information and enjoyment lie close at hand. One may come in to read the newspapers or magazines, check an atlas, look something up in an encyclopedia. One may think of the library the way George Bernard Shaw thought of marriage, as combining the maximum opportunity and the maximum temptation. Databases may have everything available and up-to-date that I have described, except the context. Browsing in a database--a form of play that is "rather expensive"--will never be the same as walking through a space with so many different temptations drawing the eye. The library user--often called a patron--identifies what he is looking for; if he cannot find it he goes to a librarian for help. The librarian engages in conversation with the patron, drawing out more about his interests and needs. The patron may be shown where to find what he wants; taught how to find it and things like it in the future; or helped to see that he actually wants something very different. That is, to think of the college situation, in the process of describing his interests or his assignment, and learning what the library is best equipped to provide, the patron may have his wants refined and redirected. The process helps him frame his question better. That clarification process can be helped by computer searches, but I think its most important aspect is that it is a conversation between two people face-to-face. More than information is transmitted in that conversation; attitudes, values, tone of voice, respect, and human interest all are part of that conversation. Every research project needs something to give it human scale. That is research as a social activity.

Such a library provides a learning milieu that is ideal for independent study--for both the beginner and the experienced researcher. The librarian acts as a facilitator, giving a great deal of help and advice but leaving the patron to do the actual work. As a general rule, the librarian is not involved in evaluating the researcher's performance.

The library I am describing has seminar rooms, typing rooms, lounges, a faculty lounge, smoking rooms, a variety of carrels, tables, and chairs for people to use in their reading and writing. There are rugs on the floors in some places, and it is not uncommon for us to see a student napping on the floor with books and papers beside him. The library has Xerox equipment and computer terminals, a language laboratory, and other audiovisual facilities. All this is available for people to take from as they wish, subject only to those rules about control of material and etiquette that make things available to the greatest number of users.

    I want to emphasize my point here. I am not conceiving of the library as an information retrieval system primarily but as a social system, a teaching-learning milieu in which retrieval of information is only a part of the goal. Browsing, conversation, exchange of ideas, sharing and confirming values, supporting one another in the common enterprise of study, reflection, and publishing one's findings--these are extremely important to what a humanist, or any member of the scholarly community, does. Take them away, and we <u>will</u> be alienated from our work and our colleagues. Improved <u>technology</u> is a splendid help in accomplishing many of our tasks, but both the successful accomplishment of our work and the satisfaction we get from our work depend on the links with the community of scholarship.

    I am arguing that the library is not merely a place or a collection of functions but a living symbol of value and rich human relations. One can listen to a church service on radio or television and be inspired by the sermon and the music; one can go to a drive-in church and see the service firsthand, while sitting in one's own "solitude covered with iron," as Robert Bly describes the automobile. But I find it very hard to believe that one can truly share communion by radio, television, or drive-in services. Communion, our deepest experience of self-transcendence, comes only in the closest association with other humans. And in our work as teachers and as researchers we know something of the joys of self-transcendence, being caught up in a text or a search that makes us forget ourselves, and we also know the joy of communion, of finding kindred spirits, dedicated scholars and writers who are a part of our human family. There must be places where such things can happen and be confirmed and memorialized. Universities and colleges are such places. So are libraries.

    You may know that Lincoln Steffens had developed his phrase about the Russian Revolution before he ever got to see the revolution itself. On the train from Western Europe into the Soviet Union he was practicing the phrase: "I have seen the future, and it works." If I were the Luddite I have posed as, I would be practicing my own phrase--something like, "I have seen the future, but it is down at the moment." But of course it would be fatuous to wish that brilliant inventions fail, that laborsaving devices be replaced once more by mind-wearying drudgery. We can have the benefits of new technologies, along with the benefits of the best methods and goals of the past and present, if we are reflective about what we want from the machines we have created. With wisdom and care, we can find that the new developments in library and research technology in the decade ahead help us to do our jobs better, with more satisfaction, help us become more skilled and subtle craftsmen and craftswomen, and far from alienating us from work or one another, help us find richer associations and deeper communions. If those things happen, however, it will not be because or despite of machinery, but because the human spirit can express itself in the new ways as well as the old.

References

1. F. Wilfrid Lancaster, "Libraries and Librarians in an Age of Electronics" (unpublished), p. 165.

2. Dame Helen Gardner, "The Academic Study of English Literature," Critical Quarterly I (1959), III.

THE TERMINAL AND THE TERMINUS:

THE PROSPECT OF FREE ONLINE

BIBLIOGRAPHIC SEARCHING*

John Budd

Few subjects generate more heated discussion and less agreement than that of user fees. Library literature is rife with articles by administrators and librarians advocating full charges, partial charges, or no charges. A prime cause of controversy in this area in recent years has been the prospect of charging fees for online bibliographic search services at public institutions.

At present, with well over 100 databases available for searching, library users often stand in awe at the avenues open to them. Consider the doctoral student commencing research on a multidiciplinary dissertation topic. A cursory examination tells the student that there is a wealth of information, but that the sources of the information are many and varied. Numerous long hours and considerable eye strain lie ahead. Next, consider the student's becoming aware of the time-saving capability of online bibliographic searching. Of course, the computerized search cannot totally eliminate the need for manual searching, but it is conceivable that the student's research time could be cut in half.

The doctoral student in the above example may be willing to absorb personally some or all of the costs concomitant with the online search. The issue debated by many librarians, however, is not the patron's ability to pay, but whether users should be charged for such services. Also, if the decision is made to charge, does the patron absorb all costs (direct and indirect), vendor costs, offline print costs, or some other fee formulation?

All of the libraries surveyed for ARL's SPEC Kit 62 state that they charge all users for searches [1]. The most common charge is for "direct costs." This is assumed to mean vendor fees, telecommunications costs (if applicable), and offline printing. When

---

*Reprinted by permission of the author and publisher from RQ, 21:4 (Summer 1982) 373-378. Copyright © 1982 by the American Library Association.

asked if the service is subsidized, most of those responding positively state that the subsidy is in the form of the library's absorption of equipment costs and costs for staff time [2]. This survey may not prove to be an accurate gauge of charging procedures, however, since all of the responding institutions are private.

The charging of fees does have its proponents and is the practice at many libraries. Bruce Bonta of Pennsylvania State University says, "Requesters [of on-line searching] were required to pay the charges for the on-line time, including telecommunications costs, the off-line printing charges, and a five-dollar handling fee per search" [3]. Charges at other libraries may vary greatly due to partial subsidization. For instance, at California State University, Chico, the library charges according to what it calls the

> 10-10-10 system. The library pays the first ten dollars of search cost; the patron pays the second ten dollars (i.e., $10.01 to $20.00); and the library pays the third ten ($20.01 to $30.00). All costs over thirty dollars are borne by the patron. The fee structure applies to search costs only, that is, online costs plus any off-line printing. No other charges are added [4].

James Cogswell is of the opinion that fees are inevitable and necessary for public, college, and university libraries [5]. He states that online searching is an added cost to the library; it replaces no service or reference tool. He also cites the cost in staff time as a primary reason for user fees. In actuality, staff time should not enter into a discussion of user fees. A publicly supported library should be staffed adequately to handle existing and proposed services without passing personnel time, which is an administrative cost, on to users.

Staffing can present a problem with the addition of online bibliographic search services. The time involved in training personnel and in the actual provision of the service is considerable and must be accounted for if the service is to prove useful. It may be that the addition of online searching (or any new service) can be used as a persuasive device with the funding agency or parent institution to gain staff increases. For instance, when the Sims Memorial Library of Southeastern Louisiana University inaugurated its online search service in the spring of 1981, a request was made of the university administration for additional personnel to ensure the continuation of all services. As a result, a support position was added to the Reference/Interlibrary Loan Department beginning in the fall of 1981. It may be, however, that additional staffing will not be forthcoming. In such an instance, the individual library must weigh the importance of all services to the library's clientele and decide, if need be, which to retain and which to curtail.

Cooper and DeWath state that they believe there is statistical evidence showing that searching is more efficient when the library charges [6]. Such a statement based on the Cooper and DeWath study is difficult to support, however, for a number of reasons: (1) the costs for searches during a period of free searching and a period of user charges at sample libraries are too divergent and inconsistent to draw conclusions; (2) during the pay period the patron was present during search 50 percent of the time, while during the free period the patron was present only 15 percent of the time; (3) since the free period preceded the pay period, searchers were probably more experienced, and thus more efficient, by the second year (the pay period).

These arguments in favor of charging user fees for online searching are based solely on economic reasoning. To support his claim for user fees, Cogswell states that at the University of Pennsylvania in 1977 online vendor charges to the library amounted to $7,800 [7]. On the face of it, this figure may seem to represent a rather high cost for the provision of one service. On the other hand, Judith Thompson of California State College, Stanislaus, states, "We do not charge for computer searching because we do not consider it a "specialized" service or a duplication of existing resources but rather an additional reference tool appropriate to certain occasions"[8]. She further says that in one year the library spent $6,759 for 1,200 searches, citing that the expenditure represents just another means of providing information [9].

Thompson's opinion is shared by Sara Knapp and C. James Schmidt. They maintain that for a library to provide in-depth service to 1,600 patrons for $20,000 ($12.50 each) is not extravagant [10]. This is indeed a valid and cogent point. For the large library with holdings of a million volumes or more and a materials budget in excess of $1,000,000 a year, $20,000 is not at all an unreasonable sum to pay to meet the needs of a large segment of the library's clientele.

The use of online bibliographic services at smaller libraries may be proportional to use at larger libraries (with regard to number of uses or expenditures for services). Therefore, if the library budgets are also proportional, the smaller library could have the same ability to absorb costs internally as the larger one. Along with the smaller size of the library, there will usually be a correspondingly small population to be served and thus a correspondingly small online expenditure needed. Such an occurrence is exemplified by California State College, Stanislaus, whose online budget noted above is considerably below the $20,000 figure posited by Knapp and Schmidt. Also, with a smaller population to be served there are likely to be fewer in-depth research requests made. Because of this, the number of detailed and involved online searches would be smaller. With this reducing level of online searching activity, the prospect of in-house funding for the service is enhanced. Perhaps the library's budget can be adjusted so that a portion of the materials fund is earmarked for the online search service.

This theory of diminishing need for online searching and the corresponding diminishing cost is workable to a point. The theory assumes that the library's budget is substantial enough to adjust (and that additional funding cannot be acquired). It also assumes that the library offering such a service has resources that can support the patron's subsequent demand for the documents. It is extremely difficult to determine what level of document delivery is adequate, but if the library has a materials budget of less than $100,000 a year and is able to provide less than 25 percent of the documents cited in the output of the average search, then the library could not add the service without putting a great strain on its resources and staff. The consideration of introducing online searching should involve the same critera as the consideration of adding an expensive printed index: Is there sufficient need to add such a specialized service? Can the patrons' needs be met by currently owned sources? Can the service be introduced without the elimination of other needed services and resources? If the library can only offer online bibliographic searching by cutting back severely in other areas, then that library should probably not attempt to offer the service.

This, of course, can be used as an excuse for the charging of fees, but if fees are necessary for the service to operate then the library may find itself in the position of having to seek out users who are willing to pay. There is a sizable capital outlay required before searching can commence. Personnel must be trained and hardware purchased or leased and stored. For the library whose budget is already strained, this may produce a burden that can only be eased at the expense of the satisfaction of some users in the form of curtailment of services. As noted above, even with a working operation there is likely to be an added strain on the staff and resources of the library. Adjunct services such as document delivery will experience greater demand. Also, there remains the ethical question of user fees that will be discussed later. With the high level of costs, not every library can handle practicably the addition of an online search service and so libraries should not penalize some users in order to provide online searching.

On the subject of fees for online searching (and for other services) James Rettig states, "Fees are discriminatory only when imposed differently for different individuals based on their incidental membership in groups" [11]. Thompson, however, notes that if certain subscriptions to printed sources are canceled and charges are levied for the online counterparts to these sources, such charges are indeed discriminatory [12]. For instance, if a public library cancels its subscription to Chemical Abstracts, then the only means of information retrieval for a local chemical engineer is online bibliographic searching. If the library charges for the service, the chemical engineer would have to pay for information he or she could have gotten free of charge before the cancellation of Chemical Abstracts.

It is recognized that the cost of an online search can be lower than the cost of a manual search [18]. Using Chemical Abstracts as an example--even if the printed source receives 100 users per year at a medium-size library, the cost per use is very high. Given the subscription rate of $3,800 for a college or university [14], 100 uses per year would average $38 per use. (This figure disregards any cost for the user's time, for user assistance, or processing, binding, or storing the printed volumes. These costs will vary considerably from library to library, but can affect the cost per use.) At a given library, the cost of an online search could be half as much as a manual search. Also, with the considerable saving of time, the online search is even more cost efficient.

Some libraries may be able to cancel subscriptions to carefully selected, expensive printed indexes and offer free access to online databases. In such instances, access to information would not be limited and cost to the library may be unaffected or even lessened. Wholesale cancellation of subscriptions is not advocated, of course, but budgetary constraints to free online searching could be eliminated at certain libraries by planned reductions in expenditures on reference tools. Such action must be contemplated on individual bases with user satisfaction, as well as cost efficiency, taken into consideration. If the printed index best serves a particular library's users then effort should be made to retain the index. With budgets shrinking (in both real and raw terms), some libraries may be forced to cancel some expensive indexes, regardless of online availability. Online bibliographic databases provide an affordable alternative, particularly in the case of low-use indexes.

There is also strong statutory impetus for offering online services free of charge in publicly supported institutions. Title 20 of the United States Code defines a public library as one "that serves free of charge all residents of a community, district, or region," and a research library as one that "makes its services available to the public free of charge" [15]. These definitions exclude libraries that are part of institutions of higher education. Pursuant to the above definitions, title 20 also defines public library services as "library services furnished by a public library free of charge" [16]. The implications of these codified definitions have yet to be felt but they could be far-reaching. If applied literally they would seem to preclude any charges for online bibliographic searching, as well as for some other services, at public libraries. Because of the vagueness of the wording of these sections with regard to online searching and other services that involve users' absorbing costs, the full impact of title 20 may eventually require testing in the courts.

In addition to the statements pertinent to public libraries and public library services in title 20, another section of the United States Code could have a somewhat narrower, but no less profound, effect upon services offered at some libraries. Title 44 states in part, "Depository libraries shall make government publication available for the free use of the general public" [17]. It has yet to be determined whether a government-produced bibliographic database is actually a government publication. However, if the Monthly Catalog is a government publication, it would be very difficult to consider its online counterpart as anything but the same. As with sections of title 20, title 44 has yet to be tested with regard to online bibliographic searching.

It must be considered at least anomalous that while many libraries charge for online services, librarians seem to be staunch advocates of free access to information. At the 1977 ALA Annual Conference, the membership and council of ALA voted to support free access to information, including computer database information [18]. Following this, at the White House Conference on Libraries and Information Services a resolution was passed: "The White House Conference ... affirms that all persons should have free access, without charge or fee to the individual, to information in public and publicly supported libraries" [19]. These statements are explicit in wording and in intent. They do not, however, carry with them any action of forced compliance. They are merely statements of resolve that are ignored by many libraries that insist upon the imposition of fees based on some claim of economic need.

Some who favor charges for online searching recognize that such fees can act to discourage users from taking advantage of the service. Pauline Atherton and Roger Christian state that, while some users may be unwilling to pay fees,

> a library that imposes token fees, or none at all, runs the risk of being inundated by an increasing user clamor, not only for more online searching, but for a blizzard of full-text photo and fiche copies, heavy interlibrary borrowing, and an urgent re-examination of established collections [20].

The library can reduce this "clamor" by using online capabilities only for research requests and not as a ready-reference tool. It may well be that an easy-to-use printed index can satisfy the needs of a patron who wants limited information on a particular subject as quickly and effectively as an online search. The librarian must use discretion with search requests in order to ensure the most effective use of the service. If, however, the researcher demands document delivery following a search, the library should be prepared to meet that patron's needs. For this reason, the library with extremely limited budget and holdings may not be in the position to offer the service. To attempt to reduce use by limiting access to online searching is definitely contrary to the principle of free access to information and to the purpose of libraries. As Fay Blake and Edith Perlmutter write,

> Not only does the user fee limit the access of those who cannot afford the fee but it materially shifts the resources of the library without regard for the relative contributions of paying clients to the well-being of society as a whole [21].

In other words, there is the danger that the provision of information and the kind of information that is readily accessible may be geared to those who can pay for it, regardless of the ultimate use of the information.

It should be noted here that there are ways for the library to minify the costs consequent to online searching. Depending upon the library's location and the volume of searching it carries out, there are several means of handling telecommunications. It may be most advantageous to dial the vendor directly or to make use of one of the time-sharing networks. Of course the most efficient solution varies according to the vendor selected and the location of the nearest time-sharing node. It is also possible to reduce online time and thus vendor charges by obtaining equipment with 1,200 baud capacity. There is the added potential (particularly at colleges, universities, or research institutions) of the costs of some of the searches being absorbed by federal or private grants. It is important to inform researchers of the possibility of including online search costs in grant proposals.

With testimony as to the affordability of online services by Knapp and Schmidt and Thompson, and with sections (though untested) of the United States Code making statements on freedom of access to information, why do many libraries insist upon charging fees for online searching? Perhaps, as Knapp and Schmidt suggest, it is because "librarians seem to find it easier to justify expenditures for possession than for service" [22]. Vendor and telecommunications costs are easily calculable, so the search appears to come with a built-in price tag. Some libraries, though, charge for staff time and for the costs of equipment and the training of personnel. The rationale for such charges has no precedent in other library services. The librarian does not charge for his or her time when assisting patrons as part of the librarian's reference duty, even when the request requires an hour or more of the librarian's time. The library does not charge for the use of a reference tool that involves the lease of equipment, such as the Magazine Index. The cost of workshops, conferences, and seminars is not passed on to the user.

It is a certainty that online searching will continue at libraries and will probably increase in volume as a research aid. For complex searches it is a very cost-efficient means of information retrieval. As for the future, F. W. Lancaster says,

> The electronic accessibility of information resources is improving as rapidly as the accessibility of printed sources is declining and ... the cost of electronic access is falling as rapidly as the cost of printed access is climbing. Moreover, and this is the most important point, cost and accessibility through electronics will continue to improve, while cost and accessibility through print on paper can only get worse and worse [23].

It will probably come to pass that some printed indexes will be supplanted by computerized bibliographic databases. When this occurs, the library may only be required to transfer funds from resource to service, rather than add funds to handle online search services. Even at present, however, there is practical and ideological evidence in favor of searching free of charge. Indeed, budgetary planning can allow for free online searching without burdening the library's staff [24].

References

1. Association of Research Libraries, Systems and Procedures Exchange Center, On-Line Bibliographic Search Service, SPEC Kit 62 (Washington, D.C.: The Center, 1980). The volume of computerized search activity and the costs and fees charged to users for the service were the focus of a survey of libraries at Cornell, Emory, MIT, Princeton, Stanford, Vanderbilt, Yale (Medical Library and Kline Science Library), and the University of Pennsylvania.

2. Ibid.

3. Bruce Bonta, quoted in Sara Knapp, "Beyond Fee or Free," RQ 20:117 (Winter 1980).

4. Peter G. Watson, quoted in Knapp, "Beyond Fee or Free," p. 118.

5. James A. Cogswell, "On-Line Search Services: Implications for Libraries and Library Users," College & Research Libraries 39:278 (July 1978).

6. Michael D. Cooper and Nancy A. DeWath, "The Effect of User Fees on the Cost of On-Line Searching in Libraries," Journal of Library Automation 10:317-18 (Dec. 1977).

7. Cogswell, "On-Line Search Services," p. 279.

8. Judith A. Thompson, quoted in Knapp, "Beyond Fee or Free," p. 119.

9. Ibid.

10. Sara D. Knapp and C. James Schmidt, "Budgeting to Provide Computer-Based Reference Services: A Case Study," Journal of Academic Librarianship 5:13 (March, 1979).

11. James Rettig, "Rights, Resolution, Fees, and Reality," Library Journal 106:303 (1 Feb. 1981).

12. Thompson, quoted in Knapp, "Beyond Fee or Free," p. 120.

13. See Stanley A. Elman, "Cost Comparison of Manual and On-Line Computerized Literature Searching," Special Libraries 66:12-18 (Jan. 1975); Paula J. Crawford and Judith A. Thompson, "Free Online Searches Are Feasible," Library Journal 104:795 (1 April 1979).

14. Ulrich's International Periodicals Directory (19th ed.; New York: Bowker, 1980), p. 397.

15. United States Code, title 20, 351a.

16. Ibid.

17. United States Code, title 44, 1911.

18. "ALA Steps Lively through Detroit," American Libraries 8:378 (July/Aug. 1977).

19. "Cadres for the Library Future," Library Journal 105:165 (15 Jan. 1980).

20. Pauline Atherton and Roger W. Christian, Librarians and Online Services (White Plains, N.Y.: Knowledge Industry Publications, Inc., 1977).

21. Fay M. Blake and Edith L. Perlmutter, "The Rush to User Fees: Alternative Proposals," Library Journal 102:2006 (1 Oct. 1977).

22. Knapp and Schmidt, "Budgeting," p. 13.

23. F. Wilfrid Lancaster, "Whither Libraries? or, Wither Libraries," College & Research Libraries 39:351 (Sept. 1978).

24. For more on the issue of user fees for online services see Thomas James Waldhart and Trudi Bellardo, "User Fees in Publicly Funded Libraries," Advances in Librarianship 9:31-61 (1979) and Peter G. Watson, ed., Charging for Computer-Based Reference Services: Proceedings of a Program Organized by the Machine-Assisted Reference Section (MARS) of the Reference and Adult Services Division at the American Library Association Conference, Detroit, June 19, 1977 (Chicago: ALA, RASD, 1978).

IS THERE A CATALOG IN YOUR FUTURE?
ACCESS TO INFORMATION IN THE YEAR 2006*

Nancy J. Williamson

In 1957, the founding year of RTSD, the focus was clearly on the catalog. It was the eve of the Stanford Institute that preceded AACR1 [1]. It was a time for reappraisal of the physical form of the catalog and the prelude to an era of intense concentration on international agreement and standardization [2]. Just prior to this Strout, in a paper on the "Development of the Catalog and Cataloging Codes," had expressed the view that in the past, while librarians had been "intelligent and serious scholars," they had also been very "short sighted" [3]. Reflecting on this, she challenged her audience to rethink principles and practices anew, lest they take for granted things that some day "might look equally ridiculous to another age." She warned:

> We may be so blinded by ... firmly established customs that we are incapable of seeing some utterly simple alternatives which might quickly resolve our problems, and which will some day look so easy and obvious that our descendants will in turn look upon us as unseeing and unimaginative.

Twenty-five years later this statement can be both reflective and challenging. How will the information professionals of the year 2006 view our approach to the challenges of 1981 and succeeding years? Will they be able to say with conviction that we met the crises of environmental, sociological, and technological changes affecting the world of information storage and retrieval with foresightedness and determination in shaping the future? Only time will tell. It will be the speakers on the podium of RTSD's fiftieth-anniversary program who will be able to answer this question. Meanwhile, librarians must do what they can to ensure a smooth and creative transition into the information environment of the twenty-first century. In doing so, they must endeavor to play a leadership role wherever and whenever possible.

---

*Reprinted by permission of the author and publisher from Library Resources and Technical Services, 26:2 (April-June 1982) 122-135. Copyright © 1982 by the American Library Association.

Is there a catalog in our future? I am almost certain of it. But what kind of a catalog will it, and should it, be? What will it be a catalog of? What kind of access will it provide to the items it describes? What functions will it perform in relation to other tools of information storage and retrieval? While precise answers to these questions cannot be immediately forthcoming, it is important that we begin now to consider the state of the art of access to information and to assess trends, technological developments, and predictions for the future, with a view to the identification of problems and issues that must be addressed as we progress toward the year 2006.

The Catalog and the State of the Art

Traditionally, the card catalog, supplemented by periodical indexes and supported by general and subject bibliographies, has provided the primary means of access to recorded information in general, and to library collections in particular. These tools, products of the world of print, are still very much with us, and have, for the most part, been developed as separate and distinct tools, without reference one to another in terms of their content, format, and functions. In the environment for which they were originally created, they served remarkably well. However, the growth of knowledge and increasingly sophisticated needs of information seekers, combined with the technological development of viable alternatives, has called the suitability of some information retrieval tools--particularly the library catalog--into question. The catalog is very definitely in a state of transition.

Nor is our preoccupation with the state of the catalog a new issue. Developments of the past twenty-five years have seen ever-increasing efforts on the part of librarians to develop the traditional catalog into a better retrieval tool. Much of what has been accomplished has been a result of a surge of interest in cooperation that had its origins in the National Program for Acquisitions and Cataloging [4] and which has had its fullest impact in the sharing of cataloging data and the development of networks and bibliographic utilities. Instrumental in these developments has been the preparation of widely accepted bibliographic standards in the form of AACR1, ISBD, and AACR2, and in the design of a format for machine-readable bibliographic records. Without the MARC record, it is doubtful that the networks and bibliographic utilities would yet be a part of the library environment, or that, as of now, librarians would be converting their catalogs from card files to COM and online catalogs. Moreover, it is the development of networks and online catalogs that has finally precipitated libraries and information centers in the direction of total mechanization of their files. Few would dispute that all of this represents an important step forward.

Nevertheless, while significant progress has been made in some areas, the status quo is still the order of the day in others. In providing new physical formats for the catalog, for the most part we have been putting old wine into new bottles. The changes that have taken place have given the catalog a new face but have done little to alter the kinds of access to its content. Few would question the importance of the work on AACR1 and AACR2, which has given us an immeasurably sounder and more logical basis for the structuring of catalogs, but these catalogs are still prototypes of Cutter's catalog of 1904 [5]. We have perfected the catalog which has existed for more than one hundred years without significantly improving the kinds of bibliographic and subject access that the catalog might provide. Nor have we experimented sufficiently with possible new approaches to subject retrieval of bibliographic items which modern technology could support. For example, the thesaurus and the PRECIS system of indexing, the two most significant developments in subject retrieval in the past twenty-five years, appear to have had little impact on the traditional subject catalog. In brief, librarians have not responded to the potential for change in a creative way. Improvements have been cosmetic rather than substantive and the catalog remains a tool that provides limited access to information. Is this the catalog with which librarians should enter the twenty-first century? Is it the best we can do, in spite of new technology? Or should the catalog continue to represent the status quo, while we direct our energies toward the improvement of access to information in some other way?

The truth of the matter is that the utility of the card catalog is already being challenged by bibliographic tools created and maintained outside the library per se. These are the products of the commercial abstracting and indexing services, many of which are computerized, and a large number of which are accessible through online bibliographic databases. While the formal bibliographic citations in these databases may not be very different from those in traditional indexes and catalogs, it is the sophisticated access capabilities which make them more efficient search tools than traditional library catalogs. Such features as the enrichment of subject description through the inclusion of abstracts as part of the record, the assignment of multiple subject descriptors, and provision for free-text and Boolean searches make these tools infinitely more efficient than the catalog. Moreover, as time goes on, increasing exposure to online reference services may have a profound influence on the kinds of demands both librarians and information seekers make on the library catalog of the future.

Of primary importance also will be the fact that as we move forward toward the year 2006, online bibliographic databases will not be the only competitors for library catalogs. Two other modes of information storage and retrieval are just now emerging--the business information systems and the information systems which are intended for general use and which are products of the union between computers and telecommunications technology. Both function as source databases, providing direct access to data, as opposed to bibliographic citations. Systems such as these, which eliminate one step in the two-step search for information through both catalogs and online bibliographic databases, may be doubly attractive to users.

Computerized business information systems are already in the process of propelling the commercial world Toward Paperless Information Systems [6]. Such systems used in conjunction with specialized online databases could reduce the role of the catalog to that of a location tool in most instances. In contrast, the general information systems, variously described as viewdata, videotext, PRESTEL, Telidon, and Channel 2000, with few exceptions, are still in the experimental stages. Nevertheless, if fully developed, the potential is there for direct home access to information on a wide scale. Although present experiments with viewdata systems may be viewed with skepticism by some, one must not forget that the horseless carriage was the ancestor of the Rolls-Royce and the Ford Escort, the punched card was the forerunner of the CRT, and the typewriter and television both had their rudimentary beginnings. The predicted "wired city" could very soon be a reality, with widespread use of source databases that would enable information seekers to bypass the library completely for most of their information requirements [7].

Where does this leave us with the status of the library catalog in the year 2006? To feel threatened by obsolescence is not the answer. Rather, librarians must be prepared to adapt and adjust to new ways of accessing information. However, such adaptation and adjustment will not occur without careful planning and a willingness to look at access to information in an unbiased and objective way, unhampered by the knowledge of existing information retrieval systems. A first step in development of services suitable for the information seekers of 2006 should be to consider the environment into which such services will be projected.

The Information Environment in 2006: What Will It Be Like?

If we are optimistic enough to ignore those who predict doomsday by the year 2000, we must assume the presence of information and a need to provide access to it. Forecasters in all spheres of life have always taken considerable delight in predicting the future. The library world is no exception to this. As long ago as 1945, Vannevar Bush conceived his plan for a futuristic library [8]. He was but one of the forerunners of such crystal-gazers as Licklider [9], Booth [10], and Lancaster [11]. As we proceed into the 1980s, it cannot be unexpected that the forecasters on expectations for the information industry [12], libraries [13], and the future of the catalog [14] have become more numerous, and some have been brave enough to project their thoughts to the year 2000 and beyond [15]. It comes as no surprise that the predictions range from cautious optimism to doom and gloom, and that some have an excellent chance of becoming reality. Whichever pronouncements are fulfilled, given the remarkable ability of the human race to adapt to a changing environment, an optimistic approach to the catalog and its problems seems both attractive and sensible. For those who already feel that they are suffering from future shock, it will also be comforting to know that any process of adaptation or change is almost certain to be evolutionary rather than revolutionary. Changes are inevitable, and while they will come quickly, they will not occur overnight.

Barring unforeseen political and environmental catastrophe, and assuming that governments, industry, and business have succeeded in solving the energy problems, it is probable that by the turn of the century the information environment will be highly computerized at all levels of life. Our personal lives are already affected by computerization of banking, supermarkets, and airline and hotel reservations, while the word processor is rapidly replacing the office typewriter, and the personal computer is within economic and operational reach of many individuals. Given that the majority of North American homes have one or more television receivers, it is a very short step to the installation of the hardware attachments which will permit television sets to become interactive viewdata systems, and to be as common in 2006 as the conventional television installations are today.

As sophisticated computer and telecommunications technology becomes increasingly available, it is predicted that it will decrease in price, whereas the cost of paper is expected to increase, be very scarce, and relatively inefficient in terms of some types of information needs. The future information environment will certainly be one in which some kinds of information will be recorded only in electronic form and disseminated only through computerized databases. Moreover, if the conservators are correct, many of the printed publications now extant but published prior to 1950, will have disintegrated or be in perilous physical condition by the turn of the century [16]. Inevitably, expensive preservation programs will be launched for purposes of preserving the knowledge of the past which, for both practical and aesthetic reasons, is worth perpetuating. For current information, paper, when it is used, will be used sparingly and for specific purposes, perhaps with books and journals being marketed electronically and only printed on demand for specific customers. Undoubtedly, we should shed a few tears over the slow demise of the universal use of the printed book. Nevertheless, there is surely something positive in the mammoth weeding of obsolescent materials which we ourselves have found humanly impossible to accomplish up to now. And think of the diminishing size of those closed and frozen card catalogs!

In this projected physical environment, the basic needs of the information seeker may not be very different from those of today. However, these people will have been educated to the new technologies in a way in which we ourselves have not been, and will have had increasing exposure to their use and capabilities. In some ways information will be more easily accessible to individuals than it has been in the past, and such users are likely to be more sophisticated in their demands on the services of libraries and information agencies of the future. As such, information seekers may be much more finely tuned to the possibilities available in accessing information than are their 1981 counterparts--a factor to which libraries and information agencies of the future must inevitably respond.

It will not be easy for us to project ourselves into this environment which is forecast for A.D. 2000 and beyond. However utopian it may seem, we are well aware of the frustrations the computer can bring and we are already plagued with downtime from overloaded systems [17]. Moreover, the present economic climate suggests that it is unrealistic to assume that we will be able to afford the technology that is projected. However, it will be most important to remember that all things are relative. If the costs of hardware and computer time continue to decrease, while the cost of the production of printed information continues to spiral, it is not unreasonable to surmise that computer access to information will be more cost-effective than traditional methods by the turn of the century.

Toward Information Services in 2006

As we move toward the year 2006, I see a catalog in our future, but a catalog which will not be the major focal point in gaining access to information, and one which will play a diminished role in that world. While the role of the library as a recreational institution does not appear to be in serious question, its survival as an information agency will be dependent on its ability to redefine its procedures and goals in terms of the bibliographic universe as a whole. In doing so, it will be necessary to place its basic tool-- the catalog--in its proper perspective with other access tools. In brief, librarians must consider the ways and means of developing information services as opposed to providing access to specific collections or particular databases. How should librarians proceed with this mammoth task?

Logically, the establishment of such a service should begin with a plan or blueprint which identifies issues to be addressed and priorities to be established. Such a plan must recognize the realities of the information world, but at the same time it is imperative that there be response to technological change. By way of encouragement, this paper attempts to identify some of the problems of access to bibliographic information which should provide food for thought and discussion by members, committees, and sections of RTSD over the next twenty-five years.

For the kinds of information services envisioned there are at least four fundamental requirements. First of all, librarians must become information professionals as opposed to reference librarians, catalogers, or collection development librarians. As well, not only the names, but also the actions must change. The new information professional must be prepared to customize services to individual users and to fulfill a role as tutor and educator in aiding and advising information seekers in the most effective use of the services and systems available. This will require much retooling and reeducation of present library personnel and some redirection of library education. In this respect, a more interdisciplinary approach to information work and education will probably be necessary [18]. Some sacrifices will almost certainly be required. However, an adjustment and redirection of our talents and capabilities could place librarians in a much better position, not only to provide better services within the library environment, but also to market their expertise to commercial information entrepreneurs and to services in the information industry at large. The ability and desire to do this is all-important if librarians are to gain and maintain influence and credibility in the information world of the future.

A second requirement in preparing for the future is that librarians as information professionals not only act, but act decisively, objectively, and without prejudices in favor of traditional methods and practices. For if they do not, someone else will. All too often in the past, there has been a tendency toward the hole-in-the-dyke approach, in which the solution to a problem has sometimes been the cheapest and easiest one, but not necessarily the best. Already librarians may be somewhat out of step with preparations for the information requirements of the future. Information brokers and commercial indexing and abstracting services have become well established in the marketplace and home information systems are being launched, in many cases without the help and expertise of librarians. Clearly, in the competition for control of the information industry over the next twenty-five years, it will be the fittest who will survive. Even now, the more enterprising of our colleagues have recognized this fact and are operating personalized information services from their homes and small offices, in communities where libraries have not yet moved to provide such services. These librarians are the potential information professionals of the future, and will surely make it to the year 2006. Will we?

A third necessity is that future planning must be done on the basis of sound analysis of problems and issues backed by thorough research. There are many unanswered questions on which librarians sometimes make sweeping statements, but about which they really have insufficient factual information upon which to base their actions. All too often the solution to an important problem is based on an assumption. Assumptions will not be sufficient basis for the preparations necessary for a successful and smooth transition into the information environment of the year 2006. Nor should they be. With such facilities as online databases and the emerging online catalogs and viewdata systems, librarians have at their disposal the material for investigation and research hitherto unavailable to them. We must make the best possible use of this opportunity in the earliest stages of the transition from the traditional to the new electronic systems.

Finally, it seems to this author that it is time that the operations of storage and retrieval were considered as functions of one single operation. That these processes are reciprocal is well known in practice and well documented in the literature [19, 20]. Yet in the day-to-day activities of libraries, their problems are usually treated separately. Surely those who know the most about storing information should also be best qualified to know how to retrieve it most successfully, and vice versa.

A number of the components of the storage and retrieval process will need to be examined with these four requirements clearly in mind. Among these are the information seeker, the role and function of the catalog, the nature of the bibliographic record, and the kinds of access to information that will be required.

The Information Seekers

Any attempt to reshape the storage and retrieval process in anticipation of the future must begin with a reassessment of information seekers and their potential needs. It seems probable that library users of 2006, like their 1981 counterparts, will have two basic types of information needs--the need to locate a particular document about which they have some information and the need to retrieve successfully information on a particular topic. However, as a basis for redefining the roles of various retrieval tools (including the catalog), information professionals will need to know more about the effects of the machine environment on users' requests than they do at present. If it is true that users tend to tailor their requests to the kind of information they believe a system can provide, will they pose the same kinds of questions as they did with manual systems? Will their questions be more precise? Will the emphasis be bibliographically oriented or subject oriented? Which kinds of retrieval tools have the potential for heaviest use? Will it be the bibliographic and source databases or the online catalog? Whatever the answers to these questions, various factors will be instruments of the results--such factors as user familiarity with different types of retrieval tools, the scope of the tools, ease of use, success in retrieval, and efficiency in information and document delivery. As amply demonstrated in the past, valid user studies are not easily achieved, but an understanding of both the what and the why of information-seeking behavior is crucial to the design and use of all kinds of retrieval tools, including the library catalog.

The Catalog

As we progress toward the twenty-first century, it can be readily surmised that proportionately less of the world's information will be accessed through online catalogs than through other kinds of online databases. Thus, there is a very real possibility that we will soon again be debating that timeworn question, Should the catalog be a finding list, or a bibliographic tool?

As finding lists, most catalogs could well suffice if they displayed records with minimal-level description and a limited number of access points per record. On the other hand, as reference tools, it could be desirable, and perhaps necessary, to enrich the catalog record with fuller bibliographic descriptions and a greater number of access points than is customary at present, to permit sophisticated access and search capabilities such as those investigated in a recent study by Pauline Atherton Cochrane [21]. In brief, a vital question to be addressed is, Where should concentration of time and effort be placed on enriching source and bibliographic databases, or in creating a supercatalog? Small local libraries, whose primary function is to provide recreational reading, may be able to take some comfort in the fact that they may be able to continue to provide "a good book" from a local catalog. Larger information and research-based institutions will almost certainly be in quite a different position. Present trends suggest that the databases could easily take precedence over library catalogs as the first place to search when accessing information.

The Bibliographic Record

In the kind of information service envisioned for the future, the role that is defined for the catalog should determine the nature of the bibliographic records it should contain. The development of various levels of detail in bibliographic description, first suggested by Cutter [22] and rediscovered for AACR2 [23], is the first step toward tailoring a standard record to a variety of information systems. As we progress, the second step will be to identify which levels of bibliographic description are best suited to which retrieval tools, and the reasons for this. There is every reason to believe that in 2006, there will continue to be a need for MARC, or MARC-like, records, universally available somewhere on demand. Indeed in this future store, records could be more detailed and more complex in their content than are the present standard records. Nevertheless, libraries and other information agencies should be in a position to exert as much flexibility as possible in the creation and formatting of records for their own use--records that would be cost-effective for an agency's specific requirements. In each institution, the information professional would be cast in the role of an assessor of the requirements of a particular information service, with the authority to prescribe the kinds of records needed to satisfy those requirements.

Access to Bibliographic Records and Source Data

The content of a bibliographic record is but one side of the coin. The other is the provision of various kinds of access to it. Online files of all kinds offer infinite possibilities for the extension and enrichment of access to information, over those provided by the present manual catalogs. While enthusiasm for these possibilities may be tremendous, wise exploitation of them will require answers to a number of important questions. What kinds of access are needed? Which databases should provide which kinds of access? How can access capabilities best be distributed through a number of retrieval tools, so as to provide the most cost-effective overall information

service? Moreover, serious attention must be given to studying the
need for increasing the amount of access, particularly with respect
to the subject content of documents. Among the variables that should
be taken into account are the following:

1. The kinds of access needed;
2. The requirements for formatting and structuring any output, including any subfiles or spinoff files which are expected to be created for display.
3. The search algorithms to be used; and
4. Interface and compatability among files and databases created by different agencies.

It is unlikely that one solution will be suitable for all situations. It
can be assumed that the variables might be combined in any number
of configurations depending upon the type of agency, the combination
of retrieval tools, and the kind of service to be given.

The reassessment of bibliographic access will raise once
again--dare we say once and for all?--the question of the validity
of the main entry concept, which has been a primary feature of
catalogs up to the present. Is it possible to dispense with the main
entry? Under certain circumstances, the answer to this question
could probably be yes. It is true that in a machine environment,
where the only requirement is to gain access to records, the main
entry loses its significance. Nevertheless, consider the problems
of retrieving organized subsets of bibliographic files for purposes
of creating separate bibliographies. Wherever there is need to produce single-entry lists of bibliographic items, the process of structuring those lists will presuppose some method of identifying principal access points. However, by the year 2006, the main entry,
as presently known, may have disappeared completely, and its function be transferred to machine identifiers or tags which could be
used, when necessary, to permit retrieval of structured single-entry
bibliographic lists.

Nor is the main entry the only time-honored cataloging tradition that could be challenged. Will it always be necessary to identify variant names of persons and corporate bodies and variant titles
of documents with preferred forms of those names or titles? Present trends in technology suggest that the answer to this question is
probably no. In the past, catalog codes, with some exceptions, have
emphasized the use of preferred names and titles to gather related
records in the catalog for ease of use by information seekers. Technologically, it is now possible to provide online browsing capabilities
that minimize the problems presented by slight variations in names.
Moreover, the invisible linkage of variants could facilitate the retrieval of works by the same author or editions of the same work
without the use of the "preferred form" principle. However, as in
the case of main entry, unless the needs of information seekers alter
significantly in the future, the logical display of subsets of a file will
still need to be provided for in some way.

Lest catalogers despair at the loss of the heart of their work, it should be pointed out that the intellectual challenges of organizing information and retrieving it will not disappear. New problems will replace old ones and the decision and judgment of the new information professional will still be required--perhaps on a more challenging plane than before. Control of data will still be important, even though it may be accomplished through new methods and devices. For example, in the new information environment, authority files could assume an increasingly important role as control mechanisms, although their format and content may be significantly different from the authority files with which we are currently familiar.

Subject Access to Information

Potential for the most dramatic changes lies in the methods and devices used to provide subject access to information. Such changes could have their origins in the exposure of information seekers to online databases, viewdata, and other high-technology information systems. Crucial to the design of new information systems will be the development of more effective methods of subject description and retrieval than have been used in the past. It is true that there have been significant attempts over the past few years to develop a theory of indexing [24, 25] and to design new indexing languages in the form of thesauri, faceted classification schemes, and string indexing systems such as PRECIS, as well as to experiment with automatic methods of classification and indexing [26, 27]. Nevertheless, these innovations have had little impact on the widespread use of traditional subject headings and enumerative classification schemes as the major instruments of subject retrieval in libraries. It would be folly to try to transfer old methods to new technology without an objective investigation into ways and means of using the advances in technology to improve subject retrieval which in the past has often been barely adequate. Thus it is imperative that there be study and research into all aspects of subject access to information--the needs and requirements of the information seeker, the indexing process, the generation and development of indexing languages, as well as the creation of efficient search strategies and retrieval techniques commensurate with new information environments.

Basic to successful subject retrieval is effective subject indexing and cataloging, the requirement for which is competent indexing, based on an understanding of the relationships among users, documents, indexing languages, and the available technology. If, in recent years, there has been criticism of subject cataloging and classification, it has been due largely to the fact that we have been unable, and perhaps in some cases unwilling, to seek out the appropriate balance among these factors needed for optimum results. Two assumptions have contributed to this problem--the assumption that subject indexing and cataloging are easy (when indeed they are not), and the assumption that one system can be adapted with equal effectiveness to a range of different information environments, large and small, general and specialized.

As identified by Elaine Svenonius in her recent article "Directions for Research," it will be necessary to know a great deal more than we now do about the indexing process and its problems if subject access is to be more effective in the future [28]. Not only is there a need for a better understanding of the factors that determine the "aboutness" of a document, but there are also a number of related questions for which answers might contribute to improved results [29]. Should the documents or their contents be indexed? What level of indexing is suitable for which kinds of documents? Under what conditions?

Moreover, the indexing languages themselves are a source of many of the deficiencies of contemporary subject retrieval. Our present subject catalogs provide for retrieval at the minimum level, with the standard subject heading lists and classification schemes encouraging a "mark and park" approach to subject indexing [30]. The result is often that a document is described in terms of the system and the descriptors provided. A more useful approach would be to give a document an accurate description based on its content and require the system to respond to its subject. Such a system would change and evolve as documents or subjects are added and as the needs of the user population change. Machine methods are much more amenable to change than manual systems, and growing sophistication in technology suggests that such flexibility will be possible before the year 2006.

If as a result of new technology information seekers become more intensely aware of the potential for improved subject access to information, subject retrieval systems will be expected to respond to their demands. This implies enrichment of the subject description of documents as well as the development of more effective indexing languages. Terminology is important, but so also is the structure of the language. It is essential that any subject retrieval system be equipped to provide information seekers with both direct access to information and the alternative of browsing among subjects for purposes of selection and choice of items. Thus provision for Boolean searches alone will not be sufficient to meet all requirements. Systematic searches for information must also be possible.

Will the indexing languages of the future be highly controlled or completely uncontrolled? More research is needed into all kinds of indexing languages, from natural language systems that facilitate free-text searching, to highly structured languages such as thesauri and PRECIS strings. It is probable that neither of the extremes will be completely acceptable as the ideal system. Present predictions suggest that natural language will play an increasingly important role in the subject retrieval systems of the future, but that in a majority of cases there will need to be at least simple synonym control through online thesauri, with perhaps some hierarchical search capability [31]. In contrast, the systems requiring complex and time-consuming search strategies for retrieval purposes will probably be the exception rather than the rule for several reasons.

Among these are the cost in time and effort of maintaining the systems, the direct interrogation of online systems by users who cannot be expected to be experts in complex search procedures, and the need for the information professionals to be able to move quickly and efficiently from database to database without having to reorient themselves significantly. This is not to say that there will not be some use of indexing languages with sophisticated syndetic structure, but for ease of use the structure may frequently be machine controlled and invisible to users. In summary, either the completely unstructured or the rigidly controlled subject retrieval system could prove to be less than satisfactory in the overview, and some middle-of-the-road approach most acceptable in many cases.

As a particular kind of indexing language, classification can be expected to assume a new and important role in the information environment of the future. Unquestionably, classification is likely to continue to function as a shelving device as long as open-shelf access to library collections is desirable. However, with increasing amounts of information browsable only in online systems, the role of classification in information systems has exciting new possibilities. The multidimensionality of subjects has always been one of the problems that shelf classification has been unable to overcome; however, browsing through an online classified catalog would be more effective than searching open shelves because of the ability to represent a document in multiple places in a classified file of surrogates. Moreover, the application of the principles of classification--"the other half of the retrieval process"--will be essential to user-friendly systematic browsing of online systems. Helpful order as well as direct access is fundamental to the best retrieval systems, and one of our problems in designing subject retrieval systems in the past has been our failure to recognize fully the essential relationship between the structure of helpful order based on the principles of classification and the inherent order of the alphabet.

Standards and Standardization

The cohesive factor in all of this is standardization. In this era when our lives seem fraught at every turn with standards, they cannot be passed over without comment. For those who feel that the saturation point has been reached, this author cannot offer the comfort that standards will go away quietly. Quality control will still be an important factor in the world of the future. Although I do not predict AACR3, there will be yet another code, which it is hoped will be designed with complete independence from the constraints of present philosophies and rules and that will be the result of sound and careful research into the characteristics of the online environment and new developments in high technology. As well, in the next few years much time and effort will be expended on addressing the problems of interface and compatability among various databases. Already work has begun on developing yet another standard, a "common communication format," which may provide a switching device to facilitate the linkage of several kinds of databases for more efficient use. The development of new techniques will not make it any easier to make a silk purse out of a sow's ear, but perhaps a new attitude towards standards will ease some of the frustration. Standards are important as conditions and guidelines within which to work in a particular information environment, rather than as ultimata for production lines which produce carbon-copy results for every situation in every institution. After all, the automobile has a common set of standards which enable drivers to operate different models and kinds of cars, but think of the variety that exists in those vehicles. Standards are, and will remain, essential, but it should be as a source of usefulness not as the basis for trauma and nervous breakdown.

Conclusion

The predictions are not for an easy time in the transition to 2006, but for a challenging one. In Lewis Carroll's Alice in Wonderland the Mad Hatter asked "But my dear, was there progress?" and Alice earnestly replied "Well, there was change." In our wonderland of the next twenty-five years there must be progress as well as change. In the marriage between new technology and access to information, let us not be left standing at the alter [sic]. Let us begin to move now in creating the "information bridge to 2006." We have the best opportunity we have ever had.

References

1. Institute on Cataloging Code Revision, Stanford University, 1958, Working Papers (Stanford, Calif., 1958).

2. Dorothy Grosser, "The Divided Catalog: A Summary of the Literature," Library Resources & Technical Services 2:238-52 (Fall 1958).

3. Ruth French Strout, "The Development of the Catalog and Cataloging Codes," Library Quarterly 26:255 (Oct. 1956).

4. N.D. Stevens, ed., "National Program for Acquisitions and Cataloging: A Progress Report on Developments under Title II C of the Higher Education Act of 1965," Library Resources & Technical Services 12:17-29 (Winter 1968).

5. Charles A. Cutter, Rules for a Dictionary Catalog, 4th ed., rewritten, U.S. Bureau of Education, Special Report on Public Libraries, Part II (Washington, D.C.: Govt. Print. Off., 1904).

6. F.W. Lancaster, Toward Paperless Information Systems (New York: Academic Pr., 1978).

7. Phyllis A. Richmond, "The Future of Classification," Drexel Library Quarterly 10:109 (Oct. 1974).

8. Vannevar Bush, "As We May Think," Atlantic Monthly 176:101-8 (July 1945).

9. J.C.R. Licklider, Libraries of the Future (Cambridge, Mass.: MIT Pr., 1965).

10. Andrew D. Booth, "The Geometry of Libraries," Journal of Documentation 25:28-42 (March 1969).

11. Lancaster, Toward Paperless Information Systems.

12. Carlton C. Rochell, ed., An Information Agenda for the 1980s: Proceedings of a Colloquium, June 17-18, 1980 (Chicago: American Library Assn., 1981).

13. Carla Funk and others, eds., "Into the '80s ... The Future of Technical Services," Illinois Libraries 62:583-640 (Sept. 1980).

14. S. Michael Malinconico and Paul J. Fasana, The Future of the Catalog: The Library's Choices (White Plains, N.Y.: Knowledge Industry Publications, 1979).

15. Harold Wooster, "The Bibliographic Libraries of the Year 2000," Library Resources & Technical Services 25:104-9 (Jan./March 1981).

16. Joyce R. Russell, ed., Preservation of Library Materials (New York: Special Libraries Association, [1980]), p. 1.

17. "Downtime Plagues Both OCLC and RLIN Networks," LJ/SLJ Hotline 10:1 (May 11, 1981).

18. Pauline Wilson, "Impending Change in Library Education: Implications for Planning," Journal of Education for Librarianship 18:159-74 (Winter 1978).

19. Barbara Kyle, "Information Retrieval and Subject Indexing: Cranfield and After," Journal of Documentation 20:55-69 (June 1964).

20. F. Wilfrid Lancaster, Information Retrieval Systems: Characteristics, Testing and Evaluation, 2d ed. Information Sciences Series (New York: Wiley, [1979]), p. 8.

21. Pauline Atherton Cochrane, "Improving the Quality of Information Retrieval Online to a Library Catalog, or Other Access Service, or Where Do We Go from Here?" Online 5:30-42 (July 1981).

22. Cutter, Rules for a Dictionary Catalog, p. 11.

23. Anglo-American Cataloging Rules, 2d ed., ed. by Michael Gorman and Paul W. Winkler (Chicago: American Library Assn., 1978), p. 15.

24. Harold Borko, "Toward a Theory of Indexing," Information Processing & Management 13:355-65 (1977).

25. J.E.L. Farradane, "Scientific Theory of Classification and Indexing and Its Practical Applications," Journal of Documentation 6:83-99 (June 1950).

26. Karen Sparck Jones, Automatic Keyword Classification for Information Retrieval (London: Butterworths, 1971).

27. Gerald Salton, Automatic Information Organization and Retrieval (New York: McGraw Hill, 1968).

28. Elaine Svenonius, "Directions for Research in Indexing, Classification, and Cataloging," Library Resources & Technical Services 23:88-103 (Jan./March 1981).

29. M.E. Maron, "On Indexing, Retrieval and the Meaning of About," Journal of the American Society for Information Science 28:38-43 (Jan. 1977).

30. Richard J. Hyman, Shelf Classification Research, Past, Present-Future? (Champaign, Ill.: Graduate School of Library Science, University of Illinois at Urbana-Champaign, [1980]).

31. "Third International Study Conference on Classification Research," International Classification 2:39 (1975).

QUESTIONS SHEEHY CAN'T ANSWER:

REFLECTIONS ON BECOMING

HEAD OF REFERENCE*

Mary W. George

There was a time when I honestly believed that being head of reference required super-, or at the very least, preternatural talents. The incumbent, I assumed, would combine the wisdom of Solomon, the patience of Job, and the reference expertise of Isadore Mudge, and would by definition be a polyglottal polymath with powers of bilocation.

Well now I know better. My previous fancies have been borne out in fact--especially the preternatural part, which, you recall, means "beyond normal" (translation: you have to be more than a little crazy to take, let alone thrive in, such a job!). The aforementioned characteristics are all essential for the head of reference in any size or type of library, but since no one was ever a paragon on day one, you find you must continually struggle to acquire and perfect the necessary skills. It is the sheer job of juggling an infinite number of variables, of forging ahead when you're not always sure where "ahead" is or whether you're being followed-- or by whom--that makes the challenge of the position so rewarding.

So, for what they may be worth, I would like to share my realizations, reflections, and insights over the past few months, my new understanding of the special requirements they leave out of vacancy announcements (or disguise by a masterfully vague phrase such as "demonstrated ability to communicate" but which are even more critical to success in the job than are education and experience.

When, early in the fall of 1980, I first began to think about the transitions involved in becoming head of reference, I was still in a state of innocence, winding down my previous job as one of a dozen or so reference librarians in the Graduate Library at the

---

*Reprinted by permission of the author and publisher from The Reference Librarian, 1:3 (1982) 5-13. Copyright © 1982 by The Haworth Press, Inc. All rights reserved.

University of Michigan. I wondered whether, because I was moving to an older and considerably smaller private institution, Princeton, there would be substantial differences in the reference work. Much to my relief that has not been so. Reference is reference. Yes, there are certain variations in reference use and demand between Michigan and Princeton, but the same goals exist both places, the universal reference goals shared by all libraries whatever their location or clientele: to provide excellent service to all users, maintain up-to-date materials and an approachable atmosphere, integrate online technology with traditional methods, develop a flexible instruction program, and on and on. The presence of six new professional colleagues, a different building, and another collection seem natural and "right," stimulating rather than irritating. As a consequence I've concluded that place is not a crucial factor in determining the abilities called for in anyone who is head of reference.

Having said this much, I would like to discuss what really have been major revelations for me, things that have little or nothing to do with the particular institutions from and to which I've moved, but which strike me now as common concerns inherent to reference management. How will a new head of reference respond to these concerns and what leadership style will result: those are the questions Sheehy can't answer.

The term "middle management" itself is perhaps the best key to my perceptions. I had never given the words much thought, taking them literally and graphically to mean positions appearing in the middle of an organization chart, halfway between the "big boss" and the "little people." Now suddenly my eyes have been opened and I realize that to be a middle manager means to be poised at the fulcrum, delicately balancing the interests of two mighty powers, those who do and those who direct. It is the most sensitive point in the organization, demanding continual first-hand experience of all aspects of the work involved, together with a broad appreciation of the issues and pressures facing librarianship in the 1980s. Most importantly, being a middle manager means being a dynamic and constant communicator--horizontally within the reference unit, vertically between reference and the administration and back, diagonally and spherically with all groups in the library, the community, and beyond; all simultaneously. Openness with colleagues and mutual respect and trust within the reference unit must be established from the first day and reinforced each day thereafter, so that the views of reference (always including any dissenting opinions of individual staff members) can be fairly and readily presented to the administration and so that "higher-up" decisions will be received without suspicion when they are transmitted through the head of the department.

Some types of communication are, of course, easier to initiate and sustain than others. Regular informational, educational, and issue-oriented staff meetings; frequent appointments with individual staff members; daily ad hoc chats with each person about specific reference questions or projects; the routine circulation of minutes, memos, conference announcements, and other items of general interest: these are the basic, second-nature procedures which are absolutely essential for keeping the social and professional reference machine running smoothly.

Harder to achieve yet equally important for the long-term health of any reference department are the less common or more sensitive areas of communication: acknowledging errors, counseling staff both as to performance and career, and making outside contacts. It is, for example, never pleasant to admit your own serious or embarrassing mistakes, especially to colleagues who may feel their impact, but to conceal setbacks from those who are directly concerned is an affront to the principle of openness and furthermore denies others the chance to contribute ideas on ways to handle a crisis.

Even more difficult for some people is the inevitable necessity of correcting or censuring staff performance. Waiting for a mandated time, such as the annual salary review, to point out chronic deficiencies or irregularities in behavior on the job is doing a disservice to the individual involved. Coaching and scolding yield opposite results, and the head of reference who castigates without also working with a staff member to devise and implement a plan for self-improvement--with a clear understanding of the consequences of failing to do so--is the head of reference who needs help. In cases where the apparent cause of the difficulty lies outside the library, the situation is even more awkward and may require the intervention of outside specialists. Most reference librarians are not trained social workers or psychologists and should remember that fact when confronted with human problems in those dimensions. It does no one any good, least of all the troubled staff member, to deny that a personal problem exists or to refuse to attend to it with the best talents available, while respecting the individual's right to privacy and discretion.

Another sensitive sort of personal communication between the head of reference and individual staff members concerns the latters' career goals generally and the enhancement of their reference skills and experience specifically. It is a breach of professional and managerial duty in any organization, I believe, but especially in one with humanistic aims such as a library, to ignore the needs for continual challenge, growth, and promotion shared by all but the most passive staff members. The latter should be responding to the communication discussed in the previous paragraph. Reference presents a paradox in that the work involves infinite, unpredictable variety and permits unlimited creativity, yet by its one-to-one idiosyncratic nature it lacks both standard evaluation criteria and the range and hierarchy of internal responsibilities found in technical services. If for no other reason than to compensate for these characteristics the head of reference owes it to staff members to display a genuine interest in careers, a willingness to actively promote personal professional goals and special talents. Not only will staff morale be heightened by this consideration, but the library will undoubtedly benefit from improved staff knowledge, innovative spinoffs, and wider professional contacts. Yes, it will sometimes happen that particularly ambitious and gifted staff members will become so attracted by the new horizons or possibilities opened before them that they will "fly the coop" and leave reference, the library, or even the profession altogether. That loss is bound to be society's gain, and in the long run librarianship will profit from having nurtured some of the "best and the brightest." Reference work is intrinsically mind-expanding and cannot afford to be career-confining. The risk of tempting good people to move up or out is more than offset by the risk of burnout or it's perfunctory relative, fadeout. While it may not always be comfortable to talk with staff members privately about their visions of their own future, doing so makes the head of reference more aware of people's aspirations, so that when opportunities arise to participate in special training, research projects, state or national professional activities, discipline-sponsored conferences, or publishing efforts, the appropriate individual(s) can be designated, nominated, or encouraged. This is not to imply that the pursuit of anyone's personal aims should ever take precedence over achieving the general goals of the reference unit within the larger organization, or that prodding should substitute for individual initiative, but rather to point out that enhancing staff competence and satisfaction is a significant communication responsibility of any head of reference. The same responsibility exists for the support staff in reference; the "perfect secretary" who is never called on to develop new skills or take on new tasks will not remain perfect forever, or even for very long.

Compared with other areas of communication, the imperative that the head of reference keep in close and continual contact with other middle managers in the library as well as with key "client" groups may seem obvious or trivial. Obvious--but never trivial!-- it may be, but that does not make it an easy duty to carry out. Familiarity with all other library operations, friendship with those in charge and with as many staff as possible may take months to establish. It is difficult without a rigorous self-imposed timetable to set up close ties with departments in the institution, with organizations in the community, and with heads of reference in the region and nation. "Know thy sources," a fundamental commandment of reference work, expands for the head of reference to "Know thy resources, peers, and counterparts." The interpersonal networks so constructed are in many instances more valuable, and reliable, than a whole room full of encyclopedias and directories. Fortunately, "reference types" are a gregarious lot so that this responsibility is not so much onerous as it is time-consuming, as is the corollary sacred duty of keeping up with the reference journal literature and with developments in the world at large. Any "spare" time the head of reference has can be devoted to reading, and better yet to contributing to, the literature in some particular discipline. Publishing in scholars' own journals is the only way we have to reach beyond the one-to-one constraints of the reference interview to explain to specialists how their communication patterns are captured and traced in reference tools.

Communication is the most serious and certainly the most pervasive responsibility I have recognized in my new role. While that was not exactly "news" to me, there are two other matters which were real surprises. One is the fact that older, wiser, and much more experienced librarians now seek my advice or defer to me with regard to reference works or unusually involved questions. I am hardly a walking Guide to Reference Books--who is?--and I still occasionally make errors--don't we all?--in conducting reference interviews or get stuck thinking of alternative suggestions for complex research problems, so I am both flattered and embarrassed by this behavior on the part of my colleagues. A second surprise arises from my desire to work regular hours at each of our three service points versus my need for more time than ever before to accomplish other things--all further complicated by staffing emergencies when all prior plans must be scrapped so desks can stay open. I knew this would be a challenge before I moved, but I didn't realize how great a problem it can be; there are days when I need a second quiet eight hours to finish tasks that simply could not be done at the reference desk where I spend most of my time. Delegation of the extra workload would seem to be the obvious solution, but when it comes to distributing extra hours, the boss can't duck a fair share.

As for the textbook components of management, those activities which are said to be common to any business whether the product is knowledge or noodles, I discovered that all of them appeared within my first few weeks on the job and have now become an integral part of my world. Reduced to six, these functions are (1) personnel and organization, (2) problemsolving, (3) policy- and decision-making, (4) planning, (5) implementing, and (6) control of the work of the reference department. Looking at this list I am amazed that each element shades into all the rest and that none can be accomplished successfully without many types of communication. A seventh basic management task; financing, I am spared by the larger organization. Other than responsibility for the reference book fund I am not directly concerned with budget matters, and so will omit that operation in the following discussion. As best I can recollect, my consciousness of each function comes from a different impression which I will attempt to re-create.

Personnel and Organization

Starting as I did in the middle of the 1980 fall term, all the reference staff were already "in place," as President Reagan's advisors would say, when I arrived. So my immediate colleagues and their individual duties were givens: I appeared on the scene to add my strengths and weaknesses to theirs with what everyone hoped would be a salutary and energizing result. Getting to know staff members and their talents might have proceeded in a slow and casual fashion, except for my first challenge as a manager. When students left campus for the holidays it was necessary to re-configure the shelving and hence virtually the entire collection in reference.

Certain bookcases were to be removed for reasons of aesthetics and
to permit more natural light to enter study areas, other cases were
to replace them, aisles between shelving units were to be broadened
to wheelchair-width: in short, several ends were being accomplished
simultaneously but with a net loss of some hundred linear feet of
shelves and the fact of having actually to remove most of the collection to the floor, tables, and window sills. A further complication
is unique to Princeton, an architectural peculiarity of the reference
room which I would not wish on my worst enemy in the profession,
namely, that there is a balcony holding several thousand volumes,
all in the Z classification, accessible only by two narrow staircases.
Originally intended in 1948 as the browsing area for current periodicals, the balcony was constructed without an elevator anywhere in
the vicinity. What does this design nuisance have to do with personnel? Well, we professionals formed chain gangs of two people
downstairs and two in the balcony, one hanging at some peril over
the railing, to pass heavy bibliography volumes up to their new location. Voilà! an instant opportunity to work closely with my new
colleagues, observing how they could pull together as a team; how
well they were able to tolerate dust, stress, and anxiety and--of
greatest interest--how they would interact with me as a leader and
compatriot, disheveled as we all were. I learned more from this
otherwise inelegant exercise than I would have from six months without it. The challenge brought us together and gave me early and
invaluable insights about individuals and the group (not to mention
the collection!). I would go so far as to recommend engineering
such a physical group endeavor to anyone just beginning as head of
reference at a new institution--which is not to say I want to repeat
the experience myself!

Problem-Solving

This is where the wisdom of Solomon and the patience of Job come
in. I cannot begin to count or recount the number of times per day
I am called on to settle some not-usually-very-thorny matter for
someone. Often the issue is deployment of staff when someone calls
in sick; other times it is making a quick assessment of the amount
of time or money a special project may take; sometimes it is in response to an issue raised by another library unit. When my colleagues feel unable to carry a reference question any farther they
will appeal to me for advice, as I mentioned earlier, and that too
is a form of problem-solving. The revelation to me has been how
constant this demand is. I find I need to remind myself occasionally
that, since I cannot possibly foreseee all the problems that will
arise in the course of a week, a day, or even an hour, I cannot let
myself get tied up in knots, Gordian or otherwise, trying to solve
them in advance. Yet, on the other hand, I know I cannot close my
eyes and refuse to consider matters that are bound to come up sooner
or later (usually sooner!). The line between preventive maintenance and first aid is very fine.

Libraries and Librarians   135

Policy- and Decision-Making

In some respects this would seem to be a non-function of a middle
manager in an organization as closely and hierarchically structured
as a library, since most policies are formulated at a higher level.
Yes and no. Within reference there are always policy issues which
occur and recur and which should be resolved within the unit, for
example, how to handle excessive phone calls from private companies
for look-ups in the catalog. As for the larger decisions, Princeton
is very open and participatory, so that I find myself frequently consulted about, or asked to serve on committees concerning, matters
of considerable impact to the entire library system. I happen to
believe that it is not merely a managerial nicety but a necessity to
bring all but the most sensitive or top-secret issues to the reference
staff. Time and again my colleagues have had advice or perceptions
which have significantly strengthened, or sometimes changed, my
own view of a problem. I subscribe to the maxim that the best decisions are made after knowledgeable people have spoken, and I am
blessed with staff who speak wisely and well, so I am confident that
the outcome will be in everyone's best interests.

Planning

This has always been my favorite activity, the one I feel I do best.
Now I find with some dismay that it is also the one most easily
pushed aside when daily crises take over. I am exceedingly lucky,
however, in having an immediate supervisor to whom I can suggest
seemingly outrageous futures and who helps me focus on the most
realistic parts of impossible dreams. Still, I can now appreciate
why some organizations institutionalize a formal planning process or
schedule annual planning retreats. The best I can seem to manage
in the hurly-burly of it all is to project ideas and "what ifs" a few
months ahead--the truly long-range goals are literally out of sight,
which is why I've resolved to set aside specific periods for my own
and my colleagues' contemplation of our goals, speed, and direction.

Implementing

In major corporations managers make decisions based on data supplied by others, then pass the task of implementation along to still
others, only becoming involved again if the project's costs get out
of line or if there is a potentially disastrous problem, as in marketing or public relations. Virtually all of the production, the physical
and intellectual labor, is delegated. I was never naive enough to
assume that the head of reference could withdraw from the firing
line and run the operation from an office remote from both the collection and the service desks. But neither did I imagine that it
would be quite so difficult to delegate little chores to others. I
find there are many things--for example, checking reference orders
in the public catalog or trying to track down everyone on the staff
to relay important news personally--which someone else could do

equally well, if not better, but which I think I can do more efficiently myself or should do myself for some other reason like staff morale. Big tasks, it turns out, are much easier to delegate than small ones, but small ones add up in the course of a week to appalling proportions, so that I am aware more than ever before of the need to use time well. There is also another side to delegation: some responsibilities which I would dearly love to undertake myself, such as giving a lecture or doing a data base search, I now must refer to others in the department. That's been a disappointment, reminding me each time it happens that there is at least a moat if not a chasm between the reference librarian I was and the reference librarian I am. The best I can do is keep the bridge across in good repair at all times.

Control

The last of the major management duties is also the most difficult when it comes to reference. Constant vigilance is required to assure that the staff, collection, and most importantly the service rendered are always as close to perfect as it is possible to be. Combining the critical faculty with the corrective instinct is the hardest task I have so far encountered. More has been written with less good result about evaluation of reference service than about any other facet of librarianship, and I will not reinforce the point by rehearsing it. I knew that evaluation would be rugged, and I wasn't wrong. Not only are there no widely accepted evaluation methods to draw on, but being continually aware of my own fumbles and inadequacies at the desk, I feel presumptuous judging and rating colleagues. Yet I realize that to permit the status quo is to permit mediocrity in some cases, perhaps to promote disservice in others. The dilemma is made worse by the fact that it is impossible, given our staffing patterns, to work closely at a desk with every student assistant and regular staff member. I am left wondering how to go about objective, positive evaluation and reinforcement, especially in regards to the conduct of the reference interview and the follow-through of complex questions.

Becoming head of reference is no Cinderella story. Nothing magical happens the first day on the job--nor, fortunately, do colleagues and collections turn into mice and pumpkins at some enchanted hour. Better than magic, what occurs is that ability combines with circumstances to answer the multitude of questions Sheehy, the text, never asked.

Part II

COMMUNICATION AND EDUCATION

WHO CAN OWN WHAT AMERICA KNOWS?*

Anita R. Schiller and Herbert I. Schiller

Appropriation of public resources for private enrichment, long familiar in the American experience, has now come to the newest valuable resource, information. With almost no public notice, the national stock of information, created through heavy public expenditures over the years, is steadily being removed from government custodianship and transferred to private ownership and control.

Actively promoting the privatizing of information on behalf of the new and already influential corporate information sector is the Information Industry Association. Founded in 1968, the Washington-based I.I.A. numbers among its more than 150 members some of the most powerful information companies in the country, including I.B.M., Time Inc. and divisions of The New York Times Company and the Chase Manhattan Bank. On its board of directors are representatives from McGraw-Hill, Dow Jones, Lockheed, Xerox, Mead Data Central and The Washington Post Company.

The I.I.A., whose members produce, package, transmit and disseminate information, claims that its primary goal is "to promote the development of private enterprise in the field of information and to gain recognition for information as a commercial product." Commonplace and benign as that may appear, it represents the reversal of a national commitment to the ideal of public knowledgeability and the informed citizen. "Information as a commercial product" is information that is produced for profit. Who can pay for it and how much it will cost become questions that affect everyone.

• • •

Information today is being treated as a commodity. It is something which, like toothpaste, breakfast cereals and automobiles, is increasingly bought and sold. It is every bit as much a physical asset as a pool of oil--it has become an essential factor in the running of the modern American economy--and indeed, supplies of the former are coveted by the business world nearly as much as the latter.

---

*Reprinted by permission of the author and publisher from The Nation, 234 (April 17, 1982) 461-463. Copyright © 1982 by The Nation, Inc.

Of course, information had commercial uses and was sold long before we realized we were living in an Information Society. What is different today is that a much wider range of information has become profitable because it can be flexibly processed, selectively rearranged, and quickly transmitted and disseminated by a virtuoso new technology.

The new reality is evident everywhere. Books are "products," the Supreme Court has ruled, holding that publishers' book stocks are no different from general commercial inventories. In some cases, scientific and technical information has been placed under export control. Productivity measures have been applied to colleges and universities. Educational institutions have signed agreements with private corporations selling the rights to exclusive use of research findings.

The bulk of the national information supply is gathered by Federal agencies or is paid for by the government's large research-and-development expenditures. The cumulative holdings in the government information reservoir--census data, Congressional hearings and reports, consultants' research, departmental studies--are immense and of increasing economic value.

The private information venders are now turning to these holdings systematically and diligently. Undaunted by the widely held belief that the public has a right to information that it has paid to have produced, they have substituted the notion that nothing that can be done privately should be undertaken by the government. They--and their representatives at the I.I.A.--supplement this wisdom with the insistence that information has to be sold at a profit. Social need is regarded as irrelevant.

In the process, control of the national information base is being rapidly shifted from the public domain into private hands. If the information industry has its way, no public facility or institution involved with information will be spared.

• • •

One of the leading targets of the demolition effort is the Government Printing Office. The G.P.O. historically has been the publisher and disseminator of government-financed and government-generated information. Although it never really fulfilled its responsibility for getting information to the public, in recent years the G.P.O. has been severely constrained and its role dramatically reduced. Budget cutbacks have hurt; so has the failure of many government agencies to use the G.P.O. as the publisher of their materials. Most damaging was the creation in 1964 of a parallel agency in the Department of Commerce, the National Technical Information Service.

N.T.I.S. has taken over a great share of government publishing activity while adhering to the I.I.A. standard of operations.

"All the costs of N.T.I.S. products and services, including rent ... salaries ... and all other usual costs of doing business," runs a brochure the service issued "... are paid from sales income, not from tax-supported Congressional appropriations." But even that is not enough for the I.I.A. It is now urging that N.T.I.S. be dismantled and that its publishing duties be performed by private information firms.

The G.P.O. was also dealt a harsh blow by a provision of the Federal Paperwork Reduction Act, signed into law in December 1980. The act gave the Office of Management and Budget discretion over what publications the G.P.O. should publish. Government documents librarians at that time pointed out the dangers of this arrangement: "To have an entity [O.M.B.] which is typically preoccupied by matters of cost and which is perceived as one of the government agencies least accessible to the public, establishing policies regarding citizen access to government information requires some guarantee of balanced decision-making regarding the collection, management, use and dissemination of information."

In April 1981, President Regan and the O.M.B. ordered a moratorium on new periodicals, pamphlets and audio-visual products. In November, it was reported that more than 900 items had been canceled--with more cuts expected this year--many of them concerned with food, diet, health, energy, social welfare and other matters of daily life.

In January, the Public Printer announced his desire to close twenty-four of the twenty-seven G.P.O. bookstores around the country because, he claimed, they compete with the private sector and are not profitable. The widely distributed monthly release "Selected U.S. Government Publications," issued free by the superintendent of documents of the G.P.O., announced in the same month that its January issue was its last. It offered this consoling alternative: "For those who want more comprehensive information about sales publications, we suggest you subscribe to hard copy <u>Monthly Catalog of United States Government Publications</u> ($90.00 domestic; $112.50 foreign per calendar year) or the microfiche <u>GPO Sales Publication Reference File</u> ($125.00 domestic; $156.25 foreign per year)." The justification the G.P.O. gave for terminating this useful tool was that it was not self-sustaining as the law requires. That is another instance of the I.I.A.'s success in having laws interpreted in a way that facilitates the destruction of public information.

• • •

The efforts of the private information industry are not limited to crippling the G.P.O. Information firms have been trying to compel the National Library of Medicine to impose higher fees for the use of its computerized information services. The I.I.A. helped force the National Institute of Mental Health to phase out access to its database, which had been available at relatively low cost and included material on social aspects of mental health literature not available elsewhere. (Although this phase-out has been attributed to budgetary cutbacks, it had also been sought by such groups as the I.I.A., which accused the institute of competing with a private operation.)

There has also been increasing pressure on the National Depository Library System to introduce market forces in making acquisitions for the more than 1,300 libraries it serves. In existence for more than a hundred years, the depository system "provides for a class of libraries in the United States in which certain Government publications are deposited for the use of the public."

The I.I.A. has urged replacing this arrangement with a system of cash payments by which depositories could choose privately prepared information packages. Under that plan, however, there is no guarantee that any depository would maintain the comprehensiveness of its collection, and they would all be subject to a wide variety of competing interests. If they succumbed to corporate blandishments, that would have the effect of encouraging more and more firms to privatize more and more information. To date, the I.I.A.'s views have not prevailed, but its pressure is unrelenting.

Other government information activities as well are under attack--an attack so heavy that in January the Washington, D.C., office of the American Library Association, in a document titled "Less Access to Less Information By and About the U.S. Government," could point to "what seems to be an emerging pattern of restricting citizen access to government information."

Various censuses, surveys and reports are being discontinued or threatened by budget cuts. The Federal statistical system is in disarray. Crucial national income data are threatened. Compilations by the Social Security Administration of basic data on industrial and occupational classifications of workers may be discontinued. The Federal Trade Commission is considering stopping its quarterly financial reports. The Census Bureau has delayed some population reports, and in February it laid off 500 employees.

Federal data of use to business is also in jeopardy, but here the private sector is eager to help. When the Census Bureau canceled its plans to release reports by zip code, a consortium of large companies was established to buy the computer tapes from the bureau and compile the information for its members.

• • •

To be sure, the public interest is being manhandled by the market in many related fields: public mail service is weakened by the switch to electronic mail; cheap and reliable telephone service succumbs to A.T.&T.'s desire to concentrate on trunk lines and computer hardware; commercial television declines as networks sell their most popular programming to pay-TV. Yet the damage in the information sector threatens to be greater and longer-lasting.

Once withdrawn from its social context and made into an item for sale, necessary information may just not be available. Not because of censorship, though this is no small concern, but because it will be controlled by the marketplace. Information we should have or might need may never be gathered, much less organized and transmitted. And if it is, it will have to be purchased.

With the destruction of public information, the basis of democracy disappears. In the new era, the upper tier is for the "information rich," more abundantly supplied with images, symbols and information than ever before. Below, in the pit, are the "information poor," the "have nots" in the Information Society. Democratic participation in the processes of government will surely suffer.

THE LONG ROAD FROM BYBLOS*

Wallace Stegner

On the eastern shore of the Mediterranean, about twenty miles north of Beirut, is a drab little Syrian village built of the broken stones of a far more ancient community. When civilization was young, before Tyre and Sidon became echoing names, a city grew up here. It traded wood and resin with other cities of the Mediterranean Basin and with Egypt, and its sculptors and shipwrights were known as far as traders ventured. Inscriptions on earthen pots fired in Luxor Egypt in the third millennium B.C. refer to it as a place of importance. Its Temple of Baalat, the Phoenician Aphrodite, built about 1900 B.C., was famous for three thousand years, until it was destroyed by fanatical Moslems in the 12th century A.D.

Alexander conquered the city in the 4th century B.C., Pompey took it three hundred years later, Crusaders captured it in 1103 A.D., only to lose it back to Saladin in 1189. On a promontory which from earliest times forced travelers and conquerors through a narrow pass between the headlands and the sea, Phoenicians, Greeks, Romans, Jews, early Christians, Crusaders from England and Burgundy, left names, initials, messages, and signs. Like Independence Rock and Register Cliff on the Oregon Trail, but over a vastly longer period, the bluff was used as a roadside post office, billboard, and message center.

The name of the modern village whose goats browse among broken columns and mounds of rubble is Jebeil, from the Arabic word jebel, meaning a hill or mountain. But the name of the ancient city was more portentous. It was called Bublos, or Byblos, and because of certain capacities of its inhabitants (in what is now called communications) the name was later applied to a papyrus or scroll, and so gave rise to the Greek word biblion, book.

The association was not accidental. Nine royal tombs have thus far been excavated in the Byblos necropolis. One of them is that of King Ahiram, who was a contemporary of Rameses II of Egypt. On his sarcophagus, which is Egyptian in everything but its

---

*Reprinted by permission of the author and publisher from Soundings, 13 (1982) 5-19. Copyright © 1982 by the University Library, University of California, Santa Barbara.

inscriptions, is Phoenician writing four hundred years earlier than
any other thus far found. Many of the letters have since undergone
transformations in their long migration down the centuries and
through many languages, but here is a recognizable ancestor of our
alphabet. Perhaps it was adapted from an even earlier Semitic alphabet, perhaps it originated here, as the city's name suggests. In
any case, Byblos not only gave its name to the thing we call a book,
but was an important center in the creation or perfection of a new
system of writing. That system, which replaced cuneiform, hiero-
glyphs, and all kinds of picture writing, as well as the clumsy syl-
labaries that developed on Cyprus and elsewhere, made possible a
quantum extension of the human mind across space and time. There
ought to be a modern temple at Byblos, dedicated to something more
even than Aphrodite.

  Language is the greatest human invention. Near the beginnings of our species it made possible the transmission of perceptions, feelings, memories, myths, duties, all the complexities of
individual perception and social relationships. The pressure that
the impulse to speak put on our hominid ancestors may well have
been a principal agent in the remarkable development of the human
brain. The left hemisphere of the brain, which controls speech
functions, is larger than the right, and the brain case bulges a
little on that side. Similarly, according to Richard Leakey, the
brain cases of fossil men, Ramapithecus, Australopithecus, and
homo habilis, all show that the left hemisphere was larger in our
earliest ancestors, too, as far back as two and a half million years.
Those half-men must have talked, and talking enlarged their brains,
and their more complex circuitry made possible more complex talk.

  Both as cause and effect, language is probably inseparable
from the development of human intelligence, and certainly it has
been of primary importance in the growth and transmission of cultures. Even as oral tradition, among tribes which have not invented
a means of writing, language holds families and bands together, and
gives every member his identity and his context, and gives the culture its memory. The first books, in the sense that a book is a
collection of human experience, thought, and feeling, were human
minds. On an island off Dakar, in West Africa, where slaves were
once gathered pending shipment to America and elsewhere, there is
a haunting scribble on a wall. It says, "In Africa, when an old
man dies, it is as if a great library had burned." Who put it
there, slave or slaver, doesn't matter. It has the resonance of a
perceived truth.

  But though oral language makes and preserves cultures, only
written language, especially when it makes use of a phonetic alphabet that is readily translatable from tongue to tongue, makes high
and fully communicable civilizations.

  In social and linguistic as well as in biological evolution,
flexibility is of the essence. Animals such as the titanothere, a
Tertiary mammal with big grinding teeth for chewing mushy forage,

became extinct when the climate turned dry and the forage became brittle and hard. Cultures that are exquisitely adapted to specific conditions, as Eskimo culture is, have trouble surviving environmental change. As for language, I have heard Frenchmen lament that the French language is so elegant and impeccable, and that the purism of the French Academy discourages corruptions and borrowings. They half wish French were as flexible as English, as adaptable and as easily corrupted, for those qualities make English a more useful <u>lingua franca</u> in a disunited world, and a more likely universal language if the world should ever unite.

Precisely what the alphabet provided the ancient world was a flexible and adaptable instrument; and when Gutenberg in the 15th century added the equally flexible mechanism of movable type, so that books could be swiftly and economically reproduced, he made possible the modern world.

Hence my short respectful pilgrimage to Byblos, whose name reminds us that "book" and "bible" once meant the same thing. A certain weight and reverence clings to the word--either word--even in these times when books are often debased to trivial or emetic uses. We aren't bothered when old magazines are shredded, but when we learn that publishers are shredding books, we wince. We will start the fire with the <u>New York Times</u> or the <u>Yale Review</u>, but we consider the burning of books to be the act of barbarians, philistines, and tyrants.

It is not print that we hold sacred, but the book, for the book has traditionally meant written language put to its highest use. In books, not only all civilized continuity but all human technology is preserved. A Zen poet once told me that if civilization were destroyed, all human achievements could be duplicated through meditation. Maybe, but it could take as long as it would take that legendary monkey with a typewriter to produce by random pecking the works of Shakespeare. A much quicker and surer method would be intense study of whatever books survived the cataclysm. I take meditation to be important, but literacy is more so. At the heart of every institution of learning is a collection of books and of men and women who love and use books. The reverential collecting of libraries as a richly rewarding activity is what this annual gathering and the Edwin Corle Awards are all about. Mr. Corle was a man who loved good books, wrote good books, collected books, and Mrs. Corle has found the perfect memorial for him.

Yet it is a fairly common notion, often blamed on Marshall McLuhan, who was after all only reporting his observations, that we are in the twilight of print, that easy, universal modern communications are returning us to the oral and immediate condition of a primitive village, and that the world village will shortly find more use for TV screens, tape recorders, cameras, loudspeakers, and computer terminals than for libraries. And on the whole, this argument says, the decline of books is not necessarily a disaster. Oral and pictorial communications are warmer, faster, more social, and more humanized than cold, private, distant print. Also easier, and humanity is congenitally lazy.

Of this position I will say two or three things. One is that I don't believe much of it except that print is harder than its contemporary substitutes. Another is that non-print is neither as profound nor as lasting as print. Communication through a book can bring a reader a sense of intimacy unencumbered by vanity, diffidence, or pride, a relationship with the projected mind of the writer that is more personal than most personal relations--or interpersonal relations, as the jargon goes. Finally, to the extent that our enthusiasm for electronic gadgets, our indifference to history, our attempted democratization of education, and our preference for the simple over the complex, the easy over the hard, have led us down this path away from books, they have led us toward a depreciation of our civilization and a lessening of the quality of our lives. Hence the demoralizing SAT scores of California high school graduates.

Certainly more direct communication than print is available, both as sound and picture. We no longer have to read the dialog of movies; we hear it. We no longer have to visualize the colors; we see them. We no longer have to read Moby Dick or War and Peace; we can see them bigger than life on the screen, with everything left out but the plot.

Photographic journalism? It began in the early thirties. I remember the first issue of Life, and the sensationalism that promoted it. (See a tiger killing a man!) For a while in the forties I worked for Look, and learned that picture-communication is minimal, unsubtle, and often misleading. We used to say around the office that Look was published for people too dumb to read Life.

As for sound communication more elaborate than the telephone, I remember long nights during the twenties when I sat with earphones on, scratching with a wire at a crystal and trying to extract something intelligible from passing airwaves. I remember even back of that, to the cylindrical Edison Records, or the Victor records projected through a tin horn bearing the picture of a cock-eared terrier and the legend, "His Master's Voice." All that is within the memory of millions of people still living. We began giving up print, in favor of sound, not much more than sixty years ago.

Theoretically, recordings and tape are as effective ways to store knowledge, history, literary art, or music as printed books and printed scores, and they demand no special skill in a complex symbolic system as reading does. Recorded oral history preserves the very tones of people who changed the world. Poets go barding around because poetry spoken aloud is more immediate than poetry on the page. Without recordings of books, blind people would be thrown back to the awkwardness of Braille. And reading aloud, though not as common as it once was, is still one of the best ways to tie a family together or to educate a child.

Nevertheless, just as I don't think pictures an adequate substitute for print, I don't think recordings which are indispensable for music, an adequate substitute for books. Any recording exists in time, like a concert. It will not hold still while we pause for thought, it won't let us backtrack to a remembered passage without exasperating delays, and it won't permit the comparison of page with page. We don't have it in our hands, under our eyes, as we have a book. It is a performance, a supplement to the book, but secondary, and no substitute. What is more, even though most modern books are printed on paper that won't last fifty years, it is likely that tapes and recordings will not last even that long in storage.

Trying to use a tape recorder for research, I have always had trouble. This year's machine won't play last year's tapes. I can never find the place I want--my finger is always on the fast-rewind or fast-forward button. The only way I can work with tapes is to make laborious transcripts of them and work from those, which puts me back where I would have been if I had submitted to working from books and taking written notes in the first place. I keep remembering that when Marshall McLuhan made his case against print, he made it not on the air or on a recording, but in books.

Admittedly reading and writing, which involve an enormously complex symbolic system, are hard to learn and even harder to become expert in. By the same token, print communicates better and more clearly because its production enforces greater care than any oral statement. No matter how we may yearn for the easier over the harder, the social over the private, the impromptu over the considered, we still go to books when we want a close grapple with another mind. A library is the shrine and symbol of the private, studious, unencumbered intelligence, by comparison with which the talking heads of TV or the throwaway discourse of newspapers and magazines, is trivial. "When a man writes to the world," Milton said in Areopagitica, "he summons up all his reason and deliberation to assist him." He tries to be important; he tries to write for more than his own time. And what writers do, readers must follow or be lost. Writing and reading are a single linked action, like skating in pairs.

To some, Milton's view of the book seems impossibly lofty. "A good book," he said--or rather wrote--"is the precious lifeblood of a master spirit, treasured up on purpose for a life beyond life." He went so far as to believe that before a man could write a great poem he must first be one. Not everyone, nor every writer, would link character and literary worth so closely. Oscar Wilde, that master of misleading epigrams, remarked that the fact that a man was a poisoner had nothing to do with his prose. But notice that he spoke only of the prose, the instrument. The tunes it plays are something else, and Oscar Wilde's tunes do not keep their rating as time passes. Even when self-revelation is unconscious, the exposure in a book is pitiless. The prose is only a decoration, a tool, a disguise, a weapon; and as Conrad said--or wrote--the

possession of a firearm doesn't make a warrior or a hunter. A
writer's book is at bottom only as good as he is.

As for me, I wish the word "book" could be reserved for
those writings, poetic, dramatic, fictional, historical or whatever,
in which a gifted and trained writer has done his best to express
what he knows and feels; in which he has gone through the long
labor, through months and often years, of learning, considering,
selecting, shaping, ordering, and revising; in which he has checked
himself for accuracy and the precise shades of emphasis, bolstered
his text with illustrations and corroborations, and tested his imaginary world against his total personal and social experience: in short,
his wisdom.

I wish we had a publishing and distributing system that would
make such books more readily available to all who are hungry for
them; a reviewing establishment that would consistently tell us the
difference between the worthy and the trashy, a critical establishment free of cliquishness and with a sense of history, and a larger
reading public which wants from books not merely entertainment and
time-killing, but some revelation of the human capacity for thoughtfulness, compassion, and growth. I wish the usual marketing lies
could be eliminated. I wish words like "great" and "masterpiece"
and "superb" could be reserved for the handful of books each decade
that deserve them. I wish that the media--and to a degree therefore the public the media serve--would quit trying to make celebrities out of writers. One of our troubles is that we are awash with
celebrities most of whom last a few months, at most a few years.
Celebrity-consciousness is only one more manifestation of our addiction to the oral and impromptu. Media celebrity-making of authors is not based on the books themselves, but upon spectacular
book sales or on some news value in book or author or on some
personal scandal or notoriety in the writer's life. Whether the media realize it or not, there is a difference between a serious writer
such as Saul Bellow, whom you will never see on these programs,
and some writer who aspires to appear beside Hugh Heffner and
Stevie Wonder on the Johnny Carson show.

If some such happy transformation could come over the American book world, then the book itself, which started on its long, devious, civilizing journey around the world from Byblos four hundred
years before the Trojan War and two hundred before Homer might
regain some of the respect that we know we owe it but too often
pay it in lip service only.

Unfortunately, none of those wishes has been granted, or is
likely to be. Making books universal we have made them less important. We try to teach all children to read, but too often fail to
develop in them standards of taste that would make their reading
selective at the highest level each reader is capable of.

Chaucer's Clerk of Oxenford would levere have at his beddes
heed twenty bookes, clad in blak or red of Aristotle and his philosophie

than robes riche, or fithele, or gay sautrie. But that was the 14th century, when books were made with painstaking care by hand. All the processes of the 20th century, so much better in so many ways, are at odds with the difficult and elite cult of the book. We have democratized too many books down to the lowest common denominator. In Chaucer's time, when both books and readers were few, readers read reverently what was thought important to their life-- Bocaccio, Boethius, Froissart, Marie de France, the Thomistic disputations of the Church fathers, books of hours, the Imitation of Christ. These days, when nearly everyone can read, some of us would levere have at our beddes heed twenty bookes of Flash Gordon, Superman, or Mickey Spillane than all the wealth of Widener or Alexandria. Some of us don't read at all, some read only newspapers and magazines, some read only pictures, some read only novels calculated to stir up the hormones. And publishing, distribution, and even reviewing are so linked to high-powered marketing that serious readers have to hunt through landslides of trash to find the broken body of the one small bit of integrity they are looking for.

The last time I looked, 45,000 titles were published annually in the United States. In the whole English-speaking world the figure must be astronomical. A few of them are truly distinguished, quite a few are important, many are amusing or practically instructive. But some are muddleheaded, and some are froth activated by a galvanic twitch, and some are poisonous.

Books find their own level, and when a popular culture which is virtually mindless is the target of publishing--when books are calculated to compete with TV entertainment or hard porn--the level of the average is villainously low. Within the entertainment world, reading is a joke. The jiggle-TV sex kitten, asked what she is doing tonight, says she is going to curl up with a good book, and gets guffaws.

It is hard to tell whether we are dealing with cause or effect, whether the reading public gets what it deserves, or is being victimized. The past is always more intelligible than the present because time has sifted out the sludge. But many people applauded last fall when Barbara Tuchman, in the New York Times Magazine, took issue with the decline of quality in every aspect of American life. "In culture the tides of trash rise a little higher by the week: in fast foods and junky clothes and cute greeting cards, in films devoted nowadays either to sadism or teen-agers and consequently either nasty or boring; in the frantic razzle-dazzle of Bloomingdale's and its proliferating imitators; in endless paperbacks of sex and slaughter, Gothics and westerns; in the advertising of sensation-fiction which presents each book as the ultimate in horror, catastrophe, political plot or world crime, each by an unknown author who is never heard of again--fortunately." (I would quibble; many of them are heard of again--unfortunately.) Examining our life for things she labels Q or non-Q--for Quality and Non-Quality--Miss Tuchman is led to wonder if some sort of Gresham's Law might not be operating, if in the affluent and hyper-stimulated democracy bad money of all kinds might not be driving out good.

It is a fair question. The leveling and stereotyping of mind and culture has been a fear of students of democracy since the Revolution. De Tocqueville remarked on the possibility; British travelers such as Mrs. Trollope stridently asserted the social and intellectual consequences of levelling. Now the cheapening and sensationalizing forces have begun to pay a dangerous attention to the book, once an object of respect.

One of the disadvantages of a society which undervalues history and tradition, courts the spontaneous, and aspires to a life style that is all present tense is that it is hard to get a perspective from anywhere within it. In an attempt to do that, I want to trace some of the steps by which books have been progressively degraded in my time. I am old enough so that when I die it will be as if a modest library had burned, and I do remember some of the corners around which we have come.

When I was in college in the twenties the principal resource of penniless but bookish students was the Modern Library--well-printed, stoutly-bound reprints of so-called "classics," ancient and modern. Most of those books were worth a reader's time; and they cost $1.25 and were made to last. I have some of them yet. There were other inexpensive reprints--Everyman Library, Loeb Classical Library. We had no paperbacks except for a few treasured French books and the Tauchnitz editions published in Germany. They too were well-edited and printed; there were people who had them hardbound and put them on their permanent shelves. Even the places that dispensed saucy books to eager readers--The United Cigar Stores, among other places--dealt not in pornographic trash but in literature. My copies of Petronius, Rabelais, and yes, Oscar Wilde, I bought at the United Cigar Store.

Nothing much visibly changed through the thirties--depression-- or the early forties--war. But two developments, in retrospect, seem significant. One was the birth of the Book-of-the-Month Club, out of whose example have come all the other mass-distribution mail order schemes. The effect of book clubs was in many ways good, for they did get books into the hands of people who lived where there were no bookstores, they promoted interest in reading, buying, and owning books. Their danger was that they promoted the sale of more and more copies of fewer and fewer titles, and though they did publish some good books, their marketing necessities made them lean toward the popular. Mass distribution is always under the temptation to seek the easy and undemanding. The natural dead end toward which the book club as an institution tends is Reader's Digest Condensed Books--shortened and trimmed and simplified fast food of the mind, about the literary equivalent of certain speed reading systems which will teach you to read Shakespeare's <u>As You Like It</u> in twelve minutes and <u>War and Peace</u> in an hour.

The second cloud on the horizon of the early thirties was the birth of Simon and Schuster, a new kind of publishing house. It did not publish authors, as the old line houses did. It published books, and it aspired to make every book a best seller. Traditional publishing was a cottage industry run by gentlemen with literary tastes. Simon and Schuster were aggressive merchandizers of books which half the time were thought up in the office and hired out to writers. They didn't always succeed, but they succeeded pretty often, and they were an ominous sign. They introduced something nonliterary into the publishing business. They reduced the book to merchandise.

The next stage came just at the end of World War II. It derived some of its impetus from the paperback Armed Service Editions printed by the government and shipped to millions of our men overseas. That experience taught all publishers the advantage of big press runs. It also encouraged them to look toward a world in which mass-produced cheap books would be as widely distributed and as expendable as magazines. That was the start of the Paperback Revolution.

The revolution did not hit its full stride until the early fifties, but it did what its prophets said it would. It encouraged the reading and buying of books, often for what was in them rather than for some sensational quality they were supposed to possess. At first it tended to reverse the tendency of the book clubs, for it made many titles available instead of specializing in promoting a few. It expanded the outlets in which books were sold to drugstores and airports and newsstands. And it didn't seem to have the effect of making the book as expendable as an old magazine. What it did was confirm old habits. Magazine readers treated paperbacks like old copies of Woman's Home Companion; book lovers more often kept them on their shelves and built useful if somewhat impermanent libraries of them. Some paperback series, especially those designed for classes, were obviously made for keeping, paperback equivalents of the old Modern Library.

So far, so good, as the man who fell off the roof said as he passed the 18th story. But the culture has twisted paperbacks into its image. Not only has the standard price jumped from fifty cents to six or seven dollars, but the level of excellence in available mass-distribution paperbacks has sharply declined. Try to find a book you want to read in an airport newsstand. University bookstores and many private bookstores do pretty well, but a lot of titles once available in paperback are no longer there when a teacher comes around wanting thirty copies for a class. The heightened desire for big profit has eliminated them. Books that a few years ago, after a modest critical success, would have sold to the paperbacks for ten or fifteen thousand dollars and been on the shelves for several years, now never even make it into paperback. The cheaper they are, the better their chances.

On the other hand, competitive bidding for sure-fire sex and violence thrillers can go up into the millions on the basis of movie tie-ins, authorial promotion nationwide, and exposure of the author on talk shows. The quality of a book begins to be unimportant. Some of these block-busters are sold on the strength of an outline, the author's past record of hitting the jackpot, and a couple of sample chapters.

What has happened in a very visible part of the publishing business, as Whiteside pointed out in a three-part article in New Yorker last October, is that it has moved into the area of mass entertainment and adopted the methods of the entertainment industry. Most name publishers are no longer cottage industries but arms of big conglomerates with big money resources and little interest in books as books. They belong, too often, with the movies or the rock recording industry. Or boxing. Remember Roberto Duran's manager's tactics when he struck the New Orleans Superdome with a multi-million dollar price for the second Duran-Leonard fight, the one that Duran walked out on when he felt he had contributed his 8-million dollars' worth? The Superdome got caught in competitive bidding, and paid the price, and lost a bundle, because it was afraid Caesar's Palace would pick off the plum, just as Bantam and Fawcett pay the price rather than lose out to New American Library.

Once books begat movies; now movies beget paperbacks that ride on the wave of movie interest. As with commodities such as breakfast food, there is a lot of deceptive packaging. As with cars, there is built-in obsolescence. Increasingly, the old-fashioned bookstores which would order a single copy of any book you wanted give way to chain stores which sell in quantity and order by computer. The computer, which is created by the jobbers, gives them a choice among authors who have a track record of big sales, have appeared on Today or the Johnny Carson Show, and are likely to be market winners. Many good books never even make it to the computer, any more than they make it to the paperback racks.

These marketing techniques inevitably influence reviewers, critics, bookstores, even readers. Decline in Q, indeed. What then becomes of good books, modern or ancient, that appeal to discriminating audiences over a long period of time? There are other lions in the path: the IRS and our inheritance tax system. Once family libraries passed from father to son, mother to daughter. Now a son can't _afford_ to inherit his father's library. The inheritance tax folks will put so high a money valuation on it that he can't afford to pay the tax. So private libraries are under constant threat of being wiped out every generation. They get sold off to second hand dealers, or are willed to university libraries. In either case they retain their usefulness, but they give none of the continuity and personal satisfaction that an heir gets when he inherits the assembled and purified mind of his ancestors.

As for the IRS, it has lately ruled that inventories of books in publishers' warehouses are taxable in the same way as tools or farm machinery inventories. Nowadays even old-line publishers with a conscience have to send to the shredder all those books, good and bad alike, that remain unsold at judgment day. Thornton Wilder's sister told me a few weeks ago that her brother's last novel, The Eighth Day, had just been shredded. If it happens to Wilder it can happen to anyone, for Thornton Wilder was for several decades one of America's finest writers, winner of the National Medal for Literature, the highest award an American writer can win, and moreover a writer who had with every book a very large audience considering how good he was.

The book business, somebody should tell the IRS and probably has, is not at all like the tool business. It is two-thirds inventory. Its virtue inheres in keeping a great tradition alive. It has a cultural obligation and a cultural effect. The IRS ruling that forces publishers to shred books is as barbarian and philistine as any bookburning.

That is the gloomy part of this discourse. The rest is more upbeat. For despite the discouraging signs all up and down the book trade, it seems that Quality does not turn belly-up, but insists on surviving, like Christians hiding from the Moors in the caves of Spain.

It does not survive by demanding suppression or censorship of trash or obscenity. The First Amendment guarantees the right of even trash, even poison, to exist. The moment we resort to censorship we have gone over to the camp of the enemy. But we can keep a channel open simply by being discriminating in what we read and buy. I am not a supply-side economist; I lean toward the demand side. If we work at it, we can make demand create supply rather than the reverse. We have to learn not only to pick our books, as you are being encouraged to do by the Corle competition, but pick our bookstores. We have to resist bandwagon tactics and the lure of advertising hype. We have to keep our feet firmly planted and hold our skirts down in this Fun House. We have to hang on to, and never slacken our grip on, the traditions of seriousness, wisdom, and permanence that have brought the book from Byblos to here.

To some extent, by individuals, small book groups, college communities, we do. Whiteside's gloomy picture of the publishing business was a little overdrawn, in spite of all its truths. For as contemporary paperback houses engage in throat-cutting competition for sleazy merchandise, and as good but unsensationalized books disappear from popular paperback lists and newsstand shelves, writers and readers of quality keep their noses stubbornly above water. Small presses and university presses, never able to compete in the big-time trade marketplace, happily take on good books as the mass-paperbacks let them go. These presses edit their books better, print them better, and bind them better than the marketplace ever did. They charge more, too, but what they charge for is something of value. They can keep a book in print practically forever, being (at least the university presses) exempt from the IRS inventory ruling. They don't have to discard a book because it is only going to sell 5000 copies. They can print it happily.

What is beginning to happen in book publishing is very like

what happened in the theater when Show Business got too sleazy: objectors created the Little Theater movement. Historically, when publishing opportunities for new and untried writers seem to be closed, there has been an inevitable outburst of little magazines. They are not to be disparaged because they reach only small audiences and last, generally, no more than a year or two. There is hardly a writer of real quality in this country who didn't find his first publication in a little magazine, and through its pages make contact with the beginning of his audience. In the years to come, I think you will be able to find, in any really good bookstore and certainly in nearly every college bookstore, the books of enduring value that as students and as adults will most satisfy the intellectual and spiritual hungers. I think you cannot stop writers from writing, publishers from publishing, and readers from finding good books. I take it that every student who has competed for the Corle Award in this university, and every person from Mrs. Corle on down who has stimulated and encouraged that award, is of the true tribe of Benjamin. Instead of being imprisoned in the present and stimulated only by the cultural equivalent of cattleprods, you can look back down the long corridors of time and know what the pilgrimage of man has been. You should be congratulated. You are of the Elect.

ON BIOGRAPHY*

Stanley Olson

When, in 1911, Edmund Gosse described biography as a mere subgenre of history--"a study sharply defined by two definite events, birth and death"--he was not simply stating the obvious, he was expressing the predicament proposed by any definition of the craft. Biography is neither fully history, nor literature. It resides somewhere in a halfway house between the two, subject, however, to critical blasts from both sides. It is history conveniently scaled-down to fit within the borders of an individual life, neatly focused on one person, and as reliant on the devices of literature as on factual precision. The rudiments of portraiture and the stringent requirements of history do merge in biography, and thus permit it, as a form, to embrace art, to become an acceptable literary form. Gosse avoided the cruel dilemma provoked by the intrusion of art because he, like biographers today, placed biography outside the realm of literature. Both have miscast it as a document of reference, and much evidence exists to support this opinion.

Biography will always remain an imprecise form: by means of some peculiar alchemy a jumble of facts and impressions is transformed into a life, resurrecting the dead. The biographer and the painter have steadily oscillated between the broad options available to perfect this stunt. The subject can either be suggested by quick, deft, brave, perhaps audacious sweeps of line and colour--the technique employed by Strachey, Boldini, and Sargent--or he can be stated, firmly, determinedly, deliberately, with equal attention turned on spots, blemishes, wrinkles, and fundamental characteristics, with near-photographic accuracy--the technique preferred by Michael Holroyd, Ted Morgan, and Jamie Wyeth. Both approaches achieve the same conclusion. Strachey disrobed his subjects of hagiography, allowing them to assume a more human scale, and modern biographers amass such a quantity of facts that their subjects are restrained (by the weight of material) from progressing beyond fallibility. But Strachey was closer to painting: he saw that no biography could be definitive, final. Painters have never been fazed by previous portraits of their subjects--there are five portraits of Marchese Casati; two by Augustus John and one each

---

*Reprinted by permission of the author and publisher from Antaeus, (Autumn 1982) 168-174. Copyright © 1982 by Antaeus, New York, N.Y.

by Boldini, Marenetti, and Bakst. Their versions are subjective--
but biographers tend to cloud this possibility by dragging excessive
evidence into written portraits. There will probably never be another biography of Henry James after Prof. Leon Edel's five volumes or of Proust after George Painter's two volumes. Strachey's
attitude that biography was a partner, an acceptable partner, of the
novel and belles-lettres has not survived because modern biographers
have teamed up with the compilers of the encyclopaedia and dictionary, happily seizing on the notion that chronicle passes for a rendition of a life. Thus biography has become overambitious, making
a bid for permanence, and long, too long.

Because the unfortunate consideration that biography is, <u>tout
simple</u>, a means of arresting material on its way to oblivion has
gained currency, some appalling misdeeds have occurred. Desmond MacCarthy claimed that a biographer was "an artist on oath,"
an imaginative writer tethered to accuracy, and Michael Holroyd
has called the biographical process a collaboration between the biographer and his subject. Yet both broad definitions have been either flagrantly abused or ignored. The biographer sees himself as
the servant of posterity, not of the higher considerations of art.

Surely no "artist on oath" would care to portray a subject
who asked to have no biography. Somerset Maugham said NO to
biography in the loudest and firmest voice he could muster. People
knew exactly why he made a bonfire of his private papers. T.S.
Eliot, W.H. Auden, George Orwell, and George Gissing--the list,
not surprisingly, is ever-increasing--have all said NO to biography.
These pleas have had no effect whatsoever. Gissing's biographer,
Gillian Tindall, overrode his instructions by claiming to have a
"special" relationship with the man whom she had never met. How
"special" can this relationship have been if she blatantly ignored
such a fundamental entreaty? Orwell's request has resulted in two
biographies; Auden has not been overlooked, nor, it seems, will
T.S. Eliot.

While a subject's opposition cannot exclude biography, it does
go a long way to create bad biography. Somerset Maugham's urge
for anonymity has resulted in a string of shoddy biographies. Because he refused to cooperate, he gave his enemies' voices more
importance because they could not be balanced by his own. Ted
Morgan's Maugham shows the unfortunate effect imbalanced material
has; Morgan gave too much space to the recital of senile activities
because the sources covered, more numerously and reliably, the
final years of the life. Whether Mr. Morgan grew to dislike Somerset Maugham or began by disliking him, the biography goes to considerable pains to support his antipathy. Perhaps Somerset Maugham
is to blame for this, but if his biographer bothered to listen and
accede to Maugham's wish, there would, of course, have been no
book at all.

If biography is history, lives of reluctant subjects ought to
be written. People like Maugham, Eliot, Auden et al. were

important because they made striking contributions to the development of letters. They are not entitled to select anonymity. They cannot commit themselves to oblivion. And, as in law, these figures have no say from the grave. But the historical contribution of <u>enforced</u> biography is dubious. The absence of vital sources helps to create bad biography, which is perhaps better than ignorance, and if readers might not enjoy fine biography of reluctant subjects, they might at least enjoy history.

Biographers have a distorted belief that their work is making a profound contribution to scholarship. Strachey knew clearly and simply what he was doing when he produced <u>Eminent Victorians</u>, <u>Queen Victoria</u>, and <u>Elizabeth and Essex</u>. He appended the briefest bibliography imaginable. Today, however, no biography is allowed publication without the heavy, ponderous, burdensome trappings of learning. A page has become little more than a veritable minefield of asterisks, footnote numbers, and square brackets. No inverted comma escapes citation, often double citation. No opinion is unbolstered by a reference. Pages of notes have become the final chapter. The standard of scholarship has become frighteningly high without producing greater clarity in the portrait. This academic precision has driven the biographer closer to his sources and made him more cautious about his opinions. Notes and cross-references exist primarily to soothe the subsequent scholar and hinder the casual, interested reader. The biographer is obliged to work harder than ever before. He is forced to carry very heavy luggage into his narrative. His job, difficult in any case, has been made more strenuous. The hours of research are testing for any stamina. The grinding solitude is unattractive. The sheer effort required to meet the exhausting demands of bibliographical excellence is unfathomable. Though one is highly sympathetic, all this is part of the biographer's job, and attention inevitably falls on the subject.

Biographers have had subtle, but effective, encouragement to lapse into Victorian hugeness in the pre-Strachey tradition of long biography. They have moved closer to their sources through the grueling process of research than to their subjects, while at the same time they know that the subject of a biography invariably sells the book, first to publishers and then to readers. The biography becomes the channel to save endangered material. The author need not concern himself with the refinements of technique, writing, or imagination because these literary devices play slim importance in the recital of facts, the revival of a reputation. When Norman Mailer's biography of Marilyn Monroe appeared, critical attention turned on the subject and not the extraordinary manner in which she was portrayed. Critics do not consider the form of biography, they merely reconsider the life.

Unwittingly, the biographer has thus been encouraged to travel where, in other circumstances, he would be wiser to avoid. His cause has been made plain, his purpose simplified. He merely retreives personalities. Literary estates have tried to make provisions

that might blunt the biographer's curiosity. Legal prohibitions have
been instituted to defuse enthusiasm. But strictures like the "closed
archive" have since become as ineffective as the pharaohs' attempts
to block post-humous intruders. Our interest in Bernard Berenson
gave one of his biographers enough courage to ignore the fact that
she did not have access to his private papers. Being Bernard Berenson
was executed without consulting papers that do exist and without
seeing papers that will, in time, be made accessible--his correspondence
with Lord Duveen. This fundamental omission gravely
flawed the book, made it unreliable, and yet it was sufficiently admired
to be rewarded with a nomination for the Pulitzer Prize. If
august bodies like the Pulitzer committee are willing to disregard
such considerations, biographers see no reason why they ought to
be the only upholders of standards. Still, the second volume of Dr.
Samuels' biography of Berenson prudently and sympathetically awaits
the end of the embargo that separates both halves of his book by
many years. The biography of Lady Ottoline Morrell appeared shortly,
too shortly, after her vast correspondence with Bertrand Russell
was accessible. This practice of sailing in the face of obstacles
which ought to pervert the course of biography is not even history,
but entertainment.

    The unfortunate equation of fame and biography has always
existed, but today biography has descended to the capacity of a servant
to press offices, public relations, and advertising. Thus biography
makes a considerable contribution to gossip, moving further
away from the limited asset of history. The number of movie-star
biographies has become legion and slightly absurd. Joan Crawford's
name is well-known and therefore she is a suitable subject for biography.
Her daughter has a vendetta against her; the form it assumed
was biography and the result was a best-seller. Norman
Mailer has returned Marilyn Monroe's name to such prominence that
she has secure entry into the new supplement of the Dictionary of
American Biography. He has even gone an ambitious distance that
permitted him to write her autobiography! Actors are nortoriously
feeble subjects for biography, but no author, save Gertrude Stein,
has shown quite how unsuitable a subject is by writing a document
the subject failed to consider. Mr. Mailer defended himself in a
mock trial transcribed for the readers of New York magazine; had
the production of the "autobiography" been a justifiable activity, he
would not have required such a florid defense.

    Few biographers have dared to be as audacious as this, and
fewer have put themselves before their subject. Perhaps Mr. Morgan's
Maugham is an implicit version of a biographer's conceit,
since he believed he knew better than Maugham. But the few authors
who have appreciated that the sources for biography are insufficient
though the subject himself sufficiently fascinating, have
entered the narrative in a supporting role. Such a duet is frank
proof of Michael Holroyd's collaboration theory. A.J.A. Symons'
The Quest for Corvo, though superseded by longer and more academically
acute biographies, is as striking as Las Meninas. Symons
draws his readers through his own progress, eloquently,

trying to unravel the tangled and often contradictory strands of evidence and debris that, once collected, collated, and interpreted, constitute a life. This is unashamedly Symons' Corvo. It possesses no pretense to be anything other than a biographer's working log. The book shows that biography is possible in face of obstacles. S.N. Behrman had no difficulty in bringing Lord Duveen to life, by means of five brilliant essays, without religious dependence on archives, without lengthy quotations.

Paradoxically, the modern approach to biography is more than just a relapse into Victorian hugeness, a return to pre-Strachey fashion complete with academic sanctity; it is overabundant proof that biographers have not strayed from the prevailing ideas of Messrs. Mason and Boswell in the earliest days of the craft: the only true index of the subject's thoughts (i.e., life) and actions is found in his letters, diaries, and other primary sources. This belief commits the biographer to years of detective work and throws the whole nature of his perspective off balance. The subject's opinions advance the biographer's. The prop of primary material does rather give a lie to any concept of objective history. If the biographer withstands the temptation to agree with his subject in all instances, readers accuse him of hating the subject. If the biographer gives way to his subject's opinions, he is accused of lacking perspective and loving his subject to the exclusion of accuracy. The elevated status of primary material (which is more or less fostered by the difficulty of obtaining it) harmfully intoxicates biography.

The biographer's reverence for letters and diaries, etc., does not remain content merely to inflate biography to unmanageable proportions, it shoves the sources of biography into unsteady independence, and effectively separates modern biography from the tradition established by Strachey who relied exclusively on secondary sources. Eight years ago Vita Sackville-West's autobiography was printed as part of <u>Portrait of a Marriage.</u> The editor, her son, was brave, and advanced the theory that she wanted it published. There were no stated instructions covering the pencil-written manuscript which for many years had happily collected dust in a locked Gladstone bag in a corner of her tower-room at Sissinghurst. There were no corrections on the sheets. The manuscript remained untouched throughout Vita Sackville-West's lifetime--some four decades after it was written. Because she had omitted to destroy it, her son assumed she wanted it published. It could not stand on its own, but it was published, thus distorting its importance, its importance to biographers.

In some cases, however, the removal of biographical sources to independent publication is a welcome addition to literature. Virginia Woolf's letters and diaries (amounting to twelve volumes) show her to be one of the finest letter-writers, equal to Mme. de Sévigné and Lady Mary Wortley Montagu, and diarists, rivalled by Creevey, Greville, Pepys, and Hickey, in any language. Even if there were not the exaggerated interest in her life and friends that produced the phenomenon of the "Bloomsbury Group," there would be substantial reason to publish so many volumes. On the other hand, the publication of three volumes of Strachey's essays (published and unpublished), spurred by the enormous interest in him sparked by Michael Holroyd's biography, is simply a miscalculation of their importance. The endless stream of F. Scott Fitzgerald's scrapings is no addition to literature. Flaubert claimed that a writer's work was all, but in these cases he was unaware that the work was elevated to prominence only after biography.

As long as the biographer sees himself as a researcher who writes rather than a writer who can research, he will be consigned to the minor importance of an historian in miniature. He will not return to the field of portraiture. He will become redundant, elbowed from his insecure perch by Ph.D. students who possess the tireless energy for research qua research and thereby merit a degree. He might always be needed to supply dates, locate lost manuscripts in attics, and grow old in libraries, yet he will not have advanced on Gosse's vague and easily satisfied requirements for his metier. He will not be able to insinuate much apart from the bland rope-ladder of chronology, and perhaps will deserve to be unemployed.

The great achievements in modern biography display the biographer's urge to bring literary skills into predominance, to advance from mere historical skills which depend on time and patience. William Murphy's life of John Butler Yeats, Prodigal Father, and Jean Strouse's Alice James are major biographies. Perhaps relatively unknown subjects afforded both biographers the luxury of seeing their lives free of reputations which needed justification or refutation. While both satisfied the historical desire to resurrect lost figures, they employed artistic and not catalog talents to bring them back to life. And both biographies prove conclusively that a fine biography is its own justification and not the fame of the subject. Both Miss Strouse and Mr. Murphy have deployed the novelist's skill to interpret and understand their subjects; they have not depended on the force, weight, and aggregate of evidence to vitalize characters.

The atmosphere which favours fame as the biographical excuse allows no space for biographies of unknown people. This climate has assisted the production of biographies that have no merit beyond the merit of the telephone directory. They might satisfy curiosity. They might fill in the areas ignored by newspapers. But these biographies have served to supplant the natural order of literary excellence--and because biographies depend on words, literary standards have a place--an excellence from which biography has surpassed the modern novel while, in an unjust, extraordinary way, exonerating itself from the one basic requirement that measures all fiction--quality. The fact that biography rests as nonfiction is no reason for it to enjoy the safety of history. It ought to be as vulnerable as fiction.

THE CASE FOR QUALITY BOOK SELECTION*

Murray L. Bob

The ultimate justification for on-demand book selection is that it gives people what they want. And what could be more democratic than that? The problem with this notion is that it overlooks the fact that consumers' tastes are largely shaped by what is available, which, in turn, is governed by economies of scale. Things, including such intellectual commodities as books, bought by many people can be produced more cheaply than those bought by a few. To render production cheap, the producer attempts to extend his market: he can do this best by catering to tastes shared by the greatest number and usually the most unsophisticated and simple-minded the taste, the wider the market. By catering to these desires, the seller creates the conditions necessary for reaping economies of scale, cheapening the product and making it accessible to more. At the same time, he discriminates against the more educated taste and pulls down the average level of public taste. We are all familiar with the blessed effects of ideological mass production on the TV wasteland. In the last decade or so, there has been a tremendous effort to extend these blessings to publishing and indeed to make publishing into a wholly-owned subsidiary of what used to be called "subsidiary rights"--the film industry, its acolytes, auxiliaries, and offshoots. This tendency, now spreading to the retailing end of the business with the emergence of giant mass marketing book chains, is finally and most inappropriately reaching libraries which, in the final analysis, have nothing to sell--a very revolutionary proposition to make, but one which I will attempt to support.

  To return to the anachronistic notion of consumer sovereignty, which is the ultimate justification for giving readers "what they want": in our age of mass production, virtually nothing gets produced that cannot be produced in the thousands. The notion of consumer sovereignty overlooks the fact that tastes are easily manipulated, influenced by suggestion, custom, example, and constantly changed, being modified by factors such as price and relative availability, not to mention advertising. If American producers spend,

---

*Reprinted by permission of the author and publisher from Library Journal, 107:16 (September 15, 1982) 1707-1710. Published by R.R. Bowker Co. (a Xerox company). Copyright © 1982 by Xerox Corporation.

let us say, $55 billion a year on bending and shaping consumer preference, it becomes clear that consumer sovereignty is largely a myth. The notion of consumer sovereignty also overlooks the question of consumer competence and education, or the lack thereof, and the fact that there are vested interests hyping--which is to say, lying--about products in order to sell more. That people exercise choice does not mean that they exercise sovereignty, which would involve choosing what is available. There are, after all, millions of consumers. Are they equally sovereign? In fact, it is the need to sell more goods, more cheaply made, for higher prices, that provides advertising with its main purpose: to promote consensus, otherwise known as conformity, to the greatest extent possible and thus achieve economies of scale. The advent of mass advertising uncoincidentally coincides with the blossoming of mass production and mass marketing. End of Lesson One of Economics 101.

Let us now descend (not ascend) to specifics--Nora Rawlinson's "Give 'Em What They Want!" which appeared in Library Journal, November 15, 1981, p. 2188. I hope to be forgiven for embarking on a detailed critique of this essay, but I do so for two reasons: 1) It is the only way to deal with the issues involved in a responsible and comprehensive way; and 2) her article is the first justification I have seen in print by one the savants of the current movement to turn public libraries into fast-food chains of the mind. Rawlinson writes: "Looking around for a tool to judge a book's usefulness, BCPL saw an old standby in a new light--circulation." But circulation is about as valuable for indicating usefulness as the number of Big Mac's, fries, and cokes sold is for indicating the general nutritional level of the population. I would insist on the exactness of the analogy. Just as the increased sale of junk foods weakens us physically, the increased circulation of schlock diminishes us intellectually.

Circulation is not a synonym for usefulness. High circulations are not necessarily useful, except perhaps to libraries seeking bigger budgets, administrators seeking to épater le bourgeois, and selectors trying to change what must be an act of judgment--selection--into a simple mechanical matter of playing the numbers. The question, after all, is always: Useful to whom? Utility, as people conversant with the concept know, is one of the most difficult terms to define. In fact, a strong case can be made that the most useful books are likely to be not those that circulate the most, but those that make the most difference in our lives.

BCPL thinks it has discovered something new, whereas it is just a matter of their doing something that librarians concerned with ideas and intellectual diversity and substance simply wouldn't have ever thought worth doing before. It is but another sorry sign of the times that a major library system would stoop that low--and that others are prepared to follow. The mission of public libraries never was and does not have to be the same as that of mass market merchandisers. We cannot--and should not--compete on that level. We need to find higher ground--for ours is an educational institution, basically--and our service is to individuals. "Finding the right book for the right person at the right time"--remember?

Since my position is certain to leave me open to the charge of elitism, perhaps I had better define that word as well. Elitism is when you hold people's capacities in contempt. As librarians, we show our contempt for people's capacities by over-emphasizing the lowest common denominator. In the book world, the lowest common denominator is very often the best seller.

What is wrong with BCPL's selection is perhaps best illustrated by the example Rawlinson chose to prove that her library system is not solely best seller oriented. She writes: "As the person responsible for buying BCPL's new adult titles, I am constantly reminded of the diversity of our patrons' reading interests. I was dubious about buying Emmanuel Leroy Ladurie's Carnival in Romans, but found that Montaillou had done quite well, and bought ten copies for the 22 branch system. Three copies were placed in one of our larger branches where they have circulated 18 times since January. Since our systemwide aim is for an annual turnover of seven, I would say this title will definitely earn its keep." Thanks a lot. Lawrence Wylie, who should know (I hope Rawlinson knows who Wylie is), called Montaillou "a new classic in both history and anthropology ... the most comprehensive historical study ever made of a community." And, by the wwy, Wylie said this in the Washington Post Book World, which Rawlinson presumably follows, if she is as interested in responding to her community as she claims to be. Reviews of Montaillou generally held it to be a masterpiece, withal charming, humane, and not at all pedantic. Indeed Ladurie, as a leader of the Annales school, has completely revised our notion of history, which also means that he and they have cast a genuinely new light on the way we must regard the present and the future.

The point is that Ladurie's books belong in libraries, whether or not the magic number of seven (why not six or eight?) circulations is reached. Public libraries owe it to patrons to make readily available those books which reshape each era's picture of the world. If Rawlinson doesn't know that or doesn't know which writers are recharting the intellectual map which enables us to find our way, how can she be the "person responsible" for buying new adult titles for a large library system? The "person responsible" cannot, by definition, be a responsible person if she lacks knowledge. In the New York Review of Books, Lawrence Stone said of Ladurie: "There cannot be much doubt that in the last twenty years Emmanuel Ladurie has been one of the most--if not the most--original, versatile, and imaginative historians in the world." This is rather like Max Planck complimenting Einstein. Isn't such informed judgment worth a little more than lucky sevens? And, by the way, it figures that truly original writings are not likely to find a wide market immediately. Is that a reason to buy such books? Or is it rather a very good reason indeed to buy them?

Since Rawlinson is so concerned with giving the taxpayers what they want, I must ask: do taxpayers want to pay a professional salary each year to a librarian to do what a page could do just as well--select books by the numbers? The real question is: what is a library for? To give taxpayers what they want--when what they want is what they are manipulated to ask for by mass media hype, huge advertising budgets, phony best seller lists, endless "fixed" look-alike TV talk show interviews? There is an issue at stake here, as fundamental as it is hoary: do libraries exist to serve a mass or to serve individuals? Are they yet another imitative and redundant instrument for massification, or is their's a unique mission, one that is not wastefully duplicative--one which serves the purposes of individuation and differentiation?

All of Rawlinson's attempts to lighten the picture only succeed in darkening it. Thus, she writes that beyond the best sellers "quality is a factor. The first consideration must always be whether a book is likely to be of interest to our patrons. This immediately eliminates esoteric and very specialized items." If one can only know what is "likely," how can one "immediately eliminate"? Haven't we learned that one man's "esoteric and very specialized" is another man's daily bread? Or that today's "esoteric" is tomorrow's commonplace? Before the Iranian hostage capture, how many books would BCPL have chosen on Iran? In fact, all that Rawlinson can really know is what is on the best seller list. What she doesn't seem to know is just how suspect, dubious, manipulated, artificial, ephemeral, and limited all such lists are and how often they have been exposed as such.

The last place we heard about giving people what they want was the American automobile industry--and look where it got them! Perhaps, instead, libraries ought to be a little more interested in giving people what they need--even if it does take some time, thought, and knowledge to determine that. Japanese automakers were able to figure out what people really needed or would need in a short time rather than what they said or thought they wanted at the moment. Popularity polls are poor guides to utility. And there is no way to avoid judgment in book selection--and selectivity. Judgment in this case requires extensive, in-depth, on-going book knowledge. BCPL preens itself on patron satisfaction. But we all know, and studies have shown, that patrons are satisfied with libraries--no matter how bad they are. Why not? Public libraries cost relatively little and impose not at all. So long as they do not charge for service, and thus are not continually abrading public sensibility by raising prices, and so long as they are not mandated--people will be generally satisfied.

Rawlinson believes that BCPL policies and practices are valid because of the small numbers of interloans compared to circulation and because her system receives more interloans than it loans. Could it be that patrons have given up trying to get the "esoteric" from BCPL? Nor does the small number of interloans compared to circulation prove anything except the obvious, which is that people will readily borrow what is immediately available. When Rawlinson says "esoteric or very specialized" titles are too expensive for the limited use they will have, she is begging several questions. It is no more true that these titles are necessarily expensive than that expensive titles are necessarily esoteric. A very much thumbed reference book in our library (which never made any best seller lists) is a little privately published book on the subject of locks for antique trunks--and it costs $3. Moreover, even the "limited" use of what is used to the limit can be very useful indeed to individuals and the community at large.

Rawlinson's hyperbole is disconcerting. It consists in setting up straw men, the more easily to demolish them. "A book of outstanding quality is not worth its price if no one will read it." No one? Well, obviously. But isn't that precisely the question--whether any one will in fact read it and over what span of time? Or, are we governed by the same immediate turnover rules of the mass book chains that have already turned book stores into fast-food chains of the mind? Indeed, which books, other than best sellers for which demand is often manufactured, can we know for sure will be read widely and immediately? The hyperbole continues: "By purchasing more and more copies, popular items were duplicated so that patrons could read the year's best sellers today, rather than next year." Next year? The best sellers? Well ... not exactly, for on the next page we read: "Making a large number of people wait four to five months for a book is not fair service." Now a year has been reduced to four to five months. But if we wanted--really wanted--to be "fair," I suspect that in the case of best sellers, it might be more true to speak of waiting, on an average, three or four weeks. Maybe I'm old-fashioned, but somehow, it does not seem an unmitigated disaster if people wait three to four weeks for a best seller--if, at the same time, staff attention and the book budget are seriously directed to nurturing intellectual diversity and anticipating real needs as opposed to pandering to the "need" for instant gratification of what is so often banal and trivial.

The religion of numbers, of which the fetish of circulation is the library world's homegrown example, has pressured some libraries into confusing their mission. It should not be that the greater the circulation the better, but the greater the range of materials, ideas, and expression the better. This is the essence of the library's commitment to intellectual freedom--to freedom of choice--and it is this, I am afraid, that BCPL's commercialization of the public library would jeopardize.

To prevent misunderstanding: we are dealing with the problem that many (not all) best sellers are mediocre at best. That doesn't mean libraries should not buy them. The question is solely as to the limits that should be observed.

I have made what I said was a revolutionary statement: libraries have nothing to sell. Because libraries do not charge for their services, by definition they have nothing to sell. Of course,

they are paid for by taxes and so you might think that they have to
sell themselves or their purposes to the appropriating jurisdictions.
But then what is their purpose? Is it to circulate the greatest possible number of items? I never heard this described as the purpose
of the library--certainly not the main purpose. So what is the purpose? Public libraries are publicly supported to serve as agencies
of informal, self-motivated, self-regulated self-education; as adjuncts
to agencies of formal education; as organized repositories of written
and other forms of the culture's communication--all of this to be
freely available to all, offering material useful or potentially useful
to all, over the longest possible time.

Public, i.e. tax, support is certainly not primarily given to
libraries in order that they act as purveyors of perishable and popular items of interest and use to only a small segment of the population, for a couple of weeks or months--no matter how much circulation is achieved. Indeed, if public authorities pay any attention whatever to circulation, it is because librarians foolishly keep talking of
only that. With light romance, formula fiction, pornography, westerns, mysteries, science fiction, and comic "books," we can always
raise our circulation--but to what end? We all know that in an
economy of scarcity, overemphasis on the purchase of certain kinds
of books, e.g. best sellers, must work to the disadvantage of other
kinds of books, of interest to other kinds of people, at other than
the present moment. Public support is not given to public libraries
as a function of the number of items they circulate, since they can
obviously circulate a lot to a few, which is wholly undemocratic.
Insofar as circulation is of concern, it should be a matter, as said
before, of circulating the widest variety of items to the most diverse
clientele, over the longest period of time--the exact opposite goal of
both the mass marketing and planned obsolescence so characteristic
of so much of the commodity economy. Because public libraries
need not charge for services, they need not focus on short-term
gains, immediate satisfaction, and the provision of the same few
things that the marketplace offers again and again, at the same time
that it offers them. Since the repository function remains basic
(contrary to myth, it never was the sole basis), such circulation as
is achieved is inherently predicated on a concept of usefulness over
time. At today's prices and in light both of what Thor is doing to
blacklists and what thieves, cheap paper, and the polluted environment do to collections, books should be regarded as an investment,
as a library's capital, and their extended use is more important
than ever. Given the popularity of expensive security systems, one
is forced to wonder why acquisition of the evanescent is important.

Since Baltimore talks incessantly of circulation, let me talk
about it, too. I think a library can have too high a circulation.
Heresy? I guess so. I would suspect something terribly wrong if
our circulation were as high as BCPL's. If you focus exclusively
on one thing, you can always achieve spectacular results--in that
one thing, and at the expense of others. What of the other functions
of a library? What of other measures of service? And what of
all the inherent improbabilities, absurdities, inconsistencies, and
inaccuracies of circulation counts:

1. Some of the most useful and popular items in a library's collection may not circulate: e.g. reference books, browsing items, newspapers, current journals.
2. Circulation statistics are more questionable than is generally supposed; the same items are not counted the same way by different libraries.
3. The period of time for which an item circulates can make an enormous difference in the circulation count. The quickest way to increase a library's circulation is to contract the loan period.
4. Physical location, hours of opening, and age of facility are other factors that have more to do with circulation than the collection.
5. A "no fines" or "low" fines policy can affect circulation, as can a friendly or unfriendly staff.
6. Perhaps the most important factor in circulation is the educational background of the library's users. "Real" readers will read almost anything they can get their hands on. On the other hand, buy all the copies of best sellers you want and see how much difference that will make in a low-reading, inner-city branch library. It is easy enough to get big circulation out of the "information-rich." What of the information poor, whose needs may be the greatest? Is it best sellers that are the most needed materials for the disadvantaged? "Best seller libraries" may be circulating ever more books to the same number and kind of people. If that is not wasteful, what is? Annual circulation increases without annual increases of new borrowers amounts to little. Registration statistics, although notoriously as unreliable as circulation statistics, are every bit as important, and outreach is as important as inreach.
7. And then there are the problems consequent upon equating circulation with utility: we have no measures to tell us the percentage of books that circulate but are left unread or partially read, much less the percentage of those circulated that are misunderstood. Can a book which is circulated but not read or understood be useful? It may be useful to a library building its circulation statistics, but does that make it socially useful?
8. Studies have shown over and over again that one major reason that people don't find what they want in a library is "simply" because books are so often misshelved, stolen, uninventoried, overdue, etc. You can gain quite a bit on the problem of inadequate circulation by taking care of some of these problems-- without touching your principles and methods of selection.
9. Circulation is not the same as either use or activity. The latter measure is likely to be better, because it is more comprehensive and the truth, after all, is

in the whole. If you feel you must use numbers to persuade, try an automatic counter. Far more people enter and variously use the library than borrow materials from it.

10. Whether increased circulation is to a growing, stable, or declining population is a matter of some import. Of course, per capita circulation is supposed to take care of this. Experienced librarians know about the vagaries of per capitas, especially when these are used for comparative purposes: are your per capitas measured in the same way as the library you are comparing yourself with? Is the service area, the city, the county, the surrounding areas? Does your location enable you to draw from a wider area than your "competitor," irrespective of any other factor? How current are your numbers? How current are his? Obviously, my faith in numbers is something less than unbounded. The final truth about statistics may have been stated by Mark Twain.

Studies have shown again and again that patrons select their books primarily by browsing. What is available is what they take out. If we restrict the range of what is available, we do a disservice to the free circulation of the widest range of ideas, information, materials. Nor does the possibility of inter-library loan remedy this. To think so would be to equate possibility with actuality. In any event, interloans are, typically, one percent or less of circulation.

If we fetishize the current and popular at a time when national bookstore chains dedicated to the quickest turnover of the smallest number of titles proliferate, when the Thor decision jeopardizes the maintenance of healthy publisher's backlists, when book prices are skyrocketing beyond the means of many who are suffering from an economic decline, and when the emphasis on blockbusters threatens to eclipse midlist books--then we are not attending to our business, which is not the same as that of commercial entities. If there are good books and libraries don't buy them, who will? Libraries have a responsibility to ideas, to nurturing, sustaining, preserving, and making readily available the intellectual capital of our society to anyone who may want or need it, now or in the future. Collections are built to serve over time. By doing that we show responsibility to the citizens who pay for the service.

I worried when I read Charlie Robinson's statement that "whereas Baltimore used to buy 15,000 titles annually, it has cut that figure to 7,000. I suspect we could get that figure down to 3,000 ... and that's still a lot of titles."

Well, some people would think 300 is a lot.

THE PUBLIC LIBRARY AND THE ALTERNATIVE PRESS*

Celia Minoughan

Introduction

Censorship in libraries is a neglected issue within the British library profession. This is apparent from a comparison of the large volume of writing on the subject which has emerged from the United States with the scant treatment the issue has received in Britain. The only statement by the Library Association was made in 1963 and has not been updated. It stated:

> The function of a library service is to provide, as far as resources allow, all books, periodicals, etc, other than the trivial in which its readers claim legitimate interest. In determining what is a legitimate interest, the librarian can rely on one guide only--the law of the land. If the publication of such material has not incurred penalties under the law it should not be excluded from libraries on any moral, political, religious or racial ground alone, to satisfy any sectional interest. The public are entitled to rely on libraries for access to information and enlightenment upon every field of human experience and activity. Those who provide library services should not restrict access except by standards which are endorsed by law [1].

This statement dodges such questions as whether the law should be changed which became obvious in 1978 when the Williams Committee asked the Library Association for submission of evidence. There has been little else published in Britian to compare with the literature in the United States which adopts a more progressive point of view, eg The Library Bill of Rights adopted in 1948 and the more recent parallel document The librarian's intellectual freedom creed [2] both take a more positive view of the library's role vis-a-vis intellectual freedom: the librarian should actively defend it. As the Library Bill of Rights states: "Libraries should co-operate with all persons concerned with resisting abridgement of freedom of expression." This active defence of intellectual freedom is lacking in

---

*Reprinted by permission of the author and publisher from Librarians for Social Change, 10:2 (1982) 7-30. John L. Noyce, Publisher, Brighton, E. Sussex, U.K.

British library literature except in the only British monograph on the subject by A. H. Thompson, Censorship in public libraries in the U.K. during the twentieth century [3], and the regular exposé of incidents of censorship in the journal Librarians for Social Change. As Thompson says:

> Problems and inconsistencies will arise until there is a firm commitment to intellectual freedom by all librarians and until legislation makes it clear beyond doubt that censorship by library authority edict is contrary not only to the public library ideal but also to the law.

This investigation focuses on the attitudes of public librarians to the 'alternative press' which has been defined by Hudson as "Periodicals which are produced on a voluntary basis and/or which portray unconventional attitudes to life" [5]. This is also an area which lacks examination in library literature with only a few periodical articles to bridge the gap. Standard monographs on serials librarianship do not give the 'alternative press' much attention. Although Donald Davison in The periodicals collection makes the useful comment that in the past these periodicals have almost totally escaped the attention of librarians and that the legal deposit regulations have been largely unsuccessful in bringing this important material into the deposit libraries [6], other standard works such as Ross Bourne's Serials Librarianship [7] lack any comment at all. The journal Librarians for Social Change has established a reputation for providing a radical point of view in librarianship and, most recently published an article entitled The provision of alternative materials in public libraries [8] which introduces the subject, suggesting that conservatism leads public libraries to exclude such materials from their collections and then explores ways in which these materials can be obtained by libraries. An anthology of articles which appeared in LFSC during 1972-5 published under the title Censorship in libraries [9] and John Noyce's Censorship in public libraries [10] both contain examples of public libraries attitudes to the alternative press. Assistant Librarian have also published articles on the alternative press, eg The alternative press in 1977 [11] and Out of the mainstream: notes on suppliers of minority and 'alternative' literature and information [12]. A recent dissertation The development of the women's movement in England since 1969 and the consequent rise in demand for women's information, and the implications for librarians [13] deals with the issue from a feminist point of view. These observations need to be followed up by more systematic studies of individual library authorities' attitudes and policies towards 'alternative' material. The case studies of Newcastle-upon-Tyne and Gateshead library authorities included in this investigation are an attempt to do this for a limited area of the North-East. This investigation is set within the context of the development of the alternative press, in particular in the North-East.

Critique of the Commercial Press

Providing a different picture of national and local events and social and political trends to that in the commercial press is the main motivating factor in the production of alternative newspapers and magazines. Criticisms of the content of the commercial press have centred around two issues. Firstly, selection: what is selected and what are the critera in selection?; and secondly, around objectivity in presentation: how does the selection made and the way it is written reflect the real world?

The Selection Process

The Marxist critique of the commercial press explains the exclusion of certain types of news items--those dangerous to the status quo--as being rooted in the ownership of the media by such interests: in all advanced capitalist societies such ownership has become increasingly centralised. In this model the media and journalists are working directly in the interests of the owners whose interests are in turn quite opposed to the public at large and to any true presentation of events in the world. While this model is too simplistic in its understanding of the conception of news, the opposite view suffers from a similar deficiency: the free market model also regards news as a 'natural' category of events, although in this case instead of manipulation of news, market forces are meant to ensure objective reporting and a free media. While both of these models have accurate elements they are too simplistic and other factors in the newsgathering process must be considered besides that of ownership.

The first process of journalism--how the reporter discovers news items--is also important. Unsought information from casual sources is rare and because of the pressure on journalists, caused by lack of time, they rely largely on a 'beat' of sources who very often prepackage news. Routine news sources are only too happy to offer their services to journalists. Thus, politicians provide advance copies of speeches; press conferences are scheduled at convenient hours so that reporters may meet deadlines; press agents write news releases in story format and media contacts are assigned the job of working with journalists who cover their agencies. By adopting the schemes of interpretation and relevance employed within these agencies, journalists tend not to challenge an agency's idealisation of what is happening. Without time or resources to do any investigation journalists have little opportunity to follow up on their doubts about officially formulated versions of events, and, therefore, tend to assume that a bureaucracy functions normally, ie according to its own idealisation. It is not so much that the media convinces news consumers that all is well with the present social and political order, but that this type of routine news leaves the existing political order intact, even at the same time as it enumerates its flaws. The governmental-bureaucratic structure itself cannot be doubted as a whole without radically upsetting the routines of journalism. The ideological character of news and its legitimating function need not be the result of 'conspiracies' of newspaper and magazine owners.

Many of the alternative newspapers and magazines specialize

in investigative journalism, eg Duncan Campbell in New Statesman has long exposed examples of the dangers of nuclear waste in its transportation around the country, and also of the dangers of the development of computer data banks in their use by police and others in the state, to the privacy of the individual. In the North-East the best example of this type of journalism is by Durham Street Press, eg the article early in 1982 on County Hall plans to axe three out of four day centres for the elderly and handicapped and the closure of geriatric hospitals and homes throughout the region, in spite of the fact that present day care falls well below the level recommended by the DHSS [14]. They have also highlighted the education cuts in the locality and predicted the closure of Durham pits [15]. The paper also has a regular column 'Telling it like it isn't,' a regular look at the local media.

There are other factors which inhibit the journalist both in the commercial and alternative press alike. These are the threats posed by the laws of contempt and libel, and the Official Secrets Act.

Libel: This law applies to defamatory words published and broadcast. The idea that the law protects innocent individuals from an all-powerful Press is a myth. Libel laws only protect those with enough resources for a costly legal action since legal aid cannot be obtained to initiate or defend a libel action. It is, therefore, a serious restriction to freedom of expression. Newspapers may choose not to publish a news story which they know to be true but could not substantiate if challenged (perhaps because a source of information would not wish to be identified). It particularly restricts small alternative newspapers and magazines specialising in investigative journalism, many of which survive on shoe-string budgets. Libel also applies to wholesalers and distributors, although not merely to the display of materials so libraries cannot be prosecuted, although an item may be removed from the shelves if it is 'sub judice.' This is, for example, the procedure at Newcastle-upon-Tyne City Libraries.

Contempt: This law is designed to eliminate any interference with the administration of justice: from disobeying a court order to attempting to influence a jury. As far as the press is concerned, once legal proceedings have begun, public discussion of the case is forbidden so that nothing is published which would prejudice a fair trial. This is open to abuse since court proceedings are sometimes started to delay or even prevent press comment.

Official Secrets Act (1911): This is superficially concerned with spying and national security but much 'official' information has no bearing on either of these. Sometimes political interests are confused with the national interest and the government may use the act to withhold information which may be politically embarassing. The danger for journalists lies not only in publishing 'secrets' but also in obtaining them. The 1978 A.B.C. Secrets Trial when Duncan Campbell, Crispin Aubrey (two journalists), and John Berry (an ex-soldier) faced charges under the Act for the compilation and publication of information on Signals Intelligence which monitors foreign communications including commercial, private and diplomatic messages contrary to international law. Although the journalists were cleared and Berry given a suspended prison sentence, and renewed pressure brought to bear to reform the Act by introducing 'freedom of information' legislation similar to that already passed in the United States, no reform has been achieved to date.

D-Notices: These were established in 1912 to guide the press away from the pitfalls of the Official Secrets Act. They cover the main areas of defence concern and although they have been recently revised by John Nott, Defence Secretary, and reduced from twelve to eight, the Commons Defence Committee which inquired into the system in 1980 said that it had failed to fulfill the role for which it was originally created and that it hardly serves any useful purpose.

All of these four pieces of legislation hamper the journalist in investigative journalism and so affect the selection of material for publication.

Presentation of News

The models of presentation used by the press are also an important area for consideration in this analysis of the craft of journalism. It is here that accusations of bias have particularly been levelled: that the papers' models of social reality, including both human behaviour and political ideology, are conservative. This has been demonstrated in studies of both the national and provincial press. An example in the national press is the treatment of militant mass demonstrations. In an article on this subject in The manufacture of news Graham Murdock made a case study of the mass demonstration against the Vietnam War in London on 27th October 1968 [16].

These events were a point of transition for the British Left: young radicals were moving increasingly away from the 'reformism' of the Labour Left and of the Peace Movement and towards the more radical perspectives, developed by the international student and anti-war movements. (This is a parallel development to that in the Labour Left today). Over a month and a half before the event The Times carried a front-page story headed "Militant Plot feared in London", describing how detectives had discovered that 'militant extremists' planned to use the main march as a cover for attacks on police and public buildings. From this point onwards the press led the public to expect violence and in stressing the expected participation of students to the neglect of other groups involved, the event became defined as essentially part of a passing fashion, rather than arising out of permanently structured conflicts of interests. The newsworthiness of the event was identified with the expectation that 'militant students' led by 'foreign agitators' would use the cover of the main march to engage in extensive street fighting with the police and to attack police buildings. The main march itself was emptied

of all its radical political content and defined as a performance--
bizarre, but within the framework of consensus politics. On the day
there were relatively few incidents of confrontation between the police
and the demonstrators but having committed themselves to a news
image based on this expectation, the newspapers proceeded as though
the event had been characterised by street fighting, eg (The Times
headline "Police win Battle of Grosvenor Square as 6,000 are repelled," and the Daily Express: "Fringe fanatics foiled at big demonstration--what the bobbies faced." All the papers except The Times
featured on the front page a photograph of a policeman apparently
being held by one of the demonstrators and kicked in the face by
another.

    The preoccupation in the media with the reporting of events
rather than the presentation of social, political and economic trends
which take longer to unfold has several important consequences.
Firstly, that news ignores the underlying content of situations; secondly, these situations will appear to be short-lived and transitory;
and thirdly, in the absence of any analysis of the underlying situation, events are presented as being 'caused' by the intervention of
natural forces or by the immediately preceding actions of particular
individuals or groups. Radical political activity appears therefore
as essentially ephemeral and confined to a small group of outsiders
rather than as the product of historical and continuing inequalities
in the distribution of power and wealth.

    To consider now the provincial press, a recent study [17] concludes that it too is an essentially conservative medium. Broadly
speaking, it endorses capitalistic assumptions and the Protestant
ethic. It strongly upholds family and institutional life; it demands
discipline in relation to penology and education; and values conventions and traditions. This study indicated that about 40 percent of
evening newspapers and up to 90 percent of weeklies take a non-partisan position, although these are likely to uphold the conservative
assumptions outlined above. Only a very small minority of the commercial press support a radical ideology. In theory minority opinions can be voiced through the correspondence columns, but in practice editors do screen out particular categories of correspondence
on the grounds that they lack wide public interest. Letters expressing extreme political views from both right and left would probably
be excluded therefore.

    In Newcastle the two Thomson newspapers the Journal and the
Evening Chronicle are examples of this 'conservative' type of paper.
A survey of the treatment of the Labour Party by these papers in
the last six months indicates this. One of the issues which has attracted the most attention in the discussion of the Labour Party in
the media is the position of the Militant Tendency within the party.
It is not that Militant supporters are not interviewed or space given
to their comments. It is in the presentation of attitudes towards
Militant in other sections of the Labour Party that the articles can
be criticised. The views of the right wing of the party are given
space, but not those of the centre left. In the Evening Chronicle,

for example, the following comments are typical in their presentation
of non-Militant opinion: "The great bulk of Labour supporters are
totally opposed to them, ie Militant and their activities which have
undermined the Party. They appear to have vast financial reserves
and more full-time organisers than the Labour Party itself", and an
emotive statement: "I think there is an element of the looney
Left" [18]. In February 1982 "Labour Party and Militant: a Journal Inquiry" also investigated the issue and a similar presentation
of non-Militant opinion can be observed. While one of the Militant
organisers, Dave Cotterill, is given space for comments, other opinions reported are from the right wing of the party as before, thus
emphasising any divisions of views within the party, eg "I think they
should be thrown out of the party ... They are just destroying the
Labour Party. They are trying to turn it into the Socialist Workers
Party. The SWP is already formed. Why don't they join that and
test the electoral strength there? That's the general consensus at
Fawdon." The reporter also commented on Fawdon branch: "the
branch had suffered as a result of Militant influence there" [19].
(my emphasis). Neither of these articles gave any indication that
the centre left of the party do not actively oppose Militant as the
right wing does, nor of the fact that Militant supporters have been
very hard working in Newcastle in building up membership of the
party and are often in the majority at ward and General Management
Committee meetings because other sections of the party are not so
diligent in attendance. In East Newcastle Labour Party, for example,
right wing members in control have allowed membership to decline.
Byker Phoenix have sought to expose the situation in their local Labour Party, eg indicating when councillors are not attending council
meetings and holding surgeries. This side of the story is not generally presented in the commercial press.

Explaining the conservative nature of the commercial press
is more complicated, therefore, than merely pointing to the ownership of the press by interests whose advantage lies in support of the
status quo. The processes involved in journalism described above
are equally important in explaining conservatism and bias. It is
very often this misrepresentation by the commercial press which
leads individuals and groups to publish their own newspaper or magazine. The next two sections describe the development of the alternative press and alternative methods of production and distribution.

The Development of the Alternative Press

The Nineteenth Century

Current alternative newspapers and magazines have their roots in
the mass popular papers which emerged at the beginning of the nineteenth century. These independent papers, eg Poor Man's Guardian
and the Chartist Northern Star, were, however, increasingly pushed
to the margins of journalism, as the commercial national press, fi-
nanced by large-scale advertising, made its impact at the end of the
nineteenth century. As control of popular journalism passed into the

hands of successful large-scale entrepreneurs who alone now could reach a majority of the public quickly, attractively and cheaply (prices were one-quarter of what they had been), on a national scale, the contradictions within popular culture were deepened: those publishing and printing these papers became separate from or opposed to the people whom this popular journalism served. Popular culture has always been an uneasy mixture of two very different elements: the maintenance of an independent identity, often associated with political radicalism and movements for social change; and secondly, ways of adapting from a socially and economically disadvantaged position to a dominant social order, finding relief inside it.

The 1960s

Since the nineteenth century the alternative press has remained on the fringes of the publishing industry with some popular successes. The mid-1960s, however, marked a significant breakthrough: a new wave of the alternative press emerged as a part of a whole new cultural wave, involving a regeneration of radical and innovative work in writing, music, fringe theatre, cinema and video. Technological, economic, political, and cultural factors combined to account for this new development of the alternative press. The introduction of the relatively cheap and simple process of offset litho printing made it possible for groups of ordinary people to raise the capital necessary to start their own papers, a situation which had not operated since the nineteenth century. The economic affluence of this period meant that state benefits were more than adequate as a living wage, enabling people to be involved in 'lifestyle politics' more easily--squatting, claimants unions, etc. Middle and upper class involvement in the independent and alternative press meant that inherited wealth was often used to launch new publications. <u>Oz</u>, <u>IT</u> and <u>Frendz</u> are examples of these new papers of the 1960s.

At the same time the birth of community organising in the 1960s--which provided a focus for the non-aligned left--and the initiation of locally-based projects on such social problems as housing and welfare, particularly in inner-city areas. These new forms of political activity needed to develop new methods of communication and looked towards the alternative newspaper. During 1967/68 the first local radical papers were founded--in Cambridge, Bristol and Glasgow. By 1969 there were over 10 and by 1975 over 60 [20]. The state was not altogether outside the development of community organising, eg the Community Development Project, funded by the Home Office, was set up in 1969 to identify the primary problems of decaying inner-city areas. The closure of the CDP came in 1976 just as the radical implications of its work became clear: the project teams found the basis of urban decay to lie in fundamental national, social and economic inequalities and were beginning to encourage the development of radical groups in the areas which were mounting opposition to state policy.

This growth of community organising is a significant development in the history of the alternative press as it led to the increasing involvement of 'professionals' in their production: Community Arts, STEP, Inner-City Development, Community Development workers and librarians. The involvement of these--mainly middle-class--community workers had led to a tension in the production of these papers: that is, whether they are being produced 'for' the people or 'by' the people, since one of the main aims of this type of self-publishing has been to demystify the process of producing a newspaper or magazine and to give local people the opportunity of producing something for and about themselves. At the same time, however, many of the local alternative newspapers have had problems in attracting local residents to make a longer-term commitment particularly in the production, printing and distribution process. Fellin' Times and Byker Phoenix are examples of recent papers which have experienced this type of problem. In many cases when there was a choice between closing down a paper or continuing through the involvement of community workers, the latter path has been chosen, eg Fellin' Times had the back-up of the Town Teacher organisation and Byker Phoenix had the assistance of community arts workers. In fact, both of these papers were closed down eventually when renewed attempts to involve ordinary members of the community in the running of the papers failed, since both papers felt that community involvement was one of their principal aims.

The Workers' Writers Movement

A parallel growth to the development of national and local alternative newspapers and magazines has been the Workers' Writers Movement (leading to the establishment of the Federation of Workers' Writers and Community Publishers in 1976), whose aim is to "further the cause of working-class writing and community publishing by all means possible, including workshop organization, local and national performance, fund-raising, and liaison with such persons and bodies as may be appropriate" [21]. There are four types of groups: writers' workshops, people's history groups, literacy study groups and community publishing groups. Examples of the last category are Centerprise in Hackney, London, Bristol Broadsides, and People's Publications and Strong Words in the North-East. People's Publications have published Our Streets, Our Lives which is a collection of poems and articles by young people from the Stanhope Street (Arthur's Hill) area of Newcastle; and also No Regrets and To Struggle is to live, both working-class memoires. The criteria for selection of material is not just a local, working-class perspective, but they aim to publish material pointing out the wrongs in society and making some attempt to suggest what can be put right: a socialist perspective. The FWWCP have had protracted disagreement with the Arts Council who will not give financial assistance to the Federation through its Literature Panel, and would only give grants to individual member groups through Community Arts whom the Federation regard as a secondary tier of the Arts Council: "... a sort of jumble sale or bargain basement, where prices and distinctions are slashed, where everything is possible and all mixed up as long as it's cheap" [22]. The Arts

Council Literature Panel judged Federation writing "... of little, if any, solid literary merit" [23]. A member of the Federation countered this comment in this way:

> How long can we divorce 'literary merit' from the life and people that literature should represent and transform? Can we accept that the great majority of working men and women should rely on those who love and leave them to write on their behalf, while what they write themselves is disregarded? Can we accept that there is just one Literature and set standards for all, and these should be fixed by a little minority, who, in refining their writing skills to the standards of a relatively leisured class, remove themselves from the life and language of the majority? We want the chance to develop our own standards, standards possible to people who work long, un-intellectual, ill-paid hours; to people whose intelligence cannot be simply highjacked from the circumstances--the scope and the limitations--they share with most of the un-Literary public. These circumstances may not favour the codes and constructs of conventional Literature, but they may evoke new forms more fitted to a content that Literature largely ignores [24].

The current state of the alternative press

Alternative newspapers and magazines should not be regarded as a separate development from the type of working-class publishing represented by the FWWCP. Many community newspapers are subsidised through the publication of more commercially viable working-class memoires in pamphlet form, eg Aberdeen People's Press' other publications include Aberdeen in the General Strike and Fascism in Aberdeen: street politics in the 1930s. The alternative press takes a variety of forms and the subject coverage is wide-ranging: this is indicated by the variety of categories and titles listed below, both national and local publications, commercially and voluntarily produced.

National

Politics/Current Affairs: Periodicals relating current affairs from a political or party political perspective which is usually radical or socialist. Monthly publications include Marxism Today, New Socialist Standard. Weeklies include New Statesman, Labour Weekly, Socialist Worker and Militant.

Unconventional lifestyle: periodicals portraying unconventional attitudes to life and society, usually of a minority group, eg alternative approaches to production and the consumption of the world's resources, such as Vegetarian, Ecologist, Undercurrents, and Practical Self-Sufficiency; and those concerning sexual politics including Gay

News, Spare Rib, and Scarlet Women (the journal of the socialist current of the women's liberation movement).

Pressure groups: those publications from campaigns putting pressure on government for a change in policy and legislation, and more generally to change public opinion, eg the Peace Tax Campaign Newsletter, and Sanity from the nuclear disarmament movement.

Local

Newsletters of national groups: of both political parties, eg Northern Notes (from Newcastle North Labour Party), and from pressure groups, eg Jesmond C.N.D. Bulletin and Peace Action Newcastle Newsletter.

Unconventional lifestyle: local magazines on sexual politics include Women Wise and Manchester Women's Paper. A new magazine Northern Lights covers issues including ecology and the environment, natural health and astrology, in the context of events and developments in the North of England.

Community newspapers: these may be politically neutral, 'radical' or explicitly socialist, and covering either a borough/county eg Tyneside Street Press (now defunct), Durham Street Press, Leeds Other Paper, Hackney Peoples Press and East End News; or secondly those which cover smaller towns and suburbs of cities, eg Cramlington Orbit, Byker Phoenix, Kenton Keyhole and Blakelaw Roundabout, all in the North-East [25].

What's On Sheets and Magazines: some community newspapers include these to help sell their papers, eg Durham Street Press, often emphasising 'radical' meetings and events. Others include Pulse (Newcastle), City Limits and Time Out (London), which also include articles on current affairs from a radical standpoint.

The Library and Community Publishing

Although public libraries have been involved in publication of local history material for some time, involvement in other kinds of community publishing is a more recent development. The increased emphasis on community involvement in the profession has led to libraries adopting more positive attitudes to supporting community ventures and even initiating projects themselves, eg the support Gateshead Libraries have given to Fellin' Times and the financial and organisational backing they gave to get off the ground a magazine for and by local young people. Peter's Scott's article about Gateshead Libraries in Fellin' Times is a good example of the way libraries can improve their image by their involvement in local alternative papers.

Your local library is alive and well

From Fellin' Times

This short extract is aimed at dispelling a few of the myths about your local library and at letting you know what we are getting up to these days. Like everyone else we are changing with the times. Gone are the days of middle-aged spinsters and bespectacled academics who jump down your throat for opening your mouth and who think your presence in the library is an intrusion. Gone are the days of dusty old Victorian buildings that were so cold and damp that you did not dare hang around too long in case you contracted something. Libraries nowadays are bright and clean places and the staff are a friendly, welcoming bunch, some serious but mostly zany who are there to provide you with the best service they can offer. We like to feel that we belong to the community just as much as the local pub or corner shop and we want to play our part in making the community we serve that little bit nicer to live in. We are not just in business to lend dusty outdated tomes from the shelves-- we can now offer you a whole range of services not dreamed of by our ancestors, anything from televisions to talking books, and they hardly cost you a penny.

And that's not all. Libraries in Gateshead, and that includes Felling, Leam Lane and Pelaw, are becoming increasingly involved in community activities. We like to contribute to, for example, local carnivals etc., or go out and give talks to local societies and we have the considerable backing of the whole library system to help us. You see, for too long librarians have been content to sit on their backsides in their comfy office chairs and expect people to come flooding through the doors, not realising perhaps that what they were offering in terms of books and services was just not what local people wanted and not understanding why only 30% of the population at the most could be bothered to make the trip. Well in Gateshead we have decided to change from the traditional library image. We are beginning to offer services which interest some of the other 70% of non-users and instead of sitting back we are going out into the community and making our presence known to more people. Books are no longer the be-all and end-all of our work and we like to think that nowadays you can come into your local branch and have most of your questions answered. If we cannot answer them then we should be able to point you to someone who can.

Just to illustrate, you might like to know that the Libraries Dept. is organising an interbranch 5-a-side competition for children aged 11 and under to take place at Gateshead Stadium on Sunday, March 15th (afternoon). So why not go along and support your local library team.

Watch this space for other thrilling future events!

P.S.: You can buy your copy of Fellin' Times from us too.

Peter Scott, Branch Librarian, Leam Lane.

Communication and Education   181

Alternative Production and Distribution

Collective Production

This is mainly a feature of local alternative publications which are usually run by volunteers. Collective production includes the rotation of tasks to reduce the 'division of labour', to use the Marxist term. Editing will either be done collectively as at <u>Durham Street Press</u>, or by individuals taking turns as editor as in <u>Cramlington Orbit</u> where the editor changes every three years and an open editorial meeting assists in making editorial decisions. This is an attempt to democratise the production process, with the emphasis on the involvement of ordinary people, and in so doing to demystify the journalistic process. Many of the nationally produced alternative periodicals are run on similar lines to commercial publications, with full-time workers and the division of tasks, although <u>Spare Rib</u> is a good example of one which is run on collective lines.

Printing

Alongside the growth of alternative publishing has been the parallel development of alternative printing organisations such as Tyneside Free Press Workshop and Rochdale Alternative Press. In the main it is local alternative newspapers and magazines with smaller print runs of up to 3,000 who use this type of 'free press'. Those with larger print runs normally use commercial printers since alternative printers, most of whom are smaller localised ventures, cannot cope with larger print runs like that of <u>Spare Rib</u> whose circulation is 25,000. Feminist print shops, mainly all-women organisations, have developed side by side with the other alternative presses, eg Moss Side Community Press (Manchester), Onlywomen Press (London) and Sheffield Women's Printing Co-op.

Tyneside Free Press Workshop, typical of this type of alternative press, was established c.1972 with involvement and help from the local Trades Council, WEA, Benwell Community Development Project and Friends of the Earth. Their policy has all along been that of a non-profit-making co-operative, doing work mainly for non-commercial bodies, particularly community associations, although there is a 'grey area': commercial organisations such as wholefood shops for whom they will work. They are politically neutral, but they will print nothing which is racist or sexist, and each individual has the right to refuse to handle an individual piece of work. At first all their three full-time and other part-time workers were unpaid, although subsequent funding from the Arts Council, Inner-City Partnership Fund and Manpower Services Commission enabled them to extend their equipment and pay wages to their full-time workers. They are associated with several small local publishing groups, eg Iron Press, Bloodaxe Books, People's Publications, and Strong Words. <u>Byker Phoenix</u> and <u>Workers Chronicle</u> are among the local alternative newspapers printed at Tyneside Free Press.

Distribution

Since 1946 there have been three Royal Commissions on the Press but none have dealt with the problems of access and distribution, even though the latest (1977) had as its terms of reference:

> To enquire into the factors affecting the maintenance of the independence, diversity and editorial standards of newspapers and periodicals and the public's freedom of choice of newspapers and periodicals, nationally, regionally and locally [26].

In 1978 another government body, the Monopoly and Mergers Commission, looked into the wholesaling of newspapers and periodicals. But not only did it exclude from its terms of reference "refusal to supply particular newspapers or periodicals, by reason of their content or publisher", it also concluded that "the monopoly structures which exist ... do not ... operate against the public interest" [27].

The reluctance of mainstream distributors to handle alternative material indicates that this issue does merit inquiry and that the best solution to the problem would be state intervention to make it mandatory for wholesalers to distribute periodicals of any size circulation regardless of content, as has been the case in France since 1947.

Currently, however, there are two routes to establishing the general availability of the alternative press:

- by breaking through into the commercial distribution and wholesale network

- by setting up a comprehensive alternative wholesaling and distribution network for the alternative press. Scottish and Northern, and Southern Distribution, two alternative distribution co-operatives, are a partial answer to this.

The first route is extremely difficult to achieve. There have been few (and often temporary) successes in infiltrating the commercial system. Spare Rib was until recently distributed nationally by Moore Harness, a large, independent, London-based distributor. When Moore Harness developed financial troubles in 1979 Spare Rib lost £5,000, although they were then approached by a much larger organization, Comag, through whom the magazine is now distributed. Gay News is also distributed nationally through independent wholesalers. It did go through Smith's and Menzies for over two years but they both dropped the paper around the time when Gay News was taken to court on a blasphemy charge. Camerawork, Undercurrents and The Leveller enjoyed a very short relationship with Surridge Dawson (third in the league of leading wholesalers) but were axed after one issue because of an offending article in Undercurrents on cannabis. Private Eye, originally distributed by Moore Harness and now distributed through its own set-up, has never been taken by Smiths or Menzies. The significance of being accepted or rejected by W.H.

Smith, John Menzies or Surridge Dawson is that these three leading wholesalers have a stranglehold on the distribution market, with 69% control of the magazine market in England and Wales, and in Scotland John Menzies alone have 93% of the Scottish magazine market. The difference that distribution by Smiths and Menzies can make is illustrated by the cases of New Socialist and Marxism Today, who have both been accepted recently. Marxism Today has trebled its circulation from 7,500 to 22,000 after acceptance by Smith and Menzies. New Socialist are able to sell three-fifths of their print run through newsagents thanks to acceptance by Smiths and Menzies, who have also been able to expand their circulation. Wholesalers' influence also extends to an important say in where new newsagents can be set up. Before opening a newsagent an agreement has to be made with the local wholesale house to supply them and if the firm will not agree then the newsagent cannot open.

The reluctance of wholesalers to handle alternative material, both national and local, is mainly due to the law of libel, since they can be sued along with authors and publishers. This is no problem with large newspapers and magazines who have enough resources to make up any loss suffered by wholesalers as a result of libel action. Small periodicals can give no such guarantee. Libel is not the only concern of wholesalers, however. They are much more sensitive to what they regard as offensive in radical magazines and newspapers than, for example, Britain's top-selling tabloid newspapers such as the Sun, which no doubt offend many people but are worth the trouble financially compared with the small papers which they regard as more trouble than they are worth.

Are alternative distributors the answer then? Publications Distribution Co-operative was set up in 1976 by a group of radical publishers and after considerable expansion split up into two autonomous co-operatives on a geographical basis: Scottish and Northern Book Distribution Co-op, based in Manchester and Edinburgh, and P.D.C. London. The latter works as two groups: Southern Distribution for books and pamphlets in London and the South, and Full-Time Distribution for periodicals across the country. While they reach alternative bookshops (of which there are 150) plus wholefood shops, newsagents are a much harder market to break into. During the period 1977/78 P.D.C. were distributing to well over 100 newsagents and selling nearly 1,000 copies of some titles, but this is just scratching the surface since there are nearly 40,000 newsagents in the UK. The majority of newsagents are supplied by Smiths and Menzies for most of their titles, and find out about new titles through their wholesalers and also by trade journals such as Retail Newsagent. Newsagents also face the threat of libel as well as the possibility of complaints and even attacks on premises if they stock politically contentious material.

For locally based alternative newspapers and magazines the alternative distributors described above are of little use but organising their own distribution system can be time-consuming and expensive. Supplying individual newsagents involves collecting unsold copies

and money from sales. In addition to this obstacle, independent
newsagents are on the decline, and their takeover by large chains
means that individual managers have little say in what they stock.
Many chains are owned by the local commercial press, eg Ricafeg
newsagents, owned by the Liverpool Daily Post and Echo, were forbidden to sell Liverpool Free Press (for several years the biggest-
selling local alternative newspaper) which regularly attacked the Post
and Echo. Other towns with similar publisher-owned chains include
Birmingham, Bristol, Portsmouth, Peterborough, Bournemouth and
Wolverhampton. There is opposition too from the National Federation of Retail Newsagents, whose secretary, Ken Peters, wrote an
article in 1979 warning his members that if they sold radical papers
like Nottingham Voice they risked being sued for libel, quoting possible costs of £5,000 [28].

One result of these problems is that local alternative papers
have difficulty in reaching a working-class audience. It is much
easier to reach the politically committed middle classes who do not
anyway suffer to any great extent from the inequalities many alternative papers exist to expose. The only community newspaper which
succeeds in the North-East in achieving blanket distribution is Cramlington Orbit which is delivered with The Leader, the local advertising sheet to every home in the town. The Orbit, however, takes a
neutral line politically and its criticisms of the local council are not
very far-reaching. One can speculate that the printing and distribution arrangements they have with Northern Press would not be as
easy to maintain if they took a more radical line politically.

Whether politically committed or not, the larger the area the
local alternative paper is aimed the more difficult distribution is.
For those papers aimed at a suburb or small town distribution by
individuals to newsagents, community centres and even door-to-door
is feasible. For papers such as Durham Street Press trying to
reach a much larger area (in this case the whole of Durham County)
acceptance by trade distribution would be very advantageous. It must
be said, however, that it is not only problems of distribution which
prevent these papers reaching a working-class audience, but also in-
frequency of publication and inaccessibility of style. Often not enough
lighter material is included to balance the heavier probing articles,
not enough 'human interest' stories; and the material is not written
in a simple enough way. This reflects on the background of those
involved in production--mainly middle-class activists--who are often
out of touch with working-class life and interests, although the difficulties which papers such as Byker Phoenix and Fellin' Times have
faced in involving working-class people in predominantly working-
class areas must be borne in mind and shows that it is often not
for lack of trying.

The issue of distribution has implications for librarians who
tend to obtain the majority of their material from library suppliers
who themselves are very selective and use mainstream distribution
channels. Library suppliers will also send material for inspection
and 'service' books with plastic jackets, etc, where desired. It

can, therefore, be laziness as well as conservatism and ignorance which prevents acquisition of alternative materials by libraries. The situation is changing, however: as many librarians are developing community information systems and in so doing using alternative distribution channels and alternative bookshops (such as Grass Roots Bookshop in Manchester whose community information catalogue is used by librarians throughout the country) they are becoming more aware of the wide range of alternative materials and other means of distribution. Some libraries also sell local alternative publications, eg Byker Phoenix and Fellin' Times were both sold in their local branch libraries.

Finance

Lack of finance is the single most important factor after distribution difficulties in explaining why alternative periodicals find it hard to succeed and establish themselves over a longer period of time. There are several elements in this problem:

- although state aid has become increasingly available many alternative publications would not accept state grants since they wish to retain their independence of the establishment and fear that this type of financial backing would inhibit criticisms of local and central government. An example of a paper which has retained its independence in spite of financial problems is Durham Street Press who have a continuing deficit of £300. Several community newspapers in the North-East receive state assistance of various kinds. Northern Arts supported the now defunct Byker Phoenix and Wallsend Forum and also some current papers including a new community newsletter in Sunderland. Local district council and County Council grants of £2,000 and nearly £1,000 from Cramlington Development Corporation support Cramlington Orbit.

- other means of finance, such as by taking advertising, are possible but this entails other problems. Advertising may be withdrawn if the political stance of the paper is regarded as offensive, and if the paper's publication is intermittent then advertisers will be harder to attract. Fierce competition from local commercial publications, including free advertising sheets, can take advertising away from local alternative papers. This was the case in East London where the weekly alternative paper East End News saw its resources draining away due to undercutting in advertising rates by East London Advertiser. This meant that for several months the shortfall between advertising and the cost of producing the paper was £1,500 per week. Consequently it has reverted to monthly publication for the time being.

- if the paper has problems in distribution then this can deplete the paper's small resources: distribution by car is expensive because of increasing petrol charges and distribution by volunteers is slower and not so reliable.

Lack of finance has been the main reason why the possibility of establishing a local radical weekly in the North-East has been dropped for the time being. Discussions to investigate the feasibility of such a venture took place through the North-East Campaign for Press Freedom group. This group (not now functioning as a body) concluded that a paper run on volunteer labour was out of the question: they thought the product would be second-rate, since alternatives run on shoestring budgets were in danger of being insular and ill-informed and very often failing to reach a wide market. The problems faced by East End News in London gave some indication of the problems. This paper started with a launch fund of £19,000 and raised another £25,000 in the course of their first nine months and yet this was not enough to ensure their financial security because of the problems they experienced over advertising described above.
The TUC has also done research into the possibility of backing local alternative weeklies, having abandoned for the time being the idea of a new labour daily because of the enormous cost (£10 million) of launching such a newspaper and uncertainties over the potential market for it.

The Public Library and the Alternative Press

It is within the context of library policies towards periodical acquisition and display that the case studies of Newcastle-upon-Tyne and Gateshead library authorities' attitudes to the alternative press are presented. Examples of censorship in these two and other public library authorities are exposed and the libraries' policies towards use of display space and meeting rooms are also explored.

Periodical Acquisition Policy

Neither Newcastle nor Gateshead libraries had any kind of policy statement about periodicals selection and acquisition. A study carried out in 1972-73 of periodical acquisition and use in British public libraries reveals that this is a wider trend [29]. This survey revealed not only that there is little evidence of a systematic policy in this area but also that knowledge of demand is not a particularly common criteria for selection and retention decisions in public library systems. This is to be compared with non public library systems for which the periodical problem is well documented, eg some studies of periodical management have applied some sophisticated mathematical analyses, using the 'laws' of scatter and obsolescence. Whether this is a suitable approach for public libraries will not be considered here. It is important, however, that compared with special and academic libraries the use of periodicals in public libraries is a neglected area of study. Even Oldman and Davinson admit that the scale of their study (fourteen library systems studied) was such that "it was only possible to scratch the surface of many

Communication and Education   187

interesting and research-worthy problems and raising more questions than were answered."

This investigation also concluded that standards for periodical provision such as the Survey of Serials commissioned by the Library Advisory Council, Working Party on Periodicals in 1971, were unrealistic and perhaps unhelpful because they used quantitative measures, suggesting how many titles should be taken by libraries serving different population sizes. Qualitative research, examining for example the relationship of the use of books and periodicals, has been neglected in public library studies. Oldman and Davinson found that surveys into periodical usage were rare, and that although libraries claimed annual revision of their periodicals lists this type of revision was not particularly systematic. Newcastle and Gateshead Libraries also fell into this type of pattern. Neither library authority did any kind of systematic survey into periodical usage for information for use in selection. Newcastle's 'management information' comes from the assistant who shelves the current issues of periodicals daily, and they claimed continuous revision on this basis. Gateshead's periodicals librarian reviews their list annually.

The next area for investigation was to consider who is responsible for periodical selection and where ultimate responsibility lies. Newcastle have two teams for periodical selection, based at Central Library, one with responsibility for science and technology and the other for social sciences and humanities, who 'vet' requests from branches. Selection at Gateshead is less centralised, the librarian with responsibility for periodical selection at Central Librarary having much more of a co-ordinating role, with complete freedom for branch librarians within financial limits. In both cases the ultimate authority rests with the relevant committee in local government (in Newcastle the Arts and Recreation Committee and in Gateshead the Libraries and Arts Committee). Although periodical holdings in Gateshead and Newcastle Libraries do not seem to have been significantly cut back in spite of cuts in library budgets, other libraries have responded to cuts in their budgets by savagely cutting back on periodical acquisition. Durham County Library is an example of one such library authority.

Censorship in the Public Library

Both Newcastle and Gateshead Libraries emphasised that the library committee did not take part in the selection process unless a controversial item was specifically brought to their attention by the library itself or by a member of the community. It is to examples of such controversies that this report now turns, both in Gateshead and Newcastle, and in other library authorities.

In Gateshead in January 1975 the National Front applied to have the library display their monthly publication Spearhead and their bi-monthly news-sheet Britain First with the argument "... we are the fourth largest and fastest growing political party in Britain. And we feel that as such we should be represented in the library" [30]. The Council backed the libraries' decision not to take or display either of the items requested, the reason given being that the National Front was not a democratic organisation and therefore it would be undemocratic to make their publications available to the public. Another example in 1975 from Gateshead Libraries was their refusal to allow Gateshead Street Press (from the other end of the political spectrum) display space in the library. This was also referred to the Libraries and Arts Committee of the Council whose chairman Fred Johnson explained the decision in this way: "We felt Gateshead Street Press was too political and too extreme and that it wasn't the function of a public library to provide a platform for political organisations" [31]. (This was also given as a reason for not keeping the National Front material.) As the article in Gateshead Street Press protesting at the decision points out, the library at that time also took papers of such political organisations as the Labour Party (Labour Weekly) and of the Communist Party (Morning Star). Gateshead Street Press (now defunct) was not the organ of a political party but rather "a forum of radical left-wing opinion in the area." A survey of three issues of Gateshead Street Press (which eventually ended up in Gateshead Libraries' Local Studies Collection!) indicate that this description is accurate and the paper could no more be accused of being 'extreme' than Morning Star, Socialist Standard or Militant which Gateshead Libraries took at that time too. Gateshead Street Press acted as a forum for news and articles on local single issue campaigns, eg in the first issue (July 1974) they included articles about 'Battered wives' and Gateshead Claimants Union. This is the traditional role of the local alternative paper and reactions of libraries to this type of paper have varied widely. Another example of an exclusion of a local alternative paper was in Sheffield when, also in 1975, the City Council's Libraries and Arts Committee decided that the library would not take Sheffield Free Press [32].

These examples seem to be clear cases of censorship. In addition the reason given at Gateshead for exclusion on the grounds of the library not taking or displaying material from political parties are contradictory. The library, then as now, takes periodicals from the whole span of political comment, including those published by political parties as indicated above. These examples occurred in 1975 and both the Borough Librarian and his deputy at that time have left Gateshead Libraries so the Library is not able to comment currently on these decisions. It would be useful to discover how far pressure was exerted on the library from above (ie from the Library Committee) or whether the library did not want Gateshead Street Press and the National Front material either.

It would appear that liberalisation has occurred in recent years, in Gateshead Libraries. The present Deputy emphasised that there was no censorship of a publication from a political point of view, except in the case of National Front material where the reason was the undemocratic and divisive nature of the organisation, which seems to separate it from the political censorship of the type that excluded Gateshead Street Press. National Front materials and posters are excluded from both Newcastle and Gateshead Libraries, and the organisation is not allowed to use library meeting rooms in either authority. Both Newcastle and Gateshead Libraries, while aware of their position in the local authority, were anxious to retain their independence vis-à-vis rights to selection, stressing the importance of keeping selection in the hands of the professionally trained librarian. It would be interesting to discover whether the Library Committee in the local authority exercises or attempts to exercise more or less pressure on the library regarding the selection of materials than in the era 1974-75 when more examples have come to light of political censorship.

Another example from that period is of the banning of Gay News from a number of libraries. In Richmond public library authority, for example, the library agreed to take Gay News for a trial period of six months after pressure from local members of the Campaign for Homosexual Equality, the subscription being paid for by a local ratepayer. The Amenities Committee of the local Council agreed to continue the papers' display after the trial period since it was well used, until the political composition of the Council changed the following May. The predominantly Conservative Committee then rejected Gay News for its allegedly immoral influences, thereby contravening the Council's own policy statement on the library service of 1965 in which the evidence of public demand was to be the main criteria for selection [33]. This 'conservative' type of decision to ban Gay News also occured in Sheffield. Newcastle City Libraries referred the question of whether to stock Gay News to the City Council Arts and Recreation Committee in anticipation of problems rather than reacting to complaints. The Committee approved the paper's display and no complaints have been made to the library about its retention. Newcastle's policy is also that of no censorship of materials on the grounds of its political content alone (besides National Front material, already mentioned above).

It is at this point, however, that one reaches the difficulty of distinguishing between censorship and the professional task of selection. Unless an item has been referred to the Library Committee and singled out in that way or an individual librarian admitted to censorship of a particular item, it is difficult to identify examples of censorship. Exclusion of material can be for a number of reasons: these include normal selection critera (Is the material poorly researched, inaccurate or poorly presented?), as well as personal political views of librarians allowed to intrude into professional work, and the fact that the librarian might not look beyond the library suppliers lists. To form a general impression of a library authority's periodical policy in relation to the alternative press other factors must be borne in mind besides individual examples of censorship. Firstly, the whole of the periodical stock must be considered. Both Gateshead and Newcastle libraries come out well as far as representation of a variety of opinion is concerned. Both represent a wide range of political opinions in both newspaper and magazine form, from the Daily Telegraph and Spectator through to New Statesman and

Morning Star. On other subjects each library has its different strengths, eg Newcastle's comprehensive collection of periodicals on alternative lifestyles including Vegetarian World and the Ecologist, and Gateshead's good representation of periodicals on social policy including Voluntary Forum Magazine, Youth and Policy and Youth in Society. Secondly, the library's other activities should also be considered. Gateshead comes out ahead of Newcastle as far as involvement in and initiation of community activities. As far as the alternative press is concerned, there is the library's backing to get off the ground a young people's magazine and the contribution of an article to and further support of Fellin' Times by Peter Scott, librarian at Leam Lane branch.

Display of Material and the Use of Library Meeting Rooms

As far as display of posters is concerned Gateshead comes out ahead of Newcastle. Gateshead Libraries will accept posters from political and religious groups whereas up till now Newcastle have not, although the new chief librarian is in favour of liberalisation. Examples of censorship in Newcastle include their former rejection of posters from homosexual pressure groups because of the anti-homosexual views of a member of the library staff. Recent indications of liberalisation at Newcastle include the CND exhibition mounted at the Central Library by Tyneside for Nuclear Disarmament, and the exhibition 'Youth Unemployment in the West End of Newcastle' mounted by the Tyneside May Day Committee with photographs by Tish Murtha. As far as use of other library rooms by political and other pressure groups both Newcastle and Gateshead Library allow this, eg the local European Nuclear Disarmament group in Gateshead regularly use Caedmon Hall in the Central Library to hold special meetings; and in Newcastle, Sandyford Ward Labour Party regularly hold their monthly meetings in the Community Room in Heaton branch library.

As far as display of periodicals is concerned neither Newcastle nor Gateshead would keep any item behind the counter for any reason except security or lack of space. They would not, for example, as Manchester Reference Library do, class a number of alternative magazines (eg IT, Oz, Mole Express, Gay News, etc) as "rare books" which means they can only be consulted after completion of a lengthy form; permission is only granted by personal notification which takes a week. The official reason is that so many of them are stolen but since they have never been on open access this is unlikely. Local alternative papers are taken and displayed (and sometimes sold) at the relevant branch libraries, eg Kenton Keyhole at Kenton branch, in both Newcastle and Gateshead. They are also kept in the local studies collections at Newcastle and Gateshead Central Libraries, although not on open access for security reasons. Examples can be found from other parts of the North-East of both positive and negative attitudes to the local and national alternative press. Cramlington Library give away spare copies of the Orbit to newcomers to the town as part of the Information service.

Durham County Library service have a censorious attitude to their library stock as a whole. Without actually banning books, Durham operate a three-tier system of removing 'offensive' material from open access: some having warning slips about possibly offensive language, some are kept in individual libraries' reserve stock and some are kept at County Hall. Among titles which are kept on closed access are The Women's health handbook, the Which guide to contraceptives, abortion and VD, and a photographic book about pregnancy and childbirth described as 'instructive' by the American Medical Association's journal [34]. While other examples of censorship of literature with sexual content have been documented (eg the placing of D.H. Lawrence's Lady Chatterley's Lover on restricted issue by Leeds public libraries [35]), it is surprising that books about women's health, childbirth and contraception should be put on closed access and only available on request. While librarians have always been quick to respond to complaints about material with explicitly sexual content or extreme political views, particularly left wing views, they have not been so open to the possibility that other types of material could offend members of the community, eg sexist material. This is indicative of the conservatism so widespread in the library profession.

Conclusion

Although it is generally recognised that many librarians carry over their own conservative attitudes into selection of library materials, it is difficult to pin down individual examples of excluded items to this and the other reasons described in detail above, unless individual cases are referred to the Library Committee of the local council, and excluded on the basis of reasons openly discussed at these meetings. From this point of view this investigation has provoked more questions than it has answered.

One must not either put all of the blame on the library for not finding out about all material published. Alternative publications, particularly local examples, should also bring their existence to the notice of librarians. Awareness of libraries differed greatly among local alternative papers in the North-East. Durham Street Press is probably the most aware, eg in their last issue they pointed out the examples of censorship at Durham County Library described earlier; they wrote to the Chief Librarian earlier this year to find out his views on his position as Information Officer with a place in the nuclear bunker in the event of a nuclear war; and thirdly, they send a copy to the British Library Newspaper Library at Colindale, London, under the legal deposit regulations, which few other alternative publications, particularly local ones, would be aware of.

Finally, to come back to the theme of the introduction of this study, librarians should be prepared to combat individual attempts at censorship from above--the library committee, etc--as well as from minority opinions within the community. The profession as a whole should give a stronger voice than is heard at present in support of the democratic right of the freedom to read.

Appendix A: Local Alternative Papers in the North-East

This list includes past and current papers. Frequency of publication is mentioned only when it was regular. Final dates are given for those which have ceased publication.

Broadside   monthly   1979-81
Byker Phoenix   monthly   1975-82
Cramlington Orbit   monthly   1972-
Durham Street Press   bi-monthly   1977-
Fellin' Times   monthly   1980-81
Gateshead Street Press   1975-76
Grapevine (Kingston Park Community Association)   1978-
Grapevine (Elswick Community Newspaper)   1976-79
Kenton Keyhole (North Kenton Residents' Association)   1978-
Northern Democrat (Campaign for the North)   1975-
Quay News: the voice of the unemployed   monthly   1978
   (Newcastle Trades Council Centre for the Unemployed)
Roundabout   quarterly   1980-   (based at Blakelaw School)
Throckley Community Association Newsletter   1974
Tyneside Socialist Centre Bulletin   monthly   1979-81
Tyneside Street Press   monthly   1977-79
Upper South Tyneside Community Association: the local news
   monthly   1974-76
Wallsend Forum   monthly   1979-81
West End Tenants Newsletter   1967-73
Westwords   bi-monthly   1980-   (West End Resource Centre: Benwell
   Law Project)
Walker Talker   1980-
Women in Durham   monthly   1980
Workers Chronicle   bi-monthly   1974   (Newcastle Trades Council)
Womenwise   quarterly   1982-

References

1. Liaison, May 1963, p. 61.

2. The librarian's intellectual freedom creed in Oboler, EM, Defending intellectual freedom: the library and the censor (Greenwood Press, 1980).

3. Thompson, A.H. Censorship in public libraries in the UK during the twentieth century (Bowker, 1975).

4. Ibid.

5. Hudson, A. The alternative press, Assistant Librarian 70:5, May 1977, pp. 82-85.

6. Davinson, D. The periodicals collection (Deutsch, 1969).

7. Bourne, R. (ed). Serials Librarianship (Library Assn., 1980).

8. Fergus, G.M. The provision of alternative materials in public libraries. LFSC 8:3, winter 1980, pp. 10-18.

9. Noyce, J. (ed). Censorship in libraries: an anthology of articles contributed in Librarians for Social Change, 1972-75 (Smoothie Pubns/Noyce, 1975).

10. Noyce, J. Censorship in public libraries. LFSC 15, 1977 (also published as a pamphlet: Noyce, 1977).

11. Hudson, A. op cit.

12. Kearns, C. Out of the mainstream: notes on suppliers of minority and alternative information. Assistant Librarian 73:2 Feb. 1980, pp. 27-28.

13. Leach, A.J. The development of the women's movement in England since 1969, the consequent rise in demand for women's information and implications for librarians. Dissertation submitted for BA, North London Polytechnic School of Librarianship, 1978.

14. Durham Street Press 28, Feb./March 1982, p. 6.

15. Durham Street Press 25, Aug./Sept. 1981, pp. 6-7.

16. Murdock, G. Political deviance: the press presentation of a militant mass demonstration. in Cohen, S. & Young, J. (eds). The Manufacture of news: deviance, social problems and the mass media (Constable, 2nd ed. 1981), pp. 206-25.

17. Jackson, I. The provincial press and the community (Manchester U.P., 1971).

18. Evening Chronicle, December 11, 1981, p. 18.

19. Journal, February 1, 1982, pp. 1 & 8.

20. Aubrey, C., Landry, C., & Morley, D. Here is the other news: challenges to the local commercial press (Minority Press Group, 1980), p. 10.

21. Federation of Worker Writers and Community Publishers. Report, 1981-82.

22. Greg Wilkinson interviewed in Morley, D., & Worpole, K. (eds). The republic of letters: working class writing and local publishing (Comedia/Minority Press Group, 1982), p. 135.

23. Ibid., p. 132.

24. Ibid., p. 134.

25. See Appendix B: a directory of local radical papers in Aubrey, C., et al. op cit., p. 76-80.

26. Quoted in Berry, D., Cooper, L., & Landry C. <u>Where is the other news: the newstrade and the radical press</u> (Minority Press Group, 1980).

27. Ibid.

28. <u>Retail Newsagent</u>, March 23, 1979.

29. Davinson, D., & Oldman, C. <u>Usage of periodicals in public libraries: an investigation carried out in 1972-73</u> (Leeds Polytechnic School of Librarianship, 1975).

30. <u>Journal</u>, January 31, 1975.

31. <u>Gateshead Street Press</u> 3, summer 1975, p. 8.

32. <u>LFSC</u> 10, winter 1975-76, p. 18.

33. Thompson, A.H. op cit., pp. 220-223.

34. <u>Durham Street Press</u> 29, May-June 1982, p. 5.

35. <u>LFSC</u> 10, winter 1975-76, p. 16.

PHOTOGRAPHY AS HISTORICAL EVIDENCE AND ART:

STEPS IN COLLECTION BUILDING*

Juan R. Freudenthal and Josette A. Lyders

> "The illiterate of the future will be ignorant of pen and camera alike."
> Lazlo Moholy-Nagy.

Photography and History

That photography was more than a mere technological breakthrough was clear to its inventors but not to their contemporaries or generations after. The fast visual appropriation of "reality," the sudden transformation of this reality into an image which mirrored our world, gave us a new lease on immortality. From its inception, photography became an act of assertion and vainglory and biographers could study the psychology of a face as well as the depth of the soul. Walt Whitman once wrote: "I've been photographed, photographed, and photographed until the cameras themselves are tired of me." (As quoted by Justin Kaplan. Walt Whitman. A Life. Simon & Schuster, 1980). From Whitman's ego trips to the forced smiles in that brief but powerful scene in the film, Ordinary People, when family soul-searching is captured by the click of a camera, the world around us is preserved and mythologized. Photography is witness to history and art, and shapes our lives as well. In a recent interview, Mikhail Baryshnikov stated that as a dancer he had been influenced not only by other choreographers but by "movies, musicals, [and] photo exhibitions." (The New York Times, June 28, 1981, p. 6). Thus, photography becomes archival material, for it speaks of the human adventure in all its diversity.

   The future of the library profession hinges on the way we perceive visual communications and come to grips with the nature of visual codes, for photography (and electronic communication among other media) is altering the idea and nature of libraries. It is believed that approximately ten billion photographs are taken in the United States each year by some ninety million people who own

---

*Reprinted by permission of the author and publisher from Collection Building, 4:1 (1982) 6-20. Copyright © 1982 by Neal-Schuman Publishers.

cameras. As time sifts through this prodigious documentation, much will remain for librarians and archivists to cope with.

One of the most important primary source materials for the historian and scholar is photo-archives. These repositories exist everywhere in the world but only recently have they come to the public's attention. Visual syntax has changed not only the way people communicate and perceive their lives, but it has also had profound effects on the way scholarly research is pursued and libraries and information centers are organized. The problem then is twofold: there is a sudden overload of visual materials pouring into libraries, archives, and research centers of all kinds; and librarians know little about the nature, procurement, organization, and dissemination of these unique resources.

The rise of photography is evident through innumerable museum exhibitions, collecting craze, auction and art galleries sales, newly created photographic repositories in institutions of higher learning, major public libraries, and specialized documentation centers. The most popular photography show in our times was Edward Steichen's "The Family of Man," first viewed in the Museum of Modern Art in January of 1955 and since then seen by over nine million people in 69 countries. Photography had finally taken root in the public's consciousness. The known photographs of the old West, the Civil War, and those commissioned during the Great Depression added a new dimension to our knowledge of U.S. history. The clarity of a 19th century Bonfils photograph of a grocery store outside the Jaffa Gate, Jerusalem, reveals, under a magnifying glass, labels on merchandise. This type of documentation has become a new means for economic historians to learn about imports in a period when smuggling flourished.

Presently, the impact of the medium on our awareness of malnutrition and poverty worldwide, the graphic horrors of Vietnam and Cambodia, or how the photographs which have been taken from space have stimulated the ecological movement in this country cannot be dismissed lightly. Photography is intimately related to the technology of our present and near future: home video, with its capability for projection on regular TV screens; phototherapy, which allows images to elicit emotional responses from patients; videodisks, which already can store 108,000 images of visual or written text in one disk (and which may allow us to leapfrog the whole world of micrographics) and so on. Photography has definitely influenced the directions of history, art, and technology.

Photography: The Beast or the Beauty?

The invention and history of photography has been investigated with enthusiasm and thoroughness. Yet, there are areas which need further elucidation and some controversies still capture our attention. The Frenchman Joseph Nicéphore Niépce succeeded, in 1826, in fixing an image on a pewter plate through the process known as heliography. On February 28, 1835, the Englishman William Henry Fox Talbot wrote the following sentence in his notebook: "In the Photogenic or Sciagraphic process, if the paper is transparent, the first drawing may serve as an object to produce a second drawing, in which the lights and shadows would be reversed." The American scholar and formerly Curator of the Royal Photographic Society of Great Britain, Gail Buckland, concludes that modern photography derives from this technical milestone. (Gail Buckland. Fox Talbot and the Invention of Photography. David Godine. 1980).

In the meantime, another Frenchman, the painter Louis Jacques Mandé Daguerre (who exchanged information and collaborated with Niépce for several years) continued his experiments which led to the invention of the daguerreotype and which was officially announced in the Academy of Science in Paris on January 7, 1839. Talbot, in no haste to publicize his findings, presented his work to the Royal Institution in London on January 25, 1839. A mere fifteen days later, but it is mostly for this reason that people still believe that we owe the invention of photography to Daguerre and not to Talbot. In 1844, the latter published his now classic The Pencil of Nature, the first book illustrated with photographs, and an essay on the nature of the new medium.

The French painter Paul Delaroche is reported to have said that the daguerrotype would make painting obsolete, while Baudelaire declared that photography was "the mortal enemy of art." It is true that the new medium could do a faster, less expensive, and more accurate job at representing nature, yet the great painters of the times and turn-of-the-century who suspected the all pervasive power of photography, continued to produce great masterpieces. Photography did not put painting out of business but helped many artists "to fix an image" for later use in their studios. A symbiotic relationship between painting and photography had started.

The fin de siècle bourgeoisie viewed photography as commercial banality and too technical for artistic pruposes. "... Instead of photographs of Chartres Cathedral ... [she would inquire whether some great painter had not depicted them, and preferred to give me photographs of 'Chartres Cathedral'] after Corot ... which were a stage higher in the scale of art." (Marcel Proust, Remembrance of Things Past, Volume 1, Random House, 1981.) Painters turned into photographers and used pencil and brush on the paper negative to change tonal values, in an effort to elevate photography to a higher status. On the other hand, photographers used oil pigments on their prints. Edward Steichen and a score of other photographers before and after him, imitated the tonal values of a Titian, Rembrandt, Velasquez, Degas, Whistler, etc.

That photography was an art, there was almost no contestation among photographers, but it took almost a century to make the general public aware of this phenomenon. The stormy history of the question of photography's right to a place among the arts has been documented consistently. Alfred Stieglitz helped the cause with the foundation, in 1901, of the Photo-Secession Group and with the publication of Camera Work between 1903-1917. But it was not until 1930, when the Museum of Modern Art bought a photograph by Walker Evans entitled "Lehmbruck: Head of a Man" and MOMA's 1932 exhibition "Murals of American Painters and Photographers" that the medium was given the mantle of respectability which could be accepted by the public at large. Its ultimate consecration came in 1977 with the publication of Susan Sontag's On Photography, a brilliant group of essays which shattered our complacency about the medium.

Libraries chose to wait, apparently for the day when the question would be answered, for classifying photography among the arts was avoided until very recently. It was safely classified as a technology in the Dewey and LC reflecting, no doubt, the general acceptance of the medium as a scientific achievement. The Art Libraries Society of North America addressed this problem in 1972, seeking to establish a place for photography in the category of fine art. In 1974, the Society made available its publication NH Classification for Photography: An Alternative to TR. Many academic libraries have since begun to use this scheme.

Photography has been seeking a secure place among the fine arts virtually since its discovery before 1839. Between the early 19th century and June 1979, when the first conference on the History of Photography took place in Britain, much has happened. For the librarian, sorting out the growing printed literature and visual documentation on the history of photography and its progress, it has become a difficult task with few acknowledged guideposts. Helpful suggestions are widely scattered. Further complicating the process of collection building in photography are the questions of how to classify these works and how to store and preserve them. Finally, it will be useful to briefly explore the presence of photography as documentary evidence and art in our professional bibliographic and evaluative tools.

The Presence of Photography in Bibliographic and Reference Sources

It is only during the later part of the 1970s that photography as art has been acknowledged in some reference and bibliographic sources. Among these, the following works point out the reality of photography's long period of neglect among the arts. Mary Chamberlin in her Guide to Art Reference Books (ALA, 1959) mentions a few national and foreign photoarchives and sources of reproductions of works of art. This has been partially corrected in Etta Arntzen and Robert Rainwater's Guide to the Literature of Art History (ALA, 1980) which includes an entire section on photography and covers bibliographies, dictionaries, encyclopedias, handbooks, western countries as well as China and Japan, and photography in the 19th and 20th centuries. Philip Pacey's Art Library Manual: A Guide to Resources and Practice (Bowker, 1977) presents a lengthy state-of-the-art section on "photographs and reproductions of works of art" and "photographs as works of art." It includes an array of sources useful for library collection development. The entire volume is written primarily from a European point of view.

Gerd Muehsam's Guide to Basic Information Sources in the Visual Arts (Norton/ABC-CLIO, 1978) has a chapter on photography, offering commentary on the history and development of the medium, along with a selected annotated list of retrospective and current books, reference sources and journals. Donald Ehresmann's Fine Arts: A Bibliographic Guide to Basic Reference Works, Histories and Handbooks (2nd ed., Libraries Unlimited, 1979) does not include photography. Art Design Photo (London, Institute of Contemporary Prints, 1972, Annual), international in scope, is a bibliography documenting in detail over 5,000 of the year's books, exhibition and sales catalogs, periodicals, newspaper articles and some other publications. In 1972 it offered five pages on photography while in 1975 it had grown to almost eleven pages, with emphasis on photography as art.

The latest issues of ARTbibliographies Modern (ABC, 1973- Semiannual) provide nearly double the number of pages devoted to photography in earlier volumes (also available online). RILA, Répertoire International de la Littérature de l'Art (College Art Association of America, 1975- Semiannual) has given very meager coverage to material under the heading of photography until the most recent issues. Eugene Sheehy's Guide to Reference Books (9th ed., ALA, 1976) lists photography under "Applied Arts" and includes ten items with emphasis on bibliographic and technical aspects. The 1980 Supplement adds four entries, still with emphasis on photography as technology. Coverage is poor, considering that Sheehy is consulted in virtually all types of libraries. The American Reference Books Annual 1980 (Libraries Unlimited, 1980) reviewed nine items related to photography. Art Index (Wilson, 1929-) indexes a negligible amount of photographic periodicals. Coverage of the medium in Books for College Libraries. A Core Collection of 40,000 Titles (2nd ed., ALA, 1975) is minimal. Most entries belong to the Library of Congress TR section. The thirty items on the history and aesthetics of photography have been chosen rather haphazardly and are not necessarily "core" items. The Reader's Adviser; a Layman's Guide to Literature (12th ed., Bowker, 1977), does not mention photography.

The Public Library Catalog (7th ed., H.W. Wilson, 1978) and supplements cover photography as art quite adequately although it could be more up-to-date. Coverage in The Junior College Library Collection (Bro-Dart, 1970) is poor, for it focuses mostly on the technological aspects of photography, mentions only five items under the history and aesthetics of photography, and lists seven miscellaneous periodicals. Although Library Literature has regular entries under "Photography" and "Archives, photographic" with various sub-headings, a glance through the years 1978-1980 reports virtually nothing on collection development or photography as art. Library and Information [Science] Abstracts for the same period fares no better. Photography is discussed almost exclusively in its role as documentation of art history in "Art Libraries and Collections" in the first volume of the Encyclopedia of Library and Information Science (Marcel Dekker, 1968).

Among the general reference sources, one in particular deserves special mention: the 1973 Britannica Encyclopedia of American Art. It was the first work of this type to fully acknowledge photography as art with innumerable entries on the medium and its major practitioners, including illustrations of their works. It includes a nine-and-one-half page entry on photography by Van Deren Coke.

With exceptions, most bibliographies, reference, and evaluative sources are characteristically late in introducing the contemporary documentation of the humanities. The bibliographic organization and access into these disciplines, however, and particularly in the art field, have progressed steadily with the availability of such indexes and abstracts as Art Design Photo, ARTbibliographies Modern, RILA and a few other tools (consult our subsequent list), several of which can also be searched online. Thus, there is hope that in the very near future, photography as an aesthetic experience will be fully documented and widely represented in our major access points to the literature.

Access to the Literature of Photography

The following annotated checklists focus on the most up-to-date, comprehensive and useful sources for a thorough overview of photography as historical evidence and art. Items from the 1971 and 1978 Choice bibliographies were duplicated only if they were considered "classics," or if new light could be thrown onto a resource, or in cases in which serials or periodicals have continued to grow in importance. Thus, a great proportion of the entries listed below have copyright dates between 1978 and 1981. These last few years have seen a proliferation of monographs, newspaper, and journal articles on the recognition of photography as an aesthetic experience, plus several photoexhibitions in museums, art galleries, libraries, and spectacular auction sales as well. A survey through the Publishers' Trade List Annual (1980 ed., Subject Index to Publishers--Photography), the 1977 Photography Market Place, and the January 21, 1980 issue of AB Bookman's Weekly (which describes the background and collection emphasis of photographic dealers in the United States) demonstrates that photography is well entrenched in the realm of publishing and collecting.

Further Indexes, Bibliographies, Bibliographic Essays

Art Books 1950-1979 (Bowker, 1979). A visual art bibliography which will prove useful for acquisitions, selection, and research. It covers 37,000 books indexed under approximately 14,000 subjects. Includes a sizable checklist of publications on photography, many still in print. Albert Boni, ed., Photographic Literature 1960-1970 (Morgan and Morgan, 1972). Volume I, published in 1962, covered 233 years of book articles and papers, spanning the years 1727-1960. Volume II, though covering merely a decade, contains more listings, but not as many under aesthetics. George M. Craven, "New Light on Photography," Choice 14:1603-1614 (February 1978). The explosion of interest in the history, technology and aesthetics of photography is cited and some reasons put forth. Over 100 items divided into reference sources, texts and manuals, histories, contemporary artistic photography, journalistic and documentary photography, applied photography, photographic technology, series, and major periodicals.

William S. Johnson, ed., An Index to Articles on Photography 1978 (Rochester, N.Y., Visual Studies Workshop Press, 1979). This is the second edition of a volume that grew out of a regular column in Alterimage. It indexes articles from almost 100 photography and art magazines. Excludes technical articles. The author hopes to make this work an annual. Martha Moss, Photography Books Index: A Subject Guide to Photo Anthologies (Scarecrow, 1980). Indexes 22 of the most widely representative and most commonly available photo anthologies. Includes indexes by photographer, subject matter, photographed individuals. Ten of these titles are duplicated in Parry's work (see below), therefore the usefulness of this work will depend on the extent of individual library holdings.

Beaumont Newhall, The New Encyclopedia Britannica/Macropedia (15th ed., 1974, volume 14, pages 306-327). Superb article and bibliography by an expert on the history of photography. Illustrated. Pamela J. Parry, Photography Index: A Guide to Reproductions (Greenwood Press, 1979). Indexes nearly 90 English language photographic anthologies, histories and exhibition catalogs, including the Time-Life series, Newhall, Gernsheim, and Beaton. Indexes by photographer, subject and title. 107 subject headings and many geographical location entries. Chronological index to anonymous photographers.

Histories, Encyclopedias, Essays, Guides, Handbooks, Directories

Cecil Beaton and Gail Buckland have edited The Magic Image (Boston, Little Brown, 1975). A personal but fascinating selection of nearly 100 photographers and numerous examples of their works. Encyclopedic in scope, focuses on photography as an aesthetic experience. Milton W. Brown et al., American Art: Painting, Sculpture, Architecture, Decorative Arts, Photography (Abrams, 1979). Good general art survey covering the Colonial Period through the contemporary scene since 1960. Helmut and Alison Gernsheim, A Concise History of Photography (McGraw-Hill, 1969). A history which is regarded as "a classic" in the field. Information-packed text amplified by 285 illustrations, spanning the years 1760-1965.

Ralph Greenhill and Andrew Birrell, Canadian Photography:

1839-1920 (Toronto, Coach House Press, 1979). A new and revised edition of Greenhill's Early Photography in Canada published in 1965. A history of photography and photographers in Canada, with direct links made between Stieglitz and the Photo-Secession, and amateur photographers in Toronto and Montreal. Judith A. Hoffberg and Stanley W. Hess, Directory of Art Libraries and Visual Resource Collections in North America (New York, Neal-Schuman, 1978). Compiled for the Art Libraries Society of North America, this directory is divided into three parts: 1. Art Libraries, 2. Visual Resources Collections, and 3. Index to Institutions. For photography holdings, see under "Art-Photography." Eugenia Parry Janis and Wendy MacNeil, Photography Within the Humanities (Danbury, New Hampshire, Addison House, 1977). Edited transcripts of a symposium at Wellesley College in April, 1975, concerning the role of photography and its connection with other fields. The speakers: John Morris, Paul Taylor, Gjon Mili, Robert Frank, Frederick Wiseman, John Szarkowski, W. Eugene Smith, Susan Sontag, Irving Penn and Robert Coles. Illustrated with the photographs each speaker chose to illustrate his/her point of view.

Beaumont Newhall, The History of Photography from 1839 to the Present Day (Museum of Modern Art, 1964). The history of photography as a fine art, this revised edition includes nearly 200 black and white photographs and is also acknowledged as a "classic." Photography Market Place (2nd ed., Bowker, 1977). Includes an annotated list of picture books dealing with "aesthetic and pictorial aspects of photography as an art ..." Also includes a list of 88 professional journals covering all aspects of photography. Susan Sontag, On Photography (Farrar, Straus and Giroux, 1977). A most brilliant tour de force by one of America's foremost essayists. Her ultimate criticism is scathing, projecting a negative feeling as to photography's "right" to be among the fine arts. John Szarkowski, Looking at Photographs: One Hundred Pictures from the Collection of the Museum of Modern Art (Museum of Modern Art, 1973). One photograph from each of 100 photographers with a commentary about each artist and his analysis of the visual impact of the photograph. His style is refreshing and deeply perceptive. By the same author, Mirrors and Windows: American Photography since 1960 (Museum of Modern Art, 1978). Catalog of an exhibition held at the Museum of Modern Art, July 28-October 2, 1978, and other museums through March 2, 1980. Szarkowski has arranged the pictures in two sections to suggest a critical thesis, which is that there exists a fundamental dichotomy in contemporary photography between those who think of it as a means of self-expression and those who think of it as a method of exploration.

William B. Welling, Photography in America: The Formative Years, 1839-1900 (Crowell, 1977). A 430-page history of photography in the 19th century, heavily illustrated. Many pages are black background, evoking a feeling that the book and its subject are one. Johann Willsberger, The History of Photography: Cameras, Pictures, Photographers (Doubleday 1977). The theme of the camera itself, revealed in magnificent photographs, runs like an attractive golden thread throughout the volume. Close-up, full-page photos of cameras and other photographic paraphernalia as well as large and clear pictures revealing the history and personalities in the world of the medium. Camera models from 1839 to 1975 are appended.

Periodicals

What follows is a brief and representative sample of well-known photography periodicals that publish fine photographs and some of the best writing on the technical and creative arts of the camera. They run the gamut between the venerable British Journal of Photography (1854) to the recent Camera Arts (1980), a magazine dedicated to the aesthetics of photography and which includes some striking portfolios. Beyond the selection tools (indexes, abstracts, guides) mentioned already, the reader should not forget two other sources for acquisition and selection. Bill Katz and Berry G. Richards Magazines for Libraries (3rd ed., Bowker, 1978), provides a well-annotated and well-balanced selection of 29 photographic journals. Ulrich's International Periodicals Directory (19th ed., Bowker, 1980) provides a greater scope for selection but does not include annotations.

Also worth consulting are two informative current awareness bulletins. Picturescope, since 1953, a quarterly of the Picture Division, Special Libraries Association, grew from a mere booklet to a full-fledged journal in 1981. The Fall 1980 issue starts a new column entitled "Periodicals," which includes citations drawn from a variety of scholarly, small presses, or fledgling art and photographic publications. The less conspicuous but important The International Bulletin for Photographic Documentation of the Visual Arts (formerly MACAA/VR Newsletter) since 1974, is a quarterly edited by Nancy De Laurier, Art and Art History, UMKC, Kansas City, Missouri, and gives current information on all aspects of slide and photograph collections.

To build retrospective collections of photographica, including rare 19th century periodicals, check dealer's advertising in AB Bookman's Weekly, January 21, 1980, volume 65; Afterimage, 1972- 10 issues a year; Aperture, 1952- q; British Journal of Photography, 1854- w; Camera, 1922- m; Camera Arts, 1980- 6 issues a year; Camera Canada, q; Creative Camera, 1963- m; History of Photography, 1977- q; Modern Photography, 1937- m; Petersen's Photographic Magazine, 1971- m; Photograph, 1976- m; Popular Photography, 1937- m; Untitled, 1972- q.

Articles

This selection of annotated articles of scholarly and popular interest deals with the impact of photography on modern art scholarship and contemporary life, and serves as a sample of the type of information which is readily accessible through a great variety of reference tools.

One of the most conspicuous and popular sources of information on photography has been The New York Times, particularly its Sunday "Arts and Leisure" section, which features "Photography View," a sometimes in-depth review and criticism of exhibitions and theories on photography as art, and a more popular column entitled "Camera." The latter covers such topics as how to photograph children or pets or weddings; pointers on choosing and using color films or filters; the use of electronic flash; grants available for serious photography; lists of "how-to" books; a directory of U.S. photographic organizations; different ways to learn about the art and craft of photography; checklist of schools, courses, seminars, workshops; well-known instructors-photographers; and in-print texts on photography.

  A. Bowman, "Has Photography Any Claim to be Considered a Fine Art?" British Journal of Photography 124:786 (September 16, 1977). Reprint of a paper read at a meeting of the Glasgow Photographic Association on October 4, 1877 "... in which he defends the artistic potential, individuality and technical excellence of the photograph." John W. Dower, "Japan's Photographic Legacy," The New York Times Magazine, March 8, 1981, pp. 37-48, 54. After the late 1850's Japanese photography not only captured the final days of a warrior class, but bore witness to the traumatic course of the modern Japanese state. In recent years, the Japanese have begun to assemble their own photographic heritage. Several photographs accompany the text.

  William A. Ewing, "Canada's Artists with Cameras," ARTnews, 77:82-85 (April, 1978). Comments on the recent developments and attitudes toward photography as a fine art in Canada. Mentions government and commercial support and includes a discussion about ten contemporary Canadian photographers and their works. Wolfgang Freitag, "Early Uses of Photography in the History of Art," Art Journal 39: 117-123 (Winter 1979/1980). After studying several options on the use of photography in the history of art by eminent art historians and critics, Freitag can write that "it appears that for teaching, study, and serious scholarship in most fields of art there is still no better reproductive medium than the carefully printed black-and-white photograph, taken of course by an art-historian/photographer from the correct point of view and under the best lighting conditions."

  Hilton Kramer, "The New American Photography," The New York Times Magazine, July 23, 1978, pp. 8-13+. Commentaries on an exhibition at the Metropolitan Museum of Art, that opened July 28, 1978, as an attempt to "provide a coherent account of contemporary photography in the United States." Kramer goes on to state that "photography has now been welcomed to the aesthetic sanctum of our culture on a scale that even its most devoted champions of an earlier day might have hesitated to predict." John Perreault, "Photo-Realist Principles," American Art Review (November 1978) pp. 108-111. Describes the intimate, mechanical/technical relationship between painting and the camera, in this school of art which employs grid transfers, slide projections, etc., to produce a painting from a photograph. William B. Walker, "Art Books and Periodicals: Dewey and L.C.," Library Trends 23:451-470 (January 1975). Describes the benefits and drawbacks in each system for art books and periodicals and specifically discusses the place of photography.

Monographs

Gail Buckland, Fox Talbot and the Invention of Photography, (Boston, David R. Godine, 1980). Considered an important new book by Hilton Kramer. Buckland's expertise and perception enhance the subject. Robert Doty, Photo-Secession: Stieglitz and the Fine Art Movement in Photography (Dover, 1978). Concise, clear details on the background, personalities, exhibitions, and nature of the fine art movement in photography. Shirley Glubok, The Art of Photography (Macmillan, 1977). One of the few books on artistic photography geared to the elementary grades. The history of photography, emphasizing the great pioneers and contemporary artists. Many illustrations complement the text. Conclusion: "... today, as in the past, the camera alone cannot take a significant picture. It requires an artist with a special vision to make a photograph a work of art."

Vicki Goldberg, ed., Photography in Print: Writings from 1816 to the Present (Touchstone, 1981). This illustrated collection of pieces on photography ranges over the entire spectrum of the history of photography and the aesthetics of the medium. A third of the choices are 19th century; in the 20th, the 1970s bulk largest, yet earlier decades are not neglected. Nearly 75 essays from American, British, French, and German sources. Estelle Jussim, Slave to Beauty: The Eccentric Life and Controversial Career of F. Holland Day, Photographer, Publisher, Aesthete (David R. Godine, 1981). This is the first biography and the first representative portfolio of one of America's most influential proponents of photography as a fine art. The publisher and the author have to be commended also for the superb, tasteful layout of the book. Janet Malcolm, Diana and Nikon: Essays on the Aesthetic of Photography (David R. Godine, 1980). A series of studies most of which appeared in the New Yorker between 1975 and 1979, on exhibitions, books and specific photographers. Reminiscent of Sontag's On Photography, Malcolm is more positive and encouraging, writing in a provocative, perceptive style.

Marianne Fulton Margolis, ed., Camera Work: A Pictorial Guide (Dover Publications, 1978). A chronological inventory of all illustrations (advertisements excepted) appearing in the 50 quarterly issues of Camera Work. A Photographic Quarterly (1903-1917). All the reproductions are in black ink, four to a page, and include some of the finest and best-known works by American and European artists such as Edward Steichen, Paul Strand, Van Gogh, Picasso, and Rodin. The editor has written an essay on Stieglitz, his character and influence, and the magazine. Three indexes by artist, title, and sitter (which applies to portraits only). Beaumont Newhall, ed., Photography, Essays and Images. Illustrated Readings in the History of Photography (New York Graphic Society, 1980). Selections range chronologically from 1760 to a 1971 transcript of Walker Evans discussing his work with students. Each article is accompanied by comments and illustrations.

Penninah Petruck, The Camera Viewed (Dutton, 1979), 2 vols. Nineteen essays in each volume, this anthology emphasizes 20th century sources of historical significance and avoids the strictly biographical or technical. William F. Robinson, A Certain Slant of Light: The First Hundred Years of New England Photography (New York Graphic Society; Little, Brown and Company, 1980). A technical, social, and aesthetic history of photography in New England, reminiscent of Robert Taft's pioneering Photography and the American Scene (1938, reprint 1964). Among the photographers mentioned: Southworth and Hawes, F. Holland Day, Paul Strand, and Walker Evans. Chapters take a topical approach: pioneers, portraiture, scientific applications of photography, illustrated books, landscapes, twentieth-century propaganda, etc.

Collecting, Preservation, Storage

Photoimages are more sensitive to the ravages of time than paper products. Among the most recent attempts to provide a forum for discussion and extend awareness of this problem are the seminars on the preservation and restoration of photographic materials sponsored since 1977, by the Graphic Arts Research Center (GARC) at the Rochester Institute of Technology (which should not be confused with nearby Kodak and the International Museum of Photography at the George Eastman House, all of them located in Rochester, New York). GARC has published since March 1979 a quarterly newsletter entitled Photographic Conservation to disseminate information and exchange ideas.

Landt and Lisl Dennis, Collecting Photographs: A Guide to the New Art Boom (Dutton, 1977). An excellent handbook for the novice collector of photography as an art. Lists of dealers, galleries, auction houses, picture collections in museums and libraries, information on conservation, fluctuation of prices, what is collectible, the famous names and the big collectors. Antje Lemke and Matthew Hogan, "Preservation of Visual Resources: Selected References for Art Librarians and Archivists," ARLIS/NA Newsletter 8:162-163 (October 1980). Offering some 50 references divided into six sections: organizations; commercial sources of advice and supplies; books; journals and series; online services; preservation institutes and seminars. Ten references cited deal exclusively with photography. Frank and Ellison Lieberman, "A Future for the Past: Collecting Old Photographs," Vermont Life 35:34-39 (Winter 1980). Although this is from a rural point of view, its perspective shows that the boom of collecting important photographs is not just in the big cities. Some of the greatest recent "finds" have come from out-of-the-way places such as Vermont.

Preservation of Photographs (Eastman Kodak Company, 1979).

A 61-page handbook for librarians, archivists, collectors and curators, it is concerned with all aspects of preservation, cleaning, mounting damage due to water, temperature controls, dust, list, [sic] and even a section on filing and classification. Susan G. Swartzburg, Preserving Library Materials. A Manual (Scarecrow Press, 1980). Chapter 9 is entitled "The Care and Conservation of Photographic Materials, including Photograph Collections, Movie, Film and Slide Collections." Also by Swartzburg is "On Preservation," ARLIS/NA Newsletter 8:175-177 (October 1980). Council action at ALA in 1980, preservation colloquia, symposia and meetings, extensive list of recent publications on conservation and care, and highlights of news from the world of preservation. The author edits an ongoing column on preservation in this Newsletter. Time-Life Books, Caring for Photographs: Display, Storage, Restoration (New York: Time, Inc., 1972). Divided into five sections packed with technique and examples; excellent photographs aid the text. From cleaning, retouching, uncurling to drying, goldplating, chemical toning and other archival treatments.

Robert A. Weinstein and Larry Booth, Collection, Use and Care of Historical Photographs (Nashville: American Association for State and Local History, 1976). Organizing, cataloging and maintaining an historical photographic collection. Emphasis is on photography as visual history. Authoritative and conveniently presented. Lee D. Witkin and Barbara London, The Photograph Collector's Guide (New York Graphic Society; Little, Brown, 1979). Extremely useful book, combination directory, subject biography, bibliography, and connoisseur's guide. It encourages photography buffs to collect, appraise, and identify photographs. Among the many useful features, it includes key dates in the history of photography, a glossary, advice on the preservation of photographs, lists of important and well-known photographic organizations, country and active dates for over 7,000 photographers, and about 300 half-tone illustrations.

Some Major Photography Collections
in the United States

Picture libraries of all types abound in this country and a wide variety of them are listed in volume two (under "Picture Libraries") of Margaret and Harold Young's Subject Directory of Special Libraries and Information Centers (5th ed., Gale Research, 1979, 5 volumes), in Picture Sources 3: Collections of Prints and Photographs in the United States and Canada (Special Libraries Association, 1975), and in Photography Market Place. Other sources helpful for the identification of collections are the Directory of Special Libraries and Information Centers (6th ed., Gale Research, 1981, 2 volumes); Lee Ash, Subject Collections (4th ed., Bowker, 1974), under "Photographs" and "Picture Collections"; and Judith Hoffberg and Stanley Hess, Directory of Art Libraries and Visual Resource Collections in North America.

The following are some of the best known photograph collections and archives in the United States. International Museum of Photography at George Eastman House, Rochester, New York. According to Newhall, the largest museum of photography in the world. In the United States, the broadest collection of photographs and photographic negatives, and a comprehensive library on the technical, historical and aesthetic aspects of the medium. Publishes the George Eastman House Newsletter, a quarterly with notices and brief articles on the activities of the center. Library of Congress, Prints and Photographs Division, Washington, D.C. Although founded as early as 1897, photographs were not systematically collected until the 1940s. The division claims eight million photograph prints and negatives in about 800 different collections.

Metropolitan Museum of Art. Department of Prints and Photographs. It includes the celebrated collection of Alfred Stieglitz originals. The Spring 1978 (volume XXXV) issue of the museum's Bulletin is a monograph written by Weston J. Naef to accompany the 1978 exhibition of the Stieglitz Collection; 54 works are reproduced. Museum of Modern Art, Department of Photography. Although this museum has collected photographs since its inception, a separate Department of Photography was formed only in 1940. It has pioneered photography as art since then. New York Public Library, Local History and Genealogy Division. An important collection of photographs on the history of New York City (1870s to 1970s). 54,000 of these pictures are now available in microfiche through University Microfilms International. Smithsonian Institution. National Museum of History and Division of Photography. Includes collections on the technology and processes as well as photography as fine art. University of Arizona, Center for Creative Photography. Founded as recently as 1975, this archive contains over 100,000 photographs of Ansel Adams, Wyan Bullock, Harry Callahan, Paul Strand, Frederick Sommer, Aaron Siskind, etc.

University of California at Los Angeles, Department of Special Collections. Better known for the Albert Boni Collection on the History of Photography. University of California at Berkeley, Bancroft Library-Pictorial Collections. Founded in 1905, collections number well over 750,000 photographs. University of Texas, Humanities Research Center, Photography Collection. It includes the collections of Helmut and Alison Gernsheim on the history of Photography, with emphasis on European photography of the Victorian era. University of Washington, Special Collections Division, Photograph Collection. Famous for its history in photography of the Pacific Northwest and Alaska. University of Louisville, Kentucky, Photographic Archives. More than 650,000 photographs dispersed in various collections dating back to the 1850s.

Additional collections of fine photographs can be found at the Art Institute of Chicago; the San Francisco Museum of Art; the Oakland (California) Museum; the Amon Carter Museum of Western Art in Fort Worth, Texas; and the very specialized but rich collections of the Bettmann Archives in New York, and the national Geographic Society, Illustrations Library, in Washington, D.C. which contains over seven million published and indexed transparencies, photographs, and original paintings.

SWEET DREAMS FOR TEEN QUEENS*

Margo Jefferson

It seems appropriate to begin a piece on books for teen-age girls with the words of the adults who produce them.

"After years of being deluged with young adult books dealing with the unhappy realities of life, such as divorce, pregnancy outside of marriage, alcoholism, mental illness, and lately child abuse, teenagers seem to want to read about something closer to their daily lives." (Wildfire Romances)

"Caprice Romances are contemporary young adult first-love novels that will express the restlessness of youth and the wonder of falling in love."

"Each Sweet Dreams romance features a heroine who is about sixteen years old--an ordinary, middle-class suburban girl, with a family to match. The romantic interest, a boy of the same age or a little older, should appear early in the story--the sooner the better."

"The tension in these novels lies in the heroine's struggles with common adolescent problems, her romantic fantasies as opposed to the realities, and in her desire to define herself.... The ending of a First Love, though, is always upbeat."

"Wishing Star ... plots should deal with some of the more serious problems of young girls today, like divorce, school difficulties, loneliness, death, parental things, etc. No books will deal with sexual matters, like abortion, unmarried pregnancy, affairs. There should, however, be a romance in every book."

"Our young people are not unaware of sex. They 'make-out' and may have the first stirrings of sexual desire but description must be sensitively handled and they will not follow through on their desires." (Caprice)

---

*Reprinted by permission of the publisher from The Nation, 234:20 (May 22, 1982) 613-617. Copyright © 1982 by The Nation, Inc.

"Lastly, there should be no profanity, no religious references, and no explicit sex. We endorse hugging and kissing, of course. Where would romance be without them?" (Sweet Dreams)

You can find these books in the young adult sections of bookstores, sometimes displayed in white plastic racks, sometimes in boxed sets, prettily done up in pink with touches of blue, mauve and dove gray. You can also find them in shopping malls and advertised in the brochures of teen book clubs owned by Xerox and by Scholastic Books, which brought out the first of these series, the Wildfire Romances, in 1979. Teen romances bring their publishers millions in sales, and the publishers are willing to lavish millions on advertising in return. Although the romances were originally marketed through schools and libraries, Bantam, Simon and Schuster, Scholastic, and Grosset and Dunlap have now captured a large trade audience as well. They have an eye to the future and say they want their girl readers to experience a literary upward mobility that will allow them to move (eventually) from Small Town Summer and I'm Christy to Wuthering Heights and Jane Eyre.

These books, which cost less than $2 for some 200 pages of text where words that exceed two syllables are kept to a tasteful minumum, reproduce rapidly, at the rate of two new titles per series each month. Bookstores usually shelve them very near their adult romance counterparts, but you can distinguish between them immediately. The covers of adult romances feature illustrations of exotic fantasy; the teen ones offer photographs of adolescent models gazing into a boyfriend's, a mentor's or the camera's eye with tender, lively or sweetly mournful expressions. Grown-up girls are expected to kick off their shoes and abandon reality with a defiant toss of the head. Teen-age girls are supposed to wander in a state of suspension where fantasy and reality cannot be torn asunder. You fix your hair, put on a record, turn a few pages of In My Sister's Shadow, watch television, go through your Sweet Dreams slumber party kit, call your best friend, try to decide whether to wear the pink, the yellow or the white sweater tomorrow and gaze at the face on the cover of Terri's Dream.

If, dear adult reader, you're confused as to which decade you're in, you'd be no less so if you'd actually read a few of these books. I did, and I found that they're grown-up nostalgia repackaged for the young, very like those remakes of 1950s and 1960s songs done by people in their 30s and 40s pretending to be ten or twenty years younger. It's the silliest sort of ventriloquism: sentimentality about one's own past, piped through the mouths of another generation. The titles alone betray their authors' generation. Remember Ray Milland in The Lost Weekend when you read about teen-agers on a farm in An April Love Story. Fuse the Gershwin brothers with the Jefferson Airplane when you read Please Love Me ... Somebody or Someone To Love. One writer is named Veronica Ladd (all these writers are women, or at least all have women's names--the girls' and ladies' book world has always supported a few men who use female pen names). V.L. dedicates her novel to "L.L.: Romantic Hero, Leading Man in My Private Movie."

Listen to the voices of these modern teen-agers as they are rendered by the writers of young adult fiction in a language taken from old soap operas and magazines: "'Lisa, beautiful Lisa,' Rick murmured as he turned her toward him, 'You will always be surrounded by flowers and love.'" "Dan seemed to be mine, all mine," one heroine declares. Another meets the boy of her dreams when he seeks shelter from a storm in her "simple country kitchen."

> "I'll get you a towel." Another crash of thunder interrupted her words.... "The lightning's close," she shuddered, frozen in place.
>
> "As long as we're inside we're safe," Jeff reassured her soothingly.
>
> (Terri's Dream)

One pair of aspiring teen rock stars dreams of being the new Sonny and Cher, but their school dances feature The Bump, The Hustle and The Funky Chicken, all nearly ten years out of date.

Yes, but if these books are so false, why do teen-age girls buy them? And why was I unable to put any one of them down once I'd begun reading, despite being enraged or sickened? Well, they're written according to a formula, and the formula is as neat and efficient as that of sitcoms or pop songs or the advertising ditties we commit to memory in spite of ourselves. But the formula also reflects our earliest learning experiences--the belief that good behavior brings rewards, bad behavior punishments; the notion that a threatening world can be made benign and orderly through external means (magic and fate) or internal means (conformity and submission).

Fairy and folk tales depend on these primitive notions, as do any number of literary classics that appear on the approved reading lists of high-schoolers. Think of Dickens, the Brontës, Jane Austen, and Shakespeare's comedies: fortunes are whisked away and rebestowed, lost parents and relations are found suddenly and lost again if necessary, siblings are joined in matched-set marriages. But of course there's so much more; the classics permit a range of responses and readings. The young adult romances allow only one of two responses--you can either reject them or comply with them, and they offer no compensations of setting, character or style.

Still, they do have one virtue that may be worth all their faults. They ease fears by offering just enough of the real to make the unreal seem irresistible and attainable. The reader of teen romances feels like Dorothy in <u>The Wizard of Oz</u>, lulled to sleep in the poppy field, or like one of those fictional children who trudge through snowy woods longing to lie down and sleep forever. Somehow the torpor of these romances, the lassitude of their writing and

plotting, accommodates the beguiling somnambulance of adolescence--
form trots obediently after function. It's all here: the yearning to
be as conventional as possible, which coexists with the desire to be
singled out as particularly worthy of love, admiration and success.
Not that the books aren't filled with moral lessons; it's just that
the lessons are small and dainty, like the feet and hands pretty girls
were once supposed to have. Don't be slothful, snobbish or deceit-
ful. Be a nice person and be well groomed. If your girlfriends
and boyfriends are from a higher social class than you are, that
proves people are just people. If they're from a respectably lower
one, that proves the same thing. (The lack of mise en scène helps
shield the mythologies of class difference from the realities.) Once
a heroine has learned to be herself--to make good grades and get
along with her parents and cultivate her athletic or artistic gifts
diligently but without undue extravagance--she'll be given a boyfriend
and a future full of vague promise. Happily ever after is the time
it takes to finish one romance and begin another.

"Rumpelstiltskin" and "The Three Spinsters" are fairy tales
that feature girls of humble birth who are hustled off to palaces to
win princes with their spinning skills. Teen romance writers are
spinning into straw whatever gold exists in our childish longings,
but the raw materials of fairy tale and teen romance are the same.
Dutiful daughters get good boys. The nastly little men and the ugly
old women have been banished. The heroines are always talking
about "learning to be me," but what a richly rewarded little me
that is. I know that teen-age agonies, however shallow--not buying
the right dress, not getting a place on the cheerleading squad--are
genuine sorrows, but I wonder if they're not also propitiations of a
sort: if we're not hoping, while we suffer, that this may be all life
demands in the way of trials and tribulations. I noticed that even
those teen romance heroines who are aspiring Olympic athletes or
gifted fledgling artists never ask themselves what every teen-age
girl would, has and does: Am I really talented? What will I do if
I meet someone who has more talent? ("You must say what you
really want most," Laurie tells Jo March in Little Women. "Genius,"
Jo answers, "don't you wish you could give it to me, Laurie?")

What happens when self-discovery has to be its own reward,
when talent isn't enough and parents thwart one's wishes while boyfriends sulk and pull away? When Louisa May Alcott wasn't dashing
off pseudonymous thrillers or--her words--"providing moral pap for
the young," she wrote Work, a spirited and earnest look at the opportunities for employment, love and self-respect available to
nineteenth-century middle-class women in America. What happens
when teen-age girls discover what Work's heroine, Christie Devon,
did: that "it's so hard to be patient and contented when nothing happens as you want it to, and you don't get your share of happiness,
no matter how much you try to deserve it." Our young adult romance writers remain silent on these points. Their publishers assure us that inexperienced young adult readers prefer it that way
and are better off if such questions aren't asked.

Critics of teen romances, notably the Council on Interracial

Books for Children, have excoriated them for sexism, racism and class smugness. All true, but it's fascinating to watch how the books try to accommodate modern views on such issues without endangering the status quo. Boys are offered as rewards here because they bring out the best in girls who are struggling to find themselves. Some of the boys are shy and sensitive, others are jock heroes eager to bring their shy, sensitive sides to light. The boy encourages the heroine to pursue her talent; he nurtures her efforts to be honest and independent. I'll be the feminist for you, he seems to be murmuring in soft but manly tones--I'll be man and woman for both of us. Parents are usually supportive and sketchily drawn, providing sitcom-style reproaches and rapprochements. Only divorced or separated parents, most often mothers, are given any dimension. That the writers only feel free to criticize those parents who have broken the marriage bond doesn't alter the fact that they are the most interesting parents in the books. Most broken marriages are mended by the book's end, of course, which is quite an accomplishment. A girl who reads more than three of these books will not only feel worthless if she doesn't have a boyfriend; she will feel worthless if her parents can't be reconciled in the real-life equivalent of 200 pages.

Given this landscape, it's hopeless to expect minority groups to be portrayed intelligently. Jews aren't mentioned directly, though an occasional Jewish-sounding name drifts across the page. (For instance, I found Jason Steiner, rejected as a possible date for Frannie Bronson in The Popularity Plan because he was "too loud.") Hispanics appear in walk-on parts and are treated with that squeamish courtesy that marks the appearance of a new Token in Our Town: Dr. Gomez, the "dark-skinned" physician, Mrs. Lopez, the art teacher "with just a trace of a Spanish accent." Blacks, who have had token status longer than Hispanics, play larger roles in several books--as school friends, as neighbors who behave like tough but loving housekeepers, or as maids who behave like loving but tough mothers and teachers. I came upon one Native American (the best friend of a wealthy white businessman's son) and no Asians.

Both a blind and a paralyzed girl appear in books from Wishing Star, the self-declared line of contemporary "non-sexual problem" books. So does a lot of wishful thinking. Blind Lee finds a shy, sensitive beau and passes for sighted at his school dance; paralyzed Andie finds a protectress in the mother of the drunk driver responsible for her condition. In not one of the books is there a whisper about homosexuality. Writers who feel obliged to countenance the occasional member of a minority group draw the line at homosexuals. And even if writers and publishers could decide what line to take, homosexuality would still raise the issues of sex--its force, its repercussions, its effect on identity--far too clearly.

The guidelines are distinct: the only lust allowed is the lust for romance and stability. Otherwise, titillation must suffice. And so heroines feel warm sensations and unbearable thrills at "his touch"; they are transfixed by his gaze and prey to "stabs" of

excitement when he passes them in the hall. Dreams, which are
"like being with him all night," are good for a few illicit snickers,
and so are sports, especially horseback riding ("Maura lifted into a
hunt seat, squeezed her legs into Blackfire's sides, and the rhythm
began--up, over, land, squeeze.") Only a few books mention "going
all the way," and I found myself wondering, given the rising number
of girls reading these novels and the rising number of girls getting
pregnant, whether there was any overlap of the two constituencies.
It is not impossible; it is, in fact, likely. What these books are
really marketing is wishful thinking--the state of mind many teen-
age girls are in when they experience intercourse, pregnancy, abortion or childbirth.

What do the writers of these books actually think about their
products? I'm not sure, but they display a certain anxiety of influence, rapping the adult romances their readers will graduate to in
a few years firmly on the knuckles. "He didn't have a rock jaw or
Roman nose or pearly teeth, or any of the stock attributes of the
heroes of the romantic novels she read by the dozens," says the
heroine of I've Got a Crush On You. She's speaking of her high
school English teacher, who will praise her poetic gift, admit that
he could fall in love with her, but leave her free to pursue college,
fame and a local boyfriend instead. Adult romances soften the brain
and teach you a lot of outdated slang, a friend tells the heroine of
Dreams Can Come True, who later exclaims, "Why couldn't things
be the way they were in books? She had met the most important
man in her life and he hadn't even looked at her.... Wryly, she
thought of her silly little dreams she'd written in her secret notebook."

I'd like to leave you with brief summaries of my two favorite
teen romances. Honey (Wishing Star) is about a young girl who lives
with her mother in a Boston suburb. Father left them years ago;
now all mother, who is from a fine old New England family, does
is whine and read adult romances. Hone, who is a promising art
student, cooks and cleans for both of them. Into this drudgery comes
the family next door--the elegant Redfields of Mississippi, with their
maid, Vanilla. Vanilla, as her name playfully indicates, is black,
and not really a maid. The Redfields discovered her singing in a
Las Vegas club to earn money for college tuition and were so impressed that they brought her into their home so she could earn her
Boston University tuition by working for them. Suddenly, Honey's
father returns, eager to make a new life for his family in Maine.
The Redfields go off to Europe and Honey stays behind for a while,
feeling deserted by everyone. But Vanilla, who has just graduated
summa cum laude, sits her down and explains a few things about
love and mothering. Honey's self-absorbed mother is only one slice
of a "Mother Pie," Vanilla says; other slices are teachers, mentors
and friends, even men. And, of course, "mean old chocolate Vanilla." So Honey goes happily off to Maine, leaving behind a boyfriend
who will visit her regularly and taking with her the knowledge that
it is still possible to make a loving mammy out of a college-educated
maid.

P.S. I Love You (Sweet Dreams) tells of young Mariah and her dream of being a famous novelist like Rosemary Rogers or Kathleen Woodiwiss. She meets Paul Strobe in Palm Springs where she, her mother and her sister have gone to house-sit for the summer. Paul is from a wealthy but enlightened and artistic family; he befriends a Native American and his father writes novels and owns a bookstore. Paul wants to be an architect, and it is he who encourages Mariah to look beyond romantic novels to realistic ones. But shortly after they fall in love, Paul is stricken with cancer, and when Mariah returns to California he enters the hospital. She is loving and loyal throughout his decline, and when he dies her mother reminds her that "no true love story has a happy ending." But this one does. Mariah has grown through her pain; she is young and pretty, her parents are getting back together and she has a new typewriter. We know that when she is a little older her love story with Paul will be the subject of her first novel. She will take it to Paul's father, who, remembering her kindness to his son, will get it published and sell it in his bookstore.

And that's where we began--in bookstores, where First Love, Caprice, Sweet Dreams, Wildfire and Wishing Star will be joined this month by Windswept, a "contemporary gothic" series. If I were a 16-year-old, would I buy these books? Well, perhaps if I had limited financial and emotional resources, knew about rising unemployment among teen-agers and cutbacks in college loans and scholarships, had at least heard of liquor and drugs, felt uncertain about sex, had some awareness of divorce and the correlation between poverty (genteel or crude) and single women (with or sans children), and didn't want to think too much about any of this--yes, I would buy these books.

And if I were an adult writer, editor or publisher who knew all of this and had experienced some of it, and perhaps wanted to recreate my memory or fantasy of a carefree adolescence--a memory that would not only soothe and please me but would see to it that, for their own good, teen-age girls were no more prepared for the world than I had been and made no fewer mistakes than I had-- well, I'd write, edit, advertise and sell these books.

LIES, DAMNED LIES, AND CRIME STATISTICS: THE FBI STORY*

Joe Morehead

Introduction

In late 1980 a perennial item from United Press International appeared in newspapers across the country:

> WASHINGTON--Serious crime jumped 10 percent in the first half of 1980, with sharp rise in robberies, rapes and rural thefts helping to account for the worst overall crime increase in five years.... Final 1979 data showed a 9 percent overall crime increase. Crime rose 2 percent in 1978 after leveling off the previous two years. According to the figures the number of robberies increased by 13 percent.... Reported rapes, which have risen steadily for more than a decade, surged by another 12 percent. Murder increased 3 percent, aggravated assault 7 percent, burglary 12 percent, larceny-theft 9 percent and motor vehicle theft 4 percent.... In rural areas, overall crime rose 14 percent, mainly because of a 14 percent rise in burglaries, a 17 percent jump in larceny thefts and a 15 percent increase in property crimes.

Over the years we have all read that same wire service story; only the percentages change. Indeed, on some occasions the data have shown a decline in reported crime. Because we venerate statistics as much as misuse them, all of this sounds very professional and correct. But if Voltaire's assertion that "l'histoire n'est que le tableau des crimes et des malheurs" is true, it is unfortunate that history's latter-day registrar is the Federal Bureau of Investigation. For numerous studies have demonstrated that the figures released by the FBI are neither reliable nor valid, and this revelation may be as melancholy as the data themselves.

In his _Autobiography_ Mark Twain attributes to Disraeli--

---

*Reprinted by permission of the author and publisher from _The Serials Librarian_, 6:1 (Fall 1981) 7-16. Copyright © 1982 by The Haworth Press, Inc. All rights reserved.

whose epigrammatic virtuosity rivaled that of Oscar Wilde--the trenchant apothegm, "There are three kinds of lies: lies, damned lies, and statistics." How reassuring that pinprick in the balloon of mathematical certitude is for those of us who wander forlorn among the silicon chips and geometries of this algorithmic age. In an imperfect world the flawed nature of crime statistics suggests a rough justice. My motive in examining these data and the reasons for their unreliability is prudent: to alert librarian and user alike to the serial publications that bear this misinformation. As I proceed, it will become evident that the FBI as issuing agency is not the sole culprit in this endeavor. Devout craven that I am, I do not want the avenging ghost of J. Edgar Hoover to accost me on some dark street in a high crime neighborhood.

A Very Brief History of Crime Reporting

According to scholars, the theoretical foundations of crime statistics originate with L.A.J. Quetelet's A Treatise on Man, published in 1835. Working with archival data, he found that the constancy of different crimes occurring in France suggested a certain "criminogenic propensity" in the species, but his findings did not embrace phenomena like law enforcement manpower problems, a constant jail capacity, arrest quotas, etc. In the United States no crime statistics were collected until the mid-nineteenth century. New York, Massachusetts and Maine were the first states to collect criminal statistics, but they were largely based on known arrests or evidence of criminal trials. For the most part, "crime statistics before the twentieth century have little or no relation to crime rates.... Data on indictments, convictions, and acquittals were collected, not numbers of reported offenses or complaints to the police."

The federal government entered the picture in 1870 with the passage of P.L. 41-97 (16 Stat. 162; 28 U.S.C. 501,503) that created the Department of Justice. A provision of that Act required the Attorney General to make an annual report to Congress on "the statistics of crime under the laws of the United States, and, as far as practicable, under the laws of the several States." The following year, at a convention that created that National Police Association, a resolution was adopted which called for the compilation of crime data for police use. Historians have termed it the "first advocacy of uniformity in police crime records."

It wasn't until 1927, however, that a Committee on Uniform Crime Records was established by the International Association of Chiefs of Police (the successor to the National Police Association). This committee devised uniform crime reporting criteria, a task made difficult by the fact that "no two states defined all crimes alike." But a system was developed, and by 1929 many police departments throughout the country were collecting crime data. The IACP recommended that an agency of the Department of Justice house, analyze and report these data, and by congressional ukase that activity fell to the Federal Bureau of Investigation. It is perhaps no coincidence that J. Edgar Hoover, director of the Bureau, served in an advisory capacity to the Committee on Uniform Crime Records. In January, 1930, the IACP began collecting uniform crime data. That same year marked the appearance of the first issue of the now famous (or infamous) <u>Uniform Crime Reports for the United States</u> [1].

The Uniform Crime Reporting Program

Although agencies within the Justice Department have developed other statistical methodologies for crime analysis, the <u>Uniform Crime Reports</u> (UCR) are said to represent "the only source of data on the magnitude and trends of crime in the United States." As a result, they are "heavily relied upon by administrators, politicians, policy and opinion makers, the press, and the public at large" [2]. Based on a cooperative effort by over 15,000 law enforcement agencies across the nation, UCR's stated objective is to "produce a reliable set of criminal statistics for use in law enforcement administration, operation and management" [3]. Annual issues carry the title <u>Crime in the United States</u>, but virtually all writers on this subject use the series acronym UCR. It is a depository item for designated libraries and is available for sale by the Superintendent of Documents (J1.14/7; Item 722). The FBI also issues a quarterly <u>Uniform Crime Reporting</u> series (J1.14/7-2), but it is neither a sales nor depository publication. Because of UCR's central importance in delineating a national view of crime, it may be useful to consider the salient features of the annual.

Police statistics are submitted either directly to the FBI or through state uniform crime reporting programs. Offenses have been divided into two categories. Part I crime consists of eight types of serious offenses reported to the police. Because of their gravity, frequency of occurrence, and liklihood of being reported, these are known as "Crime Index" offenses: murder and nonnegligent manslaughter, forcible rape, robbery, aggravated assault, burglary, larceny-theft, motor vehicle theft, and arson. In 1978 Congress passed legislation mandating that arson be classified as a Part I offense, but the latest (1979) data available to me were insufficient to establish reliable trends regarding that crime. Part II offenses comprise some twenty-two categories of "less serious" crimes excluding minor traffic violations. Arrest data, which include the age, sex, and race of those arrested, are reported for both Part I and Part II offenses by crime category. The number of "actual offenses known" in Part I is reported to the FBI whether anyone is arrested for the crime, the stolen property recovered, or prosecution undertaken.

The editing, manipulation and analysis of these data generate a host of charts, tables and graphs. One striking illustration is a "Crime Clock" depicting the frequency of offenses. The clock for 1978 statistics gives the alarming impression that most crime is of a violent nature. One "Crime Index" offense was committed every

3 seconds during that reporting period, one violent crime every 30 seconds, one property crime every 3 seconds. Specifically, the "Crime Clock" diagram shows one murder every 27 minutes, one forcible rape every 8 minutes, one robbery every 76 seconds, one aggravated assault every 57 seconds, one burglary every 10 seconds, one larceny-theft every 5 seconds, and one motor vehicle theft every 32 seconds. Yet other tables in the UCR show that homicide, for example, represented less than one percent and all violent crimes less than ten percent of total Part I offenses. And a note at the base of the "Crime Clock" schema cautions us to interpret these frequencies with care: "This mode of display should not be taken to imply a regularity in the commission of the Part I offense; rather, it represents the annual ratio of crime to fixed time intervals" [4].

Indeed, caveats abound in the UCR regarding the interpretation of the crime statistics set forth. But that has not dampened the enthusiasm of the news media for glibly designating a particular city each year as the "crime capital" of the nation. Scholars have insisted that one should not compare "the statistical information of one individual community with that of another." For instance, cities with excellent police-community relations tend to have a high rate of crime reporting by citizens. It is a flagrant disservice to interpret a "UCR indicated crime rate ... as a ranked designation in the national picture." The decision to begin collecting crime statistics decades ago was motivated by adverse press coverage about "crime waves" that unduly stirred public fears. That systematic collecting has not curbed the media's propensity for facile, simplistic explication is ironic [5].

Newspaper, radio and television distortion aside, the <u>Uniform Crime Reports</u> suffer from many limitations. As noted, internal comparability is unwarranted. Crime estimates are lower than actual frequency. Not all local law enforcement agencies report to the FBI. Some police departments do not follow the definitions of the crime categories, hence there is less "uniformity" than desired. Moreover, some police departments "report information to the UCR which is totally unlike that which appears in their own files." The result is an "undetermined level of incompleteness, bias, and contamination that may never be fully measurable." By its very nature, crime is difficult to measure; but the inadequacies that are translated into UCR data exacerbate the problem [6].

Victimization Surveys

In the 1960s the first victimization surveys were conducted under the sponsorship of the 1966 President's Commission on Law Enforcement and Administration of Justice. In 1972 the Law Enforcement Assistance Administration (LEAA), with the help of the Census Bureau, instituted the National Crime Surveys (NCS). They have aroused public interest by their contrast with official UCR figures, and the victimization survey has become an alternative or supplement to FBI reported crime data. Because NCS figures projected almost twice as much "actual" crime as the annual UCR data, the latter information was made to seem even more disreputable than skeptics had been proclaiming.

NCS are household surveys of a representative national sample, interviews with thousands of occupants of housing units. The surveys focus on certain criminal offenses, whether completed or attempted: rape, robbery, assault, and personal larceny for individuals; burglary, household larceny, and motor vehicle theft for households. Characteristics of victims are tabulated in typical census fashion--by sex, age, race, marital status, income, locality, etc. Crime characteristics include time and place of occurrence, rates of reporting to police, use of weapons, and the like. Out of this have come annual reports with the inevitable abundance of appendixes, charts, tables and graphs [7]. The compilers admonish us not to compare these data with the figures in Uniform Crime Reports. For one thing, NCS statistics include crimes not reported to the police, as well as those that are reported. Moreover, the surveys do not measure some offenses included in police statistics: homicide, kidnaping, commercial burglary or robbery, shoplifting, and employee theft. "Comparisons are odious" was a well-known phrase in the 14th century. But the urge to compare NCS and UCR data has been beyond the self-control of those who make commenting on crime figures a hobby or a business.

An obvious advantage of NCS methodology is the revelation of the "apparently substantial number of crimes that are not reported to the police." But as criminal justice researchers began to evaluate NCS techniques, they found several methodological shortcomings. As Levine pointed out, information given by respondents "may be incorrect due to misunderstanding about what transpired, ignorance about legal definitions, memory failures about when crimes occurred, and outright prefabrication." Moreover, "organizational imperatives ... may cause interviewers and coders to skew the data toward a showing of greater criminality" than was actually the case [8]. The use of sample surveys to study crime grew out of a profound dissatisfaction with the accuracy of FBI data and the paucity of information those data reveal. What a dreadful irony it is that NCS figures spawn considerable disaffection as well.

White-Collar Crime

Of all the categories of information about criminal activity, none is murkier than that of "white-collar crime," roughly defined as the antics of rich and powerful corporate and professional groups in our society. In testimony given in hearings before a House subcommittee on crime, professors Gilbert Geis and Donald R. Cressey--experts on the subject--presented a passionate brief for more vigilant law enforcement efforts in this area. Both scholars found white-collar crime far more damaging to society than the incidents of "street offenses" that find their way into the pages of UCR and NCS statistics. Indeed, as Geis pointed out, it "is quite possible that more people have died from corporate-conducted or corporate-condoned violence--involved in things such as the knowing manufacture of defective cars and private planes--than have been victims of more traditional kinds of murder." Whether the offense is unnecessary surgery, the death toll among asbestos workers, income tax evasion, marketplace deception and consumer fraud, or pollution for profit, the consequences of white-collar crime have been overlooked and underplayed.

Moreover, when the offending corporation or individual is occasionally caught, the punishment is less severe than that given the shoplifter or burglar. For much corporate crime a typical punishment is a consent order in which the accused says, in essence, "I didn't do it, but I won't do it again." Spiro Agnew was able to plead nolo contendere. Huge corporations are "punished" by being ordered to contribute a sum to charity. The small time crook has a much better chance of going to jail than his white-collar counterpart.

Cressey stated the problem in unequivocal terms. There is "not a shadow of doubt that so-called white-collar crime is by far the most important crime problem in the United States. White-collar crime results in inflation, unemployment, international political scandals, bankruptcies, and even ill health. So far as costs to the nation are concerned, income-tax evasion alone dwarfs all other crimes put together. All our social problems, including problems of the young, the old, the poor, and the black, are somehow related to white-collar crime." And since the victims of white-collar crime rarely report it, there are virtually no meaningful statistics in public documents or in the files of law enforcement agencies. "An orange juice manufacturer can water his product and cheat each of us out of only a few cents a year and reap millions of dollars in criminal profit.... We expect to be cheated, and feel impotent about protecting ourselves" [9]. When my father was mugged a few years ago, he became a UCR statistic. To my knowledge he has not participated in a victimization survey. But when it comes to white-collar crime, we are all victims at one time or another.

Serials and Periodicals Related to Crime

In addition to the annual UCR and crime victimization surveys, LEAA and the National Criminal Justice Information and Statistics Service of the Justice Department have been issuing an annual Sourcebook of Criminal Justice Statistics. This is a large compendium of criminal justice and related statistics currently available from a variety of government agencies and private sources. The data included are national in scope. Primary sources of information on the nature and extent of criminal activity are the UCR and NCS studies, but many other sources are cited. The compilers review hundreds of research reports, journals, books, and government publications in selecting data for the Sourcebook.

Periodicals concerned wholly with crime information include

the FBI Law Enforcement Bulletin and Justice Assistance News, both monthlies. The former carries signed articles on topics such as firearms courses for police, public relations programs in law enforcement agencies, occupational stress in police work, crowd control strategies at athletic events, psychological profiles of arsonists, and the like. Contributors include FBI personnel, police in local agencies, and academicians. Standard features include legal analyses of various police problems (e.g., search warrant requirements) and the notorious "Wanted by the FBI" list.

Justice Assistance News, formerly titled LEAA Newsletter, publishes news notes and items about LEAA activities in the areas of that agency's responsibilities. A recurring feature is called "Publications," brief annotations of books, pamphlets, training manuals, and reports issued by associations and research institutions in the field of criminal justice and related disciplines. The FBI Law Enforcement Bulletin is not a sales item but is available to depository libraries. Justice Assistance News is sold by the Superintendent of Documents and is also a depository item.

The many faces of crime are revealed in the large number of articles that appear in other government magazines: Access, Aging, Alcohol Health and Research World, American Education, Black News Digest, Civil Rights Digest, Direction, Forum, Postal Life, Survey of Current Business, Synergist, Worklife, etc. Most frequently cited in recent issues of the Index to U.S. Government Periodicals were Drug Enforcement, the FBI Law Enforcement Bulletin, and the excellent Federal Probation. Subjects in these periodicals suggest the range of crime activities: cigarette bootlegging, computer crime, mail fraud, car repair ripoffs, narcotics control, "sting" operations, rape and alcohol abuse, illegal aliens, victim restitution, auto theft, probation management, burglary, prison violence, child pornography. That the above represents a mere sampling of criminality can scarcely bring feelings of joy to the contemplative heart.

An Agency's Demise

Recent federal budget cuts have forced the restructuring of the Law Enforcement Assistance Administration and the Office of Justice Assistance, Research, and Statistics (OJARS). The reorganization strengthens the National Institute of Justice and Bureau of Justice Statistics, but would reduce LEAA to a small role in managing existing grants and closing programs. According to LEAA's chief officer, the retrenchment would involve "nearly $1 billion of federal funds" and "the jobs of approximately 30,000 state or local employees working on programs in every state and major unit of local government" as well as some 500 Justice Department employees. However, the Bureau of Justice Statistics "will broaden its collection and analysis of criminal justice statistics" [10].

The New York Times editorialized that LEAA, which was "born in 1968 of liberal reformers, driven from door to door by political enemies, has finally been left for dead by friend and foe alike." The agency's failure to "stamp out crime," according to The Times, "was part of the case for terminating [it]. That was never a fair test, for it misconceived the agency's broad mission. Direct crime reduction was part of it, but the more basic aim was to help local law enforcement help itself, something which might not pay off visibly for a long time." Mourning the agency's apparent demise, The Times conveyed the "spooky feeling that LEAA is being buried alive" [11].

Conclusion

Skogan avers that the "presence of error of considerable magnitude is not unique to measures of crime, although a half-century of continuous criticism has focused more attention upon the errorful nature of crime measures than enjoyed by most social statistics." Unfortunately, the discrepancies between FBI reports and survey figures do not tell us where the error lies. "Every statistic ... is shaped by the process which operationally defines it, the procedures which capture it, and the organization which processes and interprets it [12]. Of what value, then, are these much maligned data reported by the FBI and other agencies, criticized by professors, unfairly depicted by the news media, used shamelessly by cynical politicians, and worried over by a confused, concerned public? Concerning UCR data, one student of the discipline, while acknowledging that the figures "are besmeared with numerous limitations, including incompleteness and bias, and clearly fall considerably short in reporting the full extent of crime that actually occurs in the United States," finds something positive to say. The data can be used "to construct a portrait of the directional nature of specific offense patterns" and to forecast "more appropriate directions for law enforcement machinery" [13]. The prestigious Scientific American magazine noted that one useful finding arising from victimization surveys was that, for the majority of Americans, crime of the type surveyed is not, in fact, "an important personal problem--compared with issues such as inflation, unemployment, educational costs or race and sex discrimination." Even if the surveys cannot measure "actual" crime, they can "provide important information about the distribution and social consequences of crime and also data relevant to specific issues such as gun control and compensation for victims of crime. And by exploring public attitudes about crime and criminal justice the surveys could help to dispel the ignorance, misunderstanding and irrational fear that now so often characterize public debate and discussion of crime" [14].

Critics have a right to complain, in a responsible way, about the distortions and inaccuracies of UCR and NCS data; those in the safe, academic world of criminal justice research have an obligation to devise methodologies that would reduce the margin of error and include more relevant crime categories. Suppose, however, that one fine day we were able to achieve a report that included all crime and criminal activity? Such a report would account for every politician taking a bribe, every merchant diddling a customer, every lawyer swindling a client, every physician carving a patient with reckless abandon, every bureaucrat promulgating a lethal regulation, everyone cheating the tax collector, and so on and so on. If this sort of crime conspectus were proclaimed to the world, verily the great stone heads of Easter Island would weep for man's depravity. Those intent on expanding the base of crime statistics may wish to reflect that Quetelet's "criminogenic propensity" applies to us all.

Thus it would appear that the pervasive nature of wrongful conduct will forever elude the slide rules of social scientists, however subtle and ingenious their methodologies become. The meliorism of the rationalists always rubs against the power and darkness of an earlier doctrine, and the theologians may possess the final word. As Chesterton said, "By its nature the evidence of Eden is something that one cannot find. By its nature the evidence of sin is something that one cannot help finding" [15].

References

1. Michael D. Maltz, "Crime Statistics: A Historical Perspective," Crime and Delinquency 23 (January 1977): 32-33, 36.

2. James A. Inciardi, "The Uniform Crime Reports: Some Consideration on their Shortcomings and Utility," Review of Public Data Use 6 (November 1978): 3.

3. U.S. Federal Bureau of Investigation, Crime in the United States, 1978 (Washington: Government Printing Office, 1979), p. 1.

4. Ibid., p. 6.

5. Maltz, op. cit., p. 32; Inciardi, op. cit., pp. 6-7.

6. Inciardi, op. cit., p. 5.

7. The surveys, called Criminal Victimization in the United States [year]: A National Crime Survey Report, have been available for sale by the Superintendent of Documents and are received by depository libraries under Item No. 968-H-6.

8. James P. Levine, "The Potential for Crime Overreporting in Criminal Victimization Surveys," Criminology 14 (November 1976): 307-330.

9. U.S. Congress, House, Committee on the Judiciary, Subcommittee on Crime, White-Collar Crime, Hearings, 95th Cong., 2d Sess., June 21, July 12 and 19, December 1, 1978 (Washington: Government Printing Office, 1979), pp. 21-24, 31.

10. Justice Assistance News 1 (October 1980): 1, 6.

11. The New York Times (City Edition), October 20, 1980, p. A18.

12. Wesley G. Skogan, "Measurement Problems in Official and Survey Crime Rates," Journal of Criminal Justice 3 (Spring 1975): 18.

13. Inciardi, op. cit., p. 14.

14. "Science and the Citizen," Scientific American 237 (July 1977): 58.

15. G.K. Chesterton, All Things Considered (London: Methuen & Co., 1908), pp. 191-92.

GIRLS' AND BOYS' READING INTERESTS:
KEEPING THE OPTIONS OPEN*

Elizabeth Segel

As the third graders jostled their way into the room, they were unobtrusively sorted out by the pleasant woman in charge--boys to the far corner, girls to a circle of chairs nearby. It looked to me like preparations for the old sex-education lectures we had in junior high school: the Kotex movie for the girls and--come to think of it, not having a brother, I never did find out what happened in the boys' session. But this wasn't a sex-education class, it was the library period, and the woman sorting out the children was the school librarian. She did this regularly, she confided to me, taking the boys herself and reading them a story with lots of humor and action. A student intern took the girls ("they're much easier, you know"), having been instructed to choose for them a family story or a fairy tale. I was an observer at my children's school when this occurred, not so many years ago; my hesitant questioning of the sex-segregation for story time had no effect, nor did the other parents' protests. The librarian felt her years of experience had taught her all about the difference between boys' and girls' reading interests.

At that time (the mid-70s), education students came to my children's literature class under the impression that when choosing books to read to a group of children, one should pick a book that appeals to boys; they'd been taught that girls will read (or listen to) "boys' books," but boys won't sit still for "girls' books."

Assumptions about the distinctly different reading preferences of boys and girls are legacies from the Victorian Age, when male and female were assumed to be popular opposites, like hot and cold, or fast and slow. The "boys' book," as it evolved in the mid-19th Century, was adventurous, full of action and suspense, and always had a male protagonist. Often, as in Treasure Island and ... Tom Sawyer, women played no part except as representatives of the confining everyday world the boy hero escaped from. The "girls' book"

---

*Reprinted by permission of the author and publisher from School Library Journal, 28:7 (March 1982) 105-107. Published by R.R. Bowker Co. (a Xerox company). Copyright © 1982 by Xerox Corporation.

was, on the other hand, domestic in setting and in subject, and featured female characters, though males were included. Physical courage and enterprise won out over countless dangers in the boys' book; the taming of "tomboy" impulses and acceptance of the self-effacing domestic role was the most common theme of the girls' book. Over the years, books about sports, war, detectives, spies, and science fiction joined the boys' book category. The girls' book never achieved that kind of variety: it was domestic, above all -- the family story for younger girls, the "young romance" theme for older. Within the territory of the girls' book, only the subliterature of Nancy Drew and her like provided a wider arena.

It was soon observed that girls not only read "their own" books, but also devoured a good many that were labeled "boys' books." Boys, it was believed, did not read girls' books. (Some, in adulthood, have confessed that they once shed a few tears over their sister's copy of Little Women, but surreptitiously.) As this suggests, the root of the matter was the relative status of matters male and female in our society. For girls, no onus was attached to reading a boys' book, since boys were the privileged sex (though having to trespass on territory marked out for boys must have reinforced their sense of second-class citizenship). For the boy, however, the pressure to avoid and even to hold in contempt things feminine ruled out a great many books. One of the most serious results of the division of children's books by gender was that, except for those few sneaky brothers willing to risk their reputations for a good read, boys did not have the experience of reading about girls. (Any book with a female protagonist was automatically labeled a girls' book.) If, as I believe, one of the highest functions of literature is to enable us to experience life from a perspective different than the one we are born to, this is a serious loss indeed.

Given all this, it's not surprising that publishers preferred to print stories with male protagonists and "boys' themes." They sold better. (As late as 1980 the textbook Teaching Elementary Language Arts repeated the truism: "It has been found that boys will not read 'girl books,' whereas girls will read 'boy books.'" It concluded, "Therefore the ratio of 'boy books' should be about two to one in the classroom library collection." [Dorothy Rubin; Holt, p. 183]). In particular, elementary school textbooks and early-reader trade books were male dominated, since Johnny rather than Janey was likely to have trouble learning to read, and thus it seemed particularly important to offer at this level stories that appealed to boys.

In the decade just past, the imbalance was noted and pressure exerted on publishers to provide more female protagonists. And because librarians and parents were willing to purchase better books when they became available, change was rapid. Many fine books about female characters engaged in a much wider range of activities are now being published. No one, I trust, labels a display "boys' books" or "girls' books" these days. Even the librarian at my children's former school no longer reads to boys and girls separately. The progress is real.

Does this mean that each child is now free to choose any book, governed only by her or his interests and tastes as an individual? That no child is effectively denied access because of gender to certain books that she or he might enjoy? Not necessarily. Though few professionals talk of boys' books and girls' books today, much attention is focused on reading preferences of the two sexes. This interest stems from good intentions--after all, our job is to get "the right book to the right child," isn't it? To do that, we have to know what that child likes.

Alas, these good intentions have yielded a remarkable quantum of foolishness. Take the recently revised Books and the Teenage Reader by G. Robert Carlsen (Bantam, 1980). Carlsen soberly elaborates extensive differences between boys' and girls' preferences in plot (girls "tend to prefer ... a neat, tightly organized plot"), setting (boys like outdoor settings, girls indoor), time span (girls like "a defined temporal setting ... a summer, or a school year"), and style ("Males generally prefer realistic style to romanticism"). Besides deploring the sheer wrongheadedness of this (how does one square the last pronouncement with the success of Treasure Island through generations of boys?), one wonders: why bother making such statements? Would anyone screen books for a "defined temporal setting" before offering them to girls? The only comfort is that all this represents an improvement over the first edition's even wilder generalizations on the subject (Bantam, 1967).

Supposedly objective studies of reading interests also leave much to be desired. Most hinge on the child's selecting a term that describes the kind of book she or he likes to read--a technique that probably tells us more what children think they should like than what they actually read. Some studies ask children to rank categories that are grossly inadequate as descriptors of the range of available reading. Even George Norvell's relatively sophisiticated study, The Reading Interests of Young People (rev. ed., Michigan State Univ. Pr., 1973), admitted at the outset the questionable reliability of its design: "The plan chosen was to examine the reactions of boys and of girls toward a list of selections, each of which was dominated by a single factor, and to depend upon the minimizing of the potency of other factors through cancellation. Undoubtedly the method has pitfalls, since cancellation may not function as expected." Yet from his dubious data, Norvell drew sweeping conclusions about the dominance of sex as a determinant of young people's reading choices.

Obviously, a well-designed analysis of children's actual reading would be much more revealing than any of these studies. Yet even a methodologically sound study would have to be viewed with caution. For one thing, studies of sex differences, by definition, stress the dissimilarities and ignore the similarities between the sexes; universal human interests are shortchanged. We must also keep in mind that in studies such as these, significant numbers of children do not fit the dominant pattern; we need to resist the natural tendency to regard those outside the established norms as deviant.

What weight, then, should we give to apparently gender-related reading interests as we try to help each young reader to find pleasure in reading and to develop as a unique person? First, we can be discriminating. Although we see evidence every day that some types of books are read by more children of one sex than the other, we should recognize that some of these preferences are more open to change than others. For instance, the still prevalent tendency of boys to shun books with female protagonist probably testifies more to the power of peer pressure than to any difficulty of cross-gender identification. After all, if a boy can participate imaginatively in Peter Rabbit's adventures, he surely can share those of Laura Ingalls. But how to break down the resistance? Not by pressuring a boy to check out a book that he fears being teased about. No, our best opportunity to introduce to children books they wouldn't choose themselves is reading aloud. Moreover, one of the proven benefits of reading aloud is the broadening of children's reading interests. Resist the stale advice to "play it safe with a boys' book," and you'll find that oral reading sessions provide the perfect chance for boys occasionally to experience life from a feminine perspective. (Keep this in mind, too, when teachers or parents ask you to recommend a book for reading aloud.)

Another chink in the macho armor is children's loyalty to an author who has provided them with a favorite book. Boys who have enjoyed Beverly Cleary's Henry Huggins (1950) or The Mouse and the Motorcycle (1965; both Morrow) can be persuaded to try the Ramona books. Boys who appreciate Betsy Byars's perceptive accounts of growing up male in our society, such as The Midnight Fox (1968) and The Eighteenth Emergency (1973), are usually willing to give Summer of the Swans (1970; all Viking) or The Night Swimmers (Delacorte, 1980) a try.

We need to recognize, too, that some of the old "truths" about gender-linked differences in reading interests were more in the eye of the beholder than in the children themselves. Take the observation that primary school girls choose family stories while boys of the same age read sports fiction. Did you ever notice that a great many sports stories--Alfred Slote's baseball stories, for instance--hinge on the relationship of the boy to his parents? Here is a clear case of different labels obscuring the similarities in girls' and boys' interests at a particular age.

The sports book suggests another pitfall. Don't peg today's children by those of a generation, or even a decade, ago. A 1979 update of a 1971 study (by Joan T. Feeley et al.; ERIC/RCS Document ED 172 167) showed that girls identified sports much more frequently as a reading interest than previously. One school librarian noticed that since her elementary school began to include girls on the track team, the rush to books about running has been coeducational, too. As sports become an important part of more girls' lives, girls become more interested in reading about sports.

Though different studies have made much of the slight

differences between girls' and boys' ranking of books of humor, adventure, mystery, animals, historical fiction, and biography, I believe that these categories, too, have virtually equal appeal to today's girls and boys. Even war stories, once considered quintessentially masculine, are read by girls, especially if they go beyond the old "coward or hero" theme to more varied psychological and ethical issues (as many war stories do today). Fairy tales are still regarded in some circles as feminine fare, but if children are introduced to heroes as well as to heroines, and to tales of humor and adventure, not just the old romantic standbys, they will recognize fairy tales as the universally satisfying literature that they are.

The association of science fiction with the male sex will probably be harder to overcome, partly because one is dealing with older, more thoroughly acculturated children than the audience for fairy tales. Science, technology, even speculative thinking, have been labeled--subtly or not so subtly--boys' territory. Many are committed to changing that message, but change will be slow. No doubt, too, the dominance of male authors and characters in early science fiction has contributed to girls' lack of enthusiasm. That, too, is changing; we can hasten this change by finding the best non-sexist examples of the genre and introducing them to girls, so that they do not miss out on this intellectually challenging and entertaining form. (Of course, some girls just won't have a taste for the genre--as some boys don't. The point is that they shouldn't be channeled away from it.)

The genre that seems most exclusively an enthusiasm of girls is the teenage romance. The strictly female appeal of these books reflects a difference in the rate of psychosocial development for girls and boys, however, not an absolute difference of interests. Girls, of course, mature physically earlier than boys. As they cope with rapid physical and emotional maturation, they often turn to books about adolescent girls who are facing the same unsettling but exciting changes. Unfortunately, when boys--a few years later--develop similar interests and anxieties, they find very little fiction about dating written for young adults from a male point of view. Of course, by then the more advanced readers are reading adult novels like The Catcher in the Rye, which depicts a male coming to terms with his sexuality, but the less able readers miss out.

I've left for last what may be the most far-reaching difference between the reading choices of boys and girls. An experienced school librarian said to me recently: "The biggest difference I notice between girl and boy readers is that after about fourth grade, most boys check out only informational books, while girls go on devouring fiction." I haven't been able to find studies confirming this phenomenon, but other librarians I've talked with corroborate the observation. Middle-grade boys love manuals, science nonfiction, photographic essays--they even grab the sports superstar biographies and leave the sports fiction sitting on the shelf. And one librarian remarked wryly: "You know, my husband's the same way." In fact, the phenomenon isn't confined to the young. Publishers have always considered women the chief consumers of novels.

Girls' socialization, particularly as adolescence approaches, seems to breed an interest in human relationships, the fundamental subject of fiction. As Letty Cottin Pogrebin describes it: "While boys are shooting baskets or BB guns, girls are talking, sharing secrets, confessing fears, and comparing fantasies ... they are continually practicing 'self-disclosure' ... and refining the art of knowing someone else inside out." She acknowledges that "Boys have feelings too, of course. They experience sadness, love, anger, and fear exactly as girls do. But their sex role demands action and not emotional expression (Growing Up Free: Raising Your Child in the 80s. McGraw, 1980). Each socialization mode has its advantages: girls are prepared for intimacy; boys for accomplishment. The problem is that we want our girls and our boys to accomplish things; we want both to successfully develop intimate human relationships. Mightn't knowing intimately a range of fictional characters supplement a typical boy's limited interactions with other people? Mightn't exposure to outstanding informational books stimulate a girl's curiosity about the world and enhance her sense of competence in dealing with it?

Or is this divergence in reading behavior a symptom of an even greater problem? Maybe all those boys are choosing nonfiction because they have only a minimal interest in reading at all. If they must check out books, they'll choose those with lots of pictures and little text. Of course, significant numbers of boys are literate and enthusiastic readers all their lives, but large numbers of males in our culture have always viewed reading itself, and certainly literature, as effeminate. If this is still the case, then here is surely one of the most serious penalties we pay for the legacy of narrowly defined gender traits, and one of the greatest incentives to challenge their influence on children's reading.

RESEARCH ON LIBRARY SERVICES

FOR CHILDREN AND YOUNG ADULTS:

IMPLICATIONS FOR PRACTICE*

Shirley Fitzgibbons

Introduction

During the 1970s, there has been a great deal of "gnashing of teeth" over the scarcity of research concerning children and young adult services in public libraries by those who have attempted state of the art reviews of research (Gallivan, 1974 [1]; Shontz, 1982 [2]); and those who have written about the importance and need for such research (Billeter, 1975 [3]; Kingsbury, 1977 [4]; Fasick, 1978 [5]; Lukenbill, 1979 [6]; Furman, 1979 [7]; and Fitzgibbons, 1980 [8]). Gallivan in her review of research published from 1960-1972 identified only fourteen studies on public library service concerning the preschool age group through age fourteen. She recognized that school libraries have far more frequently been the object of research than public libraries, identifying thirty-two such studies for her review. There are also several outstanding reviews of school library research; Gaver (for the period up to 1960, 1962, 1969 [9]) Lowrie (1950-1967 period, 1968) [10]; Aaron (1967-1971, 1972) [11]; Barron (1972-1976, 1977) [12] and Aaron (1977-   , pending publication, 1982) [13]. Kingsbury [4] identified six studies concerning public library services, in addition to the Gallivan group. Shontz, looking only at research related to children and young adult services in public libraries both before 1970 (earliest study was 1941) and after that date, summarized forty studies specifically designed to study some aspect of public library service to children and young adults, thirty of these studies lamenting the lack of research. This paper will suggest that it is possible to draw implications from the best major studies and from groups of small-scale studies.

It is unlikely that the 1980s will produce a greater amount of research concerning services to children and young adults, due to governmental and institutional budget problems. Service practitioners are fighting for their jobs, and for maintaining even traditional

---

*Reprinted by permission of the author and publisher from Emergency Librarian, 9:5 (May-June 1982) 6-17.

services. It is for these reasons that it is all the more important for those concerned about the future of these services to examine closely what we already know from research and to try to use this knowledge in practice. The cry has been sounded for the need for hard facts to justify services and staff, for the skills of measurement and evaluation in planning and evaluating continuing and new services; and for knowing the processes for establishing goals and setting priorities. What does research since 1970 tell practitioners?

What Is Research?

Before one can even suggest that a particular study or a group of studies provide evidence to consider in decision-making, it is important to explore briefly the definition of research. In the broadest framework, there are at least two types of research, basic and applied. More recently, a concept labeled either locally-based research, field research, evaluation research, or action research appears in library literature, as a part of the applied research area. Even though the area of basic research is fundamental to the furthering of knowledge in terms of theory building and testing, practitioners are most concerned with applied, and most specifically with field, research which helps to clarify practices and evaluate particular techniques and services in specific settings.

As in most areas of librarianship, research concerning services to children and young adults tends to be cumulative, and tends to be unsophisticated in terms of statistical techniques. Rather than be deterred by the state of the art, we will examine the best of the major studies which address fundamental problems facing services in the 1980s. Research concerning materials, such as content analysis, though pertinent for collection development, will not be included, as it is discussed sufficiently elsewhere. There will be no attempt either to review the studies qualitatively or to discuss methodology, both of which are found in review articles. References will lead the reader directly to the research report, reviews, and/or popular journal articles. References include citations to all sources available, or to only one when that is the most accessible. No attempt has been made to undertake an exhaustive research literature search, rather those studies already identified in literature available to practitioners and researchers will be the focus.

What Research Can and Cannot Do

Kingsbury argues that research "... can win support since the force of evidence is often necessary to convince people of the value of children's services" [4:132]. Fasick points out that "... (research) cannot answer questions of value; cannot tell you what your goals should be, but only indicate how you might achieve particular goals [5:345]. Though this is generally true, a Delphi study by Kingsbury (1978) [14, 15] does identify goals (trends and innovations) of national leaders of children's services. Simplistic suggestions may result from studies that do not fully take in consideration the many variables that may affect a particular research question. However, when study after study shows similar results, it is apparent that something is generally true. Fasick suggests, "Research, in the broad meaning of a careful, systematic search for new facts, should help in the task of measuring and evaluating children's services, but it is not a panacea that will solve all library problems" [5:344].

Though not correctly labeled research, the use of statistical information is important as Winnick so clearly emphasized, "Without national evaluative studies or quantitative standards for measuring public library service to children, the use of recurring statistical information could illuminate the condition and document the development of these services" [16]. She went on to say that statistics have not been collected systematically in the past, either at the national level, by state record keeping, or at local levels. A great deal of information is available today, and can be used to identify users/nonusers and needs in the local community. Practitioners need to locate this data and use it wisely.

Access to Research

Much dissertation research never becomes published as a monograph, and many of them never appear in journal articles. This is a problem that should be addressed elsewhere; but it seems important to point out an apparent bias among scholarly journals in the library/information field concerning research in the children and young adult services area. Also, our own professional journals have not been particularly research conscious until quite recently; the editors of those journals seem to want the content of the studies to be "popularized" and made "good reading" to the point that there is often little substance available to judge the quality of the research being presented, or to assess the methods and techniques to determine its generalizability and importance.

In the interim, this brief article will look at major research studies that apply to public library services to children and young adults and will tentatively make suggestions concerning what we can learn from this research.

Implications

Shontz, in her review of the forty studies of some aspect of public library service to children and young adults, presented five examples of generalizations from recent research which have implications for decision-making in public libraries:

> Public library use studies report <u>high use of the public library collection and services by young adults, and young adults' preference for using the public library over the school library.</u> (Yet young adult services and programs are not given high priority).

<u>Storytelling services and summer reading clubs have apparent positive effects on children's learning.</u> (Yet these programs are sometimes overlooked by administrators, and suffer from budget cutting).

<u>A lack of qualified personnel is a crucial problem</u> in the development of library programs for children and young adults. (Yet few library schools have responded to the need for specialized education programs in early childhood education and young adult programming).

<u>Younger children and children from lower socioeconomic levels have a greater need for audiovisual materials.</u> (Yet public libraries have been slow in developing multimedia services for children).

<u>Schools and public libraries serve essentially the same children</u> and have many common goals, and purposes. There are benefits to each from sharing knowledge, collections, and services. (Yet it is obvious that <u>they are not communicating or cooperating with each other in promoting learning in children</u>).

The rest of this article will group the studies under the following categories of research: goals and future outlook; state-wide surveys; administrative studies; reading interests, behaviour and motivation; use and user studies; school/public library cooperation; programs and services--general and services to special groups (early childhood, special children, young adults); professional image of youth librarians. Though several studies of most types will be cited, the research implications are in italics with a brief description of the findings of each major study.

Goals and Future Outlook

Two studies serving similar purposes are those by Kingsbury [14, 15] for children's services and Downen (1979) [17] for young adult services. Both use modified Delphi techniques, and assess perceptions of persons who are usually in decision-making positions. Kingsbury queried the coordinators of children's services and qualified children's librarians concerning trends, goals, and innovations in children's services over the next twenty-five years. Downen asked directors of public library systems (serving at least 100,000 people) to list the most important developments they would either expect or would like to see initiated in public libraries' programs for young adults over the following fifteen years. Kingsbury found two priorities evident on the part of respondents: <u>children's librarians must become truly administrators</u> (act as part of the planning team); <u>and they must provide services to those not already served</u> by the public library to insure the survival of children's services (preschoolers, exceptional children, and those indifferent to school). Some of these goals have since been implemented in many public libraries; all should consider them.

Downen found it highly encouraging that an overwhelming majority (81 percent) of the survey respondents felt that service to young adults should be continued and expanded; though 47 percent of these respondents were uncertain whether or not this would still be the case by the year 1993. Even though 66 percent felt it undesirable that the YA department be eliminated, 36 percent were uncertain regarding the probability. He concluded that though directors show uncertainty as to the future of YA services, they do feel it is important and a desirable function of the public library. He also pointed out reactions to alternatives to a discrete YA department: negative feelings toward placing it with the juvenile department, positive feelings of putting YA services into the adult department; and/or making it a broader area such as adult services or readers advisory. There was less emphasis on programs and more on reading and orientation toward general education/motivation for lifetime use of libraries. There was great uncertainty regarding increased bibliotherapeutic use of materials and training of the YA librarian as a quasi-counselor.

State-wide Surveys of Children's Services

The 1970s have produced several major statewide surveys of children's (sometimes including young adult) services in public libraries, including North Carolina (1972) [18], New York (1972) [19], Illinois (1978) [20], Ohio (1979) [21], Wisconsin (1980) [22], and California (1981) [23]. The major studies have usually been done in cooperation with a library school or research center, the state library association's children (and/or young adults) section, and/or the state library agency and have often had funding. Recent studies easily found in the literature to date are those of Illinois [20], and Ohio [21], and Wisconsin [22]. The studies seem to be done for a similar reason: to serve as status quo descriptions of service to the specific age group as it exists in the state; sometimes they use a sampling of libraries, all libraries, and or recommended "exemplary" libraries.

Results show similarities such as the Wisconsin study report indication of major inequities in the lack of proportionate relationship between the percent of children's materials circulated and the budget, staff, and space alloted to them. The proportion of circulation of children and young adult materials was at least 40 percent in two-fifths of these libraries; and more than 50 percent in fifteen percent of them. Equally distressing was the fact that only about half of the libraries involved their children's staff in areas of library decision-making (budget, personnel, goals). The Illinois study showed similar results to Wisconsin's with the mean percentage of total library expenditures spent on children's services at 25 percent, while the mean percentage of library circulation in children's services at 34 percent. The lack of initiative on the part of children's librarians to concern themselves with budget decisions was again mentioned, with many librarians having their first exposure to the library's annual report through the study. Fasick points out these anomalies which invite further investigation and discussion: the overwhelming rejection of suggestions to eliminate children's services coupled with a lack of interest in measurement or evaluation of these services; the apparent lack of understanding of the nature and purpose of setting library goals; the high priority given to the presentation of film programs while at the same time a lack of concern for film as a medium of artistic expression.

The Connecticut Research Documentation Project, initiated by Hektoen and as reported (1980, 1981) [24], seems to be more of a systematic gathering of statistics on an ongoing basis in order to better describe current services than research; but it's a very important effort at developing measurement instruments, after deciding what measurements were needed, and how and by whom the data could best be gathered to record use of the public library's children's services. Generalizations such as Connecticut libraries do not have enough children's materials and professionally trained librarians led to the obvious suggestion for closer work with schools. The many community service referral questions, and increased adult use of children's services indicated that there is an increasing new client group for children's librarians--the adult who works with children.

Starr and Talbot [25] surveyed the post-proposition 13 status of public library services for children and young adults in California as compared to before proposition 13. Though their response rate was poor with almost no response from school libraries, almost an equal number of children and young adult public librarians responded. A dismal picture was presented with decreases in hours, staff, inservice training, programs, etc.; but the point of the survey was to urge Californians to "use the cold figures ... provide ammunition for those who wish to fight the battle for quality library service"[25]. This seems to be a valid rationale for such a study; however these results should continue to be monitored in terms of services and efforts of professionals and interested publics in that state. Could Massachusetts or other states with similar problems be helped by the California experience?

Administrative Studies

A national study by Benne (1978, 1980) [26] tried to identify the roles and functions of central children's libraries in urban library systems in terms of the changes in cities, the changes in administrative patterns, and the priorities set in response to financial problems. Benne did not attempt to judge the quality of effectiveness of services in this exploratory survey. She found a great deal of isolation on the part of these children's librarians (not participating in departmental meetings, or on committees); the number of professional positions had decreased (more than half reported a decrease), and that qualifications had been changed (lowered) so that less occupants have the MLS degree. In a time when hours had been decreased, more than one-half the circulation from the children's collection in the central library occurs on weekends. She suggested that many problems seem to stem from a mutual misunderstanding of roles (rather than as personality differences).

It was further suggested that children's services staff seem to place a higher priority on the education role rather than the information/reference role. This includes the adult public who needs help with children's materials or programming and uses the children's literature collection frequently as a reference source. Adult publics were identified as those concerned mainly with the child and those concerned with children's literature. User groups were ranked in the following order: school aged children, preschool children, parents, and adult users of children's literature. Benne felt the educational role assumption needs to be explored more fully.

Reading Interests, Behavior, Motivation

Most reading interest studies fall into simple surveys of favorite titles, or types of books, are studies of one city or large public library system, or of one state, and seem to be mainly directed toward young adults (Goetze, 1972 [27]; Hutchinson, 1973 [28]; Campbell et al., 1974 [29]; Alm, 1974 [30]; Wynn and Newmark, 1979) [31]. It is surprising how similar the top ten lists are, whether by title, author, or subject during any time period, and despite the variety of geographical areas. These results are interesting for other libraries to consider; and more importantly, to undertake similar surveys, using the same techniques and age groups.

The most recent survey by Wynn and Newmark pointed out the importance of local surveys and some of the benefits that can result: an increased cooperation between the public library and the school (administrators, teachers, and librarians) based on the cooperative effort of the survey as well as some of the specific results; information for collection development to better meet current interests and needs of a user group; and information on specific service areas improvement. The time spent on the survey could be easily justified due to these results. The learning and discussion as a part of the process with those people who should be talking with each other is an important byproduct of research.

One study, though limited to high school students in one city (Carlson et al., 1975) [32] has become an annual survey, and appears regularly in English Journal. It is especially useful in showing trends and changes over time. Another area study which has now been accomplished three times is the Bay Area Young Adult Librarians (BAYA) survey which also shows changes over time of enduring topics, authors, and specific titles. (Minudri and Bodart, 1973 [33], 1975; Bodart, 1979 [34]). In the most recent study, it was found that four authors (Tolkien, Hinton, Zindel, and Asimov) appeared on all three lists; that Blume appeared for the first time, with two of her titles appearing, but was only popular with the younger teens. Fantasy and escapist fiction (love, mysteries, and adventure) rated the highest. Surprisingly, paperbacks were not as highly preferred as expected, especially among older teens; and TV and movies though still an influence did not specifically influence as many choices as previously.

Two national studies of reading interests of teenagers (Freiberger, 1973 [35]; Stachelek, 1977 [36]) show similar results as the local studies for similar time periods, giving a great deal of credibility to generalization from local studies. In 1973, it was found that major interests were the occult and supernatural, fantasy and science fiction and problem young adult fiction. In 1977, science fiction, romance and stories about teens endured as well as the escapist literature mentioned by the BAYA poll. Among these twelfth graders, however, paperbacks were still preferred. Generally, half of these students were moderate readers, while one-third identified themselves as avid readers (a higher percentage than usual).

A more indepth study by Greenberg (1979) [37] studied the factors that led seventh grade students to choose books. Factors contributing included: family participation and encouragement; a school library, librarian, and teachers that rewarded reading ability; friends that viewed reading positively; a public library and librarian that promoted good relations with the students; and a family income that afforded comic books, magazines, and books. Students read on the basis of personal recommendations, printed recommendations, and by the subject, title, cover, and display of the material. There are implications here for collection development, suggested topics and titles for booktalks and displays, and for librarians being willing to share books and to create a reading environment.

Many of the reading surveys could and did include questions about use of libraries, sources of books and other information, and reading patterns. Numerous studies exist in the reading field in this area--with similar results to many of the library studies. For example, Scharf (1973) [38] examined reading habits in relation to sex, grade level, and intelligence. Students with higher IQs read more. Seniors read more materials regularly, prefer public libraries to school libraries, and prefer paperback books.

Somewhat similar was the Doyen study (1980) [39] which tried to compare reading preferences of different student groups, an inner city black junior high population with an alternative racially-balanced school for the creative and performing arts. Two constants were the collection and the librarians; and by comparing the circulation figures, Doyen concluded that contrary to popular assumption, large discrepancies in reading patterns did not exist. The main difference found was that the students from the alternative arts environment read more fiction and had a positive attitude toward leisure-time reading. That the school curriculum may be less important than other factors is interesting; and needs to be explored further by both school and public librarians. From reading studies, indications that home influences, reading ability and peer influences are most important also need to be considered. Bard and Leide [40] compared reading interests of grades one to six. While boys and girls began as first graders preferring imaginative literature; boys by the third grade preferred nonfiction, an interest which continued through grade six. By the fifth grade, girls preferred realistic fiction. Sex and age differences were certainly apparent. Do librarians consider these differences as they make booklists, booktalks, and encourage the reading of quality literature?

Media influences and effects are also important for public librarians working with children and young adults. Fasick (1970) [41] compared language in books and television to determine language learning from the two media. She found that children do not appear to learn as much language (verbal skills) from television as compared with being read picture books. As she points out, more research is needed to compare the differing effects of use of the two media; however, this is an excellent rationale for targeting the preschooler and the early primary child in story hour programs with parent involvement so that reading aloud will be continued in the home environment in place of some of the many hours now spent by this age group on watching television. Film preferences of fourth and fifth graders were studied by Cox (1975) [42] in terms of differences related to sex, race, or socioeconomic status. Boys and girls' ranking were nearly identical except boys liked a type labeled action/sport/outdoors while girls like a fantasy/excitement type. There were not significant differences between sex, race, or socioeconomic status; however, all children showed a preference for certain film form/techniques such as narrative/live-action; narrative/animation: and liking least non-narrative/animation films. Film selections are an important part of both collection building and programming for children and young adults and an area we need to know more about.

User and User Studies

This one area alone could comprise this entire article but an attempt will be made to highlight the results of important studies. Several early studies need to be reviewed as base line data in interpreting the results of more recent use studies in establishing how many of the total users are youth, types of users, total percentage of circulation of youth groups, and user profile characteristics. Two major urban public library studies by Martin (1967, 1969 [43]) indicated that the young adult age group was one of the largest user groups, even though the library made only limited provision for them. In Chicago in 1969, 57.8 percent of young adults in the city were public library users; and over one-third of the users of the adult section of the library were from fifteen to nineteen years old. In an even earlier study, looking only at students in Baltimore (1963) [44], it was found that two-thirds of all high school students read an average of six books per month for school work; that school libraries did not have that substantial a subject collection; and young adults preferred to use the public library over their school libraries. This same finding is echoed in more recent studies. Wilder (1970) [46] in examining library usage by students in five Indiana cities discovered students found the public library more useful in school-related terms than school libraries and regarded public librarians more favorably. Even though Wilder found elementary aged children made up only ten percent of public library patrons, they used it with the greatest frequency and ninety-five percent were satisfied with the services.

Benford (1969, 1971) [46] reported on the now well-known Philadelphia Project which included a major survey of students in grades two through twelve in Philadelphia's public, parochial, and independent schools. Though this study is now over ten years old, many earlier and later small scale studies corroborate the findings. The rather startling news at that time was the change in attitude toward school libraries and public libraries often taking place between the fourth and 12th grades with accompanying use patterns. While 61 percent of the fourth graders enjoyed reading to fulfill teachers' assignments, only 22 percent of the 12th graders do; a drop in enjoyment of recreational reading is also evident with 75 percent of students in the fourth and sixth grades enjoying such reading as compared to 62 percent of the 12th graders. In terms of use of libraries, 42 percent of sixth and 12th graders used both school and public libraries, while 13 percent used only school libraries, 13 percent only public libraries, and 13 percent depended solely on other sources. The percent of students who only use the public library increases from five percent in the sixth grade to 21 percent in the 12th grade. While half of the students using libraries say they are satisfied, others complain about inability to find books they can read, failure to get assistance from library staff, negative feeling toward too many rules and regulations, etc. The negative feelings increase from more than half of elementary students finding nothing dissatisfying about their libraries to two-thirds of the 12th graders dissatisfied with school libraries (50 percent of them like everything about the public library).

Tower (1972) [47] in a study of changes in children's library services in Pittsburgh suburbs for the 1960-1970 period, found that as population increased, quality improved (resources, staff, budgets). School libraries showed greater change, due to federal funds and a Pennsylvania state mandate.

In an indepth analysis of fifth grader user and nonuser attitudes toward school and public libraries, Ekechukwu (1972) [48] discovered that there was a significant relationship between attitudes toward public libraries and use. Though a greater number were users of school libraries (which would be expected), a greater percentage of fifth-graders had more favorable attitudes toward public libraries mainly for the book collection (of both libraries) for books to read outside the library and secondly, for school related purposes. They most disliked the rules and regulations. Though sex was not a significant variable in terms of library use, girls had more favorable attitudes than boys toward public libraries. Apparently, negative attitudes toward school libraries began even before the junior high setting. None of these studies tried to analyze the reasons why student users formed such negative attitudes toward school libraries as compared to public libraries.

Fasick and England (1977) [49] investigated how well the collection and services of a Canadian public library met the educational and recreational needs of children from six to twelve years of age. More than ninety percent viewed the book collection as the major attraction; with nonprint drawing fifteen percent and programs, fifteen percent. Though the most frequently mentioned reason for using the library was to select books for personal reading, differences between boys and girls were apparent; boys were more likely than girls to come for informational purposes (both school and own interests). The use of library materials for school projects increases with age, and more so for boys. Implications for collection building are obvious; with circulation of fiction three times greater than nonfiction while only about 50 percent of the collection was fiction. About one child in eight expressed an interest in library programs, with film shows the most popular type.

User satisfaction was expressed in terms of finding what they were looking for with access through the catalogue though there are fewer subject headings than desired; boys offer more suggestions for changes and materials than girls. Nonusers did not present major differences as a group though school children who were interviewed in the school and classified as school users (as compared to the public library users) read less books and newspapers, had less ambitious career and educational aspirations, and had less positive self-image. Both groups viewed television frequently, enjoying the same kinds of programs, and in terms of books, both preferred fiction, especially mysteries, adventure, and horror stories. An implication of this study is that due to the similarity of users and nonusers, nonusers might be encouraged to use the library without any dramatic changes in collections or programs. One idea is to promote more nonbook materials for those who do not read for pleasure. Less than seven percent of any group named the school library as their first information source; and when asked where they would turn first for information, one half of the school sample named a person (parent, teacher, friend) with almost 40 percent of the library sample doing the same. However, more than one-third think of the library as a source of information. Sex differences were greater than user/nonuser differences for those under nine. As Fasick pointed out in her study, there is little information available about the factors which lead one child to use the public library while another does not; in 1965, Parker [50] had indicated that the adult user variables that characterize use (such as sex, age, ethnic and language background, and socioeconomic class) do not seem to relate to children as a user group. This needs to be more fully studied.

The access question is explored by Moll (1975) [51] who found that for children reading above national norms, the subject catalogs provided access to 70 percent of the juvenile books, but that only 28 percent of children's books were accessible if national findings regarding children's reading levels were applied. This conclusion that the subject card catalog does not provide effective access to information for children is disconcerting in terms of Fasick indicating that children access the collection generally through the catalogue. An interesting perspective was presented by Fasick (1978, 1979) [52] in her comparison study of views on services of librarians, parents, and teachers. Generally there was agreement on traditional services such as librarians guiding children in book selection; in developing a love for reading, and providing story hour programs, as well as the newer idea of providing experiences for children under three. Priority differences in services and programs were indicated by parents and teachers rating as higher priorities, interlibrary loans, joint programs for parents and children, and providing a place for children to meet friends; with librarians preferring as priorities helping parents choose books for children, and allowing children to use the adult section. In terms of collection development issues, parents and teachers felt more favorably toward series books and books based on popular TV series, audiovisual materials/and hardware, with librarians preferring comic books and sex education materials, and the groups agreeing on poetry, classical music, and popular recordings, toys for preschoolers, and games for children to use in the library. As one of the only studies of this type, it would be an interesting experience for local libraries to replicate in their community to help reach some consensus as a group on types of materials bought and types of programs sponsored with public monies.

A citation analysis of high school students' term papers by Mancall (1978, 1979) [53] indicated interesting implications for collection building in school and public libraries, as well as for library instruction. Students depended heavily on monographs, rather than journals or other media; references were surprisingly old; and patterns of use suggested that students think in terms of format rather than by subject needs. Though one might deduce that it is important that libraries hold certain journal titles (as these researchers suggest), the study results also seem to indicate that teachers and librarians need to instruct students in the importance of currency of materials especially in certain subject areas, to suggest that nonprint media and journals may be equally valuable as books and to instruct students both formally and informally in the access to these materials. More needs to be done in this area before too many decisions are made on the basis of one study, especially when many other variables were not studied as possible influences, i.e., lack of knowledge on the students' part.

School/Public Library Cooperation

Since 1970 when the controversial recommendations of the Commissioner of Education of New York State were issued (stating that the elementary school library should have the responsibility to meet the library needs of all children except those in health, welfare and correctional institutions), the whole issue of specific types of cooperation between these two institutions has been discussed, researched, and debated ad infinitum. Several major studies have been completed during the 1970s providing evidence of how specific cooperation can/cannot be accomplished. These studies are found in the popular literature, and should be familiar to those working in services to children and young adults in both institutional settings. The most recent studies by Amey (1974, 1979) [54], Kitchens (1975, 1981) [55], Woolard (1977, 1980) [56] and Aaron (1977, 1978, 1980) [57], deal specifically with describing the combined school/public libraries in both the U.S. and Canada, serving as directories (Amey, Woolard) as an analysis of one successful venture (Kitchens), or as case studies (Woolard), and extensive attempts to understand why some succeed while others fail (Aaron). Certain conclusions are offered: <u>success is more likely in communities with a small population</u> (Woolard); <u>one cannot expect financial savings</u> (Woolard, Kitchens); <u>common objectives must be present</u>; and for success, governance and responsibility must be well established (Woolard, Kitchens). Aaron's overall conclusion is that <u>a community able to support or now supporting separate libraries would be unlikely to succeed, but in a community with limited or unavailable services, the combined program may present a reasonable alternative.</u> The researchers suggest that it is not a panacea, and yet there are several success stories. The specific guidelines for success seem to be based on evidence and should be taken seriously when a community contemplates the shared library.

Because attitudes and common purposes are considered so important for success, three perception studies are also valuable: Amey (1976) [58], Dyer (1976, 1977, 1978) [59], and Weech (1979, 1979) [60]. Dyer's Delphi study, a large scale study assessing opinions of every group, found <u>respondents judged cooperative efforts to be more desirable than probable due to institutional rigidity, self-preservation, and protection of territory.</u> Dyer concluded that cooperation stands little chance of being implemented in the next fifteen years. Amey found that <u>school and public librarians differed in their attitudes towards the concept of combined libraries.</u> Weech found little difference in attitude between elementary and secondary school librarians, or between large or small libraries, but that <u>school librarians were more supportive of combined facilities than public librarians.</u> An earlier dissertation by Woolls (1973) [61] had a broader focus in terms of types of cooperative activities but was limited to Indiana school and public libraries. Again the finding that <u>use of school libraries did not negate use of public libraries was paramount, Woolls found little cooperation</u> including program planning, staffing, publicity, book selection, etc. A specific <u>recommendation for interlibrary loan as a cooperating effort was made by Altman (1971, 1972)</u> [62] in her study of title diversity and collection overlap in public secondary school libraries. Though Altman only surveyed school libraries, Tevis (1979) [63] describes the <u>development of a cooperative program of interlibrary loan from the public library to two public high schools through the school library.</u> It would be interesting to check on its ongoing success. This seems to be the most natural cooperative effort, yet apparently it is an unusual case.

Communication and Education   245

Programming and Services

Barass, Reitzel and Associates (1972) [64] evaluated thirty excellent public library reading and reading-related programs for preschoolers (7), elementary ages (7), young adults (6), adults (5), and multi-ages (5). They further selected twenty exemplary programs/services, provided description, a cost estimate, and an analysis of effectiveness (accomplished through telephone interviews to assess whether participants read more books, like to read more, liked the library more, watched more educational TV, or did better in school). This study provides evidence to justify beginning or continuing similar programs/services. Five major types of programs emerged: preschool group activities, bookmobiles for elementary school-aged children, outreach library collections for elementary children or young adults, separate children's collections, and group activities for young adults/adults. In terms of impact, bookmobiles for children and group preschool activities ranked the highest. Other interesting results include: preschool programs had the least cost per participant; children's bookmobiles with relaxed library procedures led to a large number of participants; outreach collections involved a high cost but attracted more participants; separate children's collections were expensive in terms of per participant cost; and group activities for young adults/adults attracted the fewest regular participants but were least expensive. Some very specific findings also have implications for public libraries: those users lacking reading skills (all ages) appreciate simplified shelving; preschoolers react well to ceremony in programs (i.e., the story candle) as compared to older children and young adults who opt for informality and spontaneity; and regular schedules for outreach and bookmobile services are important as irregularities lead to attendance loss. The study provided verification that children attending public library programs do increase significantly in reading interest and desire to learn. It also presents specific effective programs in terms of cost effectiveness and impact. The study raises fundamental questions about the appropriate roles and functions of public library systems, suggests that failure to address these questions causes less program impact but does not address the validity of objectives in judging these exemplary programs.

One example of a study evaluating creative dramatics programs as compared to storytelling in fourth and fifth graders, Ziegler (1970) [65], found that while storytelling encouraged an interest in literature and reading, creative dramatics did not.

An example of a small scale study which has important results locally, and which should be replicated in many other settings, is a study reported by Perry (1980) [66] which attempted to determine if first time users brought in by a program (in this case, summer reading programs) return and become regular library patrons. With five libraries participating in this group project, they found that of those reached for follow-up by telephone, 62 percent had returned to the public library since summer; nearly all use their school library; those coming to the public library do so mostly for use of materials, none for programs. Indirectly, other conclusions were formed including: the strong influence of parental use of public library on child use; the school library is the primary information and materials source during the school year; and children do use a traditional program such as the summer reading program and will probably continue to do so. <u>In the summers the public library has a high priority.</u> This study is not generalizable to other locales, but is an example of the type of study that can be completed by practioners for local decision-making.

Services to Special Groups
Early Childhood

A pertinent review of research, as part of her doctoral dissertation, has been presented by Smardo (1978, 1980) [67] and draws from three disciplines--reading, early childhood, and library science--to examine the need for specific library services for young children. Her own study surveyed early childhood education authorities to ascertain needed areas of services, programs, materials, physical facilities, and personnel for serving children from infants to six years of age. On the basis of the literature and the survey, Smardo recommended: <u>a focus on language arts activities, involvement of parents as active participants with their children in programs, inclusion of an educational/informational component for parents, teachers, and other childcare staff,</u> specific programs such as "making books" (child dictating story to recorder), puppet shows and storytelling <u>in outreach situations,</u> programs with authors and illustrators and children, parent education courses and discussion sessions in child development, and storytelling and reading clubs which encourage parents to read selected books to children. She summarized nine specific recommendations into two common elements: the involvement of parents (and other involved adults), and an emphasis on informal prereading activities and language arts experiences (listening to stories, talking about stories, and writing about stories). On the basis of this she recommends specifically: <u>close cooperation of public librarians with parents, teachers, and early childhood staff; and welcoming parents in short informal story/play activities with two, three, and four year old children</u> (with parents encouraged to use followup activities).

Special Children

One area that needs study is service to exceptional children, in addition to the many special bibliographies and analyses of materials available for these special groups. As early as 1970, a demonstration/research program at the Public Library of Cincinnati and Hamilton County tried to evaluate the effectiveness of library service to exceptional children. Limper (1970) [68] described the project, but the actual research is not fully described; however, it was stated that there was statistical proof of the effectiveness of the program.

Young Adults

The young adult services area is the least researched. It is not always clear in the state-wide surveys of children's services if the young adult service area is included or excluded. In a substantial research project, Gratch reported on an indepth look at young adult users and services at the Central Public Library, Rochester, New York (1980) [69] to determine use and users, problems and needs, and how young adult information needs could best be met by the Central Library. The systematic gathering of data through interviews, needs assessments, demographic data, and a series of questionnaires of teenagers (user and nonusers) was impressive in terms of data received and the rigor in the research process.

The young adult users represented at least 12-14% of the total users; were predominantly secondary school students; were represented by an equal number of males and females. Slightly less than one-half were frequent users; they used the library chiefly for school-related reasons making multi-division and multi-material usage. Between one-third and one-half of all respondents had asked for assistance. Lack of consensus by the public service staff (nearly a 50/50 split) existed regarding the need to provide differential services for young adults.

Major recommendations included: need for additional staff training; need for outreach services for the alternative educational organizations and youth-related agencies; the need for a young adult librarian position at Central: for collection development and reorganization of the teen fiction, and the identification of specific goals and objectives for planning youth adult services. It was suggested that there is a need for the central library to function in part similar to a school library for the student and teachers of alternate educational programs while acting differently in providing other services such as career and job information, information about recreational and leisure time activities; more activities (programs); and a printed resource directory of youth services. Because this study was of one urban public library system, results cannot be generalized, but the research instruments have been developed for replication. As well, libraries in similar communities may see similar problems and needs identified; and the major recommendations probably do apply. In a follow-up article (1981) [70], Gratch makes the point that research can lead to change, and indicates several of the study's recommendations have been or will be put into effect, including a young adult librarian position. Two earlier state-wide young adult services studies done by Joy (1968) [71], and Walton (1971) [72] had similar findings. Few libraries had separate young adult collections--when they did, there were limited funds for purchase of these materials. When there were young adult services, they were slanted to school and reference oriented needs rather than recreational. Problems identified include: lack of sufficient collections; a problem with identification of the group; a lack of contact with the schools even though more use was made by high school students of the public library reference collection than by adults. Adult cards in New Jersey at that time were given upon entrance to senior high school, making access a real issue for young adults.

The study of the historical development and philosophical basis for young adult services is described by Braverman (1974) [73] in her historical analysis of the 1920 to 1966 period of three case studies of major public library systems. Her conclusion shows a <u>need for young adult services development today with new library services for young adults being based on a new relationship between basic philosophy, programs, and societal elements affecting youth.</u> All of these studies show the state of young adult services today, with indications for what needs to be done to plan new services, starting with philosophical thinking, setting of objectives and priorities, and planning services based on current societal (and individual community) needs.

Professional Image of Youth Librarians

Though many role perception studies of school librarians have appeared in the literature, similar studies are not available for the children's or young adult public librarian. Three recent studies indicate new interest in this area. Calabrese (1976) [74] surveyed through a questionnaire a random sampling of children's librarians in Illinois to ascertain their perceptions of their image/status. She found a <u>direct correlation between the librarians who were consulted on library policy matters and their feeling of increased status.</u> Reasons given for perceiving themselves equal in status to other librarians included: better professional training, master's degree, recognition for contribution to community, recognition as a specialist in the area, and recognition of the "child" as having some importance within the library itself. Lower status feelings were due to: the "childlike" nature (telling stories, singing songs, etc.) of the role, lower salaries and absence of administration consultation. She suggested a similar study among heads of libraries and other department heads for comparison of perceptions of the groups.

A very unusual effort to ascertain <u>children's view of their librarians</u> was attempted by Rogers (1978) [75] who used three methods to gain children's perceptions in one public library. A one line question resulted in some positive adjectives: 50 percent felt <u>children's librarians were nice, and 29 percent felt they were helpful.</u> A two page questionnaire of users did not produce useful information; however, a discussion with the "junior critics" (ages 10 through 14) resulted in a <u>realistic view of the role and background needed for the job. They wanted librarians to know books, like children and reading, like the work, be helpful and patient, and more specifically, to be aware of current television so they could be prepared for television tie-ins requested, and to be prepared to describe interesting and new books as well as to provide annotated booklists</u> for older children. Rogers suggests that input from children is necessary, and that children's librarians should try techniques to elicit such response, though the task is more difficult than gathering information from adults. She recommends the Fasick and England technique as a model for obtaining user input from children.

The third study done by Kimmel (1979) [76] was to ascertain whether the librarian who exhibits more striving for professional recognition and status will have less regard for lower-class/lower-status clients. Kimmel found a significant relation between these two variables including librarians who work with adults, young adults, and children. She drew these conclusions which have implications for public library work with children: children are susceptible to being treated as lower status clients, the current move to spread staff responsibility for service and develop a "generalist" rather than an age-level specialist is difficult to reconcile with the special knowledge required of children's and young adult librarians and their willingness to serve particular groups (may cut off service to these groups); and the lack of leadership opportunities for children's librarians (road up is also road out of children's services especially when these administrative positions are cut).

Conclusion

After examining the conclusions of approximately 58 pertinent studies, some additional comments are appropriate. There were an even number of research studies completed between the 1970-1975, and 1976-1981 periods, approximately 29 studies during each period. Before 1975, we find a larger number of studies examining use and users, reading interests, habits, and behavior, and program evaluations. Since 1975, more studies have been state surveys, studies concerned with assessing goals and the future outlook, examining actual cooperative school/public library ventures or assessing opinions toward this issue, and assessing images of librarians working with children. There was no attempt to compare methodologies but this would be an interesting venture.

In terms of needs in the field, it would seem that we need more examination of particular services and programs especially in consideration of meeting library objectives, in meeting needs of children and young adults, and in comparison of program "effects." Basic questions on program effectiveness need to be the basis for future studies to provide information in library decision-making on programs and services. We do not need more studies looking at the combined school-public library, but we do need to have "models" for successful coordination and cooperative efforts. We need to look more indepth at which factors relate to the use of libraries by children and young adults, whether age, abilities, school curriculum, family backgrounds; we need to know more about types of media preferred and the value of different media for presenting information and literature to different age groups and to meet individual needs. The impact of professional personnel as compared to nonprofessional as children and young adult librarians on use patterns, on satisfaction of users, and on actual learning gains needs to be measured. Different patterns of display and shelving, modified access procedures and different styles of personal and group contact with users should be compared in terms of effectiveness and user satisfaction. There is much information from research to serve as the basis for future studies; we must build on past and current research in order to test our assumptions and practices.

There are implications for decision-making in public libraries from this past research. The question is--are we reading and considering the results of pertinent research as we plan library objectives, services and programs for children and young adults?

References

1. Gallivan, Marion F. "Research in Children's Services in Libraries; an Annotated Bibliography." Top of the News 30 (April 1974): 275-293.

2. Shontz, Marilyn Louise. "Selected Research Related to Children's and Young Adult Services in Public Libraries." Top of the News 38 (Winter 1982): 125-141.

3. Billeter, Anne. "Research and Evaluation in the Administration of Children's Work in the Public Library." Illinois Libraries 57 (January 1975): 10-12.

4. Kingsbury, Mary E. "Research and Children's Services of Public Libraries," in Children's Services of Public Libraries. Allerton Park Institute, 23d, 1977. (Urbana, Ill.: University of Illinois, 1978): 131-147.

5. Fasick, Adele M. "Research and Measurement in Library Services to Children." Canadian Library Journal 35 (October 1978): 341-346.
Also in: Top of the News 35 (Summer 1979): 354-362.

6. Lukenbill, W. Bernard. "Research in Young Adult Literature and Services" in Libraries and Young Adults. ed. JoAnn V. Rogers (Littleton, Colorado: Libraries Unlimited, 1979): 192-215.

7. Furman, Hazel. "Fewer Assumptions--More Research." SLJ School Library Journal 25 (May 1979): 45.

8. Fitzgibbons, Shirley. "Research on YA Library Services' Progress." SLJ School Library Journal 27 (November 1980): 53.

9. Gaver, Mary. "Research on Elementary School Libraries," ALA Bulletin 56 (February 1962): 117-124.
Also: Gaver, Mary. "Is Anyone Listening? Significant Research Studies for Practicing Librarians." Wilson Library Bulletin 43 (April 1969): 764-772.

10. Lowrie, Jean E. "A Review of Research in School Librarianship," in Research Methods in Librarianship: Measurement and Evaluation. ed. Herbert Goldhor (Urbana, Ill.: University of Illinois, Graduate School of Library Science, 1968): 51-69.

11. Aaron, Shirley Louise. "A Review of Selected Research Studies in School Librarianship, 1967-1971: Part I." School Libraries 21 (Summer 1972): 29-46. "Part II." School Media Quarterly (Fall 1972): 41-48.

12. Barron, Daniel D. 'Review of Selected Research in School Librarianship: 1972-1976." School Media Quarterly 5 (Summer 1977): 271-176+.

13. Aaron, Shirley L. "A Review of Selected Doctoral Dissertations about School Library Media Programs and Resources, January, 1972-December, 1980." School Library Media Quarterly (Spring 1982): 210-245.

14. Kingsbury, Mary. "Goals for Children's Services in Public Libraries." SLJ School Library Journal 24 (January 1978): 19-21.

15. Kingsbury, Mary E. 'Innovations in Children's Services in Public Libraries." Top of the News 34 (Fall 1978): 39-42.

16. Winnick, Pauline. "Evaluation of Public Library Services to Children." Library Trends 22 (January 1974): 361-376.

17. Downen, Thomas W. "YA Services: 1993." Top of the News 35 (Summer 1979): 347-353.

18. North Carolina Central University. A Report of the Results of a Field Survey of North Carolina Public Libraries with Regard to Their Services to Young Children. (Durham, North Carolina Central University, 1972).

19. New York Library Association. Children's and Young Adult Services Section. Public Relations Committee. Report (N.Y.: New York Library Association, 1972, mimeo).

20. An Analytical Survey of Illinois Public Library Service to Children. ed. Selma K. Richardson (Springfield, Ill.: Illinois State Library, 1970).
    Also: Richardson, Selma K. "An Analytical Survey of Illinois Public Library Services to Children: Selected Findings," Illinois Libraries 60 (May 1978): 497-504.
    Also: Fasick, Adele M. Library Quarterly 50 (April 1980): 266-267 (Review).

21. A Survey of Children's Services in Ohio Public Libraries (Columbus, Ohio: Ohio Library Association, 1979. Available $5.00, OLA, 40 S. Third St. #409, Columbus, Ohio 43215).

22. Wisconsin Department of Public Instruction. A Report of the First Statewide Survey of Children's Services in Public Libraries of Wisconsin 1981. (Bureau of Public and Cooperative Library Services, 1981.)

23. Children's Services in California Public Libraries. California Library Association and School of Library and Information Management, University of Southern California. (Research Presentation by Robert Grover and Mary Kelvin Moore. ALSC/YASD Research Forum, A.L.A. 1981 Annual Conference, San Francisco, California).

24. Hektoen, Faith H. "Researching Children's Services in Public Libraries." SLJ School Library Journal 26 (April 1980): 21-27.
    Also: Hektoen, Faith H. The Connecticut Research Documentation Project in Children's Services. 2 vols. (Connecticut State Library, 1981).

25. Starr, Carol and Talbot, Elizabeth. "Proposition 13: Effects on Library Services to Youth." Top of the News 36 (Winter 1980): 152-165.

26. Benne, Mae. The Central Children's Library in Metropolitan Libraries (Seattle, Wa.: University of Washington, 1978) ED 179 203.
    Also: Benne, Mae M. "Information Services in Central Children's Libraries." SLJ School Library Journal 26 (April 1980): 25.

27. Goetze, Henry J. Reading Interests of Junior High School Students. (Arlington, Va.: ERIC Document Reproduction Service, 1972). ED 007 521.

28. Hutchinson, Margaret. "Fifty Years of Young Adult Reading: 1921-1972." Top of the News 30 (November 1973): 24-53.

29. Campbell, Patty; Davis, Pat; and Quinn, Jerri. "We Got There ... It Was Worth the Trip." Top of the News 30 (June 1974): 394-402.

30. Alm, Julie N. "Young Adult Favorites; Reading Profiles from Nine Hawaii High Schools." Top of the News 30 (June 1974): 403-409.

31. Wynn, Vivian and Newmark, Barbara. "Doing a Young Adult Readers' Survey: Results and Benefits." Top of the News 35 (Summer 1979): 363-372.

32. "Big Change in Adolescent Reading." Intellect 104 (July-August 1975): 8.

33. Minudri, Regina, and Bodart, Joni. "Hip Pocket Books: the BAYA Reading Interest Report." School Library Journal 20 (Nov. 1973): 70-71.

34. Bodart, Joni. "The Third Time Around: BAYA Hip Pocket Reading Interest Survey III." Top of the News 35 (Summer 1979): 373-377.

35. Freiberger, Rema. The New York Times Report on Teenage Reading Tastes and Habits. (N.Y.: New York Times, 1973).

36. Stachelek, Deborah Ann. "A Comparative Study." ALAN Newsletter 4 (Winter 1977): unp.

37. Greenberg, Marilyn Werstein. "A Study of Reading Motivation of Twenty-three Seventh-grade Students." Library Quarterly 40 (July 1970): 309-317.

38. Scharf, Anne G. "Who Likes What in High School?" Journal of Reading 16 (May 1973): 804-807.

39. Doyen, Sally E. "A Comparison of Reading Preferences of Two Junior High Groups." Top of the News 30 (Winter 1980): 194-196.

40. Bard, Therese Bissen and Leide, John E. Reading Interests of Elementary School Children in Hawaii as Indicated by School Library Circulation Records. (Research Presentation. ALSC/YASD Research Forum, A.L.A. 1980 Annual Conference, N.Y., N.Y.)

41. Fasick, Adele Mongan. A Comparative Linguistic Analysis of Books and Television for Children (Ph.D. dissertation: Case Western Reserve University, 1970).

42. Cox, Carole Alice. Film Preference Patterns of Fourth and Fifth Grade Children. (Ph.D. dissertation: University of Minnesota, 1975).

43. Martin, Lowell A. Baltimore Reaches Out, Library Service to Disadvantaged. Deiches Fund Studies of Public Library Service no. 3. (Baltimore: Enoch Pratt Free Library, 1967).
Also: Martin, Lowell A. Library Response to Urban Change: a Study of the Chicago Public Library. (Chicago: American Library Association, 1969).

44. Martin, Lowell A. Students and the Pratt Library: Challenge and Opportunity. Deiches Fund Studies of Public Library Service no. 1. (Baltimore: Enoch Pratt Free Library, 1963).

45. Wilder, Philip S. Library Usage by Students and Young Adults. (Bloomington, Ind.: Indiana University, Graduate Library School, 1970). ED 046 472.

46. Benford, John. Student Library Resource Requirements in Philadelphia. (Office of Education, 1969-1971) ED 031 610, ED 031 611, ED 057 831.
Also: Benford, John. "The Philadelphia Project." Library Journal 96 (June 1971): 2041-2047.

47. Tower, Jean D. A Study of Changes in Children's Library Services for Selected Pittsburgh Suburbs Related to Their Population for 1960 through 1970. (Ph.D. dissertation: University of Pittsburgh, 1972).

48. Ekechukwu, Myriette R. G. Characteristics of Users and Non-Users of Elementary School Library Services and Public Library Services for Children. (Ph.D. dissertation: University of Washington, 1972).

49. Fasick, Adele, and England, Claire. Children Using Media: Reading and Viewing Preferences Among the Users and Non-Users of the Regina Public Library. (Toronto: Center for Research in Librarianship, University of Toronto, 1977).

50. Parker, Edwin B., and Paisley, William J. "Predicting Library Circulation from Community Characteristics." Public Opinion Quarterly 29 (Spring 1965): 39-53.

51. Moll, Joy Kaiser. Children's Access to Information in Print: An Analysis at the Vocabulary (Reading) Levels of Subject Headings and Their Application to Children's Books. (Ph.D. dissertation: Rutgers University, 1975).

52. Fasick, Adele M. What Should Libraries Do For Children? Parents, Librarians, and Teachers View Materials and Services in the South Central Regional System (Ontario). (Hamilton, Ont.: South Central Regional Library Board, 1978).
Also: Fasick, Adele M. "Parents and Teachers View Library Service to Children." Top of the News 35 (Spring 1979): 309-314.

53. Mancall, Jacqueline C. Resources Used by High School Students in Preparing Independent Study Projects: A Bibliometric Approach. (Ph.D. dissertation: Drexel University, 1978).
Also: Mancall, Jacqueline C., and Drott, M. Carl. "Materials Used by High School Students in Preparing Independent Study Projects: A Bibliometric Approach." Library Research 1 (Fall 1979): 223-236.

54. Amey, L.J. The Importance of the Role Definition in Combining School and Public Libraries. (Arlington, Va.: ERIC Document Reproduction Service, 1974) ED 148 382.

Also: Amey, L.J. ed. The Canadian School-Housed Public Library. (Halifax, Nova Scotia: Dalhousie University School of Library Service, 1979).

55. Kitchens, James A. The Olney Venture: An Experiment in Coordination and Merger of School and Public Libraries. Community Service Report no. 4. (Denton, Texas: Center for Community Services. School of Community Service, North Texas State University, 1975).
Also: Kitchens, James A. The Olney Experiment: A Venture in Coordination and Merger of School and Public Libraries. (Denton, Texas: North Texas State University, 1981).

56. Woolard, Wilma Lee B. The Combined School/Public Library Concept: Will It Work? (Arlington, Va.: ERIC Document Reproduction Service, 1977) ED 140 805.
Also: Woolard, Wilma Lee Broughton. Combined School/Public Libraries. (Metuchen, New Jersey: The Scarecrow Press, Inc., 1980).

57. Aaron, Shirley L. and Smith, Sue O. A Study of the Combined School Public Library. (Tallahassee: State Library of Florida, 1977). ED 150 986.
Also: Aaron, Shirley L. "Combined School Public Library Programs: An Abstract of a National Study." School Media Quarterly 7 (Fall 1978): 31-32, 49-53.
Also: Aaron, Shirley. Study of Combined School Public Libraries. (Chicago: American Association of School Librarians, American Library Association, 1980).

58. Amey, L.J. and Smith, R.J. "Combination School and Public Libraries: An Attitudinal Study." Canadian Library Journal 33 (June 1976): 251-261.

59. Dyer, Esther R. "Cooperation in Library Services to Children: A Fifteen-Year Forecast of Alternatives Using the Delphi Technique." (Ph.D. dissertation: Columbia University, 1976).
Also: Dyer, Esther R. "New Perspectives in Cooperation in Library Service to Children." School Media Quarterly 5 (Summer 1977): 261-270.
Also: Dyer, Esther R. Cooperation in Library Service to Children. (Metuchen, New Jersey: The Scarecrow Press, Inc., 1978).

60. Weech, Terry L. "Attitudes of School and Public Librarians Toward Combined Facilities." Public Library Quarterly 1 (Spring 1979): 51-67.
Also: Weech, Terry L. "School and Public Library Cooperation--What We Should Like to Do, What We Do." Public Libraries 18 (Summer 1979): 33-34.

61. Woolls, E. Blanche. Cooperative Library Services to Children

in Public Libraries and Public School Systems in Selected Communities in Indiana. (Ph.D. dissertation: Indiana University, 1973).

62. Altman, Ellen O. The Resource Capacity of Public Secondary School Libraries to Support Interlibrary Loan: A Systems Approach to Title Diversity and Collection Overlap. (Ph.D. dissertation: Rutgers, the State University of New Jersey, 1971).
Also: Altman, Ellen O. "Implications for Title Diversity and Collection Overlap for Interlibrary Loan Among Secondary Schools." Library Quarterly 42 (April 1972): 177-194.

63. Tevis, Ray. "Library Cooperation in Granite City: The Public Library and the High Schools, 1975-1977. Illinois Libraries 61 (January 1971): 6-9.

64. Barass, Reitzel and Associates, Inc. A Study of Exemplary Public Library Reading-Related Programs for Children, Youth, and Adults. Vols. I and II. (Cambridge, Mass.: The Associates, 1972) ED 066 197.

65. Ziegler, Elsie Mae. A Study of the Effects of Creative Dramatics on the Progress in Use of the Library, Reading Interests, Reading Achievement, Self-Concept, Creativity, and Empathy of Fourth and Fifth Grade Children. Ed.D. dissertation: Temple University, 1970).

66. Perry, Karen. "Research in Children's Services in Public Libraries: A Group Project in North Carolina." Public Libraries 19 (Summer 1980): 58-60.

67. Smardo, Frances Antoinette. An Analytical Study of the Recommendations of Early Childhood Education Authorities with Regard to the Role of the Public Library in Serving Children from Infancy to Six Years of Age. (Ph.D. dissertation: North Texas State University, 1978) ED 160 222.
Also: Smardo, Frances A. "What Research Tells Us About Programs for Young Children" Public Libraries 19 (Spring 1980): 34-36.

68. Limper, Hilda K. et al. "Library Service to Exceptional Children." Top of the News 26 (January 1970): 193-204.

69. Gratch, Bonnie. Central Library Young Adult Study Project. Final Report 1978. (Research Presentation, ALSC/YASD Research Forum, A.L.A. 1980 Annual Conference, N.Y., N.Y.).

70. Gratch, Bonnie. "Research Can Lead to Change." SLJ School Library Journal 28 (December 1981): 35.

71. Joy, Patricia L. Young Adults Service in Connecticut Public Libraries. (Master's thesis: Southern Connecticut State College, 1968).

72. Walton, Jewel. "Young Adult Services in New Jersey." New Jersey Libraries 4 (1971): 6-12.

73. Braverman, Miriam Ruth. Public Library and the Young Adult: The Development of the Service and Its Philosophy in the New York Public Library, Cleveland Public Library, and Enoch Pratt Free Library. (Ph.D. dissertation: Columbia University, 1974).
Also: Braverman, Miriam. Youth Society and the Public Library. (Chicago: American Library Association, 1979).

74. Calabrese, Alice. "An Image/Status Study." Illinois Libraries 48 (December 1976): 792-794.

75. Rogers, Norma L. "The Children's Librarian as Viewed by Children." in Children's Services of Public Libraries. ed. Selma K. Richardson (Urbana, Ill.: University of Illinois, 1978): 57-61.

76. Kimmel, Margaret M. Professionalization and the Orientation of Public Librarians to Lower Class Clients. (Ph.D. dissertation, University of Pittsburgh, 1979).
Also: Kimmel, Margaret M. "Who Speaks for the Children?" SLJ School Library Journal 26 (December 1979): 35-38.

AUTOMATION IN SCHOOL LIBRARY MEDIA CENTERS*

Russell & Mary Anne Driver

Automation of acquisitions and technical processing in the school media center is an idea whose time has come. It is an idea which has been more than 25 years in development and yet automation in schools is still not in general use. However, as more and more schools move toward automated processes, it is interesting to review the beginnings of the movement and to trace its growth. This article is a survey of the historical development of automated technical processing in schools. The impact of this automation on a number of schools and some projections for the future will be noted.

While attempting to remove the mystery of automation, McCauley (1971) exhorted school librarians to jump into the age of electronic data processing and she implied that the computer age was about to leave the timid and faint of heart behind. Her advice was basic: Discover what equipment is already available in the school system for accounting and administrative purposes, and decide what library jobs that equipment can assist with or accomplish in their entirety. Suggestions were given for updating acquisitions lists; producing bibliographies and subject guides; ordering and fund accounting; generating spine labels, shefl list cards, pockets, circulation cards, etc.; and recording serials. McCauley saw "data processing for school libraries ... not [as] examples of sophisticated information handling ... but simply good business management techniques." For the future, McCauley predicted increased centralization of processing and networking.

One of the earliest examples of automation for school use was in the early 1950s, when Baltimore Public Schools used punched cards for a basic elementary book list. With those cards a basic book collection was more easily initiated for a newly-opened elementary school (Brown, 1978). Albuquerque Public Schools moved into automated centralized processing in 1963, when cataloging was begun for five new elementary schools (Breiland, 1969). By 1968, using IBM cards, the Albuquerque Library Processing Center was

---

*Reprinted by permission of the authors and publisher from School Library Journal, 28:5 (January 1982) 21-25. Published by R.R. Bowker Co. (a Xerox company). Copyright © 1982 by Xerox Corporation.

ordering, cataloging, and processing all learning materials for 108 school libraries. Suggested buying lists were distributed to school librarians twice a year to aid in selection; a subject code was assigned to facilitate subject bibliographies and subject books catalogs. Descriptions of procedures seem cumbersome by today's standards; however, in 1968, those procedures were innovative and daring.

Walker (1969) reported on the trial-and-error process of the Ann Arundel County's (Maryland) Central Processing Department in inaugurating a workable automated acquisitions system. School librarians were presented with lists of recommended titles grouped according to pertinent grade levels and subjects. The number of copies desired was marked in the appropriate column, and the order lists were returned and compiled. After receipt of books, fund accounting was accomplished via computer, and the books were routed to the schools for cataloging. Walker suggested that although the automated system might not save total man-hours, it did give librarians more time to work with students and teachers.

A computer-based cataloging and processing system was begun in 1967 in Madison (Wisconsin) Public Schools (Holmes and Lively, 1970). All media were handled in an operation that served 52 school libraries and generated ordering lists, purchase orders, status reports of orders, fund accounting, card catalog sets, labels for pockets, and book cards.

Today this system consists of 39 schools and four central professional libraries. About half the AV items owned and stored by the local schools are computer cataloged; there are plans to get the other half on computer soon. In addition, the cataloging and booking of centralized AV materials is provided. There are plans to change the current key punch/data card entry to direct data entry and to incorporate the ISBN and LC numbering of items for sharing resources with libraries that are outside the system (Dresang, 1981).

Batch Ordering & Cataloging

Shawnee Mission (Kansas) Public Schools first designed a batch ordering and cataloging system in 1968 (Miller and Hodges, 1971). Two years later, through unification, the system's 15 schools increased to 65 schools (all with libraries) and the batch system was judged inadequate for the expanded load. Encouraged by the Computer Center to investigate multiprogramming, Central Library Processing designed an on-line ordering and cataloging pilot project using the software package acronym, FASTER (Filing and Source Data Entry Techniques for Easier Retrieval). There were three files: the disk title file, the disk copy file (with fields for circulation control), and the title index (used to determine duplicates). Before the end of the pilot project, a decision was made to go ahead with on-line cataloging for all 65 schools. This was easily accomplished because of design flexibility. The system was found to be efficient, accurate, and economical. By using an existing software package,

Shawnee Mission schools avoided the expense of developing their own software. Although the initial cost of the terminal system exceeded that of the batch system, the unit cost per item was 42 percent lower for on-line use (Miller and Hodges, 1971).

Automation of Materials

In the late '60s, work was begun in the Los Angeles City Unified School District under a U.S. Office of Education grant for a project which was given the acronym AIMS, for Automated Instructional Materials Handling System (Black, 1974). The project was a prototype, adaptable for use in other school districts with varied requirements. The goal was to design a computer-based system for the management of instructional materials through three major subsystems: selection, ordering, and control. The system was designed in two stages. Black listed the following capabilities for Stage I: inventory control with an on-line query capability; an on-line interactive booking system for 16mm films; programs for ordering all materials; a program for the management of the evaluation file; an accounting and budgeting program; and a MARC index program to support evaluation, ordering and cataloging functions. Among the capabilities for Stage II programs were expanded on-line inventory access for materials other than textbooks and the addition of on-line ordering subsystems for all materials.

Another extensive program which did not fare as well was Oregon's OTIS/OALS systems. As described by Bracken (1974), Oregon Total Information System (OTIS) was a cooperative data processing center serving more than 60 Oregon school districts, community colleges, universities, and state and federally funded education projects. As a subsystem, OTIS Automated Library Services (OALS) was set up to provide catalog production (book or media), materials evaluation reports, on-line booking for instructional materials, computerized ERIC (Educational Resources Information Center) searches, and textbook circulation and inventory control. The program met with difficulties in 1970 when crews, working to enter holdings of individual libraries, found some librarians openly hostile and uncooperative. The ordering and processing system was abandoned in 1972 when participants were unable to agree or compromise on format, quality control, and necessary accounting procedures; the data base of 75,000 print titles was stored on tapes with the hope of future use. The other functions of OALS continued to grow and respond to user needs. By late 1973, the OALS director was planning a renewed attempt to revive the ordering and processing system (Bracken, 1974). Recent information indicates that although OALS no longer exists intact, some elements have been retained and are in use by the Lane County Educational Service District. These elements include the file format for storing data for nonprint material, a book catalog for nonprint material, a booking and scheduling system for nonprint material, a catalog of professional print materials for administrators and teachers, a preview catalog, and an ERIC search system. The OALS experience should encourage persistence by those whose first attempts at far-reaching systems have proved less successful. Much of the system which has been salvaged is now functioning successfully (Jones, 1981).

Automation Programs

Individual school systems do not normally have the funds to initiate large-scale school library automation programs; they begin by tackling individual problem areas. Glidden (1977) reported the automation of audiovisual catalogs in West Bend (Wisconsin) Joint School District. Four separate book catalogs were printed (by Dewey number, medium, title, and location) and were made available in each of the district's 11 school media centers, facilitating district-wide access. Funding problems have slowed progress in West Bend in recent years; however, in early 1982 similar book catalogs for professional materials will be fully operational in the system. Additionally, West Bend now has an automated interlibrary loan system within the school district which includes parochial and private schools (Glidden, 1981). In Eau Claire, Wisconsin, Rewerts (1977) reported cataloging similar to that of West Bend, which included the entire nonprint collections of 20 elementary schools, and the production of book catalogs to promote interlibrary loan, expedite inventory, and enlarge the media collection available to each patron.

The Oak Creek (Wisconsin) Public School District is small and serves under 5,000 students in six elementary and one junior and one senior high school. With the help of the data processing center, the library processing center designed a system that aids in ordering, cataloging, and processing of books (Carmody, 1977). The district was able to provide shelf-ready books to the schools in a reasonable time. In recent years, subject book catalogs, an audiovisual catalog, and computer-generated bibliographies have been produced. Unfortunately, the project did not receive continued funding for 1981-82, due to shortage of funds in the system (Carmody, 1981).

About the same time, a much larger system, the Milwaukee (Wisconsin) Public School System, was making wider use of computer facilities. Among the functions Burke (1977) described were its automated acquisitions system and instructional resource catalog production. Two data bases had been established to support those functions: a library file and a film file. The library file was a compilation of titles previewed and recommended by staff, frequently ordered, adopted as textbooks, or listed in selective bibliographies. Those titles were added to the library file when all order information was verified, and the file was used to produce automated purchase orders, an automated book list of all titles in the file, and a catalog of recommended textbooks, audiovisual materials, and reference books. The film file was used to generate annotated film catalogs for use in the elementary and secondary schools.

SLJ (August, 1980) reported on the computer system in operation in the St. Johns Parish school library in Tampa, Florida. The

400 students in grades one through eight use the computer to find books. The computer performs other duties as well: it identifies overdue books and is used in processing new books. Carol McCammon, head librarian, reported that a three-year backlog of uncataloged books has been cleared and the processing of new books has been expedited to a fraction of the time formerly spent on these functions.

"The lack of sophisticated library automation ... should not be interpreted as a lack of need for nor a lack of interest in such systems" (Brown, 1978). Brown goes on to note that school libraries do not have the same alternatives available as do larger libraries, however more is available than is being used. A 1974 study of 1,030 Illinois school districts revealed that 72 school districts had inhouse data processing equipment and 252 shared data processing with other district functions; only ten of those 324 districts were using data processing for library functions. Of those, some used automation for listing audiovisual holdings, some for circulation, one for a book catalog, and one for subject bibliographies from cataloging data.

Networking

Most of the previous examples of automated processes in schools were the products of school district personnel working within their districts. The standards set forth by Media Programs: District and School (AASL/AECT, 1975) clearly indicate the necessity of networking in the provision of materials to support school curricula (Franckowiak, 1977). In the forefront of the networking movement have been public libraries beginning, in the late '50s, to develop regional and state cooperative systems. School media centers have lagged far behind in network development; many have moved to the district concept, and more recently, toward regional educational service centers though without a strong commitment to sharing both information and materials. At the same time, the networks developed by public libraries have been expanding to include other types of libraries, and now those networks are beginning to invite school participation. Leading networks which are opening membership to schools are the Illinois Library and Information Network (ILLINET), the Washington Library Network (WLN), and the Ohio College Library Center (OCLC).

Franckowiak (1977) noted that network participation may provide a wide range of benefits for schools. Some networks are limited to bibliographic information with emphasis on acquisitions and cataloging. Some offer access to resources and data bases, such as ERIC. The trend is toward full-service networks, offering a complete range of services from acquisitions and shared cataloging to reference and circulation. The many services available through networks can provide a significant expansion of the print and audiovisual materials available to both students and teachers.

Networking is a reciprocal arrangement, and schools must

consider what they have to offer, as well as what may be gained
through network participation. Schools have taken the lead in the
utilization of audiovisual media and have developed collections far
outstripping the holdings of most public libraries. School media
centers have worked toward the cataloging of those materials and
have the potential for significant contribution. Media center personnel have developed skills in media evaluation, selection, and utilization, and in combining print and nonprint materials to meet instructional objectives. Sharing those resources may prove to be a stumbling block, however. Franckowiak points out that most of the materials were purchased with funds from local, state, and federal
taxes and should, therefore, be as widely available as possible--as
long as their use by teachers and students is not hindered. School
media personnel must sell the concept of networking to administrators and school boards by stressing the benefits of participation.

WLN & Schools

WLN serves as an outstanding example of what a network can be
and how it could be used in a school setting. Kolb (1977) outlines
the wide range of automated services offered by WLN: on-line access to MARC records; recording holdings and local cataloging in
MARC format; ordering individualized products for processing; inquiry by keyword, author, title, subject, and other access points;
acquisitions and accounting; circulation; and serials control. WLN
membership is voluntary and offers three levels of participation.
The free _basic_ membership involves interlibrary loan, resource
sharing, and reference/referral. A _cooperative_ member contracts
to enter holdings into the data base and to purchase such products
as processing materials, bibliographies, and microfiche catalogs.
A _principal_ member purchases data processing equipment, enters
holdings into the data base, and contracts for products and services.

In 1977, about 50 school districts were WLN members, and
cooperation between public libraries and educational services districts was developing. Options for membership include cooperative
members receiving data processing through contracts with principal
members. In this option, a school district might contract with a
public library principal member for cataloging and processing, or
an education service district might be a principal member with online access and provide services such as acquisitions, accounting,
and cataloging to school districts within its area.

OCLC's Services

Some school districts have investigated OCLC as a means of achieving automated services. Twaddle (1979) reported that the Indiana
Cooperative Library Services Authority (InCoLSA) offered OCLC cataloging services to Indiana school processing centers. As its primary goals InCoLSA originally sought to institute a MARC-based
cataloging service and to create an Indiana data base. According

to Markuson (1981) those objectives were met. Additionally, InCoLSA engaged in two OCLC related research projects. The first led to the conclusion that there are advantages for small libraries which use services such as OCLC (Markuson, 1981). The second tested the feasibility of centralized processing centers for cataloging nonprint materials in schools. It was found that there was a need for that service and that satisfactory service could be provided (Alexander & Markuson, 1981). To date, funding has not been available for InCoLSA to begin the service, but some school districts decided to provide funding at the local level for their schools to become full participants in OCLC.

Deal (1977) studied methods of processing including uses of OCLC in school districts in the Cleveland, Ohio area. Lakewood Public Schools had contracted for processing through the local public library, but when the public library joined OCLC, the processing time was reduced and costs rose sharply. Rather than renew the contract, the school's processing center investigated the possibility of joining OCLC as a full member with on-line access, but because the OCLC data base did not include audiovisual materials, Lakewood Public Schools opted for commercially preprocessed materials, supplemented when necessary by locally centralized processing. North Olmsted Schools contracted for processing through the county public library, which was an OCLC member. However, through local budgeting vagaries North Olmsted found they could provide more materials if they did their own central processing. Shaker Heights City Schools, which have been using an OCLC terminal since 1974 for their centralized cataloging, found the system to be completely satisfactory. In July 1977 they began using a nonprint catalog. Other services provided include an on-line printer for book spines, labels, etc. and a catalog of student career development materials. It was reported that use of the career development materials has increased dramatically since the automation of that catalog (Stepanian, 1981).

Turn-key Systems

Another method for providing automated purchasing and processing is the use of a turn-key system such as BATAB, Baker and Taylor's Automated Buying System. Atlanta Public Schools was the first school district to employ BATAB. Walston (1975) reported its use in the Austin (Texas) Independent School District (ISD), indicating that BATAB's five major aspects for acquisitions included:

1. production of selection lists, hard copy of microfiche;
2. automatic production of purchase orders;
3. automatic production of open order reports and claiming notices;
4. automatic production of fund status reports for each school and for the district;
5. automatic production of acquisitions history and statistics.

The Austin ISD found it could obtain ten percent of the audiovisual and 80 percent of the print materials with processed kits. Cataloging and processing of those items without kits was done by the Materials Processing Center, and materials were delivered shelf-ready to the schools.

Future Projections

How will acquisitions and cataloging be handled by school media centers of the future? Specific needs, resources, and requirements will continue to be varied among schools and school districts, yet some commonality of library service will remain. The answer has to be networking. The forms which networking takes may vary, but its basis will be cooperative effort.

The Task Force on the Role of the School Library Program in Networking, appointed by the National Commission on Libraries and Information Science (NCLIS), has as its only long-range recommendation that, "Library networks in which school library media programs are full participating members be established and operational in every region, state, and area in the nation" (Fite, 1979). The task force listed some of the materials contributions which school libraries might make to a network as follows: audiovisual resources, professional libraries, specialized ethnic collections, career education collections, high interest/low reading level collections, foreign language materials, and collections for special students. According to the task force, schools can also offer services such as: ordering, processing, and cataloging; repair services; computer-assisted instruction; materials examination centers; consultation services; and delivery systems. School libraries would have much to gain through networking: the ability to provide precise and needed information for students and teachers, and the capability of giving students materials on the appropriate levels from many sources.

Perhaps one outcome of increased networking will be much-needed public and school library cooperation. Through cooperative planning of acquisitions and processing, the resources of both could be broadened by eliminating some unnecessary duplication, while recognizing the necessity of duplicating other information materials (Fleming, 1978). A number of services outside the scope of this article, such as programming and equipment purchasing, might also be planned cooperatively. These and similar efforts would result in lower costs to both institutions and could forestall a taxpayers' revolt in which libraries will be forced to combine services and/or share materials.

The reasons why more school libraries have not become involved in automating functions must be addressed before widespread automation takes place. Some school media personnel operate in an isolated environment away from the mainstream of library progress and lack sufficient understanding of what is available. Communication and documentation of the state of the art in schools is woefully lacking; we are convinced that more school systems have moved into automated functions than have been documented in current periodical literature. The future of the art demands that library associations and networks at the state, regional, and national levels disclose school library automation's best kept secrets regarding what has been done and what is possible. The library community's opinions about the school media centers' ability to contribute to networks has hampered movement by schools toward cooperative efforts. School media centers with access to automated equipment have sometimes not utilized that equipment because school administrators tend to look toward direct service by libraries, not toward internal efficiency (Brown, 1978). Schools have led the way in the multimedia approach, and the library community's slow recognition of the necessity for integrating print and nonprint media has hindered schools' embracing existing automated systems (Hicks and Tillin, 1977). Additionally, lack of standards for cataloging has discouraged the development of multimedia bibliographic data bases.

Factors such as cost will no longer be excuses for avoiding automation of functions since costs have decreased dramatically. Hoffman (1978) reported that if cost improvements in the computer business had been matched in other industries a sirloin steak would cost nine cents and a new car three dollars. The improved price/performance ratio is making school library automation more cost-justifiable.

The future may see specialized networks similar to OCLC for school media centers, if existing networks cannot or will not accommodate the unique requirements of schools. Cable television as the technology of the future may far exceed our wildest dreams; hard copies may be obsolete, and homework may evolve into a technological challenge for teachers and librarians as well as for students. If school media centers do not begin to move now, possibly the future will find students and teachers using more efficient resources, while the media center's procedures and services become obsolete.

References

Alexander, J.E. and Markuson, B.E. "A Network Approach to Nonprint Media Cataloging for Schools: A Report of an Indiana Department of Public Instruction and Indiana Cooperative Library Services Authority (InColSa) Project using OCLC System," March 1981.

Black, D.V. "The AIMS Project in Los Angeles." In H.W. Axford (ed.), Proceedings of the LARC Institute on Automation of Libraries in School Systems. The LARC Association, 1974.

Bracken, P. "Oregon's OTIS and OALS Systems." In H.W. Axford (ed.), Proceedings of the LARC Institute on Automation of Libraries in School Systems. The LARC Association, 1974.

Breiland, M. "Centralized Data Processing for Libraries in the Albuquerque Public Schools." Drexel Library Quarterly 5 (1969): 92-100.

Brown, T.M. "School Libraries and Automation Systems--Some Thoughts." Illinois Libraries 60 (1978): 420-22.

Burke, M.A. "Automated Assistant for Media Professionals." Wisconsin Library Bulletin 73 (1977): 120-21.

Carmody, J. "Computer Processing for Books." Wisconsin Library Bulletin 73 (1977): 122.

Carmody, J., Cedar Hills School, Oak Creek (Wisconsin) Public School District. Personal communication. November 17, 1981.

Deal, P.N. "A Study of Centralized Processing for School Media Centers." Drexel Library Quarterly 13 (1977): 80-90.

Dresang, E., Madison (Wisconsin) Metro Public School District Library Services. Personal communication, November 23, 1981.

Drescher, R.A. "School Library Cooperation in the Illinois Library and Information Network (ILLINET)." Illinois Libraries 58 (1976): 548-51.

Fite, A.E. & The Task Force on the Role of the School Library Program in Networking. "Report of the Task Force on the Role of the School Library Program in Networking." School Media Quarterly 7 (1979): 89-114.

Fleming, L.D. "Public and School Libraries: Partners in the 'Big' Picture." School Media Quarterly 7 (1978): 25-30.

Franckowiak, B. "Networks, Data Bases, and Media Programs: an Overview." School Media Quarterly 6 (1977): 15-20.

Glidden, I., Library Media Services, West Bend (Wisconsin) Joint School District. Personal communication, November 18, 1981.

Glidden, I. "Automation for Media Centers?" Wisconsin Library Bulletin 73 (1977): 115-17.

Hicks, W.B. & A.M. Tillin. "Libraries and Technology--Some Future Concerns." SLJ/School Library Journal vol. 23, no. 8 (1977): 27-32.

Hoffman, C. "The Computer in the High School Library." Catholic Library World 50 (1978): 10-11.

Holmes, R. & G. Lively. "Computer Processing for All Media in Madison Schools." Wisconsin Library Bulletin 66 (1970): 319-24.

Jones, L., Manager of Instructional Services, Media Services Division, Lane County (Oregon) Educational Services District. Personal communication. November 18, 1981.

Kolb, A. "Development and Potential of a Multitype Library Network." School Media Quarterly 6 (1977): 21-27.

Kolb, A. & J. Morse. "Initiating School Participation in Networking." School Media Quarterly 6 (1977): 52-59.

Markuson, B.E., Indiana Cooperative Library Services Authority. Personal communication, November 18, 1981.

McCauley, E. "Computers in School Libraries." School Libraries 20 (1971): 28-32.

Miller, E.W. & B.J. Hodges, "Shawnee Mission's On-Line Cataloging System." Journal of Library Automation 4 (1979): 13-26.

Rewerts, I. "Print-out for Progress: Eau Claire Computerizes AV Holdings." Wisconsin Library Bulletin 73 (1977): 119.

Stepanian, E., Director of Library Media, Teaching Media Center, District Library Media Office, Shaker Heights, Ohio. Personal communucation. November 18, 1981.

Twaddle, D.R. "School Media Services and Automation." School Media Quarterly 7 (1979): 257-268 & 273-76.

Walker, N.C. "Automation and Acquisitions." Drexel Library Quarterly 5 (1969): 80-83.

Walston, R.A. "A Materials Processing Center for the Austin Schools." Texas Library Journal 51 (1975): 23-25.

STATIC IN THE EDUCATIONAL INTERCOM:
CONFLICT AND THE SCHOOL LIBRARIAN*

Alixe Hambleton

For the past twenty years many excellent, rational and resounding professional statements have stoutly proclaimed the potential of school library programs. Liberally sprinkled through these statements are phrases which assert that the school library of today is "the keystone" of the educational program, a "force for educational excellence" and the "heart" of the school. Unfortunately, these phrases remain only clichés, and often the school library is still regarded as an adjunct or auxiliary service, and often, in times of fiscal restraints, is a prime target for cuts in both staff and resources. There is obviously "static" in the communication system between sender and receiver. The message is not getting through or, at best, is being distorted.

Research in school librarianship has attempted to discover the source of this static, and a trend in the research literature since the early 1960's has been continuing concentration on role perception studies, with a major focus on the school librarian's role as viewed by other members of the educational system.

Many of the findings of these studies have negative connotations. In the numerous studies carried out in the past twenty years, a number of conclusions are common: that the school librarian's perception of that role differs significantly from that of others in the educational system, that the school library seems to play only a marginal role in the total educational program, and that the low regard for the school librarian militates against a direct involvement in the instructional program of the school [1].

Role theory suggests that when differing perceptions of a role are present, the person performing that role is placed in a conflict position, resulting in a loss of effectiveness, both for the individual and for the organization.

In order to investigate the implications of such theory on the

---
*Reprinted by permission of the author and publisher from Emergency Librarian, 9:5 (May-June 1982) 18-20.

operation of school libraries within a school system, the writer carried out a research project in the elementary schools within an area of central Ontario. The objectives of the study were to determine the perceptions of principals, teachers and school librarians of the role of the school librarian; to test the relationship between the extent of role conflict and effectiveness in the performance of the curricular teaching role; and, finally, to explore the relationship between personality and the extent of role conflict.

Eighty-four elementary schools from nine school boards in central Ontario were surveyed. All respondents were asked to complete a role inventory questionnaire consisting of sixty items. Principals also completed an effectiveness questionnaire dealing specifically with the curricular teaching role of the school librarian. The school librarians responded to a role conflict questionnaire and to a personality inventory. Responses were received from ninety per cent of the teachers and eighty-nine percent of the school librarians.

It is not possible, within the scope of this article, to present a complete analysis of the data. Rather, the intent is to discuss some of the findings which may be worth consideration as possible contributors to that "static" which seems so persistently evident in the school system.

The role inventory questionnaire dealt with seven roles performed by the school librarian: Materials Specialist, Curriculum Development Teacher, Technical Services, Administration, Extra-Mural Activities and the Sub-Professional Role. Analysis of the distribution of scores indicated differences in perceptions among the three groups on all of the seven categories of the librarian's role. Of particular interest was the fact that for the items related to the Materials Specialist role (which one might expect to be the particular expertise and responsibility of the school librarian) there was a significant difference among the three groups. Also, there was no agreement on any of the items relating to the Sub-Professional role, indicating that the concept of the school librarian as a professional member of the school staff is not yet universally accepted. Though it may be tempting to explain this finding by citing the lack of clerical help in the schools, it is nevertheless true that this situation is not likely to change as long as the present perceptions of the librarian's role exist.

For all groups, the majority of responses fell most often in the preferential (Preferably Should or Preferably Should Not) category, a further indication of a lack of definite role expectations. This is a safe response, one carrying little commitment, and is also a response which indicates a reluctance to delineate priorities.

Distribution scores did not present the total picture. It was necessary, as well, to look at agreement or disagreement within each of the three groups. Variance scores for each item of the questionnaire calculated for each of the respondent groups provided results which also indicate another serious source of the static which is perhaps prohibiting successful communication. Variance scores computed for the group of principals showed that there was low agreement within that group on forty-three per cent of the items. Within the teacher groups, a low level of agreement was found for fifty-three per cent of the items. For the librarian group, a low agreement was found for fifty-five per cent of the items.

These variance scores were also categorized by the seven types of librarian's roles. It was found that principals are more consistent in their perceptions than teachers or librarians, and that they have a more "professional" view of the librarian's role. They agree on more of the items making up the Materials Specialist, Teacher, and Administrative roles, indicating that principals may be expecting more of the librarian in these areas than many librarians assume. However, principals are confused, as a group, about the Technical Services and Sub-Professional roles, and in view of the lack of agreement on the part of the librarian group, they will likely continue to be confused unless some direction is forthcoming.

Teachers, as a group, are generally in agreement on the Teacher role of the librarian, but do not agree on the curricular involvement role of the librarian. The majority of responses to the items in these categories were in the preferential rather than mandatory category [2]. Teachers seem to see teaching of individual classes as part of the role of the librarian when this is possible, but they do not see the librarian as being involved in overall curriculum development. Teachers do not agree on the Materials Specialist role of the librarian. Also there is little agreement among teachers as to the Administrative role of the librarian and much less agreement on the Technical Services and Sub-Professional role. Although the scores for items making up the Extra-Mural role indicate agreement of this role, thirty-six per cent were undecided as to whether the librarian should act as a community resource person.

Librarians as a group are in agreement on less than one-half of the sixty items. There is low agreement within the group on forty-seven per cent of the items comprising the Materials Specialist role, fifty percent of the items making up the Curricular role, fifty per cent of the Administrative role, seventy-five per cent of the Technical role, and ninety-two per cent of the Sub-Professional role. They agree, as a group, on the majority of items making up the Teacher and Extra-Mural role. A larger percentage of their responses fall in the Mandatory category than is the case with principals and teachers.

The high incidence of low agreement within the librarian group suggests that librarians themselves are not prepared to communicate a definite role to principals and teachers.

Librarians' response to the role conflict questionnaire indicated they experienced conflict as a result of unclear guidelines, a realization that different groups serviced by librarians may operate quite differently, a too heavy work load, a lack of adequate resources or manpower, and the necessity of having to work on too many assignments at one time.

If role theory is to be borne out, as differences in perceptions are great, role conflict should also be great. In statistical terms, a high correlation should exist between conflict and differing perceptions. However, when the data were analyzed on an individual school basis, a different picture emerged. When conflict scores were correlated with scores representing the difference in perception between the school librarian (the role receiver) and principals and teachers (the role senders), this expected correlation was not evident. Surprisingly, the correlation, although not statistically significant, was negative, indicating that in schools where the highest discrepancy in role perceptions exists, the conflict scores tend to be low. Unsure themselves of their role, school librarians may neither recognize nor respond to the conflicts that are present in an individual school. If conflict is not recognized, no positive attempt will be made to resolve it, and the future role of school librarians may continue to be in jeopardy.

Principals were asked to assess the degree to which their school librarian participated in tasks related to the curricular role since this has been considered one of the more controversial and less agreed upon roles. They rated their school librarian's performance on a five point scale which ranged from Almost Always to Almost Never.

In the Almost Always/Frequently group were found those items related to selection of resources, library assignments, the location of resources, the publicizing of resources to teachers, and curriculum planning. In the Almost Never/Rarely group were found those items most closely related to the teaching role including team teaching, planning and carrying out workshops, participation in staff meetings, acting as an information source for teachers, and providing innovative instructional help for teachers. School librarians were doing most frequently those tasks that have a specific connection with resources and library programs. Those tasks that require the school librarian to perform in a teaching role were not being carried out to any appreciable extent.

School librarians are seen by the majority of principals as performing "library type" tasks, as opposed to "teacher type" tasks, in spite of the fact that ninety-one per cent of the principals felt that all were tasks that <u>should</u> be carried out by school librarians.

Data on eight personality characteristics were also collected, and scores were determined for the librarians on the traits of ascendancy, responsibility, cautiousness, original thinking, personal relations and vigour. Librarians' mean scores were lower for personal relations, ascendancy and sociability than for the other traits. In a comparison of the librarians in the sample to other groups for whom norms are available (college women, female low level managers, college men), it was found that, with the exception of the cautiousness and sociability scales, the school librarians scored equal to, or significantly higher than, comparable groups on the other scales.

Paradoxically, perhaps, the school librarians rated high on both original thinking and cautiousness. School librarians with the potential for creative and innovative ideas may, in practice, be too cautious to implement these ideas. This cautiousness may also be partially responsible for the lack of cohesiveness within the librarian group, the lack of response to possible areas of conflict, and the tendency to perform most often those tasks that relate to library expertise rather than those which involve the librarian in the teaching program.

The correlation between curriculum effectiveness scores and cautiousness scores was significant and negative. Low cautiousness scores are associated with high effectiveness scores. Correlations between conflict scores and three of the personality factors were significant and negative. High conflict scores were associated with low cautiousness, low emotional stability and low responsibility scores. Since the scores on these three traits were generally high, it can be assumed that the recognition of conflicts is restricted to a relatively small group of librarians. The majority of librarians scored high on cautiousness, emotional stability and responsibility and low on conflict scores.

The findings relative to the presence of differing perceptions provide ample proof that static does exist between librarians and the school staff. The lack of agreement on the role of the librarian within the librarian group itself is certainly one of the factors contributing to such static. If a message is to be transmitted without distortion, that message must be clear and also clearly stated. If there is a confusing message, it is not surprising that the receiver of that message is also confused. The school librarian must build a relationship with teachers and the principal that is based on strong, professional expertise--an expertise that is a necessary part of the educational environment. That expertise must be defined, and defined in terms which can be understood by educationalists. Then, and only then, can a strong, clear, professional message be communicated effectively to principals and teachers.

The reluctance or the inability to recognize or resolve conflict where it does exist is another factor contributing to the static and interfering with effective communication. Here again, a firm conviction concerning role and an equally firm commitment to that role become prerequisites. Once the role is defined and is communicated effectively, it becomes easier to develop the ways and means of carrying out that role.

Communication without static will not take place in a school system without a realization on the part of all three groups that both teaching and learning go on in a school library, that the school librarian makes an important contribution to the intellectual and social growth of the student, and that this contribution is possible because of an expertise which effectively blends librarianship and teaching skills. This will be realized only when that expertise is both practised and effectively communicated in such a way that it becomes recognized as a necessary part of the educational enterprise.

As the study revealed, school librarians may be too cautious and too unsure of their role to provide the clear message that is necessary if school libraries are to fulfill their potential. This barrier to effective communication must be removed and soon, for in times of fiscal restraint a clear message becomes crucial to survival. Conflict may, indeed, be a source of static in the educational communication system; but until the nature of this conflict is realized, and until school librarians recognize their responsibility to resolve it, the school librarian role will likely continue to be marginal, and any hope of providing a "force for educational excellence" will continue to be unrealized.

References

1. See for example, doctoral theses by E.F. Tielke, E.H. Daniels, L.E. Olson, B.A. Hull, C.J. Anderson.

2. The two responses, **Definitely Should** and **Definitely Should Not** were considered **Mandatory**, while the **Preferably Should** and **Preferably Should Not** were considered **Preferential**.

Part III

THE SOCIAL PREROGATIVE

FROM ADAM SMITH TO RONALD REAGAN:

PUBLIC LIBRARIES AS A PUBLIC GOOD*

> "The purpose of studying economics is not to acquire a set of ready-made answers to economic questions, but to learn how to avoid being deceived by economists."
> --Joan Robinson, as quoted by John Kenneth Galbraith in <u>Economics and the Public Purpose</u> (Houghton, 1973)

Miriam Braverman

A specter is haunting this country--the specter of Adam Smith. It is a very unhappy specter, because, as has happened with so many idols, his ideas have been twisted and maimed by his idolators to fit their own interests and agendas. Today a queue of market-mechanism worshipers invoke their individual mantras--rugged individualism, free enterprise, free market economy--hoping to achieve the state of grace of Adam Smith's world as described in the <u>Wealth of Nations</u>. The Reagan Administration's economic programs and sympathies have made this world extremely attractive. A rash of writings emphasize the constructive role of unfettered and unregulated business, putting tax-supported institutions on the defensive. We now see strong evidence in the library field, too, of lemming-like movements to adopt business jargon and methods of evaluation. Before we librarians get too carried away by the aura of the business ethic, we should first define the public and private sectors, examining the ideas of two economists whose recent writings are concerned with library economics, and trace the concept of "public good" in library development.

In Adam Smith's world each person is essentially a creature of self-interest, and as each person follows his or her economic self-interest, there is generated a process to supply demand. This process, unhampered by the strictures and regulations of government,

---

*Reprinted by permission of the author and publisher from <u>Library Journal</u>, 107:4 (February 15, 1982) 397-401. Published by R.R. Bowker Co. (a Xerox company). Copyright © 1982 by Xerox Corporation.

regulated only by competition of the marketplace, is the "invisible hand" which will succeed in bringing ever greater productivity and progress to a nation. It is impossible in this short paper to discuss at greater length a brilliant and complex work [1]. We are concerned not so much with Adam Smith's ideas on the individual, government, and economic progress, as on how his ideas relate the market system and the public good.

Libraries as a "Public good"

Smith recognized the need for the support of public works and public institutions by the state which are "beneficial to the whole society" and "which though they may be in the highest degree advantageous to a great society, are however of such a nature, that the profit could never repay the expense to an individual or small number of individuals, and which it therefore cannot be expected that any individual or small number of individuals should erect or maintain" [2]. The areas he identifies as meeting these criteria are national defense, the administration of justice, the education of the youth (although not past a rudimentary level, since "the endowments of schools and colleges have necessarily diminished more or less the necessity of application in teachers"), and the "experience of supporting the dignity of the sovereign" [3].

There are many functions which are considered as tax-supported public goods in today's society, functions which meet Smith's criteria. Public education and national defense are classic examples. Others range from government support for research and development in a variety of fields to provision for injections against various contagious diseases for children in schools.

The basic question with regard to the public libraries and the economy is whether library services constitute a public good or a commodity. If library services are "beneficial to the whole society," and it is agreed they are not an enterprise from which entrepreneurs can profit, then they represent public good, and qualify for tax support outside the considerations of the marketplace. If, on the contrary, library services can be bought and sold at a profit, and the judgement is made that they are not necessary to the whole society, then they are a commodity, subject to the values of the marketplace and belong in the private sector. More than a century ago our society made the determination that libraries are a public good, and the most highly developed public library systems in the world were founded on this principle.

Public libraries, of course, do not exist in isolation from the private sector. They are connected to the private sector essentially by the materials, furniture, and other products they purchase. Libraries are distinguished from the private sector in that their services are not bought and sold as commodities in the marketplace.

In <u>Public Libraries: an Economic View</u>, Malcolm Getz, an economics professor at Vanderbilt University, begs the question whether libraries belong in the public or private sector. The opening chapter of the book is titled "An Introduction to Public Library Industry." One can only assume in reading it that he is not discussing the industriousness of public librarians. He is concerned with their efficiency in terms of "how many facilities to operate, how many materials to put in each, and how many hours to operate." His measure of efficiency is use. "The number of locations, hours of service, and number of new materials acquired each year should reflect a balance between additional use of the library from additional activities and the cost of additional activities" [4].

The examination of the New York Public Library (using these criteria)," says Getz, "... suggests that at the present time the library operates too many branches, each of which operates too few hours with too few new materials." Getz recognizes the library as a purveyor of public good (knowledge and culture), and states that "local tax support of public library services is appropriate (since) the benefits accrue locally" [5].

Equity vs. efficiency

It is when he makes efficiency the central concern in library operations that he begs the question. One person's efficiency (designing services for the library's middle-class and politically strong clientele) may be another person's deprivation (the constriction or denial of services to children and youth, and the poor whose political clout is limited but whose library needs remain). Getz does recognize this conflict between equity and efficiency. The two most relevant components of equity in libraries, he says, are "equality of opportunity, providing persons from lower-income backgrounds a way to improve themselves" and the provision of access to needed information. In each case, however, the test of cost efficiency is invoked. Getz's criterion of efficiency necessarily leads to a violation of equity, and relying on use alone, while ignoring a multitude of variables in library services, gives him his desired result--fewer libraries, retaining only those aimed at the "users," those who the Public Library Inquiry in 1950 called the library's "natural public," the middle class.

While we would agree that internal management questions with respect to library operations are important in determining the effectiveness of services, they do not determine library objectives or the mission of the library.

By touting efficiency in the delivery of library services as the central consideration in library work, Getz has stood the question on its head. To approach the question logically, the first task is to determine whether libraries are to be considered a public good. If they are, then the central question is how to provide this public good for the whole society. If we make Getz's measures of efficiency the central concern of libraries, we are applying business methods and measures in service delivery--and slyly negating the concept of the public good in relation to libraries.

This distortion is especially manifest in the work of Lawrence White, professor of economics at New York University, and author of "The Public Library: Free or Fee? An Economist's Perspective." White sees library services as public services only if there is "some showing of the private market's failure to provide the service in socially desirable quantities and at socially desirable prices" [6]. What both White and Getz fail to see is that success or failure of an enterprise in the private sector is not measured in "socially desirable" terms, but by the balance sheet--the measure is whether the enterprise returns a profit to its investors. By confusing market criteria with "socially desirable" functions, White takes the first step in moving libraries out of the public sector.

In an earlier article in the New Leader, White completes this process. He argues that "in our society the value of a service does not alone justify making it available at the expense of the taxpayer. The market mechanism is still the routine way of meeting consumer demands" [7]. Who are the library consumers? He cites studies to show they are essentially middle class adults, with students and children (more particularly middle class children) making up the next highest group of users. This, says White, is unfair to poor people, who pay taxes but don't use the library. Since libraries also fail, according to White, to "further education, encourage literacy (or) spread socially useful knowledge" among the general population, he suggests that we charge a fee, seven or eight cents a day, to all but students and children (the latter two groups to be supported by local taxes "keyed to usage") [8]. Some poor people may not be able to use the library, but considering "1980 incomes and prices," 49 cents a week "is not a large amount," he claims, and if people are not willing to pay this, then they "must clearly be users who place a relatively low value on reading library books." Meanwhile, poor people will not have to pay taxes toward the "0.25 percent of all government spending and slightly over 0.5 percent of state and local government spending" which go to library support [9]. (Note that White has retracted the free services for the poor that he advocated in his earlier New Leader article. The market mechanism has already started its work on this theory.)

White, like Getz, also stands the question of library support on its head. The definition of a public good is not that it becomes such because of market failure. If that were so, how come Chrysler and Lockheed, with huge infusions of public monies, can still be privately owned?

How, then, do we determine whether libraries are "beneficial to the whole society"? Getz and White measure their value by business standards. Libraries then become an industry, the value of the services they render determined by consumer demand, as are commodities in the marketplace. The history of public libraries demonstrates different criteria.

The Social Prerogative 281

The historic definitions

The founding and early development of public libraries in the last half of the 19th Century were guided by private philanthropy and fueled by local tax money. There was great variety in the way the "public good" was defined by the men of great wealth, as well as by the middle class and professional people who were active in the formation of public libraries in many communities in that time. Library historians have written about that variety in the philosophical and ideological roots of the founders of libraries. To avoid a potpourri, it is necessary to trace the concept of libraries as a public good historically, in its economic, social, and political contexts. This cannot be done adequately in a brief article. What we can do is select certain historical highpoints that serve to establish the character of the concept.

An 1852 report of the trustees of the Boston Public Library asks: "Why should not this prosperous and liberal city extend some reasonable amount of aid to the foundation and support of a noble public library, to which the young people of both sexes, when they leave the schools, can resort for those works which pertain to general culture, or which are needful for research into any branch of useful knowledge? At present if (this young person) wishes to consult a valuable and especially a rare and costly work, he must buy it, often import it at an expense he can ill afford, or he must be indebted for its use to the liberality of private corporations or individuals. The trustees submit, that all the reasons which exist for furnishing the means of elementary education at the public expense, apply in an equal degree to a reasonable provision to aid and encourage the acquisition of the knowledge required to complete a preparation for active life or to perform its duties" [10].

The most generous of library benefactors, Andrew Carnegie, felt "that the surplus of his and other great fortunes ... should be dispersed by their owners for the public good and during their lifetime" [11]. This is not to say that the library philanthropists did not filter their ideas of public good through their own value systems. They were for the most part men of great wealth, accumulated and maintained in an era of Social Darwinism. Andrew Carnegie told an audience gathered for the dedication of the library building in Homestead, Pennsylvania six years after a number of strikers and spectators had been killed at his Homestead Steel Works by Pinkerton agents called in to break the strike, that he and his wife felt "peculiar" on this occasion. He went on to "commend the library as an instrument for the elevation of the working man, promoting harmony between 'kindly and friendly capital and self-respecting labor.' "[12]

Cultural historian Vernon Parrington commented on the apparent contradiction between the business and philanthropic lives of the Boston Brahmins, among them Everett and Ticknor, most prominent in the founding of the Boston Public Library. The Brahmins "divided between State Street and the Back Bay, ran (their) lives (on) a smoothly agreeable course with no hint of potential antagonisms between exploitation and culture. (They followed so strictly the injunction, let not thy left hand know what thy right hand doeth, that the two were almost total strangers to each other" [13].

In the last decade of the 19th Century, a giant flood of immigrants arrived in this country. They provided much of the labor power in the mines, mills, and factories owned by the ruling Anglo-Saxon elite, who nevertheless viewed with consternation their bad grace in being poor, speaking in foreign tongues, wearing strange clothing and following strange religious practices, such as Roman Catholicism and the Jewish religion. Socializing their children into "American" ways was made difficult by the lack of firmly based national institutions because, after all, the United States was only a little over 100 years old and only the American Indians had had the centuries of experience in North America required to develop socializing traditions and institutions. So the established elites latched on to the public school system as the most effective instrument for homogenizing the population in its own image [14]. Public libraries replaced the early social and subscription libraries for the same purpose. As the Boston Public Library trustees had said, the reasons that applied to the establishment of public education at public expense applied as well to public libraries.

In the first decades of the new century, revulsion grew against the conditions of work and life created by unfettered capitalism. The revelations of the muckrakers on the "robber barons" were published, and the Progressive movement flourished. It was in these years that the great leaders in social work developed the settlement house movement and librarians were greatly influenced by their work. During these years, librarians played a greater role in setting policy than had their predecessors, and when the children of immigrants, encouraged often by their parents with upwardly mobile ambitions, poured into the children's rooms of the public libraries, librarians welcomed them, visited their homes, respected their cultural traditions [15]. These librarians were more effective in implementing the socialization of the young than their patronizing and mean-spirited predecessors. In the 1920's, with the growth of the adult education movement, some of these new attitudes--respect for the patrons and their quest for education and a better life--were translated by librarians into developing the library as "the people's university."

Libraries in depression

The cataclysmic depression of the 1930's, with its millions of unemployed, shook society to its foundations. The laissez-faire doctrine, which had been applied historically more particularly to the poor than to the rich, was abandoned. The government turned to the economic theories of John Maynard Keynes to help prevent total collapse. Keynes maintained "There is no 'compact' conferring perpetual rights on those who Have or on those who Acquire. The world is not so governed from above that private and social interest always coincide. It is not a correct deduction from the Principles of Economics that enlightened self-interest generally is enlightened; more often individuals acting separately to promote their own ends are too ignorant or too weak to attain even these. Experience does not show that individuals, when they make up a social unit, are always less clear-sighted than when they act separately." Keynes went on to say: "We must aim at separating those services which are technically social from those which are technically individual. The most important Agenda of the State relates not to those activities which private individuals are already fulfilling, but to those functions which fall outside the sphere of the individual, to those decisions which are made by no one if the State does not make them" [16].

Adam Smith's idea that government took responsibility for functions individuals could not carry out profitably remained in place, but the theory whereby what was good for the individual acting in his own self-interest was necessarily good for society had proved bankrupt. It was then necessary for government to intervene where the economic system failed--to Keynes, by using deficit spending, carefully controlled, to provide for the vast army of poor, and thus stoking the system back into operation.

Almost no one went untouched by the depression, and a socially sensitive response became a hallmark of many librarians. Margaret Scoggin, young adult librarian in the George Bruce Branch of the New York Public Library, reflected the social concern of the depression years, when she wrote in 1931, that librarians "must take cognizance of the problem of boys and girls out of school and out of work, with no place to go." This may be called "social work," she said, "but I am more and more convinced that the librarian's place is not behind the desk but on the street corner--or at least she should divide her time between the two" [17].

It was the Keynes tradition that the Great Society followed, and the libraries, funded by federal dollars in the 1960's and 1970's, extended library services to previously neglected populations, particularly minorities and the poor. Youthful, idealistic, and enthusiastic librarians exercised their creativity, and exciting and useful programs reached into communities. The lack of full administrative commitment to these programs, reflected in their almost total dependence on federal money, was only one of the problems contributing to their decline in recent years [18]. A major study, commissioned by the Department of Education, of how Title I LSCA funds were used found more money was channeled by state agencies into administration and networking than into programs for minorities and the poor--a violation of the act's purposes and of federal guidelines [19]. Despite these obstacles, the programs of the 1960's and 1970's established a powerful precedent for the library as a public good, with services and materials available to all communities.

The current erosion

The information infra-structure has experienced a qualitative shift in recent years. With "information ... more central to societal functioning," and libraries an expanding market for the private information sector [20], the philosophical foundation of library services as a public good is beginning to erode. The private sector is well aware of this. IBM Vice-President Lewis Branscomb, commenting on the shift in the economy "from an economy grounded in the production of capital goods and manufactured products to an economy based on information," foresaw "a deep transformation in which information is purveyed as an economic good, rather than as a social overhead" [21].

There is a danger that in our honest, if defensive, desire to be part of these current fashions in economic and political theory, librarians are adopting the criteria of Getz and White, and are thus adding to the erosion that is currently washing away at the roots that have defined public library service as a public good in America. When, for example, you decide that a fee is a good way to cover the costs of a service, you immediately suggest that that service no longer is good for the whole society, or worthy of societal support. When you decide to "ration" the use of currently limited resources and services by instituting a fee or a "price" for their use, you accept, like White, that those who won't pay, "must clearly be users who place a relatively low value on reading books." You close the library to the growing ranks of those who simply can't pay, whatever the price. When you justify shorter hours or a branch closing on the basis of internal "cost-effectiveness," without first being certain to consult with the public on those hours that branch serves, you begin the process of converting that library from a public good into a private venture for those who have the time or money to get to the location of the service when that service is available. When you stop reaching out, stop putting library service "on the street corner" as Margaret Scoggin urged, because you no longer get federal money for the purpose, you clearly undermine the case for tax support for those services that reach out to the whole society; you begin to select your users much as a private venture selects the "market" it will serve.

We must guard against the easy options that suggest that for efficiency we serve only a "segment" of our "market." Such choices ultimately provide the proofs for which White, Getz, and other Reagan economists constantly search, proofs that there is no measure of the value of a service beyond its ability to make money [22]. Public libraries are still the "people's university." The mission has grown as the society has changed, and its cost is still part of the "social overhead." We must not let our drive to be more effective or efficient transform that "overhead" into revenue and profit by adopting a "marketing" posture.

Libraries are one part of the mosaic that makes up the quality of our social, educational, and cultural life, and as Major Owens wrote, in the next 25 years "social, political, and cultural changes will be far more significant than technological changes" [23]. Let us hope that the ethos of the marketplace will not dominate in these spheres, will not undermine libraries and other institutions, and that society will not be thrown back to the pitiless age of Social Darwinism.

References

1. For a clear and concise discussion of "The Wonderful World of Adam Smith," see Robert L. Heilbroner's The Worldly Philosophers: the Lives, Times, and Ideas of the Great Economic Thinkers, Torchbooks; S.&S., 1980.

2. Smith, Adam. An Inquiry into the Nature and Causes of the Wealth of Nations. Edinburgh: Oliphant, Waugh, and Innes, 1814, p. 98.

3. Ibid., p. 159, 246, 249.

4. Getz, Malcolm. Public Libraries: an Economic View. Johns Hopkins, 1980, p. xi, 142.

5. Ibid., p. 142, 24, 170.

6. White, Lawrence. "The Public Library, Free or Fee? An Economist's Perspective," Financial Choices for Public Libraries. Public Library Assn., 1980, p. 17.

7. _____. "Sensible Economist's Guide to the Economics of Information," New Leader, December 17, 1979, p. 3.

8. _____. "Public Library, Free or Fee?," p. 30.

9. Ibid., p. 31, 19, 3.

10. Shera, Jesse. Foundations of the Public Library: the Origins of the Public Library Movement in New England 1629-1855. Univ. of Chicago Pr., 1949, p. 274.

11. Dain, Phyllis. The New York Public Library: a History of Its Founding and Early Years. New York Public Library, 1972, p. 209.

12. Ditzion, Sidney. Arsenals of a Democratic Culture: a Social History of the American Public Library Movement in New England and the Middle States from 1850 to 1900. American Library Assn., 1957, p. 157.

13. Parrington, Vernon. Main Currents in American Thought: an Interpretation of American Literature from the Beginnings to 1920. HBJ, 1930, p. 184.

14. See Robert H. Bremner, ed. Children and Youth in America: a Documentary History. Harvard Univ. Pr., 1970, 1974, Vol. 2, 1866-1932, Part 8. Robert A. Carlson. The Quest for Conformity: Americanization through Education. Wiley, 1975. For an interpretation of similar motivations of library founders, see Michael H. Harris, The Purpose of the American Public Library in Historical Perspective: a Revisionist Interpretation. ERIC Ed 071 668. 1972.

15. See Dain, op. cit. Rosemary Rubig Dumont. Reform and Reaction: The Big City Public Library in American Life. Greenwood, 1977. Dee Garrison. Apostles of Culture: The Public Librarian and American Society 1876-1920. Macmillan, 1979.

16. Keynes, John Maynard. The End of Laissez-Faire. Dubuque, Iowa: William C. Brown Reprint Library. (First published in 1927 by Leonard and Virginia Woolf at the Hogarth Pr., London.)

17. Braverman, Miriam. Youth Society and the Public Library. 1979, p. 39.

18. An excellent analysis of community work was done by Leigh Estabrook, "Trends in Community Library Services," Library Trends, Fall 1979, p. 151-64.

19. Summary Report and Evaluation of Title I, LSCA. Applied Management Sciences, January 1981.

20. Estabrook, Leigh. "Productivity, Profit and Libraries," LJ, July 1981, p. 1377-80.

21. New York Times, August 20, 1981.

22. E.P. Thompson described the market approach as the Gradgrind theory of the Victorian rich: "The laws of supply and demand were 'God's laws', and in all major affairs of society all other values must bend before commodity values ... Even excessive charity might endanger the working of these 'natural' laws, by subsidizing and encouraging poverty, and (Dickens maintained) 'the Westminster Review considered Scrooge's presentation of the turkey to Bob Cratchit as grossly incompatible with political economy' ... The market was the final determinant of value, and if there was insufficient demand to make fine architecture and beautifully planned towns pay, [and here we might add library services] this was sufficient evidence that such commodities as these were insignificant in the realm of Fact." Thompson, E.P., William Morris: Romantic to Revolutionary. London: Merlin Press, 1977, p. 9.

23. Owens, Major R., "The State Government and Libraries," LJ, January 1, 1976, p. 28.

BOOK BANNING IN AMERICA*

Colin Campbell

A censorial spirit is at work in the United States, and for the past year or so it has focused more and more on books. Efforts to remove certain titles from school and public libraries, from paperback racks and bookstores, from the eyes of adults as well as children, have increased measurably.

Two months ago, the Supreme Court agreed to review a case stemming from the decision in 1976 by the school board of Island Trees, Long Island, to remove nine books from its libraries and curriculum: Bernard Malamud's The Fixer; Kurt Vonnegut's Slaughterhouse-Five; Go Ask Alice, the anonymous diary of a young girl who died of a drug overdose; Eldridge Cleaver's Soul on Ice; A Reader for Writers, an anthology edited by Jerome Archer; Down These Mean Streets, Piri Thomas's realistic novel of Puerto Rican street life in New York City; A Hero Ain't Nothin' But a Sandwich by Alice Childress; The Naked Ape by Desmond Morris; and Best Short Stories by Negro Writers, edited by Langston Hughes. According to one of the board's press releases, the books were "anti-American, anti-Christian, anti-Semetic [sic] and just plain filthy." The anti-Semitic charge was a reference to Malamud.

A Federal Court of Appeals declared last year that it was "permissible and appropriate" for local school boards "to make decisions based upon their personal, social, political and moral views." The court thereby upheld a 1977 ban by the school board in Warsaw, Ind., against five books, including Sylvia Plath's novel The Bell Jar. The case became notorious after a local senior citizens' organization supported the board's ban on another book--Values Clarification, which discusses marijuana, divorce and other controversial topics-- by collecting 40 copies from school authorities and setting them on fire.

In Abingdon, Va., the public library has been fending off attacks on Goodbye, Columbus by Philip Roth, The Lonely Lady by Harold Robbins, Bloodline by Sidney Sheldon and other novels that

---

*Reprinted by permission of the publisher from The New York Times, December 20, 1981 Book Review, 1, 16-18. Copyright © 1981 by The New York Times Company.

the Rev. Tom Williams of Emmanuel Baptist Church calls "pornography." Pastor Williams is supported by a slim minority of county supervisors who keep threatening to cut off library funds. In a recent county election, which threw out one anti-library candidate, a supporter of the banning was nonetheless re-elected, and one supervisor who had supported the library declined to run.

Last summer in Atlanta, Ga., a recently passed state law against displaying "lewd" and "lascivious" books and pictures wherever minors might see them caused the chief book buyer for a chain of department stores, Rich's, to postpone ordering any new books. The law, which a Federal judge overturned in October, would have outlawed the "showing" of "any book ... which contains descriptions or depictions of illicit sex or sexual immorality." Faith Brunson, the Rich's buyer, said recently that the law would have required her to change the department store's purchasing policies "totally." Similar "harmful-to-minors" laws have been enacted, and are still on the books, in Florida, Pennsylvania, Maryland and Colorado.

Such cases are on the increase nationally, according to the American Library Association's Office for Intellectual Freedom in Chicago. Over the past six months, more than 100 titles have been either removed or threatened with removal from both school and public libraries in more than 30 states. During the early 1970's, the office received approximately 100 complaints a year that library books had been removed or threatened with removal. The complaints shot up to 300 a year in the late 70's, and are nearing 1,000 a year this year. (That does not mean 1,000 titles; objections are being registered to many of the same books.) And, although three years ago just 10 percent of the complaints concerned public libraries, now 20 to 30 percent concern them--a rise from a couple of dozen incidents in 1979 to more than 200 this year. There have been more and more demands as well that certain books in public libraries not merely be restricted to adult readers but that they actually be removed from the premises.

The reason that censors and would-be censors give most often is that a book is unsuitable for minors because of its vulgarity or its descriptions of sexual behavior. But the censors also condemn the depiction of unorthodox family arrangements, sexual explicitness even in a biological context, speculations about Christ, unflattering portraits of American authority, criticisms of business and corporate practices, and radical political ideas.

Significantly, there are no clear Federal laws that specify what rights school boards or local governments have to decide what books will be available in school or public libraries. That is one reason why the Supreme Court has agreed to review the Island Trees case, as a way of sorting out the conflicting rights of local authorities and readers.

In Island Trees, five high school students first took the local school board to court in 1976 to challenge its right to remove books from its school libraries. The plaintiffs argued that the board had denied them their First Amendment rights of free expression and had introduced "a pall of orthodoxy" into the school community. The board has replied that parents and elected school boards are empowered by state law and long-established custom to decide what will be taught and read in local public schools. The board has also argued that the students' rights of free speech were not denied by the removal of the libraries' books and that the First Amendment rights of minors are in any case circumscribed by law and common sense. The case could become a landmark and is being carefully watched.

• • •

Recent attempts to remove books from school libraries are better documented than attempts to remove books from public libraries and bookstores. According to a national survey sponsored by the Association of American Publishers, the American Library Association and the Association for Supervision and Curriculum Development, the following books are among those that have either been removed from school libraries or been allowed to remain only after being altered or restricted.

The fiction titles include Jaws by Peter Benchley; many books by Judy Blume, a best-selling author of sexually explicit books for children and young adults; The Pill Versus the Springhill Mine Disaster and other novels by Richard Brautigan; Manchild in the Promised Land by Claude Brown; Kramer vs. Kramer by Avery Corman; Catch-22 by Joseph Heller; Sons by Evan Hunter; Valley Forge by MacKinlay Kantor; One Flew Over the Cuckoo's Nest by Ken Kesey; The Thorn Birds by Colleen McCullough; The Godfather by Mario Puzo; Portnoy's Complaint by Philip Roth; One Day in the Life of Ivan Denisovich by Aleksandr Solzhenitsyn.

And among nonfiction: The American Heritage Dictionary; The Dictionary of American Slang; Trial of the Catonsville Nine by Daniel Berrigan; Our Bodies, Ourselves by the Boston Women's Health Book Collective; The Art of Loving by Erich Fromm; Boss: Richard J. Daley of Chicago by Mike Royko; The Electric Kool-Aid Acid Test by Tom Wolfe.

Also: A Farewell to Arms, 1984, Brave New World, The Catcher in the Rye, The Merchant of Venice, The Grapes of Wrath, Huckleberry Finn and Stuart Little.

The survey names scores of other titles. Yet only 15 percent of such incidents are ever mentioned in local newspapers, according to the survey's finding. Even fewer get national attention.

• • •

In the vanguard of this nationwide campaign to take some books out of general circulation are dozens of religious and political organizations whose names aren't necessarily familiar in the context of books. They include the Heritage Foundation, a Washington brain trust best known for its conservative position papers; the Moral Majority; the Gabler family in Longview, Tex., which analyzes textbooks and distributes a newsletter to more than 10,000 Americans; Phyllis Schlafly's Eagle Forum; the Pro-Family Forum; state groups like Parents of Minnesota; and countless local outfits like Western Pennsylvania Citizens Against Pornography in Butler County or Citizens for True Freedom in Ogden, Utah.

The fundamentalists and far-rightists among those groups have received support, at least for their ideas on school libraries, from large numbers of more traditional conservatives; from more liberal-minded people who have recoiled from the full effects of the recent, extraordinarily uncensored social environment; and, most significantly, from the courts.

The censors have also found support, and in some cases precedents, among feminists who decry pornography, blacks opposed to the ways blacks are depicted in films and history books, homosexuals organized against unpleasant images of homosexuality, Jews who believe that young people should be protected from The Merchant of Venice, and textbook publishers who have responded to shifting educational fashions by jerkily revising the facts and tone of American history.

Most local groups zero in on titles they learn about from the newsletters and direct mailings of right-wing and special-interest groups. Some organizations also provide useful ideological contexts for their efforts--such as the Moral Majority's contention that a "religion of secular humanism" has been set up in the schools, or the notion of some anti-abortionists that certain book-learned values lead to promiscuity, divorce and crime.

"We're not censors," more than one school-library critic has said; the issue, rather, is how one raises children according to society's values. Ivan B. Gluckman, general counsel to the 33,000-member National Association of Secondary School Principals, says that if school board meetings have become battlegrounds where even an author like Malamud may get shot down, well, "There's a remedy for such bad decisions--vote 'em out of office."

The defenders of books have not been trooping to court to press the honored principle of majority rule. On the contrary, they want to protect certain other principles that majority opinion may endanger. The American Booksellers Association, the American Library Association, the Media Coalition, the Coalition Against Censorship, the Association of American Publishers--whose president, Townsend Hoopes, recently testified against Georgia's "minors-access" law--these groups and others have both a commercial and a constitutional stake in the freedom of books from censors. So do those who have offered friend-of-the-court briefs and other legal aids during the litigation over Island Trees, including: the American Civil Liberties Union, the American Jewish Congress, the Writers Guild of America, the National Council of Teachers of English, the Unitarian

The Social Prerogative   291

Universalist Association, the Anti-Defamation League of B'nai B'rith, the American Jewish Committee, PEN American Center and the National Education Association.

Some of those groups, like the American Library Association's Office for Intellectual Freedom, publish newsletters that carry information about cases of book banning. All, despite disagreements, worry that books may become less available. "You just can't start taking books off the library shelves by majority vote," said Leanne Katz of the National Coalition Against Censorship.

The political passions now let loose are intense. Defenders of books have called the banners "yokels," "Philistines," "fascists." In a recent New York Times Op Ed piece, a legal adviser to The New Yorker magazine wondered out loud if school board members bent on banning books realized what troubles they might face in court. "Would you feel comfortable having to elaborate on why you find the material objectionable? ... Do you like publicity? Notoriety?" And Steven Pico, one of the five students who took the Island Trees board to court, recalls: "This one board member told me that if I had any personal property I should get it out of my name. If the district wins, he said, they're going to sue me, personally."

• • •

Mr. Pico, who was Student Council president when he first became a plaintiff in the Island Trees case, has now graduated from college. Unlike many of his supporters, he has some sympathy for what his community and its school board want to do. "They're trying to protect their children," he says. But he thinks their answers are too simple.

Mr. Pico's lawyers say the banning was a political purge rather than an exercise of the community's normal authority to educate the young. Two board members entered the high school library at night with a checklist of titles and authors they had acquired at a conservative political meeting. The school board subsequently ordered that nine books be removed from the library on the basis of selected quotations from them. Only later did the board give the books a full reading. Their decision to ban the books remained firm.

"The facts are awful," says Gwendolyn Gregory, a lawyer for the National Association of School Boards in Washington. She was using "facts" in the legal sense, and was suggesting why some organizations like hers--which would normally bend over backwards to defend a school board's authority--had decided not to join the Island Trees board in its legal fight.

Although the board's lawyers have argued that "bad taste" and "vulgar language" made the books intolerable, early attacks on them by board members seemed to make as much of the books' political and religious views as of their language. One banned book, A Reader for Writers, infuriated three board members originally because a selection in it had compared Malcolm X favorably with the Founding Fathers; one of the board's objections to Vonnegut's Slaughterhouse-Five was that it has a character who insults the name of Jesus Christ.

In an affidavit the school board's president explained his position this way: "I feel that it is my duty to apply my conservative principles to the decision-making process in which I am involved as a board member, and I have done so with regard to fiscal matters, student decipline, teacher performance, union negotiations, curriculum information and other educational matters."

Since 1976 the Island Trees board has been re-elected year after year, though at times by small margins. In the meantime, while lamenting efforts to "sanitize the library," the first Federal judge in the case, George C. Pratt, supported the board's argument that the First Amendment was not at issue. Judge Pratt's 1979 ruling also endorsed the reasoning of the Federal Court of Appeals in a 1972 case over Down These Mean Streets. The court had said then that books do not acquire "tenure" by sitting on a shelf, and that the school board is as free to remove books as it is to acquire them.

These were not the last words, however. Later in 1979 the case went to a three-man panel of the Federal Court of Appeals for the Second Circuit. With one judge dissenting, the panel last year reversed Judge Pratt's decision. It said that the First Amendment might be at stake, and that a trial was needed to decide the matter. Last spring the whole Court of Appeals met and disagreed 5-5 over whether to overturn the panel's ruling. The case was still headed for trial when the Supreme Court granted the school board's request that it intervene with an opinion of its own.

The board's latest brief was sent to Washington a few weeks ago. It repeats the argument that school boards have a right to protect juveniles from "indecent expressions." But it also observes that "all school systems carry on some form of political indoctrination in the better sense of the word" and that a public school is "an instrument of political socialization."

This puts the issue in plain terms. And--although the board's brief asserts that, in its own case, "the record" happens not to disclose any "political motivation"--it nonetheless asks the Court to comment on whether "political" thinking may be inevitable and proper in such decisions.

• • •

Lawyers for both camps in Pico v. Island Trees have come to agree: The law itself is less than clear.

The Supreme Court has said, in a 1969 decision concerning students' right to protest, that neither teachers nor students "shed their constitutional rights to freedom of speech or expression at the schoolhouse gate." Yet the Court has also said, in Epperson v. Arkansas (1968), that courts "do not and cannot intervene in the resolution of conflicts which arise in the daily operation of school systems and which do not directly and sharply implicate basic constitutional values."

Lower courts have lately afforded even more contradictory guidance. That Indiana book burning, for example, preceded a court ruling that upheld the right of school authorities to remove the volumes. Other opinions, in sharp contrast, have been more concerned with protecting the rights of readers and students. One Federal Court of Appeals held in 1976 that, once the state of Ohio and an Ohio school district had created a high school library, "neither body could place conditions on the use of the library which were related solely to the social or political tastes of school board members." Two rulings from district courts later added that a library's decisions must not be based on content, but must deal only with such "neutral" matters as shelf space.

These cases have raised other questions. Is the freedom to speak and write linked inextricably to a "right to read," as some court decisions have suggested in limited contexts? If so, does such a principle apply even to a public school, which the Island Trees board and many others argue is a "unique social structure?"

A few battlers on each side would be content to see the Supreme Court uphold their own most extreme personal views--such as that school boards should be allowed to require instruction in religion and patriotism, or that students should be allowed to test in court any number of school decisions. Yet the more widespread desire is simply for guidance. As Gwendolyn Gregory, the lawyer for the National Association of School Boards, says: "I hope they go to the heart of the matter"--of rights in conflict. One often mentioned route to compromise would be to protect school libraries from excessive community pressures by providing clearer definition of what constitutes acceptable library procedure for acquiring, removing and circulating books. The Court, for instance, might authorize librarians to reconcile local values and pedagogic values when they are in conflict. Some defenders of books, however, fear that procedural compromises might only legitimize book banning along administratively "correct" lines.

• o •

As for removing books from bookstores and public libraries, the law is also less than clear.

Lawyers who have been fighting state "minors-access" laws consider them extremely dangerous. According to Maxwell J. Lillienstein, the lawyer for the American Booksellers Association, the legal removal of books from retail shelves because they are "harmful to minors," though not legally obscene, could strip the book racks in supermarkets, drugstores, airports and other places--besides bookstores--where adults buy best sellers and classics. Michael Bamberger, the lawyer for the Media Coalition of publishers and distributors who persuaded a Federal judge to strike down Georgia's law, wonders if similar statutes might be worded subtly enough not to offend other judges.

The law is far less clear about public libraries, since few cases of removal or restriction have gone to court. Librarians do have certain rights of due process; a Federal judge not long ago ordered that a librarian in Utah be rehired after she was fired for refusing to take a book off the shelves. But this and a few state-level precedents don't weigh much.

One might assume that adults have the right to borrow whatever library books are available. But what about the "rights" of library boards and city councils to censor the shelves, as several have attempted to do? What about a local government's power to install librarians who suit its tastes in acquisitions? Most library boards across the country are either appointed by elected officials or are directly elected--like school boards.

According to a lawyer for the American Library Association, it is hard to know how such questions might be answered in court if challenges to public library books sharpen.

● ● ●

What defenders of books and their free circulation hope is that certain principles will remain firmly established. Among them:

The literary marketplace for adults must not be legally restricted in such a way that it reduces "the adult population to reading what is only fit for children." So the Supreme Court said in Butler v. Michigan (1957). The Supreme Court has also stated, in Erzoznick v. Jacksonville (1975): "Minors are entitled to a significant measure of First Amendment protection, and only in relatively narrow and well-defined circumstances may government bar public dissemination of protected materials to them." Moreover, Judge Jon O. Newman pointed out last year that even a 1972 Court of Appeals decision which acknowledged that indoctrination is "a principal function of all elementary and secondary education" nevertheless condemned "'indoctrination' in the sense of endeavoring to insist that one set of values must be accepted by the students."

As Judge Newman also wrote, removing books from a school library for reasons that appear at least partially political could easily be seen as "an official message" to the community "that the ideas presented in those books are unacceptable, are wrong, and should not be discussed or considered."

What many want to see preserved, whether through law or some deeper cultural and political consensus, is a spirit of tolerance toward the written word.

There are signs that such views will indeed weather the recent challenges. After all, Georgia's "minors-access" law was struck down. Some censorial school boards have been voted out of office; so have some local officials willing to pull books from public libraries. In Oak Lawn, Ill., for instance, a furious campaign to remove the picture book Show Me! from school and public libraries resulted last spring in elections that defeated the book-banning candidates. In half a dozen states, moreover, demands that public libraries reveal the names of those who borrow "questionable" volumes have been foiled by the passage of laws that keep this information secret.

Faith Brunson, the Atlanta book buyer, was asked what she thought the future held for censors. "I don't think they're going to get their way," she said. Two questions remain, though: whether the Supreme Court will agree and, beyond that, whether the conflicting rights, as they are now being argued, can be easily reconciled in practice whatever the Court decides.

THE ONLY GENTLEMAN*

Russell Baker

The question of what books are fit for young eyes has arisen again in the Washington suburbs, where authorities are arguing whether the Mark Twain Intermediate School of Fairfax County should drop Mark Twain's Huckleberry Finn from the curriculum. My immediate question is, what's it doing in the curriculum in the first place?

It's a dreadful disservice to Mark Twain for teachers to push Huckleberry Finn on seventh-, eighth- and ninth-graders. I had it forced on me in 11th grade and, after the hair-raising opening passages about Huck's whiskey-besotted "Pap," found it tedious in the extreme. Thereafter I avoided it for years. It had been poisoned for me by schoolteachers who drove me to it before I was equipped to enjoy it.

I had similar experiences with Shakespeare (As You Like It and Macbeth), George Eliot (Silas Marner), Charles Dickens (A Tale of Two Cities) and Herman Melville (Moby Dick). Schoolteachers seemed determined to persuade me that "classic" was a synonym for "narcotic."

Ever since, it's been my aim to place severe restrictions on teachers' power to assign great books. Under my system any teacher caught assigning Dickens to a person under the age of 25 would be sentenced to teach summer school at half pay.

Punishment would be harsher for assigning Moby Dick, a book accessible only to people old enough to know what it is to rail at God about the inevitability of death.

Huckleberry Finn can be partly enjoyed after the age of 25, but for fullest benefit it probably shouldn't be read before age 35, and even then only if the reader has had a broad experience of American society.

Unfortunately, this sensible reason for pruning the school

---

*Reprinted by permission of the publisher from The New York Times, April 14, 1982, A23. Copyright © 1982 by The New York Times Company.

The Social Prerogative

curriculum has not been advanced in Fairfax County's case for dropping Huckleberry Finn. Instead of pointing out that assigning the book to adolescents damages Mark Twain, the authorities argue that Mark Twain damages the students.

John H. Wallace, one of the school's administrators, makes the case in The Washington Post. The book "uses the pejorative term 'nigger' profusely." (It does.) "It speaks of black Americans with implications that they are not honest, they are not as intelligent as whites and they are not human."

While this is meant to be satirical, and is, Mr. Wallace concedes, it also "ridicules blacks," is "extremely difficult for black youngsters to handle," and therefore subjects them to "mental cruelty, harassment and outright racial intimidation."

I suppose a black youngster of 12, 13 or 14 might very well suffer the anguish Mr. Wallace describes, and even white youngsters of that age might misread Twain as outrageously as Mr. Wallace has in thinking the book is about the dishonesty, dumbness and inhumanity of blacks. This is the kind of risk you invite when you assign books of some subtlety to youngsters mentally unprepared to enjoy them.

Mr. Wallace thinks Mark Twain aimed only to be "satirical," but only in the loosest sense can Huckleberry Finn be called satire. It is the darkest of visions of American society, and it isn't satire that makes it a triumph, but an irony full of pessimism about the human race and particularly its white American members.

Irony is the subtlest of artistic devices, and one of the hardest for youngsters to grasp. It requires enough experience of life to enable you to perceive the difference between the world as it is and the world as it is supposed to be. Many adults have trouble seeing that the world Huck and Jim traverse along the Mississippi is not a boyhood adventure land out of Disney, but a real American landscape swarming with native monsters.

The people they encounter are drunkards, murderers, bullies, swindlers, lynchers, thieves, liars, frauds, child abusers, numbskulls, hypocrites, windbags and traders in human flesh. All are white. The one man of honor in this phantasmagoria is black Jim, the runaway slave. "Nigger Jim," as Twain called him to emphasize the irony of a society in which the only true gentleman was held beneath contempt.

You can see why a black child nowadays, when "nigger" is such a taboo word that even full-blooded racists are too delicate to use it, might cringe and hurt too much to understand what Twain was really up to. It takes a lot of education and a lot of living to grasp these ironies and smile, which is why adolescents shouldn't be subjected to Huckleberry Finn.

Now that the race issue is raised in Fairfax County though,

the only sensible thing for the Mark Twain Intermediate School to do is tackle the matter head-on, put aside some other things and conduct a schoolwide teach-in to help its students understand what Huck and Jim are really saying about their world.

When the great teach-in is over, a few might even understand why Mark Twain, if he'd surprised himself by landing in Paradise, would be watching them and laughing and laughing and laughing.

INFORMATION JUSTICE

A REVIEW OF THE NCLIS TASK FORCE REPORT:

Public/Private Sector Interaction
in Providing Information Services*

Patricia Glass Schuman

Gutenberg spent five years setting type for the Bible. Today its entire contents can be transmitted by satellite in less than one second. Whirlwind I--a pioneering computer of the 1950's--cost $5 million. A microcomputer with comparable features can be bought now for under $2000. New technologies offer unparalleled opportunities for information production, management, and dissemination.

Close to half the U.S. labor force is involved in some kind of information transfer. More than $50 billion is spent annually for information--telephone services, postal services, television, radio, satellite transmission, computers, books, newspapers, magazines, libraries, etc. The federal government paid over $6 million for data processing alone in 1981. Some 50 percent of the gross national product relates to the production, processing, and distribution of information; the information industries are growing more than twice as fast as the GNP.

"Information Age," "Knowledge Society," "Post-industrial Society"--the terms describing the U.S. economy's shift from a manufacturing base to an information base began to sound like tired clichés. The very real societal transformation they describe, though, is causing heightened tensions, increased debate, and some realignment between social goals and private interests. Recommendations and decisions are being made which will have far-reaching effects not only on information services, but on the quality of our lives and the future of American democracy.

The need for information, and its value to society, is not new. But the amount of information an individual requires to negotiate through complex social and economic structures--and the power

---

*Reprinted by permission of the author and publisher from Library Journal, 107:11 (June 1, 1982) 1060-1066. Published by R.R. Bowker Co. (a Xerox company). Copyright © 1982 by Xerox Corporation.

of that information to determine who will do well and who will do poorly--in our society is unprecendented. Theoretically, we are surrounded by an abundance of information, but the channels for obtaining specific information are complex and confusing: television, radio, newspapers, magazines, government agencies, social service agencies, libraries, data base services, information brokers, telephone services, publishers, etc. Methods of information production and delivery often cross the line between the public and the private sectors, and the conflict between the seemingly divergent philosophies of free access and free markets is escalating.

Although technology is rapidly reducing the costs of storing, producing, and processing information, the costs of the intellectual labor to create it are rapidly rising. Some segments of society are already receiving more benefits from new technologies and information because they have both the sophistication to use them and the money to pay for them. Our information society raises constitutional, social, political, and economic issues which may force us to seek new answers to some of the old questions: Is access to information a right of every individual? If it is, how will that right be upheld? Who will bear the cost? Does the First Amendment apply to all forms of information? When do issues like privacy, confidentiality, or ownership take precedence over rights of access? What are appropriate mechanisms for which kinds of information distribution, for whom, and under what circumstances? When should--or do--the laws of the marketplace apply? Though it may be a truism that an informed citizenry is a prerequisite for a functioning democratic society, the argument about citizen rights of access to information is being intensified both by the capital investment necessary to produce it and the decline in government support of public services.

The policy problem

Merging social and economic priorities has long been a subject of debate. The question of who should invest how much in what information, when and for whom becomes critical in a society in which information becomes the major force. We may be very close to the reality of the technology necessary for a true information society, but as a nation we do not have an appropriate societal framework with which to handle the complexities. There have been numerous attempts to tackle elements of national information policy. The latest emanates from the National Commission on Libraries and Information Science. In 1979, it appointed a Task Force on Public/Private Sector Interaction in Providing Information Services. Its charge was to:

> Identify and illustrate the types of library and information service functions that should be carried out by government or by the private sector; define and illustrate the criteria used to determine what information services should be supported by tax funds or by the marketplace; identify activities within government and the private sector which now

contradict the Task Force views; and identify means and
actions to be taken to correct the balance, and identify
the parties, including NCLIS, that should take them.

This charge mandated a Herculean undertaking by any standard.
Early on, Task Force members concluded that it was inconsistent
with "the actual problems of concern" and that the assignment of
functions was not the way "to guide interaction" between the sectors, since no function was the "exclusive province" of one or the
other. Instead, they focused "almost solely" on federal government
involvement, especially in distribution of information--directly or
through the private sector. Issues relating to "private copyright,
to conflicts between different private information activities, and to
conflicts between the providers of information services and purchasers" were not considered, unless they involved "the government
as a party in those conflicts." Issues related to technology or international data flow were not considered either. Rather than identifying current areas of conflict, the Task Force concluded that the
only way it could make progress was to "limit its consideration to
activities that might arise in the future," leaving the question of
existing situations to be "considered on an 'ad hoc' basis."

The Task Force

The 20 members of the Task Force, according to NCLIS, were
"carefully chosen to be as representative as possible of several constituencies involved." Seven members came from the private sector (a newspaper, and six information industry companies); one from
a not-for-profit organization with a data base product; five people
represented various government sectors; and two were former government employees. The five library community members included
two library school deans (one a past ALA President, the other a
well known consultant to the information industry), a library school
educator, a state librarian, and the director of a private research
library.

Task Force members were able to agree that "information
resources, products, and services" are "vital components of our society, of our economic productivity, of our individual growth and
well-being ... Government policy should be designed to foster the
development and use of information resources and to eliminate im-
pediments to such development and use." There were, however,
basic differences concerning the "proper role" of government as
creator and provider of information resources and products. Much
of the text of the NCLIS report focuses on this debate.

The debate

One side argued that government entry into the marketplace has a
"chilling effect" on private sector investment in information services.
They favored severely restricting the role of government, and instead

placing total reliance on competitive market forces to provide a wide choice of information services needed by society. Members who disagreed with such restrictions pointed to the need "to ensure equitable, open access by the public in general" to information supported with public funds. They argued that information needs not met by the marketplace must be met by the government; that democratic government needs informed and aware citizens, regardless of their ability to pay.

A "simplified" table summarizing "Schematic Contexts for Conflict Concerning the Role of the Federal Government in Providing Information Resources, Products, and Services" was developed. Essentially, it says that when a federal agency determines that an information service is needed, the likelihood of conflict is high if the information is extensively marketed and intended to influence policy. "There would be little, if any conflict when a function is Constitutionally defined (support of National Defense, for example)." The more specific the audience and the more able the audience is to pay, the more likely the conflict if the federal government provides an information service. "Information of high economic value is information that the private sector wants to repackage, to market, to distribute."

On the other hand, it asserts that information of high value to society as a whole--disaster information and medical data, for example--is "unlikely to be controversial." The sensitivity of the contexts escalate with the amount of "user specificity," "value added," and "form of availability." If government information services include tailoring data specifically to user needs, doing additional processing, or providing sophisticated means for access, then the likelihood of conflict increases. Among the most serious causes of conflict the report says, are governmental services which directly compete with private sector activities.

Philosophical differences among the Task Force members are abundantly clear within their report, totalling almost 100 pages. Yet, after two years of meetings, they agreed "almost unanimously" on seven principles and 27 recommendations to "guide the information policies" of the government. (See "Principles & Recommendations" pp. 303-305.)

Of these seven principles, the first four deal specifically with the extent and nature of Government's role in providing information. The Task Force "does not feel that a 'national information policy' is the answer." Instead, the federal government should limit itself to "leadership," encouraging private sector information services and products, and providing incentives to industry. Government should not engage "in commerce" unless there are "compelling reasons" to do so, and the property rights of the private sector should be protected at all times. The remaining three principles represent an attempt to satisfy the concern that "information distributable by the Government should be openly and readily available." But the prices and means for gaining access to that information should be such "that

Principles & Recommendations

Listed below are the seven Principles and 27 Recommendations included in *Public/Private Sector Interaction in Providing Information Services*, the report of the Public/Private Sector Task Force of the National Commission on Libraries and Information Science:

Principle 1. The Federal government should take a leadership role in creating a framework that would facilitate the development and foster the use of information products and services.

Recommendation #1. Provide an environment that will enhance the competitive forces of the private sector, so that the market mechanisms can be effective in allocating resources in the use of information and in directing innovation into market determined areas.

Recommendation #2. Affirm the applicability of the First Amendment to information products and services.

Recommendation #3. Encourage Congress to be consistent in the language used and in the application of principles relating to information products and services, such as those identified in this Report, when it formulates legislation and when it exercises its oversight role.

Recommendation #4. Encourage government agencies to utilize the most efficient (information) technologies.

Recommendation #5. Encourage the setting and use of voluntary standards that will not inhibit the further development of innovative information products and services.

Recommendation #6. Encourage and support educational programs that provide the professional skills needed to further the development and use of information as an economic and social resource.

Recommendation #7. Encourage and support both basic and applied research in library and information science.

Recommendation #8. Encourage and support statistical programs and related research to provide the data needed to deal with information policy issues.

Principle 2. The Federal government should establish and enforce policies and procedures that encourage, and do not discourage, investment by the private sector in the development and use of information products and services.

Recommendation #13. Identify and eliminate legal and regulatory barriers to the introduction of new information products and services.

Recommendation #14. Encourage private enterprise to "add value" to government information (i.e., to repackage it, provide further processing services, and otherwise enhance the information so that it can be sold at a profit).

Recommendation #15. Provide incentives to existing organizations, such as libraries and bookstores, that will encourage them to expand their activities in dissemination of governmentally distributable information.

Recommendation #16. Establish procedures which will create a realistic opportunity for private sector involvement in the planning process for government information activities.

Recommendation #17. Involve the private sector in the process of formulating standards relating to Federal information activities.

Recommendation #18. Create or improve mechanisms for ensuring that the actions of government agencies, in developing information resources, products, and services, are consistent with the policies, goals, and long range plans that are announced.

Principle 3. The Federal government should not provide information products and services in commerce except when there are compelling reasons to do so, and then only when it protects the private sector's every opportunity to assume the function(s) commercially.

Recommendation #19. Announce intentions sufficiently ahead of time to provide an opportunity for private sector involvement when a government agency, for reasons it regards as compelling, should plan to develop and/or to market an information product or service.

Recommendation #20. Review and approve, before implementation, any plans for the government to develop and/or market an information product or service, the review to be carried out by an agency appropriate to the branch of government (such as OMB, GAO, CBO).

Recommendation #21. Include an "information impact and cost analysis" as part of the process of review, evaluation, and approval of any plans for the government to develop and/or to market an information product or service, the analysis to cover economic and social effects, effects on existing products and services, effects on potential private sector products and services, and benefits to the public.

Recommendation #22. Review periodically to evaluate the desirability of continuation of any information product or service as a governmental activity.

Recommendation #23. Do not arbitrarily restrict the Federal government from enhancement of information products and services, even if solely to meet the needs of constituencies outside the government itself.

Recommendation #9. Conduct a periodic economic assessment of the impact of Federal government information products and services.

Principle 4. The Federal government, when it uses, reproduces, or distributes information available from the private sector as part of an information resource, product, or service, must assure that the property rights of the private sector sources are adequately protected.

Principle 5. The Federal government should make governmentally distributable information openly available in readily reproducible form, without any constraints on subsequent use.

Principle 6. The Federal government should set pricing policies for distributing information products or services that reflect the true cost of access and/or reproduction, any specific prices to be subject to review by an independent authority.

Principle 7. The Federal government should actively use existing mechanisms, such as the libraries of the country, as primary channels for making governmentally distributable information available to the public.
Recommendation #10. Encourage Federal agencies to regard the dissemination of information, especially through the mechanisms of the private sector (both for profit and not for profit), as a high priority responsibility.
Recommendation #11. Identify and evaluate alternatives to existing federal information dissemination mechanisms.
Recommendation #12. Develop and support the use of libraries as active means for access to governmental information by the public.
Recommendation #24. Announce the availability of governmentally distributable information and maintain one or more registers to help the public determine what governmentally distributable information is available.
Recommendation #25. Deposit governmentally distributable information, in whatever form it may be available, at national and regional centers, including regional depository libraries, where it may be examined at no charge.
Recommendation #26. Do not assert any Federal government copyrights on information the Federal government makes domestically available.
Recommendation #27. Use the nation's libraries and nongovernmental information centers as means for distribution of governmentally distributable information instead of creating new governmental units or expanding existing ones.

the private sector will be encouraged to create new products and services."

The leadership role specified for government is intended to preclude government management of information, which the Task Force says is "counter to the political philosophy of the country." They consider the private sector the most efficient means for information diversity because the criteria for distribution are then "economic forces, rather than political, with profit as a means of rewarding individual entrepreneurs." Many of the 27 recommendations focus on reducing the uncertainties and risks the private sector may face when it invests in information resources, and what the Task Force considers necessary steps the government should take before it engages "in commerce." Libraries, particularly public libraries, are the "safety valve" proposed to provide a means for distribution "... on a less active basis than the entrepreneur" and ensure that "ability to pay" does not prevent access to government information.

While the principles and recommendations obviously represent compromise, the Task Force report emphasizes a view of information as a "commodity, a tool--of substantial value in the marketplace ... "a product that can ..." lead entrepreneurs to the development of products and services for sale. Information is a "capital resource."

Though lip-service is paid to the societal value of information, clearly and definitively, the report favors a free market system, with as little government intervention as possible. While this conclusion is not particularly radical, given our current political climate, its underlying assumptions require careful scrutiny. Taxpayer dollars which have already paid for the initial gathering of the information that industry is so anxious to resell (if there's a profitable market) are largely ignored.

The Information Industry Association goal "To promote the development of private enterprise in the field of information, and to gain recognition for information as a commercial product" certainly receives strong support from this NCLIS report. But, as Anita and Herb Schiller point out in their recent Nation article: "Commonplace and benign as that (goal) may appear, it represents a reversal of a national commitment to the ideal of public knowledgeability and the informed citizen." [Turn to p. 138 for full article.]

With this report, NCLIS fundamentally departs from what has long been accepted by many--in the information and library community at least--as conventional wisdom. "Serious problems" are now seen in the prospect of a national information policy if that implies any kind of "management" of information by government. Cooperation between the public and private sectors may be highly controversial, because "... cooperation with government carries with it commitments to support and participate with the government, to some extent yielding the independence of action so vital for a free press."

The Social Prerogative

A rather subtle, but definite, semantic switch occurs concerning the question of access within the report. Numerous previous documents, including a White House Conference on Library and Information Services resolution, call for guarantees of "full and equal access" to information, yet the report says that the public library's view is "... that there should be equity if not equality for all users." Despite some ten pages devoted to definitions of terms, the words access, equity, and equality are not defined, though a distinction between "open availability" and "free availability" is defined, since the latter term could be interpreted as meaning "without cost." A rather revealing interpretation of access is buried within the discussion presented for Principle 5:

> The term access was discussed, and interpreted as including retrieval of prespecified (not user-specified) packages of information. It would include an ability to communicate online, but with only limited interaction with the user. Access would include availability at identified national and regional centers and depository libraries. Access by user-specified retrieval would be provided only if specifically authorized.

In other words, libraries can provide access, as long as it's not too useful to the user.

Confusing and questionable terminology abounds throughout the report. Libraries are variously included within either the public sector, the private sector--or separated out entirely. Overwritten and poorly organized, over 70 percent of the text is devoted to a rehash of broad and general discussions; the reader is offered few specifics. An appendix, designed to illustrate cases the principles apply to, presents almost meaningless examples like:

> The NTIS, as the agency principally responsible for the distribution of governmental information, provides the largest single example of governmental service to which principles and policies could be applied.

There is no further explanation; there is a hidden agenda. Those familiar with the controversy know that the information industry would prefer that NTIS disband to allow similar services to be sold by entrepreneurs.

The Task Force makes no concrete recommendations about increasing financial support for libraries. Their reasoning is revealing: "In fact, there would have been significant differences in views within the Task Force concerning the value and appropriateness of any of them."

Market solutions

Obviously, the perspective advocated by the Task Force must be read in the context of our current political and economic climate.

Many of its explicit and implicit assumptions are part of a larger national debate about economic productivity and social justice. Foremost among these is what economist Robert Lekachman calls an "American fixation on market solutions to public problems." Do we indeed have a free, competitive market situation with respect to information services that will--if left to its own devices--produce efficiency, innovation, and equity? The NCLIS Task Force thinks so. "The kind of things the private sector can do most effectively are those which respond most directly and immediately to the needs of the marketplace and thus to the consumer." Demand, they say, is measured by "voluntary payment of a price.... The decision is made in terms of "individual decisions--by the entrepreneur and the purchaser ... the cumulative decisions lead to the optimum allocation of resources to produce the products and services that the purchaser wants, not those that a Government agency determines they need."

Maybe, sometimes, but, as Martha Williams succinctly pointed out at the recent National Online Meeting:

> If the Government hadn't succeeded in some of its information ventures, no one would be concerned--nor are private sector information industry proponents concerned about those activities that have not and don't appear to be able to attract a sizable paying clientele. There are a very few successful activities but one must remember that they didn't start out that way and that if the government hadn't carried out or sponsored much of the pioneering work in the development of databases and online systems, the information industry--both U.S. and worldwide--would not have reached the stage of development it enjoys today....
>
> ... The government did more than develop technologies: it also created markets for the new technologies and it didn't happen overnight nor did it occur in competition with industry. The government filled a gap that at the time was not perceived by the private sector as being able to produce profits in the near term. Such investments by the government have paid dividends for the private sector, and no doubt this pattern will repeat itself....

NCLIS, in accepting the report of this Task Force, runs the risk of adopting a very simplistic perspective on the "free marketplace" for information.

The government itself is not only a major compiler of statistical, bibliographic, scientific, and other information, but is also a major consumer and subsidizer of information resources. Government funding for educational and library services has long provided major markets for the publishing/information industry. Government regulation (copyright, fair use) and subsidy (special postal rates for libraries and books) are an established tradition. Agencies like the Department of Defense and of Education, and the National Science

Foundation, have underwritten the production of information on a massive scale.

What happens in either sector has an impact on the price and type of services available in the other. The Reagan Administration is making concerted attempts to undercut many traditional government supports and subsidies for information. Government Printing Office reductions, cutbacks in education and library programs, the National Archives, and NTIS are only a few examples. Nevertheless, the increased budget proposed for national defense research, if adopted, will increase the government's power as a creator and consumer of information.

Another harsh reality is the increasing number of interlocking multiconglomerates (well represented within the Information Industry Association) which own both hardware and software--publishers, computer companies, data processing services, telephone services, television networks, newspapers, and the like. Some of these cross national boundaries and owe no particular allegiance to any nation. For example, Elsevier North Holland counts among its holdings Excerpta Medica, Congressional Information Service, and Greenwood Press. Information Handling Services, which recently acquired both BRS and Predicasts, is a subsidiary of Indian Head, which in turn is owned by Thyssen Bornemisza of The Netherlands. Time, Inc. owns five magazines, 17 weekly newspapers, five publishing houses, a television station, a cable system, a record firm, the Book-of-the-Month Club, and more. ITT, in addition to its numerous communications, data processing, and computer subsidiaries, also publishes books under the labels of Bobbs-Merrill, Sams, Audel, G.K. Hall, Gregg, and Twayne.

Public goods

Another problem with the pure free market approach, as Marc Uri Porat graphically illustrates in his classic study of The Information Economy, is that the private information infrastructure:

> ... operates under a mixed regime of protective monopoly (telephone), regulated competition (the specialized common carriers) and unregulated competition (computer and other equipment manufacturers). And that the major users of information technology are also subject to a multitude of Federal and State regulations (e.g., finance, USPS). And that even the competitive sectors are characterized by allegations of oligopolistic leadership. Even if our best sentiments are in favor of market solutions, the stark realities of existing market structure defy a laissez-faire approach....

The popular theory underlying the Reagan economic program holds that the only legitimate functions of government are the provision of public goods and the correction of market failures. Unfortunately, the realities of implementing these functions are dependent on political judgments. This is made abundantly clear by the 1982 Economic Report of the President. National defense is described as a "true" public good, while education is a good that "could be private." On the topic of safety regulation, the budget report states: "... the best solution would probably be to rely on market judgments about the value of safety."

A recent contretemps between the White House staff and the Department of Labor reported by the New York Times underlines the possible consequences of this skewed emphasis on market forces. The argument centered around a regulation requiring that toxic chemical hazards, symptoms, and hazard-preventing measures be listed on product containers. Labor estimated that 4000 cancer deaths annually could be prevented by this measure. The Office of Management and Budget disagreed: their estimate was only 400 cancer deaths: "... workers' 'right to know' about chemical dangers in the workplace should not be considered a 'right' in isolation from the cost considerations of the employers and manufacturers who would have to supply the information." Fortunately for those affected, OMB was finally overruled by the Task Force on Regulatory Relief.

Not a commodity

The view of information as a commodity that can and should be bought and sold represents yet another kind of problem with an unregulated free market approach. The perception of the value of information is not new. There has always been a price. Traditional ways of absorbing costs have varied from tax funds to support library services on one end of the spectrum to direct user purchase on the other. As information increases in quantity, and as information products reach new levels of sophistication, questions of value become more complex, but treating information strictly as a commodity is problematic. Edwin Parker, of the Institute for Communications Research at Stanford, summarizes the dilemma:

> Information as such is not a commodity that can be readily bought and sold. There are no satisfactory units for measuring quantities of information, or for establishing a price per unit. Physical commodities have the property that when one person gives or sells them to another, the original owner gives up possession. This is not true for information, because the seller or giver of information retains the information after he has transmitted it to someone else. Sometimes the value of the information to the original possessor is increased after it is widely disseminated.... According to neoclassical economic theory and conventional wisdom in economic policy, the production and distribution of physical commodities can best be handled within a competitive economic system. When all the assumptions of the economic theory are met, unrestricted

competition should lead to optimal total investment (even if the distribution of benefits from that investment offends our social consciences). One of the key assumptions, however, of the economic theory leading to that conclusion is the assumption of standardized products about which consumers have perfect information. This leads to impossible contradictions in the case of information treated as a commodity. If the buyer has perfect information about the information he is considering buying, he has no need to buy it. In addition, the seller cannot relinquish possession of the information because he still has it after the transaction.

Even if we were able to treat information as a pure economic commodity, would society really benefit by leaving the fate of information creation, production, and dissemination--and therefore policy--to the whimsy of the marketplace? Is quality and need determined only when people are aware of their need, as well as able and willing to pay the price? Products which can be bought and sold will certainly be bought and sold, but who will finally decide that a product is salable and therefore should be produced? Should information be held hostage to this year's bottom-line considerations alone, to what the sellers perceive we want and are willing to pay for? Suppose the marketing experts guess wrong?

This NCLIS Task Force report should be carefully examined by all interested parties, as should the activities of NCLIS itself. If the commission is truly committed to the goal it stated in 1975 to: "... eventually provide every individual in the United States with equal opportunity of access" to information regardless of his or her "social or physical condition or level of achievement," it will have to involve many more people in this particular discussion. The current Task Force membership is skewed. It represents neither the end users of information, traditional publishers, or librarians working in different types of libraries.

A weak compromise

NCLIS as a whole, as of this writing, has not yet acted on this report. It was released in February for "review and reaction." The full text, and the reasoning behind the principles and recommendations, must be read carefully to understand their full impact. All concerned with information policy should do so and react. Neither the public nor private sectors are well served by isolation. The principles and recommendations promulgated in this report represent an attempt to compromise, to gloss over the very real differences of motives and goals which exist in various sectors. The potential economic and social consequences of information policy are too crucial to settle for such a compromise.

The danger of narrowly focusing on only internal parts of the problem and coming up with short sighted "vertical" policies are aptly underscored by Porat:

Hardly a word was breathed in the 1890's about the potentially destructive effects of transportation on the environment, on inner cities, on social adjustments. Henry Ford sold cars and trucks; the suburb, the collapse of the inner city, environmental pollution, energy shortages and a stream of property damage and broken bodies emerged much later.

After the inventors work their miracles and entrepreneurs push ideas into material realities, we are left with the untidy portion of the problem: the externalities. Enter the academic economists and sociologists, who are brought in after economic and social realities are upon us, to measure the rate at which the horse left the barn. Then, as now, few with power paused to reflect on the implications of the new technology.

Satisfactorily merging questions of information access and social justice with economic profit and progress is not a simple task. We cannot unwittingly commit our future by allowing information policy to become a bread and butter issue of big business, or any other special interests, at the expense of the national interest. Equal access to information is a natural extension of democratic principles. If information is a public good, and an informed individual contributes to the benefit of society as a whole, then access to information must be guaranteed--not only in principle, but in fact. People with a competitive edge in life are those who are best informed.

Information justice

Guaranteeing a just distribution of information will require continuing debate among the various stakeholders, including the present and potential users of all manner of information products and services. Such a debate requires a much more active stance than the passivity reflected in this report, a more active stance for government, the library community, and the citizens of our nation. The simplistic, but dangerous, approach advocated by the NCLIS Task Force should not stop us from fully confronting the issues. What we desperately need is a forum which will both encourage argument on all sides and creatively channel the tensions, the conflicts, and the healthy controversies towards the achievement of long-term benefits for all-- rather than short-term profits for a few.

Bibliography

National Commission on Libraries and Information Science. Public Sector/Private Sector Interaction in Providing Information Services. Report to NCLIS from the Public/Private Sector Task Force. Stock number: 052-003-00866-1. GPO February 1982. $5.50.

Parker, Edwin B. "Social Implications of Computer/Telecoms Systems," Telecommunications Policy, December 1976, p. 3-20.

Porat, Marc Uri. The Information Economy. Definition and Measurement. U.S. Dept. of Commerce, Office of Telecommunications. GPO, 1977.

Schiller, Anita R. & Herbert I. Schiller. "Who Can Own What America Knows?," The Nation, April 17, 1982, p. 461-63.

Williams, M.E. & Thomas Hogan. National Online Meeting Proceedings, 1982. Medford, N.J., Learned Information, Inc., 1982.

ANTI-INTELLECTUALISM IN AMERICAN LIBRARIES*

David Isaacson

If the young Melvil Dewey, recently graduated from a library school, were to apply for his first library job today, he might be rejected in some American libraries for being "overqualified." This term is often a euphemism for "intellectuals need not apply." Dewey, and other singularly dedicated men and women, would be rejected not because they weren't competent, but because they are, or are perceived to be, "intellectuals." The social perception that one is an intellectual is at least as important--probably more important-- than the fact that a person actually is an intellectual, as I shall seek to demonstrate. It is sadly ironic that our profession, with its often passionate devotion to intellectual freedom, should sometimes demonstrate a patronizing bias, however subtle and unconscious, against intellectuals in our midst. It is also ironic that a profession which has been among the most vocal in combating discrimination against minorities, should itself sometimes be prejudiced against a class of people who have always been a minority, albeit a very significant one, in American culture.

Sad ironies aside, there are reasons for this prejudice. This subject has been addressed, briefly, in the context of the continuing debate about librarians' professional status, by Phyllis Dain:

> Among librarians there has been perhaps a special contempt for their professional schools. Even though they constantly deal with expressions of thought, librarians have shared with the rest of society a certain anti-intellectualism, at the same time as they themselves have been the victims of it in the negative, sexist stereotypes of librarians commonly held by Americans. Yet librarians' scorn for library schools often has a measure of justification in memories of sterile, boring, pointless courses taught by professors bereft of imagination and intellectual rigor and isolated from the field. Compounding the situation has been the recent anti-institutional, anti-academic, and anti-professional mood [1].

---

*Reprinted by permission of the author and publisher from Library Journal, 107:3 (February 1, 1982) 227-232. Published by R.R. Bowker Co. (a Xerox company). Copyright © 1982 by Xerox Corporation.

I agree with Dain that some aspects of library education have sometimes contributed to the anti-intellectualism in our profession, but a lackluster professional education is a symptom, rather than a cause of this phenomenon. Anti-intellectual attitudes do receive some encouragement from some inept library school professors, but these attitudes have their roots in a pervasive, long-established, social tradition of distrust of the life of the mind in our culture as a whole.

To understand why some librarians are anti-intellectuals, we must first agree on some definitions. A merely denotative definition of the word intellectual will not suffice, for if an intellectual is defined as a person who is committed to learning and reasoning, probably not many librarians are anti-intellectual. It is the commonly held connotative associations with the word intellectual that help us to understand more clearly why some librarians are anti-intellectuals. As Richard Hofstadter has argued in his classic study, <u>Anti-Intellectualism in American Life</u>, anti-intellectualism has often been a vague set of epithets covering a variety of sins. He describes some of the typical assumptions of anti-intellectuals:

> Intellectuals, it may be held, are pretentious, conceited, effeminate, and snobbish; and very likely immoral, dangerous, and subversive. The plain sense of the common man, especially if tested by success in some demanding line of practical work, is an altogether adequate substitute for, if not actually much superior to, formal knowledge and expertise acquired in the schools [2].

The typical anti-intellectual is suspicious of intellectuals because he believes they overvalue mental activity, and assume, to use current jargon, an "elitist" or anti-democratic bias. Such assumptions often fail to take into account what an intellectual actually does. As Hofstadter explains:

> A man in any of the learned or quasi-learned professions must have command of a substantial store of frozen ideas to do his work; he must, if he does it well, use them intelligently; but in his professional capacity he uses them mainly as instruments. The heart of the matter--to borrow a distinction made by Max Weber about politics--is that the professional man lives <u>off</u> ideas, not <u>for</u> them. His professional role, his professional skills, <u>do</u> not make him an intellectual. He is a mental worker, a technician. He may <u>happen</u> to be an intellectual as well, but if he is, it is because he brings to his profession a distinctive feeling about ideas not required by his job. The skills are highly developed, but we do not think of him as being an intellectual if certain qualities are missing from his work-- disinterested intelligence, generalizing power, free speculation, fresh observation, creative novelty, radical criticism [3].

With this distinction between the mental technician and intellectual, we can begin to see why some librarians would be suspicious, and sometimes resentful, of intellectuals. But the issue is too simply described if it is seen as an opposition between mechanistic technicians on one side and exciting, creative intellectuals on the other.

If intellectuals get hired in libraries, they may confront an environment that only pays lip service to Hofstadter's list of the intellectual virtues. The free, speculative, creative, and critical play of the mind is far too "heady" an atmosphere for many libraries; in fact, far from being stimulating, such an atmosphere might actually be regarded as unproductive. There are, after all, some practical arguments which can be made against hiring intellectuals in libraries. Let us consider these arguments first, before proceeding to see what legitimate place intellectuals do have in libraries.

Snobbish bookworms

One of the most prevalent connotative associations people often make with the word intellectual is "snob." Intellectuals, of course, don't have a monopoly on snobbery, but the common stereotype readily identifies "smart" people with such socially stupid behavior. It is clear that a person who habitually acts in a snobbish way will have a rough time getting along with those to whom he or she condescends, and an especially difficult time if he condescends to those who have authority over him. In those cases where it is clear that a librarian is a snob, that librarian will not do his or her best work, nor will anyone be impressed but fellow snobs. Even worse, if snobbish librarians are expected to deal with the public, they will be successful only with those patrons they recognize as members of their inner circle, whom they don't "patronize." A good case can be made against hiring certifiable snobs to work in libraries.

Another, more recent connotative association people sometimes make with the word intellectual is "elitist." In current parlance, this term is usually used perjoratively to mean someone with an anti-democratic bias. This word sometimes also shades into male chauvinism, though women have sometimes also been called elitist when they are perceived to be "domineering." An elitist is assumed to be "judgmental," another cant phrase, which means either to make prejudiced value judgments, or, simply, to make any judgments at all. But there is another, older, nonpejorative meaning to this word, one which is unfortunately rapidly losing its meaning. An intellectual elitist may be defined as a person who is dedicated to discovering the best idea, the most elegant solution to a problem, or the most precise answer to a question. Elitists of the first type have made it difficult for women and other minorities to be treated equitably in libraries. Elitists of the second type have made some of the most significant contributions to our profession. Some people, like Melvil Dewey, have elitist characteristics in both the positive and negative senses of the word, but Dewey's most lasting contributions, such as advancing the cause of public libraries and mass literacy, and implementing his classification scheme, derived, in part, from his positive elitist attitudes. To be concerned

The Social Prerogative

about quality does not necessarily mean one has to neglect a concern for equality.

Another connotative association with the word intellectual is that persons so labelled have such a firm dedication to a special area of expertise that they are oblivious to other concerns. When this dedication supports a cause that is relatively uncontroversial, such as Dewey's efforts to make libraries more accessible to the common man, or his system of classifying books, then intellectuals get a good press. But when intellectuals support what may be perceived to be misguided, or even harebrained, like Dewey's scheme for spelling reform, then they are regarded as narrow-minded specialists. It is important to realize that not all intellectuals are consistently intelligent or successful in promoting their ideas. Some intellectuals are dogmatic, even fanatical (as Dewey sometimes was), but it is wrong to assume that the cultivation of intellect necessarily leads to mere expertise in a specialty.

Another mistake people often make is to assume that intellectuals necessarily conform to a certain personality type. It may be assumed that because the intellectual likes ideas, he or she is bookish, preferring to spend most of his or her time reading rather than interacting with people. To the extent that this stereotype is sometimes true, this person may have trouble obtaining or holding a library job, especially in public services. Although many librarians are attracted to library work because they like to read, it is clear, despite the popular image to the contrary, that the responsibilities of our work allow few of us much time for consecutive reading. It is also true that one can be an avid reader without being an intellectual, and that many intellectuals are anything but introverted.

When one or more of the traits just described can be applied to an intellectual, a reasonable case can be made against having that person work in a library. Our profession, like others, can ill afford many who are snobs, prejudiced "elitists," misplaced specialists, or bookworms who are not willing to serve the public. Actual circumstances, however, are usually more complex than these stereotypes suggest.

It is difficult to combat anti-intellectualism because it is often subtle, at least partly unconscious, and associated with otherwise reasonable attitudes. Part of the problem is that our profession is still not sure enough of itself to agree on its own defining characteristics. Although much of the work we do requires mastery of a set of specialized skills, it is not universally accepted that these skills are, or ought to be, intellectual ones. Librarians are fond of comparing our dedication to public service to a similar dedication in other professions. But neither we, nor most members of the various groups we serve, would claim that our work requires a rigorous preparation comparable to the more established professions. Even if we were to agree that a two-year course of study was necessary to obtain the MLS, and even if all librarians had to be certified by examinations and re-certified by strict standards of accountability, we would not achieve the same status--even with honorific titles like information specialists--as lawyers, doctors, and other professionals. Part of the frustration, but also the challenge, of being librarians is that we have not yet established a secure identity either with the public or among ourselves. It should not be surprising, then, that some librarians feel ambivalent about intellectuals in their midst, since they may also feel ambivalent about the value of their work.

Detrimental intellect

Another reason that some librarians are anti-intellectual is that it is believed that there is an inevitable conflict between the typical intellectual virtues and the goals of administrative efficiency. The intellectual librarian may be regarded as giving his highest loyalty to ideas, as only incidentally loyal to a given library, or as temperamentally at odds with typical bureaucratic library routines. If we accept Hofstadter's description of the intellectual as someone who lives for ideas, rather than off of them, then it may be argued that many library jobs simply don't allow time for such a person to read, think, and write. It may be further argued that the qualities Hofstadter lists as essential to intellectuals are useful to some librarians, but they may disrupt daily operations, or at least contribute to inefficient service. If allowed unrestrained movement, so this argument runs, the free play of the mind might actually subvert those orderly routines without which no library could function efficiently. A librarian-intellectual who consistently demonstrates "disinterested intelligence, generalizing power, free speculation, fresh observation, creative novelty, (and) radical criticism" may be regarded as a threat, and as someone who is not an effective team member.

Notice that now the argument is considerably more serious. Now the intellectual is not being rejected because he is a snob, an "elitist," a misplaced specialist, or a bookworm, but because it is felt that intellectual skills are not necessary, and, in fact, may be detrimental to library work.

The problem is to decide how essential intellectual skills are to the management and the mission of the library. It should go without saying that intelligence is necessary for our work, but intelligence is not really the issue. The issue is demonstrable application of intellect. The question is not whether some intellectuals will be hired, by way of patronizing tokenism, to add "tone" and "class" to a library staff, but whether our work is of intrinsic intellectual interest and worth.

False dichotomies

One way this question is typically answered is to recite the theoretical foundations of librarianship. A firm grounding in the principles of library science is regarded as an intellectual necessity. But, it is often believed, the daily work of a librarian is more often "practical," not theoretical. This distinction betrays a false and simplistic dichotomy between theory (intellectual) and practice (nonintellectual). The theoreticians are regarded, often falsely, as removed from the real concerns of people working in the field, the practicing librarians are often equally falsely regarded as unconcerned with these seemingly rarefied pursuits.

It is true that some library educators are so far removed from the daily operations of a library that they don't understand the real needs of patrons, but this does not mean they are "intellectuals," only ineffectual people, who have forgotten the purpose of their profession. It is also true that some librarians have not kept up with new developments in librarianship, but these are not necessarily practically minded professionals; they may be lazy, complacent, and sometimes anti-intellectual people.

There may be reason to resent the "intellectual" cataloger so concerned with the intricacies of AACR 2 as to be unconcerned about the applications of these rule changes to the library. There is reason to resent the "intellectual" reference librarian so intrigued by the complexity of one patron's request for an explanation of the theory of relativity that he or she disdains helping another patron learn how to use Readers' Guide. There is no reason to resent, and every reason to encourage, librarians who are fond of thinking and who recognize that our work is fundamentally, unabashedly, intellectual.

Nevertheless, many librarians are insecure about, or deny that they have intellectual responsibilities. Too often, librarians apologetically say that they work with books as tools, but not in books, as scholars and readers. This dichotomy, like the one between theory and practice, does not hold up under examination. A reference librarian who is only conversant with the way a given index is organized is not nearly as helpful to a patron as one who is also acquainted with the subject matter of the question to which the bibliographic citations in that index refer. If this librarian is only interested in how the Social Science Citation Index is constructed, he or she may know the "nuts and bolts" of the craft, but he or she is not practicing fully the professional responsibilities of a reference librarian. Librarians are trained in techniques if they know that the Social Science Citation Index works differently from the Social Science Index; but they are educated in principles if they know one index is more appropriate for some questions than another, and they are dedicated to library service if they exercise judgment in selecting a source appropriate to the patron as well as to the question. To make such a simplistic distinction between working with books as tools and books as means of achieving not only information, but knowledge and understanding, is to further the still too prevalent image of the librarian as a clerk, rather than a professional.

It is often argued that our responsibility as librarians is to show patrons how to find "information," but not to interpret that information for them. This is another false dichotomy, and sometimes an anti-intellectual one. Each choice, however simple, of a subject heading in the catalog; each choice, however routine, of one reference book over another, is an act of judgment, an interpretation that requires intellectual skill. The librarian who regards these decisions merely as routines may as well be working in a grocery store.

It is not enough for the librarian to have intellectual interests, but it is often necessary for that librarian to demonstrate intellectual judgment. Unfortunately, the intellectual in action is sometimes misunderstood by nonintellectuals. The intellectual at work may seem to be impatient with those who are slower thinkers; he or she may find problems where none seemed to exist before, point out contradictions, argue, and not accept easy answers. The intellectual may turn answers into further questions. To the nonintellectual, such a person may be, or seem to be, a threat.

The point is that the intellectual should be regarded as a liability to a library only when it is clear that his or her mind is turned to nonlibrary concerns. As Melvil Dewey said many years ago:

> There is no room for those who wish to take up library work simply because they fancy it to be easier and more agreeable to one who is fond of books and cultivated society; because it will give such a good chance to read; or because there seems to be nothing else to do and so they try to get in a library. In fact, the work is not easy except in some small libraries where the pay is still easier, and though surrounded constantly by thousands of books which are handled during all the working hours there is hardly any occupation which gives so little opportunity to read. Our traditional motto is "The librarian who reads is lost." Of course I am speaking now of working hours. The librarian who does not read at other times is certainly lost to growth [4].

But it is not enough that a librarian read after hours. It is not sufficient even that a librarian be well-informed. Keeping up with the news or the latest best sellers is not equivalent to a liberal education. Too often intellect, in our popular image of it, is regarded as the same thing as a good memory. What is necessary for the librarian, is that his or her intellect be focused on library concerns. The quality of thought and the way the librarian uses his or her mind is much more important than the number of things he or she remembers.

Instead of resenting intellectuals, we should try to share some of the deep satisfaction they feel for ideas. I don't mean merely the personal satisfaction of solving problems, but the deeper pleasure of sharing with a patron the excitement of an intellectual experience. As Lester Asheim has said, the attraction of librarianship ought to be more than the "fun" involved in it: "The librarian's raison d'être lies in what we have to give to others, rather than in what we can selfishly get for ourselves. I do not think that we will earn the respect of nonlibrarians--or even that we will recruit good young people for librarianship--if we can say nothing more for our (if you will excuse the expression) profession than that it is so much fun, and you meet such interesting people" [5].

If the librarian truly respects the intellectual significance of library work, he or she takes considerable, and justifiable pride in organizing a collection of library materials That selection and organization requires considerable knowledge of the interrelationships between one subject and another and a knowledge of how these materials are likely to be used, or should be used by the groups served. A librarian is perhaps best known by the ability, only acquired after much thought and experience, not only to meet, but to anticipate the needs of patrons. If librarianship is truly a profession, then it not only has a set of intellectual skills to be learned, but a service to be performed. And these skills and service cannot be separated from one another without casting doubt on either of them.

There are library school students who, because they intend to work in a small public or a high school library, do not see why they should learn how to use resources which will probably only be found in academic libraries. Such a short-sighted attitude, if it is not anti-intellectual, is certainly nonintellectual; it is roughly comparable to a medical general practitioner who does not keep up with new developments in medicine, because patients can be referred to hospitals with more specialized resources. Such an attitude toward knowledge is not only ignorant but selfish; what we don't know may not hurt us, but it may be a disservice to our patrons.

Hiring "intellectuals"

Fortunately, the majority of library school students are not so narrow-minded. Some are eager for their first job because they realize the intellectual challenges of our profession. The decision not to hire such people ought to be based on a judgment that they are not dedicated to service, rather than the suspicion that they may outshine other members of the staff. I am not proposing affirmative action guidelines for the hiring of intellectuals, for that would be to admit the anti-intellectual prejudice that intellect is something "extra" that a person possesses, not an essential characteristic of our work. Nor am I arguing for "tolerance" of intellectuals, as if they were eccentrics one had to politely accommodate. But I am arguing that intellect is not something entirely separate from character and motivation. We should not hire intellectuals simply because they are intellectuals, but because they have a demonstrable dedication to share their mental facility with others.

To think like a librarian is not to think differently from a nonlibrarian, but it is to concentrate the mind on problems most nonlibrarians don't think about. The pleasure a seasoned cataloger derives from classifying a difficult book may be akin to that of a

taxonomist, and the structures of subject headings sometimes have
genuine epistemological intrigue. The orderly disposition of books
according to type, function, and subject offers endless problems
that may challenge quite cultivated minds. But these problems are
not only of intrinsic, abstract interest; they have, simultaneously,
considerable everyday, practical, and social implications. As Sanford Berman has pointed out for years, subject headings often have
considerable ideological consequences, and offer significant evidence
of our cultural and intellectual history. The cataloger who thinks
about the work and its significance for others has no reason to
apologize for the intellectual worth of that work.

The reference librarian who takes reference work seriously
has often been compared to a sleuth, sometimes seeming to rival
Sherlock Holmes in the ability to ferret out elusive bits of information. But reference work is more than the pleasure of problem
solving; it can often offer the deeper satisfaction of teaching. Reference problems are, after all, solved usually for individual patrons,
who may themselves "catch" some of the enthusiasm of the bibliographic search from the librarian.

Administrative work in libraries also has its intellectual attractions, not simply because the administrator is responsible for
the functioning of a place which is dedicated to serving the needs of
the mind, but because most libraries are intricate structures, the
orderly management of which calls for all those qualities of mind
Hofstadter describes an intellectual.

Library work is not for the intellectual who would rather focus on other things. If the intellectual does not recognize, for instance, that books are not only sources of information, recreation,
and knowledge, but also objects that have to be preserved, shelved,
and sometimes disposed of, then that intellectual isn't a librarian.
But to the uninitiated, and unfortunately, sometimes to librarians
who ought to know better, it is evident that the reading and writing
of books is an intellectual activity, but it is not equally evident that
the organization of books for use is also an intellectual activity.

It would be hyperbolic to claim that library work is only intellectual, but it is equally exaggerated to feel apologetic for it, as
an adjunct to already firmly established disciplines, as if we were
only "handmaidens" to the real intellectuals. As Lester Asheim
has said:

> "Handmaiden" connotes subservient response to the initiative of others, and librarians do more than perform a
> handy and convenient service. They play a dynamic and
> creative social role. They are not merely the stage
> hands--they design the set. For it is the librarian who
> makes it possible for the scholar, the researcher, and
> the casual reader to make the kind of demands they make
> with some reasonable assurance that they can be satisfied.
> It is the librarian who shapes the collection, organizes

the services and creates the atmosphere and the machinery that brings these demands into being. Thus he does more than assume the tiresome, grubbing tasks which other busier people do not have the time to assume. He does something that the others, however important in their own field, are not equipped to do, and for which they have a greater need than they know: he makes available one of the few channels through which the free access to the best in the world of ideas is kept open [6].

Pseudo-intellectuals

Let us grant that the librarian who apologizes for the lack of intellectual challenge in librarianship may not be anti-intellectual. But this self-defeating attitude may encourage an unconscious anti-intellectualism, or take on another all too familiar defense posture: pseudo-intellectualism. After all, few people will admit they are anti-intellectual, and some of the most successful and long-lasting attacks against the intellectual life have come, ironically, from those who profess to be dedicated to it. One of the most successful "philosophies" of American education, as Hofstadter points out, has been the "life adjustment" school. This movement has been well-intentioned, but openly hostile to the intellectual goals of education:

> Contrary, then, to what had been believed by exponents of the older concept of education as the development of intellectual discipline, there are no general mental qualities to be developed, there are only specific things to be known. The usability and teachability of these things go hand in hand; the more immediately usable an item of knowledge is, the more readily it can be taught. The value of a school subject can be measured by the number of actual life situations to which it directly applies. The important thing, then, is not to teach pupils how to generalize, but to supply them directly with the information they need for daily living--for example to teach them, not physiology, but how to keep physically fit [7].

Although Hofstadter is describing a movement in American secondary education which is at least two generations old, this pseudo-intellectual philosophy is still alive in some schools today, and has also taken root in higher education, including library education. All too often librarians talk glibly about our role as information managers, seeming to assume that information is equivalent to knowledge. All too often we equate sources of information, or discrete bits of data, with knowledge, forgetting that these sources are inert and these data meaningless until they are interpreted by the patron and/or by the librarian. As I have discussed elsewhere [8], this pseudo-intellectualism in librarianship is often reflected in a pseudo-scientific jargon, borrowed frequently from other disciplines, like business communications, education, and various social sciences, with which we sometimes find common cause. Sometimes the result of the use of this jargon is not to make communication easier among fellow specialists, but to confer status, bloat egos, and otherwise lay false claim to "intellectual" worth. Some of the talk about "parameters among user-populations" and "rationales for client-professional interfaces" is not only a substitute for clear thought, but a convenient, pompous way of making the simple sound complex, and for avoiding thought. Such ersatz "intellectualism," once it becomes habitual, makes it difficult to think about significant library problems. This pseudo-intellectuality, once it has become entrenched, is far more difficult to combat than the naïve resentment of the merely ignorant anti-intellectual.

For every genuinely provocative intellectual such as I.F. Stone who is invited to speak at an ALA convention, challenging received ways of looking at the world, all too many pseudo-intellectual celebrities purveying cant and self-congratulatory uplift, and making "revelations" about how if "I'm o.k. then you're o.k. too," drown out the voices who actually have something interesting to say. It is distressing to see library meetings which draw a more enthusiastic audience for a pep-talk by a representative of the McDonald's Corporation promoting the idea that selling Big Macs is equivalent to selling libraries, than they draw for a lecture by Daniel Schorr critical of the ways the mass media manage the news.

I do not criticize the intentions of pseudo- and anti-intellectual librarians, but I am trying to account for some of the barriers that have too often made intellectuals either objects of exaggerated praise as celebrities or exaggerated scorn as eggheads. Sometimes the very way intellectuals regard themselves contributes to this misunderstanding. They may, for instance, consider themselves humanists, and disdain, with a singular lack of clear thought, what they call the "technocrats," or perhaps dismiss with a sneer, those information scientists who don't know what a real library is for. The intellectual's "opponent," equally simplistically, may regard the humanist as a fuzzy-minded dilettante, spouting effete platitudes, who is also oblivious to the real purpose of a library. There is a very unfortunate conflict between at least two "cultures" of librarianship, not unlike the conflict between the humanists and scientists C.P. Snow identified [9] over 20 years ago in our society as a whole. Librarianship is a profession that combines essential elements of both the humanities and the sciences, and it is nonintellectual, if not stupid, not to recognize this. The search to discover something like regular laws of the way people search for information is scientific; the concern for the value of what libraries do is fundamentally humanistic. Neither necessarily excludes the other. Both are enterprises of considerable worth.

Value judgments

One doesn't have to regard oneself as a humanist, a scientist, or an intellectual to realize the fundamental significance of our profession.

Anti-intellectualism among librarians may not so much be the result of distrust and fear of what intellectuals do, as it is of misunderstanding. A genuine intellectual obviously enjoys thinking. Librarian intellectuals, it would seem to follow, enjoy library work because it offers opportunities to exercise the mind on significant problems.

It may be long before anti-intellectualism is eradicated in our profession, or our culture, but an unpretentious willingness to ask questions and to learn will help to keep it manageable. There is no need for all librarians to identify themselves as intellectuals, and some reason, as I have suggested, to believe that libraries cannot function if intellectuals are regarded only as thinkers, whose exclusive activity is communion with "the best that has been thought and said." Fortunately, despite the pervasive influence of anti-intellectual stereotypes, most librarians are people, not disembodied minds. It is precisely because the life of the mind is inseparable from the other activities going on in libraries that we cannot afford to be prejudiced against intellectuals in our profession. Intellectual freedom for librarians is threatened even when no other prejudice exists. It is threatened when thinking is regarded only as something experts and specialists do, and when judgments of value are not regarded as central to library work. The chief characteristic of an intellectual is the capacity ot make discriminating judgments; the chief characteristic of an anti-intellectual is to "discriminate" against that very capacity.

References

1. Dain, Phyllis, "The Profession and the Professors," Library Journal, September 1, 1980, p. 1705-06.

2. Hofstadter, Richard, Anti-Intellectualism in American Life (Knopf, 1963), p. 18-19.

3. Hofstadter, p. 26-27.

4. Dewey, Melvil, "Librarianship As a Profession for College-Bred Women." Address Before Association of Collegiate Alumnae, March 13, 1886 in Vann, Sarah K. ed., Melvil Dewey: His Enduring Presence in Librarianship (Libraries Unlimited, 1978), p. 110.

5. Asheim, Lester, "The Professional Role of the Librarian" in 2 Library Lectures (Kansas State Teachers College, 1959), p. 9.

6. Asheim, Lester, op. cit., p. 8.

7. Hofstadter, op. cit., p. 346.

8. Isaacson, David, "Let's Talk Turkey: a Librarian Cries Fowl to Libraryese," Wilson Library Bulletin, September 1978, p. 64-70.

9. Snow, Charles Percy, The Two Cultures and the Scientific Revolution (Cambridge Univ. Press., 1959).

'THESE ARE LITTLE BATTLES FOUGHT IN REMOTE PLACES'*

Nat Hentoff

If I were to name the town, most of you would have to look it up in an atlas. It's not a village--being big enough for a school population of 16,000--but it's no metropolis. Hardly any news comes out of this town that's of interest to anyone but the folks who live there, and they'd like to keep it that way.

Especially, these days, the man in charge of coordinating the English program in the town's classrooms isn't looking to be on the nightly news. A black parent has just complained to him about Huckleberry Finn, which is required reading in the ninth grade. I mean it's really required. No child leaves the ninth grade in this town without getting on the raft with Huck and Jim.

The black parent is disturbed that his child, that any child for that matter--but especially a black child--should have to read a book with the word "nigger" in it. All the way through it. At this point, the black parent is not demanding that Huckleberry Finn be removed from the curriculum and the library. He is objecting to the book being required reading.

So far, the discussions have been low-key and informal. No newspaper or wire service or broadcast station has any idea that this place may join Fairfax County, Virginia; Davenport, Iowa; Warrington, Pennsylvania; and Houston as yet another battleground over whether Mr. Twain's novel does injury to young readers, particularly young black readers.

The school official in this unnamed town agreed to let me hear him think out what he's going to do--he's not sure yet--provided I didn't name him or the town.

"You see," he said, "I've kept a file on the attacks on Huckleberry Finn around the country, and one thing that's clear to me is that as soon as the press gets into this, it gets a lot harder to keep the talks between the school and the parents low-key. Anyway, there is no story here. Yet. We're trying to figure things out. The

---

*Reprinted by permission of the author and publisher from Village Voice, May 25, 1982, 4.

parent doesn't want to come across as a censor. And I don't want to come across as being callous on this thing."

He paused, and then said slowly, "When a person is offended, a person is offended. You can't say to him, 'Well, you shouldn't have been offended, or it's ridiculous to be offended by this book.' But on the other hand, it's difficult for me to agree to allow any child to go through our school system without reading Huckleberry Finn. There's no other book I know of that is so important--in so many different ways--for kids to know. Especially ninth-grade kids. It seems to me I'd be falling down on my job if I didn't keep that book on the required list. On the other hand, I've got to be sensitive to other people's sensitivities. So I don't know what I'm going to do."

Before hearing why this schoolman feels so strongly that all kids who don't read Huckleberry Finn are culturally deprived, a note about the impact of the press on these matters. On the one hand, as I tell librarians around the country, as soon as the censor draws a battle line, go to the press. Illumination works wonders, even in those areas where most folks attend fundamentalist churches.

The majority of citizens, anywhere, do not like appearing, in newspapers or on television, as if they're being manipulated by organized pressure groups deciding for them what they and their children are going to read. Knowing this element of the American grain is how librarian Kathy Russell triumphed over the censors in conservative Washington County in Virginia. Through the newspapers and broadcast stations there, she kept reminding people that the library belonged to all of them, not just the Baptist minister and his allies who wanted to purge it. And the people got angry--at the Baptist minister.

Press attention, however, does not always have salutary effects. Last week, I wrote about the travails of Huckleberry Finn in Warrington, Pennsylvania, and the ultimate grand compromise there which took the book out of the junior high schools and removed it to the high school where it will be only one of eight titles from which teachers can choose.

In Warrington, the protest began with one set of black parents. The wire services picked up the story, followed by some of the big papers in the area, notably the Philadelphia Inquirer.

Thereupon, other black parents came forward. They reported--and this impressed school officials--that their children had not only suffered emotional harm because they'd had to read Huckleberry Finn, but their classwork in other subjects as well had been adversely affected. All because of Mr. Twain's creature.

I asked the language-arts supervisor in the Warrington school system whether there had been any such reports of damage to black children during all the previous years in which Huckleberry Finn had been on the required reading list in the junior high schools.

No, there had been no such reports.

I asked if she and other school officials had investigated this alleged correlation between Huck and those black children's failing grades. A correlation that revealed itself only after the press reports on the single initial complaint against the novel.

Well, no, the school officials had not really looked into whether such a connection could actually be demonstrated.

My own theory, which I also can't prove, is that a kind of group loyalty was in operation among the black kids who claimed to have been injured by the book. The parents of one of their own had complained about Huckleberry Finn, and in a show of solidarity, other black children began protesting against the book. And to make their points all the more vivid, they also began showing symptoms that the presence of that book was so malign that they couldn't concentrate on their other studies either.

Every one of those black children may well have thoroughly believed all this to be true. The function of the school, however, is to find out if it is true. And it didn't even try.

But let us suppose it is true, that Huck had paralyzed those black kids. All the more reason for them to get all the way into Huckleberry Finn. Otherwise, what a terrible thing for a child to learn! That he is so fragile, so vulnerable, so without intellectual and emotional resources that a book can lay him low. And that is what the teachers and supervisors of the junior high schools in Warrington, Pennsylvania, have allowed the black children in their care to learn.

To return to the conflict still aborning in the small town which I will not name. The coordinator of the English curriculum was saying one recent morning that he is riven between his desire to avoid a racial conflict in the community and his desire to "keep the best literature we can in the classroom."

If he wanted a way out, I told him, Russell Baker, among others, had given him one. In the April 14 New York Times, Baker, an admirer of Huckleberry Finn, nonetheless claimed: "It's a dreadful disservice to Mark Twain for teachers to push Huckleberry Finn on seventh-, eighth-, and ninth-graders.... Huckleberry Finn can be partly enjoyed after the age of 25, but for fullest benefit it probably shouldn't be read before age 35, and even then only if the reader has had a broad experience of American society." [Turn to p.296.]

Dr. Kenneth Clark had snorted when I read him that Russell Baker passage on the phone. So had I when I saw it. (For a more lyrical rebuttal, see Lionel Trilling in last week's column.)

But how did this schoolman--worrying about a possible racial confrontation over this book--react to what Baker had said? He

The Social Prerogative   329

could tell the black parents that on reflection, he had decided that this book was not right for any child in the secondary schools. And, for that matter, he could recommend that even on their own time, all teachers under 35 stay away from the novel.

"No," the man decided not to take this escape route. "No. Neither Russell Baker nor my concern about other people's concern over the use of the word 'nigger' is going to change my mind about what's right educationally. Huckleberry Finn is well placed, very well placed, in the ninth grade. And I'll tell you why.

"First, the story is told by an adolescent: and there are very few quality novels where a youth is dealing with adults entirely from his perspective, in his language, through his experiences.

"Second, in terms of craftsmanship and flow, it's a simple novel. At the ninth grade, students are just learning the structure of the novel. It's really our first opportunity to teach the novel as a form, and there's nothing better to do that with than Huckleberry Finn. Especially the way it's tied in so nicely with the river.

"Also, it's a chronological novel. Not all novels are. For instance, when you jump into Charles Dickens at grade 10, you've got a different, more complicated structure to the novel than you have with Huckleberry Finn. So Twain's book is a great introduction to the form of the novel.

"Then," the schoolman continued, "it ties in very well with the pre-Civil War history that this school district, and most others, are studying at this grade. Twain has a lot to say about America during that period. He gives adolescent kids a great deal to learn and think about.

"Take the word 'nigger.' It's during the adolescent years that kids ought to be dealing with that word, its history, and the kind of people who used it then, and those who still use it. Good Lord, Twain spends three-quarters of his book trying to make clear what a damnable word 'nigger' is, because it shows the whites who used it didn't see, didn't begin to understand, the people they were talking about."

I mentioned a letter I'd received recently from a librarian in Twain's home state, Missouri. She was focusing on books as a vital part of what she calls the initiation rites of children. Books, she insisted, are among the ways teenagers move into adulthood. "And," she continued, "to deny them the books that can most help them make that transition is inhumane."

"Well, sure," said the schoolman, "That's another reason I've insisted on requiring that all kids in this town read Huckleberry Finn. That book is about Huck's rites of passage. To put it more prosaically, a large part of it has to do with an adolescent's growth. But that book also has such a sweeping magnitude to it. It has so many things in it. It's about adolescence; it's about the race thing; it's about con men, the Duke and the Dauphin; it's about the murderous foolishness of pride, the Grangerfords. Oh, I could go on all morning."

The schoolman's voice became low. "It would be such a shame for a kid never to get to read this book."

I asked him how he felt about such "compromises" as the one that had been worked out in Warrington, Pennsylvania, to spare kids from Huck Finn in junior high and maybe allow them to read the book in high school. But even then, in the majority of such "compromises," Huckleberry Finn has carefully been removed from required reading lists in high schools.

"It's insidious," the schoolman in the small town said. "I mean, it's not outright censorship, so nobody has to defend himself against that charge. But this kind of 'compromise' does make it harder and harder for the kid and the book to come together. Oh, some self-starters will seek out Huckleberry Finn in the library or ask if they can choose it for independent study; but in those school districts that have compromised, most kids will never get to read the book.

"And you know what that's an extension of? The way we underestimate kids. This is a classic case of just that. We underestimate the capacity of black kids to understand why and how 'nigger' is used in Huckleberry Finn. And God knows we underestimate Mark Twain."

"Yeah, but so much of this book is Twain's satire," I said. "And John Wallace, the black administrator at Mark Twain Intermediate School in Fairfax County, said that it was asinine to think that most children understand satire."

The schoolman laughed. "What could be more perfect underestimation of kids than that? Look at what kids read on their own. Sometimes I think they live on satire."

"Well, it seems to me you've made up your mind that Huck's going to stay here," I said. "In the ninth grade. And on the required reading list."

"I don't know," he sighed. "I know I'm right about the book, but the key thing is this--you have to be sensitive to someone else's sensitivities. I can talk about the book to the black parents, just the way I've been talking to you about it now. And I can assure them we teach it sensitively, and they'll say, 'It still hurts my child.' And I'll say the child can choose another book. But what book can replace Huckleberry Finn?"

The schoolman had another appointment. "I'd say," he bade me farewell, "that it's a toss-up right now as to what's going to happen. This is just one of those little battles fought in remote places. Only we'll know how it turns out."

ARE SCHOOL CENSORSHIP CASES REALLY INCREASING?*

Kenneth I. Taylor

A current notion that schools are experiencing "capricious and irrational" censorship pressures at an increasing rate is, by now, all but taken for granted by a good segment of the American population. Librarians' appeals for help against censorship by the public, according to one source, rose 500 percent after President Reagan was elected. Censorship, according to another, is "real, nationwide, and growing," while a third warns, "America may be experiencing one of the worst waves of censorship this country has known." Like a ritualistic chant in which the word becomes real, constant repetition has given the notion such a high degree of credibility that we have come close to losing sight of its origins.

While there is little doubt that censorship occurs, we also know that it has been present at every point in American history, including several infamous, nationally organized examples. Should today's public be censoring at an increasing rate that is reaching an all-time high, we must then be experiencing an unprecedented alienation of those people whose support and participation we now so badly need.

Whenever we make charges of censorship, we are making statements about national behavior and adding critical judgment as well. As professionals, we have a moral and ethical responsibility to determine whether or not they are accurate. The purpose of this article is to examine the evidence of three nationally prominent sources of the notion of increasing censorship, which represent professional and commercial interests. Their data, it is proposed, reflect, to an appreciable degree, the perception and apprehensions of persons who are most intimately involved in providing and using school materials and, to an unreliable extent, the actions of community members. For more helpful information, it is recommended, we should be looking directly to the public in order to learn about its inquiries regarding school programs and materials.

---

*Reprinted by permission of the author and publisher from School Library Media Quarterly, 11:1 (Fall 1982) 26-33. Copyright © 1982 by the American Library Association.

ALA Office of [sic] Intellectual Freedom

For a decade and a half, the Office of Intellectual Freedom of the American Library Association (ALA) has reported on censorship of library materials. Established in 1967, it compiles records of censorship activities, reports on court decisions, and provides information and assistance to librarians who are encountering censorship difficulties. In philosophy, it appeals to authority, namely the U.S. Constitution as a guarantee of student rights and professional reviewing media as assurance of collection quality. Its distinctions between school and public library objectives are minimal.

In speeches, talk-show appearances, and press releases that provide content for sources as diverse as Ellen Goodman and the Wall Street Journal, the staff cites titles of classics, Pulitzer Prize winners, and dictionaries as its stock-in-trade proof of the irrationality of censorship. Catcher in the Rye, Diary of Ann Frank, and Huckleberry Finn rank among their favorites, whereas titles, such as Sensuous Woman and Valley of the Dolls, which have also been censored, receive scant notice.

In an analysis of the Office's bimonthly newsletter to its subscribers, Woods found ninety-one individual titles cited as having been censored at least twice in academic, public, or school libraries from 1966 to 1975 [1]. When we compare Woods' list, however, with those of national citizens groups in the late 1940s, we find that the Friends of the Public Schools of America, one of the most powerful of numerous antischool groups, listed, within a span of three years, ninety individuals in its Bulletin, apart from textbook writers and corporate entries, whose entire works were to be banned from libraries throughout the country. In this one instance, we have evidence of greater attempted censorship activity by a single group than is being reported by ALA today on American citizens as a whole.

The Office of Intellectual Freedom conducts few, if any, behavioral studies but bases its estimates of increasing censorship instead on staff perceptions, informal counts of pleas for help, and anecdotal case histories. A well-publicized count states that requests for information rose from "about" four a week to "about" four a day, or a rise of "500 percent," after President Reagan's election [2]. This, the Office surmises, is evidence of increasing conservative power and hostility toward public education.

It is clear that frequency counts of this order constitute dubious evidence of a rise in censorship. Like the compilation of national statistics on health and crime, figures rise as an agency's data-gathering techniques improve and respondents become more accustomed to reporting. A comparable increase in librarians' requests for assistance could have been predicted as the Office publicized the availability of its services. While the Office of Intellectual Freedom provides a useful service by helping those in need and periodically furnishes good copy for journalists, its statistics and press releases should not be accepted as valid indexes of censorship rate.

The Social Prerogative 333

The National Council of Teachers of English

According to the National Council of Teachers of English (NCTE), censorship is increasing in frequency and intensity, is more prevalent, and may be at its highest point in American educational history. Its position is based on two member surveys made in 1966 and 1977, each of which asked respondents whether they had experienced "objections" to books or magazines. There were, respectively, 608 (38 percent) and 630 (30 percent) returns.

Council members reported a higher frequency of objections in 1977. These results and accompanying articles were published in a best-selling monograph, Dealing with Censorship [3]. According to the report, which equates "objections" and "book censorship pressure,"

> If book censorship alone is considered, the 1977 survey shows that slightly over 30 percent of the returns reported book censorship pressures. In raw numbers, 188 respondents reported objections to books used in their schools; 427 respondents reported no objections. In contrast, the NCTE survey of 1966 showed just over 20 percent of the returns reporting censorship pressures on books. The 10 percent increase seems [sic] a significant difference [4].

This last sentence and personal judgments of other writers in the monograph form the only basis of the Council's well-publicized conclusion that censorship had increased over an eleven-year period. Press releases announced findings to the national news and professional media and supplied content for countless articles, including a feature in Parade, the most widely circulated periodical in the U.S.

"After a lapse of several years, cries of 'Ban the book' are rising again," exclaims U.S. News and World Report. "Books and periodicals that some groups find offensive are the targets of a renewed effort at censorship in the nation's schools and libraries." Quoting James E. Davis, editor of Dealing with Censorship, they continue, "Censorship demands have intensified markedly in recent months. There isn't a teacher or school board member in the country that isn't being compelled to take books out of the curriculum" [5].

In Dealing with Censorship, Davis and others refer to what they call the "benchmark" citizens' quarrel with the West Virginia Kanawha County (Charleston) School Board, which began in April 1974 and erupted in violence that drew national attention. Starting with textbooks up for adoption, the controversy developed into a county-wide class struggle wherein one group of citizens and educators was perceived as imposing subject matter and values on others who were markedly different. While the controversy was a reminder of the national pattern of community outbreaks in the McCarthy era, it did not spread, as predicted, to other school districts. Council leaders cite this event and the NCTE's two surveys as evidence of an upsurge in censorship after a brief but deceptive lull. "In my estimation," writes Edward Jenkinson, chairman of the NCTE Committee against Censorship, "there are more attempts at censoring now than ever before" [6]. According to Robert T. Rhode, in the same report, "Today, America may be experiencing one of the worst waves of censorship this country has known" [7].

We do, of course, have censorship pressures, but they are in no manner as powerful or unified as the purge of pro-British materials from the Chicago and New York City schools, as well as states such as Wisconsin, Oregon, and Oklahoma, that was inspired by the Hearst newspaper chain in the 1920s. Nor do we have employment boycotting of blacklisted writers, like Lillian Hellman and Ring Lardner, as we did after World War II.

Certain problems in the design of the two NCTE surveys are often found in others in education and related behavioral fields. We have no follow-up sampling of nonrespondents to see how they differ from or are similar to those who did respond, nor do we know their reasons for not replying. We also have a problem when comparing two surveys that are taken eleven years apart. If we were to apply statistical treatment, we would have to assume, as we would hesitate to do, that cultural and social factors in the U.S. had remained the same. This principle of statistical analysis applies also to informal interpretations of survey data, as was done by the NCTE. Did English teachers feel as free to report on community pressures in 1966 as in 1977? We have no way of knowing.

More serious, however, is the ambiguity of the term "objection" and its use by the Council to mean "book censorship pressure." An objection to a book on grounds of quality or place in the curriculum need not constitute an attempt to censor, even when it is replaced by another. Addressing English teachers and the problems they encounter in selecting materials, Allan Glatthorn writes, "Some of our choices seem just not for all the young adolescents in our classes ... I do think that some of us have made some foolish mistakes in the hope of finding relevant literature" [8]. In order to establish validity, the designers of the NCTE surveys should have defined closely related terms for respondents and field-tested the questions for clarity.

Because of these problems, the Council report is uneven in value for anyone who seeks information on public and teacher roles in appraising materials. Several of the articles are over-reactive, already dated, and, occasionally, inaccurate. For example, Robert F. Hogan's undocumented portrayal of the typical censor as a blue-collar worker, who is undereducated and fundamentalist in religion, promotes a stereotype [9]. From what we know of the McCarthy period and more current examples, critics of the schools are often successful, politically influential members of the business community or the professions, who are articulate, highly persuasive, and regard themselves as equal or superior to educators.

Several articles in the NCTE report provide psychological and behavioral insights that should be helpful to beginning teachers. One, by Allan Glatthorn, is on selection of materials and the values, rights, and privacy of the student [10]. Another is Robert C. Small's article on respect for the citizen who raises questions about materials and teaching [11]. Both are likely to be important long after the data of the two surveys.

AAP-ALA-ASCD Survey

In 1980, the Association of American Publishers (AAP), American Library Association, and Association for Supervision and Curriculum Development (ASCD) undertook a survey of school administrators and librarians that they have called "the most extensive study that has been undertaken to date" [12]. Its purpose was "to provide comprehensive data on the relationship between the censorship problem and the larger selection process." Of 7,500 questionnaires sent to administrators and librarians, 1,891, or 25 percent, were returned. As in the case of the two NCTE surveys, we have no information on nonrespondents. Respondents were asked for the number (or an approximation) of separate items that had been "challenged" since September 1, 1978. Administrators were asked to report on classroom and library materials. Librarians were to respond on library materials only.

Shortly upon receipt of the returns, the researchers found that respondents had encountered difficulty in defining the term "challenges." Several replied that they were reporting only on challenges that had involved formal complaint procedures, whereas others said they were reporting on formal and informal challenges combined. Designers of the instrument said in their summary report that they had had both in mind.

Strikingly different views of "challenges" emerge from the two groups of respondents. Whereas one in five administrators reported challenges to materials in their schools, one in three librarians did so; and whereas administrators reported that 10 percent of the challenges had come from the teaching staff, librarians reported 31 percent. Although no reasons are proposed by the researchers for these discrepancies, we might suppose, for the moment, that librarians had encountered more informal challenges from parents and teachers, whereas administrators were more aware of formal complaints. The actual reason is less important than the evidence here that questionnaire data often bear a closer relationship to the experiences and perceptions of the respondents themselves than to actual facts. In this study, we have 577 librarians proportionately reporting a much higher incidence of challenges originating inside and outside the school than did 1,314 administrators. This point is especially important to keep in mind wherever we find the researchers combining the data of the two groups, as they do, for example, in their treatment of responses on rate of challenges to materials between two two-year periods.

Referring to 1978-80, the instrument asked both groups, "How does this rate compare with the rate of challenges in the two-year period preceding September 1, 1978: lower, about the same, higher, not certain?" The treatment given these responses results in a surprisingly misleading impression of widespread increase from one two-year period to the next.

Data given on reported challenges in 1978-80 and changes in rate from 1976-78 are as follows:

- 1,891 administrators and librarians responded.
- 1,387 or nearly 74 percent did not report challenges of any kind.
- 494 or 26 percent did report challenges.

Of the 494 above who reported challenges,

- 68 or 13.8 percent were uncertain if a change in rate had occurred.
- 250 or 50.6 percent perceived no change.
- 131 or 26.5 percent perceived an increase.
- 45 or 9.1 percent perceived a decrease.

From these data, we can formulate for ourselves a straightforward conclusion of our own making (but not one made in the report): <u>Nearly 7 percent of 1,891 school administrators and librarians perceived an increase in the number of challenges to school materials over a four-year period, whereas 93 percent did not.</u>

The press release to the news media and the professions, however, reports only on the responses of the 176 persons who perceived some kind of "change," either lower or higher. By combining the 45 who reported a decrease and the 131 who reported an increase, and without furnishing raw data for independent reader analysis, the five-page press release statement for July 31, 1981, presents the following as one of its "salient survey findings":

> Nearly 75% of the respondents who indicated any change in the rate of challenges between the 1976-78 and 1978-80 periods reported that the rate had increased [13].

This has become one of the most frequently quoted findings of the study in the national press, an instance in which a 6.9 percent response has been elevated to a more newsworthy 75 percent. Given the researchers' acknowledgment of the ambiguity of the word "challenge," the obvious perceptual nature of the two sets of responses, and what may well become a classic example of data mistreatment, we cannot begin to conclude from these reported findings that an increase in challenges to materials actually occurred (a) in the schools of the respondents when taken as a group, (b) in the survey sample, or (c) in the nation at large.

We also find more than one viewpoint in the report and its accompanying press release, providing curiously divergent interpretations of the findings. In the body, we are properly cautioned against regarding challenges to be the same as censorship attempts:

> While the frequency of challenges reported in the survey is of concern ... it is important to emphasize that challenges to instructional and library materials do not necessarily constitute a threat to freedom of speech or the ability of our schools to provide quality education. On the contrary, such challenges--whether by professionals within the schools or by parents and other members of the community outside--have a legitimate place in a democratic educational system [14].

We are also advised in the introduction, "Neither the report itself nor the survey data should be taken as precise indicators of the rate or impact of censorship pressures nation-wide" [15]. Despite this precaution, the researchers (or others) then offer, in the next paragraph, an inexplicable generalization about national behavior: "What the experiences reported here do indicate is that censorship pressures on books and other learning materials in the public schools are real, nationwide, and growing" [16].

The press release, which is all that many editors and journalists receive, carries the word "censorship" in its heading: "NATIONWIDE SURVEY INDICATES GROWING CENSORSHIP IN THE U.S. PUBLIC SCHOOLS" [17]. Each of these unsupportable statements has been published by news and professional publications without data or clarification for the general reader.

The AAP-ALA-ASCD survey should not be accepted as a report on the American public. It is, inadvertently, a significantly arresting _perceptual_ study of two groups of educators who may be perceiving, experiencing, and reacting to public inquiries about materials in very different ways. With this in mind, readers should disregard any survey conclusions based on combined responses of librarians and administrators. They should also interpret findings on "reported" behaviors as "perceived" behaviors.

The report, which has been distributed by the Washington office of the Association of American Publishers, may be useful as a source of ideas for more-sophisticated perceptual studies. Among these might be an inquiry into what appears to be an unconscious or compulsive desire, by this and other professional sources, to raise the specter of increasing censorship pressures in the absence of appropriate data.

The report also contains several briefly stated but possibly helpful recommendations on selection policies, procedures for handling complaints, and community education programs   All of these, it reminds the reader, are best implemented before problems arise.

The Public and Its Schools

We find it impossible to assert from the data of any of these three sources that censorship pressures are increasing either in frequency or intensity. We learn more from these studies and articles about the perceptions of the respondents and writers than we do about the public itself. Many of them see the schools and their communities engaged in adversarial relationships, like labor and management of earlier decades. The public creates crises by exerting unwelcomed pressures on teachers and librarians.

We should be careful that our studies do not constitute what Robert Asahina calls "social science fiction," wherein an investigator begins with a notion, gathers factual and anecdotal data that concur, and interprets them to obtain a foregone conclusion. Like the Hite reports on human sexuality, to use a popular and patent example, such studies seem to elicit responses from those who are most deeply involved with or enamored of the subject and share the predispositions of the researchers. We will do better by observing and defining public behavior as precisely as possible, using historical and contemporary perspective.

Even a modest knowledge of twentieth-century history indicates that censorship has been far more powerful than at present. Although the NCTE report refers to censorship in the colonial seventeenth century, it does not mention the 1920s or late 1940s when school personnel could and did lose their positions because of "anti-American" ideas, membership in blacklisted organizations, or "anarchistic intent." While the conservative right wing might be growing in political effectiveness today, it is in no way as powerful and influential as business, religious, and patriotic groups that joined forces to launch nationwide attacks on education. We have nothing even remotely like their efforts to remove titles from every school in the nation, as was done successfully with the Rugg social studies texts in 1939 and the Building America series in 1947, both of which ceased publication because of the unified pressures.

There are also important differences between the public attitude toward schools in the first half of this century and today. In the 1920s and 1940s, the public feared schools on ideological grounds and turned to national citizen groups for leadership. The Hearst newspaper syndicate, the Daughters of the American Revolution, and the Conference of Small Business Organizations were among a sizable number of powerful special interests that encouraged attacks on public education. In 1950, Fulton J. Lewis, Jr., one of the nation's most powerful radio broadcasters, was able to begin his evening commentary with full assurance that the listening public shared his opinion about the subversive state of education, by announcing, "Now getting around to our study of un-Americanism in the textbooks of the schools and colleges of this nation...."[18]

Public concerns about the schools are now largely economic and related to teacher and student performance. Requests to cover religious doctrine, such as creationism, are overshadowed by an insistence on high performance in reading and related basic skills. We can be thankful that, when the public questions professional choices in materials, it turns to the schools rather than outside authority. It does not invite outsiders in to plead a local case. Most inquiries come from individuals rather than groups, and, instead of charging teachers with subversive purposes, it asks why certain materials are being used in relation to student maturity or school objectives.

Teachers, in turn, will be more effective if they respond without appealing to authority, either to the opinions of "experts," institutional pronouncements, or the First Amendment, and speak in terms of the individual student and parent. Nationally distributed selection tools, book reviews by persons unknown in the community, and book lists from professional and commercial sources are poor arguments as a defense of local school decisions. Librarians and teachers should be the first to point out problems inherent in national reviewing processes and acknowledge that powerful commercial influences are exerted on school libraries and textbook committees. The public wishes to know instead how educators work together in the selection process, what criteria they follow, and how they relate programs to community needs.

A mistake made by educators after World War II was to ignore early attacks on the schools, assuming that they were isolated and of little consequence, whereas they were symptomatic of a nationwide fear of foreign subversion. Today's concerns are nationwide expressions by individuals who are inquiring in the personal interest of their children. They are not anonymous faces in the community who are trying to use schools to justify their own failings, as more than one of the professional organizations in this article have publicly charged.

Schools need not fear that the public is about to turn to super-patriotic groups for help, although it may, history tells us, should the country become involved in an international conflict. Schools should be concerned instead about the public's turning to alternative programs and home instruction for the teaching and materials it regards as best, a phenomenon, interestingly enough, that may signify a decreasing need for censorship pressure.

We should be able to understand some aspects of the public's search for alternatives by examining the activities of prominent personalities, such as the much-maligned Gablers. Norma and Mel Gabler have long been known as leaders of conservative educational thought, with fans who see them as charming, attractive, and devoted individuals unafraid to speak out on controversial matters. The Gablers are not enemies of the schools, like the Lucille Cardin Crains or Allen A. Zolls of thirty years ago. They do not seek to destroy public education or replace the curriculum. They ask instead for a place for their views in the school program, not an unreasonable position to take in a democratic nation.

They do their homework thoroughly, know textbook content in impressive detail, and share their information with others. They use official state channels to make their views known in Texas at selection time, and, by their own admission in their story, Textbooks on Trial, often fail in their attempts to have a textbook accepted or rejected [19]. Their reviewing processes might withstand public scrutiny better than those of many school systems. Komoski reports that 45 percent of nearly twelve thousand teachers indicate that they had not taken part in reviewing the materials they were using. Fifty percent of those who said they had participated reported spending less than an hour in the process [20].

Activities of public figures like the Gablers tell us that those who inquire about school decisions have a high respect for the influence of materials on young minds. The Gablers believe, as did many of our Founding Fathers, that ideas in school materials can influence young readers and affect their behavior as citizens. There was a distinct preference for American-written materials in the post-Revolutionary period over those of British origin. Men, like Thomas Jefferson and Benjamin Rush, who devoted much of their writing to education, wanted schools that taught moral values and prepared students to be effective citizens. They would have been less impressed by present-day authority appeals to the First Amendment, which say that children, "theoretically at least," should have access to any and all ideas, than by our knowledge of Piagetian principles of moral, intellectual, and social development in children and youth.

Many members of the public are also worried, as educators should be, about the inferior quality of many school texts, a concern shared by Frances Fitzgerald who writes from the position of historian as scholar [21]. Librarians and others are on weak ground when they question the power of materials to influence young people adversely. Educators have an excellent opportunity instead to point to the advantages in using original sources, such as the Federalist Papers and Tocqueville's Democracy in America, or, for younger readers, colonial diaries and letters, in lieu of the secondary accounts of texts.

Parents and community members in the past have been active supporters of school library and classroom supplementary collections, as demonstrated by financial support from the local to the federal level. They have a right to inquire why and how materials are being selected for school use, whether on the basis of classroom activities in response to children's needs or because of their listing in nationally distributed selection tools. Is Catcher in the Rye, said to be the most frequently censored title, in the school library because it has a place in the instructional program or because it constitutes a part of what someone outside considers to be an ideal collection? Are stories of little girls masturbating used by the teachers and counselors or does the library media collection comprise an independent, quasi curriculum of its own in response to commercial interests?

These are the kinds of real but difficult questions that parents are asking. When they do, they are not necessarily challenging the responsibility of teachers or librarians; nor, when they inquire about the relationship of materials to the conceptual and affective development of children, are they rebuking student rights. According to Robert Small, too often "resolutions are made and passed condemning censorship with almost no understanding that protesting citizens are to a very considerable extent fulfilling the role assigned to them by the historical development of the American school" [22].

It is probably time for research on or the development of a taxonomy of questioning behaviors that can help us identify and define the multiple meanings behind the asking of why. Perhaps such behavioral inquiry will help us distinguish between serious public inquiry on the one hand and a fearful perception of censorship pressures on the other.

Acknowledgments

This article was submitted during preparation to M. Frances Klein, associate professor, University of Southern California; Robert E. Clasen, professor and chairperson, Extension Programs in Education, University of Wisconsin; and P. Kenneth Komoski, executive director, Educational Products Information Exchange. The writer gratefully acknowledges their comments by correspondence and telephone.

It will be read at the Airlie House Conference of the Journal of Curriculum Theorizing, October 21, 1982, through the courtesy of editors Janet L. Miller and Jack R. Luskay.

References

1. L. B. Woods, "The Most Censored Materials in the U.S.," Library Journal 103:2170 (1 Nov. 1978).

2. "Books and TV--New Targets of Religious Right," U.S. News and World Report, 8 June 1981, p. 43.

3. James E. Davis, ed., Dealing with Censorship (Urbana, Ill.: National Council of Teachers of English, 1979).

4. Lee Burress, "A Brief Report of the 1977 NCTE Censorship Survey," in Davis, Dealing with Censorship, p. 16.

5. "Censorship on Rise Again in Schools," U.S. News and World Report, 4 June 1979, p. 51.

6. Edward B. Jenkinson, "Dirty Dictionaries, Obscene Nursery Rhymes, and Burned Books," in Davis, Dealing with Censorship, p. 5.

7. Robert T. Rhode, "Legal Decisions and Censorship: A Game of Chance," in Davis, Dealing with Censorship, p. 76.

8. Allan Glatthorn, "Censorship and the Classroom Teacher," in Davis, Dealing with Censorship, p. 52.

9. Robert F. Hogan, "Some Thoughts on Censorship in the Schools," in Davis, Dealing with Censorship, p. 86-95.

10. Galtthorn, "Censorship and the Classroom Teacher," p. 48-53.

11. Robert C. Small, "Censorship and English: Some Things We Don't Seem to Think about Very Often (but Should)," in Davis, Dealing with Censorship, p. 54-62.

12. Association of American Publishers and others, Limiting What Students Should Read (Washington, D.C.: The Association, 1981).

13. AAP-ALA-ASCD press release (31 July 1981), p. 2.

14. Association of American Publishers, Limiting, p. 11.

15. Ibid., p. 2.

16. Ibid.

17. AAP-ALA-ASCD, p. 1.

18. Robert A. Skaife, "They Want Tailored Schools," Nation's Schools 47:35 (May 1951).

19. James C. Hefley, Textbooks on Trial (Wheaton, Ill.: Victor Books, 1976).

20. P. Kenneth Komoski, Report on a National Study of the Nature and the Quality of Instructional Materials Most Used by Teachers and Learners (Epie Report no. 76 [New York: EPIE Institute, 1977]), p. 7-8.

21. Frances Fitzgerald, America Revised (Boston: Little, Brown, 1979).

22. Small, "Censorship and English," p. 61.

HOME INFORMATION SYSTEMS:

THE PRIVACY DEBATE*

Alan F. Westin

During the 1960s and '70s, technological forecasters gave a lot of thought to the possible development of two-way households. These were interactive home information systems that might, one day, enable consumers to receive a wide array of individualized information services and also to communicate purchases, opinions, investments, and many other personal transactions outward at the touch of a button. The problem of protecting the sensitive personal data that such at-home systems could generate was widely discussed and even prompted hearings by state commissions looking into one means of wiring up the home--cable television. In those years, however, it all remained highly speculative. There were no commercial systems in operation, the technology was costly and uncertain, and it wasn't clear whether there was actually a demand for such services.

Now, in the early 1980s, two-way home information systems seem to be moving toward both technological feasibility and financial attractiveness. With pilot projects drawing enormous attention in the popular media and new entries coming on-stream steadily, it's time to look seriously at the issue of privacy raised by these systems.

About 25% of American households (and about 25 million viewers) are estimated to be wired for cable tv in 1982, with over 4,000 local cable stations in operation. Only a fraction of these stations-- a few dozen--now offer two-way service, and these are all pilot projects. It's estimated, however, that 5 million households (with 15 million to 20 million viewers) could have interactive systems by the end of the '80s, from a base by then of 50 million cable-wired households.

About 96% of American households have telephones. Many industry observers believe that home terminals linked to service-providers via the telephone network will become the most common kind of two-way home information system in the next decade.

---
*Reprinted by permission of the author and publisher from Datamation, July 1982, 100-114.

The prime terminal for these systems is the home computer. An estimated 1.5 million to 2 million microcomputers are in use today, and that number is expected to grow to 5 million by 1985 and as many as 10 million to 15 million by the end of the decade. This would provide 30 million to 50 million potential customers for home information services.

Both cable tv and telephone-based systems are currently testing the market for a wide array of consumer services; a recent Federal Trade Commission study found no less than 60 possibilities. From the standpoint of potential privacy issues, these can be grouped into eight main categories:

1. <u>Home banking</u>. By early 1982, there were almost a dozen major home banking projects in operation across the country. A recent survey by Payment Systems Inc. found that banking from the home was the two-way service most desired by American consumers. The banks developing these projects have often linked up with communication firms or information service partners. For example, United American Bank's project in Knoxville has Radio Shack and CompuServe as participants, while Southeast First National Bank is working with American Telephone and Telegraph and the Knight-Ridder newspaper group.

2. <u>Shop-at-home</u> services. In a period of high transportation costs and other inconveniences, the opportunity to choose from a wide variety of goods (including supermarket orders) and have these delivered to the home is seen as a service for which there could be a sizable middle-class market.

3. <u>Information services</u>. General and specialized information services for the home via computer or cable tv terminal are already thriving. Almost 1,000 databases are presently available to home computer owners, containing information on the stock market, public affairs, professional fields (such as law, medicine, agriculture, etc.), and many other subjects. In the cable tv system, subscribers also have access to a rapidly expanding body of videotext information displays.

4. <u>Home and personal security services</u>. Many systems offer their subscribers what one cable tv firm calls "high interest two-way services" such as fire, security, and intrusion protection, and medical emergency alert. Automatic monitoring, billing, and control of utility services is another application currently being piloted.

5. <u>Instant opinion polling</u>. Projects using this service have asked their subscribers about local community issues, national politics, social questions ("Would you favor a publicly known homosexual teaching in the school system?") and just about every kind of topic that appears in door-to-door or telephone opinion polls.

6. <u>Home study</u>. "Instant-response home study courses" are

available on two-way systems, offering the subscriber access to interactive educational programs.

7. <u>Special entertainment options</u>. While sports programming is seen as the big potential money-maker in this category, both soft- and hard-core sexual materials are coming onto the cable tv market.

8. <u>Organizational fund raising</u>. Regular cable tv already offers a variety of religious programming, ranging from a few hours per day for some religious groups to a 24-hour-a-day Christian network. Also being screened are black, Japanese, Italian, Jewish, and many other group packages. Political, civic, consumer, and single-cause groups of all kinds are not far behind. (Even the American Civil Liberties Union is currently exploring a move into cable programming.) The dream of all such organizations--which the two-way systems stand ready to fulfill--is the home pitch. "If you believe what you have just seen and heard, and share our sense of urgency, don't wait to write a check and send it in the mail. Just put your finger on the keyboard and let us receive your support immediately."

The Heart of The Issue

What these and other service options have in common is that the operators managing these systems will be collecting a significant pool of personal data from their subscribers. Into the operator's computer will flow information about checking and charge-account expenditures; purchase of reading material, novelty items, and magazine subscriptions; which special information databases are subscribed to; times owners left their homes or turned alarm systems off, and health conditions involving special alerts; viewer positions on survey questions; and home profiles produced from aggregating many individual responses, including purchases of sexually oriented films and services and contributions to various civic, political, religious, social, and charitable causes conducting home telethons.

Whether subscriber records listing use of these services will be preserved or will simply be used temporarily for transactional purposes and then destroyed is one of the key issues involved in home information systems. But, to the extent that personal data are preserved, a future subscriber who takes advantage of these enticing options would be creating a highly detailed record of personal and family data. And therein lies the heart of the privacy issue.

If there was one lesson that was learned during the first part of the computers-and-privacy debate, it was that personal information is the vital lubricant of the data-based social system we have been building since the 1950s. Knowledge of consumer preferences and behavior is central to marketing of goods and services, extension of credit, decisions about employment and insurance, and many other activities. Computerized personal information is equally sought by government for a host of rational administration purposes such as tax compliance, law enforcement, licensing, program eligibility, etc. When such personal information exists in automated form, we have learned to assume that there will be business uses made of it and there will be legal obligations created to produce it for government, unless organizational policies or new legal constraints are developed to keep such data confidential.

The potential threats to privacy fall into four main categories:

● Improper commercial use by the system operator. Here, the potential harm is that personal information supplied in order to bank, shop, vote, be entertained, or contribute to causes may be used--without the subscriber's knowledge or consent--for additional business purposes. Lists of subscribers with various characteristics could be sold to commercial marketing firms or the civic and religious organizations. In addition, lists of individuals with "derogatory characteristics" could be sold by the operator to services that would resell the information to groups such as merchandisers, credit grantors, landlords, employers, and insurers.

● Breaches of confidentiality to private third parties. Sensitive subscriber information could be obtained by private third parties through illicit cooperation of employees and executives of the system operator, or through outsider penetration of the system's security measures. Such intruders could be persons seeking data for the commercial or organizational purposes cited above. Or the intrusions could arise as part of the rough and tumble of American business, labor, and political life, which has featured extensive wiretapping and other forms of organizational espionage throughout our history.

● Pressures on subscribers to authorize release of their profile data. If home information systems store income and expenditure profiles, persons applying for credit or other financial-based opportunities might be asked to authorize the system operator to supply information to business or government organizations that the subscriber was applying to. This would add home information profiles to the list of other records that individuals are increasingly being required to provide when applying for credit, health insurance, housing, government benefits, etc.

● Investigative or litigative access by government. Telephone toll records, credit-card receipts, bank records, and other data generated by individuals and kept in organizational files have been sought for law enforcement investigations, legislative hearings, and judicial proceedings for many decades. Therefore we can assume that any personal data that government agents consider relevant to an investigation or prosecution could be sought directly from home information system operators.

Data Use Without Consent

This raises the question of whether the system operators would have to (or would be legally able to) notify the subscriber that a government demand had been made, and whether the subscriber would be able to challenge the scope or pertinency of the demand. In addition, to the extent that records of the home information system might pinpoint the location of individuals at a given time (especially where unique personal identifiers were used to authorize certain kinds of purchases or services, either from the home or from remote-terminal services), one could expect the files of home system operators to be especially attractive to government officials for surveillance or evidentiary purposes.

Until 1980, legal protection for subscriber privacy had been limited. Only one state cable commission, Minnesota's, had issued a privacy rule requiring privacy safeguards to be written into every franchise agreement issued by a municipality. In other states, some individual municipalities in the 1970s had written guarantees against use of subscriber data without consent into their ordinances on cable operations or into regulations for franchise operators. However, no general legislation (state or federal) had been enacted that gave privacy protection to subscribers of interactive cable tv (or to other forms of home-information-service systems). The Federal Communications Commission had said several times in the 1970s that it was watching the issue of privacy on interactive cable systems, but that action would not be taken because "evidence of abuse in this area had not yet come to light."

Then, in 1981 through 1982, as the pilot interactive systems spread and their uses were highlighted in national publicity, the pace of action quickened. This has been marked by four parallel developments: the enactment of more detailed municipal privacy regulations; the promulgation of the Warner Amex Privacy Code; a move to enact state and federal cable privacy legislation; and accelerated privacy protection activities by state cable commissions.

Some municipal governments began in 1981 and 1982 to issue detailed subscriber privacy protections. Lexington, Ky., for example, forbids either the grantee or the government to tap or monitor a subscriber's line "for any purpose whatsoever without the express written permission of the subscriber"; an exception is made for "sweeps" to verify system integrity, control "return-path transmission" or bill for pay services. Lexington also forbids grantees, "without specific written authorization of the subscriber involved," to provide any party with a list of names and addresses "which identifies the viewing habits of subscribers." Violation by a grantee of either of these sections subjects it to a fine of up to $10,000, and any other party violating the regulations is also subject to fine and/or imprisonment.

Milwaukee, Wis., adopted a similar general ordinance governing cable communications in May 1981. A 1981 study in Wisconsin, however, found that out of 80 municipalities served by cable, 61 had no ordinances protecting subscriber privacy. Of the 19 that had enacted some safeguards, mainly in the middle to late 1970s, only

10 dealt with the elements the study regarded as essential: bans on collecting or releasing identified subscriber information without express consent, and a prohibition on requiring such consent as a condition for receiving the cable service. The study found that even the 10 ordinances with these rules "were vague, redundant, contradictory, and, in general, poorly written." Therefore, the study concluded, adequate and uniform privacy protection for local cable subscribers needed "to be handled at the state or federal level."

Voluntary Operator Rules

In October 1981, Warner Amex, operator of the Qube system in Columbus, Ohio, announced the first comprehensive "code of privacy" to be promulgated by an operator of an existing interactive project. Gustave Hauser, Warner Amex's chairman, stated that the growing discussion of "social policy issues relating to privacy and individual rights [in cable systems] ... is understandable and welcome," and that such questions "have to be answered as part of any responsible two-way cable development program."

The Warner Amex code drew heavily on fair information practices rules developed in the '70s. Because the code was what Hauser called a "codification" of rules developed through experience in running the Qube project since 1977, its provisions are presumably practical measures that would not jeopardize the operation of a successful system.

Subscribers are guaranteed the right to "examine and copy any information developed by Warner Amex pertaining to them, and to correct such records upon a reasonable showing by the subscriber" that any information is "inaccurate." As for developing "individualized information concerning viewing or responses," the code says these will not be compiled "unless the subscriber has been advised in advance and given adequate opportunity not to participate." Warner Amex promises to keep "individual subscriber information" for only as long as is reasonably necessary, e.g., to verify billing." All third parties who provide services to Warner Amex subscribers would be required to adhere to the company's code of privacy. It is promised that individual subscriber information will be surrendered to government agencies requesting it only in response to a subpoena or court order, and that the operator will notify the subscriber "prior to responding, if permitted to do so by law."

The Warner Amex code represents a well-formulated and responsible voluntary action by a service provider, comparable to the employee privacy policies that IBM and a few other progressive companies pioneered in the early 1970s. Like those IBM policies, which were widely copied by other large employers during the '70s, the Warner Amex code is likely to be adopted by at least some other service operators. And, the New York State Cable Assn. issued a 10-point code for its members in May of 1982 that closely parallels the Warner Amex rules. However, the National Cable TV Assn.

The Social Prerogative

stated it has no immediate plans to issue an industry-wide code (a point to which we will return later).

There has been some concern that not all operators will adopt these rules, especially where they threaten to diminish income from secondary uses of subscriber data. There is also concern that the company codes do not provide for penalties to punish employee violations or proper damages to subscribers who might be harmed. It has also been stressed that no voluntary code can cope with the demands for information that government or third parties might make through legal process.

One example, widely cited to show that this is not a hypothetical concern, involves Warner Amex's own Qube system in Columbus, Ohio. A local theater owner, prosecuted on obscenity charges for screening an allegedly pornographic film, became aware that an abridged version of the same film had been offered on Qube's popular pay-movie option. The theater owner's lawyer subpoenaed the Qube records to obtain both the number of local viewers who had ordered the film and the names of these subscribers. Reportedly, he wanted to see whether the list might turn up any policemen, prosecutors, judges, city officials, and perhaps even leader of antiobscenity groups who had watched the movie in their homes.

The presiding judge, under his judicial authority to define the proper scope of a subpoena, directed the Qube management to produce only the number of viewers who had ordered the film, not the names. Warner Amex has stated that it would have appealed any other ruling to higher courts. But local judges could well rule differently in other cases, and the appellate courts might sustain those rulings where there is no statutory protection for the identified records. For example, where it is not forbidden by statute, courts have repeatedly compelled reporters to produce their notes for stories when the notes seem to be relevant in the determination of libel cases or in serious criminal proceedings, despite strong protests that such compulsory disclosures intrude upon the confidentiality expected by news sources.

Concern over such possibilities has led to the third recent development, a move to formulate new state or federal legislation.

Cable TV Privacy Act

In 1981 Illinois became the first state to enact legislation to protect individuals from invasions of privacy in the operation of cable tv systems. The Cable Television Privacy Act is relatively short, and contains the same kinds of safeguards as the Lexington and Milwaukee ordinances. It prohibits a cable tv company from monitoring "an individual subscriber's set or his individual selection of viewing fare," except for service purposes. It also forbids the operator to give anyone, without express written consent, a list containing a subscriber's name; to "conduct research for any purpose"; or to "install or maintain a home-protection scanning device in a dwelling."

In April 1982, Wisconsin became the second state to enact cable privacy legislation. Opening with a legislative finding that "the use of cable television may infringe on the right to privacy in this state," the law adopted two major regulations. The first requires operators to give any subscriber who asks for it an "on-off" device to prevent signals from being transmitted from the home. The switch is not required to interrupt constant-interval signals, such as those used for home security, fire detection, and utility service monitoring.

The second main provision forbids any person, without the written consent of the subscriber, to monitor the subscriber's cable equipment or the use of it, except for service purposes; to provide anyone with information that discloses any "aspect of behavior" of the subscriber, of members of the household, including "individual habits, preferences, or finances"; or to "conduct research that requires the response of the subscriber or a member of the subscriber's household, except by mail or personal interview," unless the subscriber is notified in writing before the research begins and "at least once a month while the research is being conducted."

Violations of Wisconsin's new cable privacy law include first-offense fines up to $50,000 and subsequent offense fines up to $100,000. Damages and injunctive relief can also be awarded to injured parties who sue under the law.

"Ours was a low-key, low-visibility effort," observed Marlin Schneider, the bill's sponsor. "But we now have a good law that can channel the conduct of this new industry in ways that observe and protect subscriber privacy."

By mid-1982, cable tv privacy bills had been introduced in Maryland, California, Missouri, Massachusetts, and New York. Since the New York bill has attracted the most attention, and promises to be a focal point for national debate over the immediate need for detailed state regulation, it is helpful to look at its origins and main provisions.

In January 1982, a month after the State Consumer Protection Board had recommended safeguards to protect subscriber privacy in two-way cable systems, State Attorney Gen. Robert Abrams submitted the most comprehensive two-way cable privacy bill put before any state legislature. Several days of public hearings were held in May 1982, and the bill is now pending.

Many of the New York bill's provisions parallel the Warner Amex code, and would seem to pose no compliance problems for system operators who have adopted that code. But the New York bill does more. It would establish a subscriber's "expectation of confidentiality" and right of access to his or her own file as legal rights, providing a clear basis for judicial treatment of subscriber privacy claims as these might arise in government inquiries or court proceedings. In addition, the bill specifies duties of accuracy in keeping personally identifiable data, and sets obligations on operators to correct inaccurate or outmoded information. There is a very detailed (and complex) notification procedure for obtaining and updating several forms of subscriber consent. The bill would also make tapping or interception of cable signals a crime under the state wiretapping statute. Finally, the bill gives authority to the state Cable TV Commission and the Attorney General's Office to issue further rules to carry out the legislation.

Standards by Law

Attorney General Abrams and his staff believe that such legislation is essential despite the Warner Amex code or even the possibility of an industrywide voluntary code with no enforcement sanctions. Robert Perry, the specialist who worked on the bill, stressed that setting privacy standards by law would put compliance costs on all system operators (not just the "good guys"); would lead to useful standardization; and would lead operators to install protective procedures more cheaply in the early stages of system development, rather than having to disrupt their systems later at what would probably be far greater costs.

California also held hearings on a cable privacy bill in 1982. Drafted by Assembly Majority Leader Mike Roos, a Democrat from Los Angeles, the California bill reduced the complexity of the notice provisions and other regulatory details of the New York bill and was written with considerable advice from the California Cable Television Assn. as well as the State Dept. of Consumer Affairs. The sponsors believe they have a bill that retains essential safeguards but is less cumbersome than the New York draft. With an interactive system about to start in Southern California, they say their measure has a good chance of passage in 1982, or at least in 1983.

Industry spokesmen are generally opposed to state legislation at this time, on the basic premise that no abuses of subscriber privacy have occurred. They oppose "premature" regulatory intervention, and especially the New York bill's threat of administrative rulemaking that could carry restrictions still further. Some also believe that if there is to be law, it ought to be federal law, in order to promote a uniform set of rules and procedures for an industry in which multistate, standardized operations are needed to turn a profit. In addition, the executive director of New York's State Commission on Cable Television sharply attacked Abrams for "frightening people and giving interactive cable a bad name." "I don't think the wolf is at the door," Edward P. Kearse retorted to the state attorney general. The problem "doesn't exist, and we already have a solution to it in our rules," which he said prohibited cable companies from collecting or disseminating subscriber information without permission.

Senate Cable Bills

Early 1982 was also the time when federal bills were introduced to provide privacy protection in cable operations. Sen. Barry Goldwater, sponsor of a general "Cable Telecommunications Act" that would give the FCC primary regulatory authority over cable, included a section on "Protection of Subscriber Privacy" that would prevent unauthorized interception of cable signals by declaring them "wire communication" protected against tapping. The act would also forbid cable operators to disclose personal information about subscribers without permission. If a court orders such disclosure, the subscriber must be notified and given at least 14 days to contest the order. A subscriber whose privacy is "violated" can recover civil damages, and cable operators who violate the privacy protections are subject to criminal prosecution. Senator Goldwater feels that even though voluntary codes are useful, basic subscriber rights to privacy need to be protected by any federal law regulating the cable industry.

In addition, Senators Ernest Hollings of South Carolina and Howard Cannon of Nevada, both Democrats, included basically similar subscriber privacy protections in a measure they introduced in late April 1982, to leave cable regulation with the municipalities. Thus both the Republican and Democratic bills proposing to create federal policy for cable operations now include privacy sections. However, the National Cable Television Assn. has said that it opposes the privacy sections of both bills, because it feels there is no problem and no legislation is needed.

While the Reagan Administration has not yet expressed a position on the cable legislation pending in Congress, Chairman Fowler of the Federal Communications Commission stated in February 1982 that, as far as the FCC was concerned, cable privacy was not yet an issue calling for federal action. In addition, a staff report done at the FCC, "Economics and Telecommunications Privacy: A Framework for Analysis," recommended that the federal government leave privacy protection to the marketplace; privacy could then be "priced" and would be supplied as a service to those who really wanted it.

Though 11 states have created state cable commissions, only Minnesota's has as yet issued broad subscriber privacy rules. The Minnesota privacy rule was issued in 1975, under a legislative act giving the state commission authority to establish rules for cable, including rules "relating to privacy." This format reflects two of Minnesota's long-standing traditions--early enactment of strong consumer and privacy protections, and broad legislative assignment of rule-making authority to state administrative agencies.

The Minnesota rule requires that any municipality franchising a cable system must enact the following privacy protections by ordinance:

●No cable signal can be transmitted from a subscriber's terminal to monitor individual viewing patterns without express permission of the subscriber. Permission must be obtained in a separate document describing fully the use to be made and cannot last longer than a year, though it can be renewed.

The Social Prerogative   353

• No penalty can be invoked for refusal of a subscriber to consent
or renew a consent to such use, and it can be revoked at any time
by the subscriber.

• No information on the viewing habits of a subscriber obtained by
monitoring a subscriber's transmission can be sold or otherwise
made available to any party other than the operator and its employees
unless authorized by the subscriber.

Since issuing this rule in 1975, the Minnesota commission has
updated it from time to time as cable technology has developed. For
example, an additional regulation clarified that sweeps to verify system integrity or to carry out billing do not require a subscriber's
permission.

A move by some of the other 10 states with cable commissions to adopt regulations similar to Minnesota's seems likely in
1982 or 1983. Forty states, however have no such cable commissions. Unless commissions are created in these jurisdictions, some
other route will have to be found to formulate and adopt statewide
administrative privacy rules for franchise operators.

Where Do We Go Now?

What observations and judgments should be drawn from this report
of quickening interactive projects and early privacy-protection responses? First of all, it helps to compare home-information-system
activity with the way that the first uses of information technology unfolded in the '60s and '70s. Then, business and governmental organizations that had manually collected personal data about clients,
customers, and subjects for many years, moved part of their recordkeeping and information uses into automated forms. Instead of adopting privacy regulations solely for the automated activity (as the Europeans have largely done with their licensing of EDP systems by data
protection boards and commissioners), the United States chose to update and expand traditional privacy expectations in these organizational settings, and apply them to all collection and uses of personal information, whether manual or automated. We did this in two ways:
by enacting some broad fair information privacy codes to cover all
federal agencies (the Federal Privacy Act of 1974), with some states
having done likewise; and, by enacting specific federal and state privacy codes to cover particular areas of informational activity (criminal justice and credit reporting for example) that needed detailed
regulation.

In this perspective, we need to ask whether--for privacy protection purposes--we should characterize home interactive systems
as being essentially an expansion of familiar activities such as telephone communications, banking, and charge-card shopping. Or,
should we regard home interactive systems as a new kind of business
requiring new privacy rules?

Despite all the recent promotional publicity of system developers and futurists, which tells us what these new home systems will soon be like, and despite the reactive conclusions adopted by privacy advocates based on such predictions, the cold fact is that home interactive systems are in such an early stage of development that many of their privacy-critical elements are still not clear.

For example, despite the fact that some conglomerate operators of interactive cable projects now include credit card firms, banks, and publishers, along with the communication organizations, the cable company may turn out to function primarily like a communication carrier, such as the telephone company. If so, specific information services would be provided by banks, department stores, and educational companies, as lessors of communication time, and they would be the organizations that kept individual subscriber records. Presumably, traditional confidentiality relationships and existing legal rules would apply between subscribers and the providers of such services. If no legal rules were in existence for a particular service, such rules could be set for the service-provider using the cable facility.

Under this possible line of delopment, neither the cable company nor the telephone company would monitor or record the content of any information passing from the subscriber to the service provider; it would only record usage levels for billing and spot check for system integrity. Like the telephone company, which now keeps long distance toll records only for the six months required by FCC regulations, a cable carrier could similarly destroy individual records after the short period needed for customer billing needs.

Should this be the route that cable and telephone-based systems take, effective privacy regulations might well be limited to: a ban on releasing any data as to what services are used by an identified subscriber, without consent; forbidding any penalty for refusing to agree to such release; rules controlling third party and government access to such subscription data; and a prohibition against tapping of cable lines by third parties.

This common carrier model, however, may not prove to be the business operation that emerges in the next decade. If, as many think likely, cable and telephone-based systems themselves decide to provide home security, utility management, medical alert, and similar monitoring functions, then privacy regulations would have to be extended to cover any records the carrier would keep about such subscriber uses.

Furthermore, if the cable or telephone-based systems decide to make use of their current conglomerate status to offer credit card, banking, news, entertainment, shopping, or other specific information services, then the cable or telephone-based operator has become, for all practical purposes, a new form of consumer organization. The new operation would bring under one administration sensitive personal information now held by a variety of separate consumer-service organizations. The subscriber profile that could be drawn from records of this unified system would be broader and potentially more extensive than anything available today.

Toward an Industry Code

Should this be the case, extensive privacy rules would be called for to provide legal rights of confidentiality and access covering the cable or telephone-based system as a new multiservice provider, as well as any outside providers that were also allowed to offer services on the system.

While it may be too early to tell which of these arrangements will prevail, one thing seems clear: the moment has been reached at which industry pleas of laissez innover are not persuasive. Enough pilot projects are under way that the National Cable Television Assn., not just Warner Amex or the New York State Cable Assn. has an obligation to be more forthcoming than it has yet chosen to be. So far, the NCTA has refused to develop an industry code and has been content to assert that because there are no fully operating commercial systems and because no operator abuses have taken place, legislators and regulatory agencies should leave the industry alone.

Moving to the substance of the privacy issue, clearer discussion would be possible if public policymakers distinguished commercial and research uses of personal data from problems of government access.

Today, names, addresses, and characteristics of persons who belong to organizations, subscribe to publications, shop at stores or use various credit services, and give money to civic or political causes are exchanged or sold by the organizations providing such services, either to other single organizations or to mailing-list brokers. Some private organizations give persons an opportunity to decline having additional uses made of their names: for example, American Express does this for its credit card customers. Most private organizations do not provide such a choice, and are not required to do so by law.

The possibility that such commercial uses might be made by home information systems operators has produced what might be called the "free market" versus "prohibitory" debate over secondary uses of subscriber data. Some industry leaders see the ability to sell lists of subscriber names and characteristics as an important source of revenue, as it is for many magazine publishers and voluntary organizations today. Privacy advocates have insisted that if this is to be done, persons should be asked in advance whether they agree to such further use, and should be able to decline without penalty. Some privacy advocates want all such additional uses to be banned outright, on the theory that people shouldn't be pressured into consents that weaken social boundaries of self-disclosure.

The free market view argues that the decision on secondary

uses of subscriber data should be left to the individual viewer, not dictated by the privacy advocates. There would be no penalty for declining, but a money benefit might be provided to those who agree to have their names supplied for contact in areas of their consumer or social interest. In my view, this kind of option should be open to subscribers, since the core of privacy is the individual's right to choose what he or she reveals to others.

The same is true for market and social research uses. Wisconsin's new law now bans any research use of the interactive system, even with full disclosure and subscriber consent, unless it is done by personal interview or by telephone. This represents the kind of paternalism and overkill that American privacy protection has not previously engaged in. It resembles the Swedish data projection board's ban on computer dating services, which the Swedes reject as too self-revealing for people to be allowed to choose. In the United States, we let people select such services, and the law steps in only if blackmail or other abuses are found to be taking place.

My own view is that legislation or regulatory-agency action dealing with commercial and research uses ought to be simple and basic at this point. It should concentrate on advance notice to subscribers of any additional uses contemplated by service providers or system operators; a requirement of consent without penalty; and rights of inspection and correction by subscribers for any identified data kept about them. Such a law could require franchise applicants and those awarded franchises to file specifications as to how they would meet these requirements, and the internal confidentiality and security safeguards they would install. It is hard to take seriously the argument that such basic protections of privacy and consumer rights would cripple the emerging industry.

Essential Access Shields

Industry representatives and privacy advocates agree that shielding identified subscriber data from "improper" government access is essential. The industry position is that adequate protection exists now through confidentiality laws governing particular consumer activities (banking, insurance, etc.) plus expected judicial protection of identified subscriber data that system operators would actively assert, as in the subpoena of identified Qube records for the obscenity trial in Columbus, Ohio.

Looking over judicial decisions of the past decade involving government access to employee medical records, drug prescription records, private social-agency client records, and similar sensitive data, it is hard to see the basis for such optimism. In almost every case in which the government has asserted that there was a compelling public interest in reaching databases, the courts have ordered the holders of the data to surrender them. And, in the banking area, where the courts flatly rejected any right of privacy by the depositor in his or her account information, it took legislation in the late '70s--federal and state financial privacy laws--to set the proper framework so that courts can now properly weigh the government's claims against the depositor's claims.

For these reasons, my view is that minimal legislation is needed at this time to set rules for government access. Such legislation should provide personal data kept in interactive systems with a legitimate expectation of confidentiality; require that subscribers be notified in advance and have an opportunity to litigate when government seeks to obtain personal data; specify the standards for courts to apply in weighing such conflicting claims (e.g., that subscriber data should be requested only if other sources of documentation are not available to the government); and bring any tapping of cable signals directly under state or federal wiretapping control laws.

If simple and basic legislation is needed now, as I believe it is, my choice would be to have this passed at the federal level, assuring national uniformity and allowing a national floor of conduct to be set for all system operators. The federal government also has the best potential resources for keeping track of the new systems as they develop, and paying attention to the effects of new technological and organizational developments.

Until such first-stage federal legislation can be enacted--and it might take some time--the states will (and should) step in. Useful experience will be gained while a federal bill is pending. But, in the long run, any industry as clearly national in character as this one ought to be under basic federal rules, with state laws able to add noncompetitive protections if these are found to be necessary. The credit reporting industry was brought under national privacy rules this way with passage of the Fair Credit Reporting Act in 1969, and that is not a bad model to apply here.

Myths of Computer Abuse

As the privacy debate progresses, it will also be important to dispel some of the false accounts of computer abuse that surface in these discussions and mislead public policymakers. During the May hearings on the New York bill, for example, James Cameron, a journalist who did a radio documentary on the Qube system for NBC News in 1981, testified about what he called serious "indiscretions" by Warner Amex's Qube operators. According to Cameron: "Data on the viewing habits of Qube subscribers has got in the wrong hands in the past, despite Warner Amex's best efforts to safeguard the computer's database. During a local mayoralty election it was revealed that the incumbent's tv viewing patterns included the soft-core porn channels that Qube offers--some of their most lucrative, best-watched channels, by the way. The candidate for mayor of Columbus, his privacy violated, admitted that the computer data were correct, but that his viewing of the channels was out of civic duty, not moral turpitude. 'As mayor,' he said, 'I should know what's on the cable tv system franchised by my city.'"

Cameron cited this as proof that the Warner Amex system couldn't be controlled by its managers and that New York should enact the Abrams bill. But a call to Mayor Tom Moody's office reveals that this information never came from the computer. A reporter was in the mayor's office interviewing him. The mayor, fairly nonchalantly, mentioned that he watched the sexually oriented channels "once in a while," to see what was being shown. When this was published, the local newspapers played it up, and that was how the fact of the mayor's practice entered the reelection campaign. So much for another lurid tale of computer abuse of privacy.

Whether industry self-regulation or public regulation will be the rule in the next few years is likely to turn on several developments. How widely will a privacy code such as Warner Amex's be adopted as an industry standard and followed by all operators? Will threats such as the subpoena of Qube-system records begin to appear in other pilot projects unfolding during this period? Can industry spokesmen show persuasively that detailed privacy protections such as those in the New York State bill would be unduly costly, restrictive, or cumbersome?

A broad consensus about the types of potential privacy violations and the kinds of rules that could meet these threats seems to be emerging in the early stages of interactive home systems. A thoughtful debate over best remedies and best regulators is already under way. This suggests that the early alarms, empirical analysis, and adoption of first-generation privacy rules that our society went through during the first era of computer use in the '60s and '70s have served us well. If we nurture that sense of necessary anticipation and timely response, we may be able to apply computer and communication technologies in the next two decades in ways that protect rather than impair the fundamental values of a free society.

NOTES ON CONTRIBUTORS

LESTER ASHEIM is among the best known, most highly respected teachers in library science. He is now at the School of Library Science, University of North Carolina.

RUSSELL BAKER often is compared favorably with James Thurber, and is one of the best of the New York Times regular columnists. There is no necessary connection between the job and the comparison.

MURRAY L. BOB is director of the Chautauqua-Cattaraugus Library System in Jamestown, NY.

MIRIAM BRAVERMAN is a well-known writer and is associate professor at the School of Library Service, Columbia University, New York.

JOHN BUDD may be found at the University of North Carolina, Chapel Hill, NC. He is a teacher and coordinator of online bibliographic services.

COLIN CAMPBELL is a reporter for the New York Times.

RICHARD DE GENNARO is another regular to this series, and when not writing may be found in the director's office of libraries at the University of Pennsylvania.

MARY ANNE DRIVER is library media specialist at the Irving Middle School, Norman, Oklahoma.

RUSSELL W. DRIVER is assistant professor of management at the University of Oklahoma.

SHIRLEY FITZGIBBONS is assistant professor at the School of Library and Information Science at Indiana University in Bloomington.

JUAN FREUDENTHAL is associate professor at the Graduate School of Library and Information Science, Simmons College.

MARY W. GEORGE is the head of the reference department at Princeton's Harvey S. Firestone Memorial Library.

DANIEL GORE is the former director of the library at Macalester College, St. Paul. He is a frequent contributor to library literature and this series.

ALIXE HAMBLETON is associate professor at the University of Regina Faculty of Education and a well-known writer in the field of education.

NAT HENTOFF, a frequent contributor to this series, is a columnist for the Village Voice, staff writer for The New Yorker, teacher, lecturer, and author of numerous books.

DAVID ISAACSON is assistant head of reference and humanities librarian at Western Michigan University in Kalamazoo.

MARGO JEFFERSON teaches journalism at New York University. Prior to that she was on the staff of Newsweek.

PAUL LACEY is Bain-Swiggett professor of English literature and language at Earlham College in Richmond, Indiana.

MAURICE LINE is the Director General of the British Lending Library Division and well-known to readers of this series. His articles often are selected for the year's best.

JOSETTE LYDERS is at the Graduate School of Library and Information Science, Simmons College, where, at the time of the article, she was a doctoral candidate.

CELIA MINOUGHAN is an English librarian.

JOE MOREHEAD may now be the country's leading authority on government documents (at any rate, there is no one around to challenge him). When not mumbling about the state of documents, he may be found in the classrooms at the School of Library and Information Science, SUNY at Albany.

STANLEY OLSON is a well-known biographer, and the author of the standard work on Elinor Wylie. At the time of this essay he was working on a biography of John Singer Sargent.

SAMUEL ROTHSTEIN is a familiar figure in reference circles, and when not commenting on the state of the art, may be found teaching at the School of Librarianship at the University of British Columbia.

ANITA SCHILLER is a regular contributor to library literature and is reference bibliographer at the University of California, San Diego.

HERBERT SCHILLER writes on information questions and has the distinction of being the husband of Anita.

PAT SCHUMAN is President of the publishing firm of Neal-Schuman and lectures at the School of Library Service, Columbia University, New York.

Notes on Contributors

ELIZABETH SEGEL is a lecturer in children's literature at the University of Pittsburgh, Department of English.

DAVID SHAVIT is professor in the Department of Library Science at Northern Illinois University, DeKalb.

WALLACE STEGNER is one of America's most distinguished writers, as well as a superb teacher and critic.

KENNETH TAYLOR is the industrial training manager for International Signal and Control Corporation and has served as school library media specialist and library educator.

ALAN F. WESTIN is professor of public law and government at Columbia University and the author of numerous articles and books on the problem of privacy.

NANCY J. WILLIAMSON is associate professor, Faculty of Library Science, University of Toronto.